THE RHETORICAL ROLE OF SCRIPTURE
IN 1 CORINTHIANS

Society of Biblical Literature

Studies in Biblical Literature

Edited by
Sharon H. Ringe

Number 15

The Rhetorical Role of Scripture
in 1 Corinthians

THE RHETORICAL ROLE OF SCRIPTURE IN 1 CORINTHIANS

John Paul Heil

Society of Biblical Literature
Atlanta

THE RHETORICAL ROLE OF SCRIPTURE IN 1 CORINTHIANS

Copyright © 2005 by the Society of Biblical Literature

All rights reserved. No part of this work may be reproduced or transmitted in any form or by any means, electronic or mechanical, including photocopying and recording, or by means of any information storage or retrieval system, except as may be expressly permitted by the 1976 Copyright Act or in writing from the publisher. Requests for permission should be addressed in writing to the Rights and Permissions Office, Society of Biblical Literature, 825 Houston Mill Road, Atlanta, GA 30333-0399, USA.

Library of Congress Cataloging-in-Publication Data

Heil, John Paul.
   The rhetorical role of Scripture in 1 Corinthians / by John Paul Heil.
       p. cm. — (Society of Biblical Literature monograph series ; 15)
Includes bibliographical references.
ISBN-13: 978-1-58983-167-4 (paper binding : alk. paper)
ISBN-10: 1-58983-167-5 (paper binding : alk. paper)
   1. Bible. N.T. Corinthians, 1st—Socio-rhetorical criticism. 2. Bible. N.T. Corinthians, 1st—Relation to the Old Testament. 3. Bible. O.T.—Relation to Corinthians, 1st. I. Title. II. Series.

BS2675.52.H45 2005
227'.2066—dc22   2005016465

---

12 11 10 09 08 07 06 05   5 4 3 2 1
Printed in the United States of America on acid-free, recycled paper conforming to ANSI/NISO Z39.48-1992 (R1997) and ISO 9706:1994 standards for paper permanence.

Contents

Abbreviations xi

1. Scripture in 1 Corinthians 1
   State of the Research 1
   Methodology 3
      Paul's Rhetorical Strategy *3*
      Audience Response *5*
   Preliminary Analysis and Overview 10
      First Rhetorical Demonstration: 1 Cor 1:18–4:21 *10*
      Second Rhetorical Demonstration: 1 Cor 5:1–7:40 *11*
      Third Rhetorical Demonstration: 1 Cor 8:1–11:1 *12*
      Fourth Rhetorical Demonstration: 1 Cor 11:2–34 *12*
      Fifth Rhetorical Demonstration: 1 Cor 12:1–14:40 *13*
      Sixth Rhetorical Demonstration: 1 Cor 15:1–58 *13*
   Outline of Scriptural References in 1 Corinthians 14

2. 1 Corinthians 1:19 17
   Old Testament Background 17
   Literary-Rhetorical Analysis 19
   Relation to the Antecedent Context in 1 Corinthians 1:1–18 22
      Opening Address in 1 Corinthians 1:1–3 *22*
      Thanksgiving in 1 Corinthians 1:4–9 *24*
      Theme and Occasion of the Letter in 1 Corinthians 1:10–18 *25*
   Relation to the Subsequent Context in 1 Corinthians 1:20–4:21 30
   Summary on 1 Corinthians 1:19 36

3. 1 Corinthians 1:31 37
   Old Testament Background 37
   Literary-Rhetorical Analysis 39
   Relation to the Antecedent Context in 1 Corinthians 1:1–30 41

    Relation to the Subsequent Context in 1 Corinthians 2:1–4:21 45
    Summary on 1 Corinthians 1:31 50

4. **1 Corinthians 2:9** 53

    Old Testament Background 53
    Literary-Rhetorical Analysis 58
    Relation to the Antecedent Context in 1 Corinthians 2:1–8 60
    Relation to the Subsequent Context in 1 Corinthians 2:10–15 62
    Summary on 1 Corinthians 2:9 66

5. **1 Corinthians 2:16a** 69

    Literary-Rhetorical Analysis 70
    Relation to the Antecedent Context in 1 Corinthians 1:21–2:15 71
    Relation to the Subsequent Context in 1 Corinthians 2:16b 73
    Summary on 1 Corinthians 2:16a 74

6. **1 Corinthians 3:19b–20** 77

    Old Testament Background 77
    Literary-Rhetorical Analysis 80
    Relation to the Antecedent Context in 1 Corinthians 1:17–3:19a 81
    Relation to the Subsequent Context in 1 Corinthians 3:21–4:21 84
    Summary on 1 Corinthians 3:19b–20 86

7. **1 Corinthians 5:13b** 89

    Old Testament Background 89
    Literary-Rhetorical Analysis 92
    Relation to the Antecedent Context in 1 Corinthians 5:1–13a 92
    Relation to the Subsequent Context in 1 Corinthians 6:1–7:2 99
    Summary on 1 Corinthians 5:13b 100

8. **1 Corinthians 6:16b** 103

    Old Testament Background 103
    Literary-Rhetorical Analysis 104
    The Chiastic Structure in 1 Corinthians 6:12–20 105
        Superscription: 6:12   106
        Chiasm: 6:13–20   106
    Relation to the Antecedent Context in 1 Corinthians 6:12–16a 111
    Relation to the Subsequent Context in 1 Corinthians 6:17–20 117
    Summary on 1 Corinthians 6:16b 122

9. **1 Corinthians 9:9–10** 125

    Old Testament Background 125

    Literary-Rhetorical Analysis 130
    Relation to the Antecedent Context in 1 Corinthians 8:1–9:8 133
    Relation to the Subsequent Context in 1 Corinthians 9:11–18 140
    Summary on 1 Corinthians 9:9–10 142

10. 1 Corinthians 10:7b 145

    Old Testament Background 145
    Literary-Rhetorical Analysis 146
    Relation to the Antecedent Context in 1 Corinthians 8:1–10:7a 147
        1 Corinthians 8:1–10:5   *147*
        The Chiastic Structure of 10:6–11   *149*
    Relation to the Subsequent Context in 1 Corinthians 10:8–11 153
    Summary on 1 Corinthians 10:7b 158

11. 1 Corinthians 10:26 161

    Old Testament Background 161
    Literary-Rhetorical Analysis 162
    Relation to the Antecedent Context in 1 Corinthians 10:23–25 163
    Relation to the Subsequent Context in 1 Corinthians 10:27–11:1 . . .167
    Summary on 1 Corinthians 10:26 170

12. 1 Corinthians 11:7–12 173

    Old Testament Background 173
    The Role of 1 Corinthians 11:7–12
    in the Argument of 1 Corinthians 11:2–16 175
        The Structure of 1 Corinthians 11:2–16   *176*
        The First Unit: 1 Corinthians 11:3–7   *179*
        The Second Unit: 1 Corinthians 11:8–12   *182*
        The Third Unit: 1 Corinthians 11:13–15   *185*
        The Conclusion in 1 Corinthians 11:16   *187*
    Summary on 1 Corinthians 11:7–12 188

13. 1 Corinthians 14:21, 25 191

    Old Testament Background 191
        1 Corinthians 14:21   *191*
        1 Corinthians 14:25   *194*
    Literary-Rhetorical Analysis 196
        1 Corinthians 14:21   *196*
        1 Corinthians 14:25   *197*
    Relation to the Antecedent Context in 1 Corinthians 14:1–20 197
    Relation to the Subsequent Context in 1 Corinthians 14:22–25 200
    Summary on 1 Corinthians 14:21, 25 202

14. 1 Corinthians 15:25, 27 205

Old Testament Background 205
    1 Corinthians 15:25 and LXX Psalm 109:1   207
    1 Corinthians 15:27a and LXX Psalm 8:7b   208
Literary-Rhetorical Analysis 210
Relation to the Context in 1 Corinthians 15:20–28 212
    1 Corinthians 15:20–23   212
    The Chiasm in 1 Corinthians 15:24–28   212
    The Role of the Scriptural Quotations in the Chiasm   215
Summary on 1 Corinthians 15:25, 27 218

15. 1 Corinthians 15:32b 221

Old Testament Background 221
Literary-Rhetorical Analysis 222
Relation to the Antecedent Context in 1 Corinthians 15:29–32a ...223
Relation to the Subsequent Context in 1 Corinthians 15:33–34 ...226
Summary on 1 Corinthians 15:32b 228

16. 1 Corinthians 15:45a 231

Old Testament Background 231
Literary-Rhetorical Analysis 234
Relation to the Antecedent Context in
1 Corinthians 15:21–22, 35–44 236
    1 Corinthians 15:21–22   236
    1 Corinthians 15:35–44   237
Relation to the Subsequent Context in 1 Corinthians 15:46–49 241
Summary on 1 Corinthians 15:45a 244

17. 1 Corinthians 15:54b–55 247

Old Testament Background 247
    1 Corinthians 15:54b and Isaiah 25:8a   248
    1 Corinthians 15:55 and Hosea 13:14b   249
Literary-Rhetorical Analysis 251
Relation to the Antecedent Context in
1 Corinthians 15:21–26, 50–54a 253
    1 Corinthians 15:21–26   253
    1 Corinthians 15:50–54a   254
Relation to the Subsequent Context in 1 Corinthians 15:56–58 257
Summary on 1 Corinthians 15:54b–55 259

18. Conclusion 261

Bibliography 263

Author Index 287

Scripture Index 295

Abbreviations

AB	Anchor Bible
ABR	*Australian Biblical Review*
ACNT	Augsburg Commentaries on the New Testament
AGJU	Arbeiten zur Geschichte des antiken Judentums und des Urchristentums
AnBib	Analecta biblica
BA	*Biblical Archaeologist*
BBR	*Bulletin for Biblical Research*
BDAG	Bauer, W., F. W. Danker, W. F. Arndt, and F. W. Gingich. *Greek-English Lexicon of the New Testament and Other Early Christian Literature.* 3rd ed. Chicago, 1999
BDF	Blass, F., A. Debrunner, and R. W. Funk. *A Greek Grammar of the New Testament and Other Early Christian Literature.* Chicago, 1961
BECNT	Baker Exegetical Commentary on the New Testament
BETL	Bibliotheca ephemeridum theologicarum lovaniensium
BHT	Beiträge zur historischen Theologie
Bib	*Biblica*
BibInt	*Biblical Interpretation*
BIS	Biblical Interpretation Series
BR	*Biblical Research*
BSac	*Bibliotheca sacra*
BT	*The Bible Translator*
BTB	*Biblical Theology Bulletin*
BZ	*Biblische Zeitschrift*
BZNW	Beihefte zur Zeitschrift für die neutestamentliche Wissenschaft
CBET	Contributions to Biblical Exegesis and Theology
CBQ	*Catholic Biblical Quarterly*
CBQMS	Catholic Biblical Quarterly Monograph Series
ConBNT	Coniectanea biblica: New Testament Series
CRINT	Compendia rerum iudaicarum ad Novum Testamentum
CTR	*Criswell Theological Review*
CV	*Communio viatorum*
EDNT	*Exegetical Dictionary of the New Testament.* Edited by H. Balz and G. Schneider. ET. Grand Rapids, 1990–1993
EKKNT	Evangelisch-katholischer Kommentar zum Neuen Testament

EstBib	*Estudios bíblicos*
ETL	*Ephemerides theologicae lovanienses*
EvQ	*Evangelical Quarterly*
ExpTim	*Expository Times*
FRLANT	Forschungen zur Religion und Literatur des Alten und Neuen Testaments
GTA	Göttinger theologischer Arbeiten
HNT	Handbuch zum Neuen Testament
HNTC	Harper's New Testament Commentaries
HUT	Hermeneutische Untersuchungen zur Theologie
ICC	International Critical Commentary
Int	*Interpretation*
ITQ	*Irish Theological Quarterly*
JBL	*Journal of Biblical Literature*
JETS	*Journal of the Evangelical Theological Society*
JSNT	*Journal for the Study of the New Testament*
JSNTSup	Journal for the Study of the New Testament: Supplement Series
JSOT	*Journal for the Study of the Old Testament*
JTS	*Journal of Theological Studies*
Jud	*Judaica*
NAB	New American Bible
NBf	*New Blackfriars*
Neot	*Neotestamentica*
NETR	*Near East School of Theology Theological Review*
NICNT	New International Commentary on the New Testament
NIGTC	New International Greek Testament Commentary
NIV	New International Version
NovT	*Novum Testamentum*
NovTSup	Novum Testamentum Supplements
NTS	*New Testament Studies*
ÖTK	Ökumenischer Taschenbuch-Kommentar
PRSt	*Perspectives in Religious Studies*
RB	*Revue biblique*
RefR	*Reformed Review*
ResQ	*Restoration Quarterly*
RevScRel	*Revue des sciences religieuses*
SBFLA	*Studii biblici Franciscani liber annus*
SBLDS	Society of Biblical Literature Dissertation Series
SBLSCS	Society of Biblical Literature Septuagint and Cognate Studies
SBLSP	*Society of Biblical Literature Seminar Papers*
SBLSymS	Society of Biblical Literature Symposium Series
SBLTT	Society of Biblical Literature Texts and Translations
ScEs	*Science et esprit*
SEÅ	*Svensk exegetisk årsbok*
SNTSMS	Society for New Testament Studies Monograph Series
SNTSU	*Studien zum Neuen Testament und seiner Umwelt*

SP	Sacra pagina
ST	*Studia theologica*
SUNT	Studien zur Umwelt des Neuen Testaments
THKNT	Theologischer Handkommentar zum Neuen Testament
TJ	*Trinity Journal*
TSAJ	Texte und Studien zum antiken Judentum
TU	Texte und Untersuchungen
TynBul	*Tyndale Bulletin*
TZ	*Theologische Zeitschrift*
VTSup	Vetus Testamentum Supplements
WD	*Wort und Dienst*
WMANT	Wissenschaftliche Monographien zum Alten und Neuen Testament
WTJ	*Westminster Theological Journal*
WUNT	Wissenschaftliche Untersuchungen zum Neuen Testament
WW	*Word and World*
ZNW	*Zeitschrift für die neutestamentliche Wissenschaft und die Kunde der älteren Kirche*
ZTK	*Zeitschrift für Theologie und Kirche*

CHAPTER 1

Scripture in 1 Corinthians

State of the Research

Several recent articles have briefly and in a general way discussed various aspects of Paul's use of the Old Testament in his First Letter to the Corinthians.[1] Some articles have focused more narrowly on the scriptural background of particular passages within the Letter.[2] Recent books devoted to the topic of scripture in Paul include treatments of and references to

---

1. D. Moody Smith, "The Pauline Literature," in *It Is Written: Scripture Citing Scripture. Essays in Honour of Barnabas Lindars* (ed. D. A. Carson and H. G. M. Williamson; Cambridge: Cambridge University Press, 1988), 265–91; François S. Malan, "The Use of the Old Testament in 1 Corinthians," *Neot* 14 (1981): 134–70; Raymond F. Collins, " 'It Was Indeed Written for Our Sake' (1 Cor 9,10): Paul's Use of Scripture in the First Letter to the Corinthians," *SNTSU* 20 (1995): 151–70; Thomas L. Brodie, "The Systematic Use of the Pentateuch in 1 Corinthians," in *The Corinthian Correspondence* (ed. Reimund Bieringer; BETL 125; Louvain: Louvain University Press, 1996), 441–57; Andreas Lindemann, "Die Schrift als Tradition: Beobachtungen zu den biblischen Zitaten im Ersten Korintherbrief," in *Schrift und Tradition: Festschrift für Josef Ernst zum 70. Geburtstag* (ed. Knut Backhaus and Franz Georg Untergassmair; Paderborn: Schöningh, 1996), 199–225; Richard B. Hays, "The Conversion of the Imagination: Scripture and Eschatology in 1 Corinthians," *NTS* 45 (1999): 391–412; Christopher M. Tuckett, "Paul, Scripture, and Ethics: Some Reflections," *NTS* 46 (2000): 403–24.
2. Jan Lambrecht, "Paul's Christological Use of Scripture in 1 Cor. 15.20–28," *NTS* 28 (1982): 502–27; Peter S. Zaas, " 'Cast Out the Evil Man from Your Midst' (1 Cor 5:13b)," *JBL* 103 (1984): 259–61; Gail R. O'Day, "Jeremiah 9:22–23 and 1 Corinthians 1:26–31: A Study in Intertextuality," *JBL* 109 (1990): 259–67; David E. Lanier, "With Stammering Lips and Another Tongue: 1 Cor 14:20–22 and Isa 28:11–12," *CTR* 5 (1991): 259–85; C. J. A. Hickling, "Paul's Use of Exodus in the Corinthian Correspondence," in Bieringer, *Corinthian Correspondence*, 367–76; Bart J. Koet, "The Old Testament Background to 1 Cor 10,7–8," in Bieringer, *Corinthian Correspondence*, 607–15; Brian S. Rosner, "The Function of Scripture in 1 Cor 5,13b and 6,16," in Bieringer, *Corinthian Correspondence*, 513–18; Joop F. M. Smit, " 'You Shall Not Muzzle a Threshing Ox': Paul's Use of the Law of Moses in 1 Cor 9,8–12," *EstBib* 58 (2000): 239–63.

1 Corinthians.³ Some recent monographs study the Jewish scriptural background of various parts of the Letter.⁴ Although commentaries offer helpful yet limited treatments, we are unaware of any current monographic, comprehensive investigation of Paul's employment of scripture in 1 Corinthians. The present study hopes to fill this void by offering an exegetical analysis of all of this Letter's various explicit quotations and references to the OT.

Furthermore, the need for a consideration of the rhetorical dimension of Paul's biblical quotations has been noted.⁵ Consequently, we aim to examine the various authoritative roles that not only scriptural quotations but also other explicit references and allusions to scripture play in Paul's rhetorical strategy in his First Letter to the Corinthians. We thereby hope to illuminate the powerful impact that the Jewish scriptures exert on Paul's implied audience at Corinth.

---

3. Dietrich-Alex Koch, *Die Schrift als Zeuge des Evangeliums: Untersuchungen zur Verwendung und zum Verständnis der Schrift bei Paulus* (BHT 69; Tübingen: Mohr Siebeck, 1986); Richard B. Hays, *Echoes of Scripture in the Letters of Paul* (New Haven: Yale University Press, 1989); Christopher D. Stanley, *Paul and the Language of Scripture: Citation Technique in the Pauline Epistles and Contemporary Literature* (SNTSMS 69; Cambridge: Cambridge University Press, 1992), 185–215; James W. Aageson, *Written Also for Our Sake: Paul and the Art of Biblical Interpretation* (Louisville: Westminster John Knox, 1993); Romano Penna, "Paul's Attitude Toward the Old Testament," in *Paul the Apostle: Wisdom and Folly of the Cross* (Theological and Exegetical Study 2; Collegeville, Minn.: Liturgical Press, 1996), 61–91; Timothy H. Lim, *Holy Scripture in the Qumran Commentaries and Pauline Letters* (Oxford: Clarendon, 1997), 124–75; Florian Wilk, *Die Bedeutung des Jesajabuches für Paulus* (FRLANT 179; Göttingen: Vandenhoeck & Ruprecht, 1998).

4. Peter J. Tomson, *Paul and the Jewish Law: Halakha in the Letters of the Apostle to the Gentiles* (CRINT 1; Minneapolis: Fortress, 1990); Brian S. Rosner, *Paul, Scripture, and Ethics: A Study of 1 Corinthians 5–7* (AGJU 22; Leiden: Brill, 1994); Kent L. Yinger, *Paul, Judaism, and Judgment according to Deeds* (SNTSMS 105; Cambridge: Cambridge University Press, 1999), 204–59; C. Marvin Pate, *The Reverse of the Curse: Paul, Wisdom, and the Law* (WUNT 114; Tübingen: Mohr Siebeck, 2000), 296–304; H. H. Drake Williams, *The Wisdom of the Wise: The Presence and Function of Scripture within 1 Cor. 1:18–3:23* (AGJU 49; Leiden: Brill, 2001).

5. Christopher D. Stanley, "The Rhetoric of Quotations: An Essay on Method," in *Early Christian Interpretation of the Scriptures of Israel: Investigations and Proposals* (ed. Craig A. Evans and James A. Sanders; JSNTSup 148; Sheffield: Sheffield Academic Press, 1997), 58: "Recent studies of biblical quotations in early Judaism and Christianity have focused rather one-sidedly on the interpretative process that lies behind the present text. In the process, the rhetorical dimension of the quotation process has been largely overlooked. . . . [A] truly rhetorical analysis of biblical quotations is needed, one that examines how quotations function in their present argumentative context." See also Christopher D. Stanley, "Biblical Quotations as Rhetorical Devices in Paul's Letter to the Galatians," *SBLSP* 37 (1998): 700–730.

Methodology

Paul's Rhetorical Strategy

Rhetorical approaches to the New Testament in general and to Paul in particular are certainly in vogue.[6] And 1 Corinthians both as a whole,[7] as well as in part,[8] has received a goodly share of rhetorical attention recently.

---

6. R. Dean Anderson, *Ancient Rhetorical Theory and Paul: Revised Edition* (CBET 18; Louvain: Peeters, 1998); Carl Joachim Classen, *Rhetorical Criticism of the New Testament* (WUNT 128; Tübingen: Mohr Siebeck, 2000), 1–44; Frank Witt Hughes, "The Rhetoric of Letters," in *The Thessalonians Debate: Methodological Discord or Methodological Synthesis?* (ed. Karl P. Donfried and Johannes Beutler; Grand Rapids: Eerdmans, 2000), 194–240; Mark D. Given, *Paul's True Rhetoric: Ambiguity, Cunning, and Deception in Greece and Rome* (Emory Studies in Early Christianity 7; Harrisburg, Pa.: Trinity Press International, 2001); Robert A. Bryant, *The Risen Crucified Christ in Galatians* (SBLDS 185; Atlanta: Society of Biblical Literature, 2001), 18–37; Thomas H. Olbricht and Jerry L. Sumney, eds., *Paul and Pathos* (SBLSymS 16; Atlanta: Society of Biblical Literature, 2001); Michael J. Gorman, *Apostle of the Crucified Lord: A Theological Introduction to Paul and His Letters* (Grand Rapids: Eerdmans, 2004), 79–85.

7. Michael Bünker, *Briefformular und rhetorische Disposition im 1 Korintherbrief* (GTA 28; Göttingen: Vandenhoeck & Ruprecht, 1984); Wilhelm Wuellner, "Paul as Pastor: The Function of Rhetorical Questions in First Corinthians," in *L'Apôtre Paul: Personalité, style et conception du ministère* (ed. Albert Vanhoye; BETL 73; Louvain: Louvain University Press, 1986), 49–77; Elizabeth Schüssler Fiorenza, "Rhetorical Situation and Historical Reconstruction in I Corinthians," *NTS* 33 (1987): 386–403; Antoinette C. Wire, *The Corinthian Women Prophets: A Reconstruction through Paul's Rhetoric* (Minneapolis: Fortress, 1990); Margaret M. Mitchell, *Paul and the Rhetoric of Reconciliation: An Exegetical Investigation of the Language and Composition of 1 Corinthians* (HUT 28; Tübingen: Mohr, 1991); Stephen M. Pogoloff, *Logos and Sophia: The Rhetorical Situation of 1 Corinthians* (SBLDS 134; Atlanta: Scholars Press, 1992); Eckart Reinmuth, "Narratio und argumentatio—Zur Auslegung der Jesus-Christus-Geschichte im Ersten Korintherbrief: Ein Beitrag zur rhetorischen Kompetenz des Paulus," *ZTK* 92 (1995): 13–27; Frank Witt Hughes, "Rhetorical Criticism and the Corinthian Correspondence," in *The Rhetorical Analysis of Scripture: Essays from the 1995 London Conference* (ed. Stanley E. Porter and Thomas H. Olbricht; JSNTSup 146; Sheffield: Sheffield Academic Press, 1997), 336–50; Anders Eriksson, *Traditions as Rhetorical Proof: Pauline Argumentation in 1 Corinthians* (ConBNT 29; Stockholm: Almqvist & Wiksell, 1998); Richard A. Horsley, "Rhetoric and Empire—And 1 Corinthians," in *Paul and Politics: Ekklesia, Israel, Imperium, Interpretation. Essays in Honor of Krister Stendahl* (ed. Richard A. Horsley; Harrisburg, Pa.: Trinity Press International, 2000), 72–102.

8. Karl A. Plank, *Paul and the Irony of Affliction* (Atlanta: Scholars Press, 1987); Duane F. Watson, "1 Corinthians 10:23–11:1 in the Light of Greco-Roman Rhetoric: The Role of Rhetorical Questions," *JBL* 108 (1989): 301–18; Peter Lampe, "Theological Wisdom and the 'Word about the Cross': The Rhetorical Scheme in I Corinthians 1–4," *Int* 44 (1990): 117–31; Hermann Probst, *Paulus und der Brief: Die Rhetorik des antiken Briefes als Form der paulinischen Korintherkorrespondenz (1 Kor 8–10)* (WUNT 45; Tübingen: Mohr, 1991); Duane Litfin, *St. Paul's Theology of Proclamation: 1 Corinthians 1–4 and Greco-Roman Rhetoric* (SNTSMS 79; Cambridge: Cambridge University, 1994); Michael A. Bullmore, *St. Paul's Theology of Rhetori-*

Broadly speaking, two different basic approaches characterize rhetorical criticism of the NT. First, we have a more historical-critical approach that utilizes the categories and devices of ancient classical Greco-Roman rhetoric. And second, we have a more literary-critical approach that utilizes modern scientific theories of rhetoric, sometimes called "New Rhetoric," to analyze texts.[9] We intend to employ the insights of both approaches as far as possible as we consider the role of scripture in Paul's various rhetorical arguments and demonstrations throughout 1 Corinthians.

Although Greco-Roman rhetoric influenced Paul, whether directly or indirectly, he employed, adapted, and transformed it in his own way and for his own purposes. But we must keep in mind that Paul also utilized distinctively Jewish rhetorical devices and techniques in his Septuagintal use of the

---

cal Style: An Examination of I Corinthians 2.1–5 in the Light of First Century Graeco-Roman Rhetorical Culture (San Francisco: International Scholars, 1995); Insawn Saw, *Paul's Rhetoric in 1 Corinthians 15: An Analysis Utilizing the Theories of Classical Rhetoric* (Lewiston, N.Y.: Mellen, 1995); Khiok-Khng Yeo, *Rhetorical Interaction in 1 Corinthians 8 and 10: A Formal Analysis with Preliminary Suggestions for a Chinese, Cross-Cultural Hermeneutic* (BIS 9; Leiden: Brill, 1995); Glenn Holland, "Paul's Use of Irony as a Rhetorical Technique," in Porter and Olbicht, *Rhetorical Analysis of Scripture*, 234–48; Gary S. Selby, "Paul, the Seer: The Rhetorical Persona in 1 Corinthians 2.1–16," in Porter and Olbricht, *Rhetorical Analysis of Scripture*, 351–73; Lambert D. Jacobs, "Establishing a New Value System in Corinth: 1 Corinthians 5–6 as Persuasive Argument," in Porter and Olbricht, *Rhetorical Analysis of Scripture*, 374–87; Maria Pascuzzi, *Ethics, Ecclesiology, and Church Discipline: A Rhetorical Analysis of 1 Corinthians 5* (Tesi Gregoriana 32; Rome: Gregorian University Press, 1997); Laurence L. Welborn, *Politics and Rhetoric in the Corinthian Epistles* (Macon, Ga.: Mercer University Press, 1997); Brian K. Peterson, *Eloquence and the Proclamation of the Gospel in Corinth* (SBLDS 163; Atlanta: Scholars Press, 1998), 144–47; Joop F. M. Smit, *"About the Idol Offerings": Rhetoric, Social Context, and Theology of Paul's Discourse in First Corinthians 8:1–11:1* (CBET 27; Louvain: Peeters, 2000); Dennis L. Stamps, "The Christological Premise in Pauline Theological Rhetoric: 1 Corinthians 1.4–2.5 as an Example," in *Rhetorical Criticism and the Bible* (ed. Stanley E. Porter and Dennis L. Stamps; JSNTSup 195; London: Sheffield Academic Press, 2002), 441–57; Joop F. M. Smit, "Epideictic Rhetoric in Paul's First Letter to the Corinthians 1–4," *Bib* 84 (2003): 184–201; Bruce W. Winter, "Philodemus and Paul on Rhetorical Delivery (ὑπόκρισις)," in *Philodemus and the New Testament World* (ed. John T. Fitzgerald et al.; NovTSup 111; Leiden: Brill, 2004), 323–42.

9. Eriksson, *Traditions*, 20: "[T]here is at present no consensus in New Testament scholarship concerning the use of rhetoric in exegesis. Historical critics see rhetoric primarily as a cultural artifact from the ancient Greco-Roman world which can give important parallels to the text of the New Testament. Literary interpreters put the emphasis on rhetoric as a theory to analyze the text and view the products of rhetorical activity as persuasive strategies in the text which affect our understanding of the text. Even if the two camps are starting to communicate and learn from one another, the different perspectives on rhetoric lead to basically different versions of rhetorical criticism." See also J. David Hester Amador, *Academic Constraints in Rhetorical Criticism of the New Testament: An Introduction to a Rhetoric of Power* (JSNTSup 174; Sheffield: Sheffield Academic Press, 1999).

Old Testament.[10] Indeed, one of our contentions, which we hope to demonstrate in this investigation, is that Paul's use and adaptation of Jewish exegetical techniques, such as *gezera shava, kal va-homer*, pesher, and targumic methods have not only interpretive but rhetorical functions.[11]

The insights but not the technical jargon of "speech-act theory" will inform our investigation.[12] According to this theory, words do not merely say something informative but do or perform something; they have a transformative effect upon those who hear them. We will be concerned with how Paul's use of scripture in 1 Corinthians does not merely inform his listeners but performs a rhetorical strategy aimed at persuading and transforming them in various ways.[13]

Audience Response

Paul, as the implied, epistolary author and co-sender (together with Sosthenes; cf. 1 Cor 1:1) of the text of 1 Corinthians, expects his implied or authorial audience to understand, respond to, and be persuaded by his use of scripture in the various rhetorical demonstrations throughout the Letter. We may presume that many, if not all, in Paul's actual, historical audience

---

10. Brad Ronnell Braxton, *The Tyranny of Resolution: 1 Corinthians 7:17–24* (SBLDS 181; Atlanta: Society of Biblical Literature, 2000), 108–9: "[A]n analysis of Paul's rhetorical techniques also reveals that his tactics of persuasion were not merely Greco-Roman but also, at times, distinctively Jewish. Paul's Bible, more than likely the LXX, informed his symbolic world and provided him a source of rhetorical tropes which could be adapted or transformed to fit and speak to new settings and circumstances.... Paul's use and adaptation of antecedent traditions were effective and long-standing *Jewish rhetorical* practices. Thus, in an analysis of Paul's rhetoric, one finds oneself simultaneously in the Greco-Roman *and* Jewish cultural worlds" (Braxton's emphasis). See also Natalio Fernández Marcos, *The Septuagint in Context: Introduction to the Greek Versions of the Bible* (Leiden: Brill, 2000), 329; Raija Sollamo, "The Significance of Septuagint Studies," in *Emanuel: Studies in Hebrew Bible, Septuagint, and Dead Sea Scrolls in Honor of Emanuel Tov* (ed. Shalom M. Paul et al.; VTSup 94; Leiden: Brill, 2003), 500, 508.

11. On Paul's use of Jewish exegetical procedures, see Carol Kern Stockhausen, *Moses' Veil and the Glory of the New Covenant: The Exegetical Substructure of II Cor. 3,1–4,6* (AnBib 116; Rome: Biblical Institute, 1989), 24–30; idem, "2 Corinthians 3 and the Principles of Pauline Exegesis," in *Paul and the Scriptures of Israel* (ed. Craig A. Evans and James A. Sanders; JSNTSup 83; Sheffield: Sheffield Academic Press, 1993), 143–64; Timothy W. Berkley, *From a Broken Covenant to Circumcision of the Heart: Pauline Intertextual Exegesis in Romans 2:17–29* (SBLDS 175; Atlanta: Society of Biblical Literature, 2000), 17–66.

12. Speech-act theory was first proposed by John Langshaw Austin, *How to Do Things with Words* (Cambridge: Harvard University Press, 1962). For a description of speech-act theory with regard to Paul's use of biblical quotations, see Stanley, "Rhetoric of Quotations," 46–48.

13. For application of speech-act theory to 1 Corinthians, see Alexandra R. Brown, *The Cross and Human Transformation: Paul's Apocalyptic Word in 1 Corinthians* (Minneapolis: Fortress, 1995), 14–30; Anthony C. Thiselton, *The First Epistle to the Corinthians: A Commentary on the Greek Text* (NIGTC; Grand Rapids: Eerdmans, 2000), 41–52.

recognized and appreciated his scriptural references, otherwise he greatly underestimated the capacities of a community that he himself founded. Rather than the actual, historical audience at Corinth, however, the implied or authorial audience of 1 Corinthians refers to the more idealized audience Paul has in mind and indeed creates in composing the Letter. The authorial audience is thus a textual construct—the audience as known by and presupposed by the text of the Letter. It is the ideal audience that Paul assumes to possess all the knowledge necessary to actualize the Letter's meaning. This is the audience—the ideal audience Paul has in mind—with which we will be primarily concerned.[14]

Determining the responses of the authorial audience is not a matter of reconstructing or speculating on how the original, historical audience at Corinth, or any other "real" audience, may or may not have responded. Rather, it is a matter of determining how the ideal audience is expected to respond based on analysis of the rhetorical strategies within the text of the Letter. But this is not an ahistorical endeavor. It takes seriously the sociohistorical and cultural location of 1 Corinthians within the world of both Paul, as the Jewish apostle to the Gentiles, and his authorial audience of Jews and Gentiles in first-century Roman Corinth.[15]

We prefer the terminology of implied or authorial "audience" to that of the conventional implied "reader" for two reasons. First, the term "audience" is more accurate and appropriate in view of the oral/aural dimension of Paul's letters. Rather than being read primarily by individuals in silence and in private, they were written to be orally performed and publicly heard by an assembly of Christians. This oral dimension is a very important but often neglected feature of Paul's rhetorical strategy. In our rhetorical analy-

---

14. For a more detailed explanation of the authorial audience, see Warren Carter and John Paul Heil, *Matthew's Parables: Audience-Oriented Perspectives* (CBQMS 30; Washington: Catholic Biblical Association, 1998), 9–14. Note the difference between our concern primarily with the audience's response to Paul's rhetorical use of scripture and the concern of Williams, *Wisdom*, 4: "Our perspective in considering Scripture texts in I Cor. 1:18–3:23 will thus be primarily from an author's perspective (i.e., what we believe Paul wrote rather than his audience's identification of all of these elements)."

15. Pogoloff, *Logos and Sophia*, 80: "[N]either the implied author nor reader is a fiction divorced from the actual author or reader. They are distinguished from the actual writer and reader not by a dichotomy of fact and fiction, but by the phenomenology of writing and reading. The Paul we meet in his letters is not the same as the historical Paul, for in his letters we encounter only the self he presents as relevant to a given rhetorical situation. . . . But the reader of the Pauline letters does construct a Paul that he or she believes represents relevant aspects of the historical Paul, who, for example, passionately believes in the importance of the crucifixion and resurrection of Christ. The implied reader is likewise the self who can, at least temporarily, share these convictions."

sis we will be concerned with the oral patterns involved in Paul's scriptural quotes and references.[16]

Second, the term "audience" more aptly corresponds to the corporate or communal dimension of 1 Corinthians. Rather than being directed to specific individuals or even particular ethnic or social groups, this Letter was intended for the entire community of believers—"to the church of God that is in Corinth" (1 Cor 1:2), composed of both Jews and Greeks (1:22–24; 7:18; 9:20–21; 12:13).[17] This is important with regard to assessing the

---

16. On oral patterns in 1 Corinthians, see John D. Harvey, *Listening to the Text: Oral Patterning in Paul's Letters* (Grand Rapids: Baker, 1998), 155–92. Joanna Dewey exaggerates Paul's orality to the point of denigrating his interaction with the written text of scripture ("Textuality in an Oral Culture: A Survey of the Pauline Traditions," in *Orality and Textuality in Early Christian Literature* [ed. Joanna Dewey; Semeia 65; Atlanta: Scholars Press, 1995], 37–65). But see the response to Dewey, in the same volume, by Vernon K. Robbins, "Oral, Rhetorical, and Literary Cultures: A Response" (75–91). Robbins states: "One of the achievements of Pauline discourse is to 'imitate written text' " (82). He suggests that there is a "rhetorical spectrum of oral-scribal texture in New Testament texts" consisting of reference, recitation, recontextualization, reconfiguration and echoes to an authoritative written text of scripture (82–88).

17. Craig Steven de Vos, *Church and Community Conflicts: The Relationships of the Thessalonian, Corinthian, and Philippian Churches with Their Wider Civic Communities* (SBLDS 168; Atlanta: Scholars Press, 1999), 231: "The Corinthian church seems to have been a very large and mixed group. Greek, Roman and Jewish backgrounds are all present, and the full social spectrum seems to be represented, including some members of Corinth's ruling elite." On the social and ethnic composition of the Christian community at Corinth, see also Gerd Theissen, *The Social Setting of Pauline Christianity: Essays on Corinth* (Philadelphia: Fortress, 1982), 69–119; Wayne A. Meeks, *The First Urban Christians: The Social World of the Apostle Paul* (New Haven: Yale University Press, 1983), 73; John K. Chow, *Patronage and Power: A Study of Social Networks in Corinth* (JSNTSup 75; Sheffield: JSOT Press, 1992); Andrew D. Clarke, *Secular and Christian Leadership in Corinth: A Socio-historical and Exegetical Study of 1 Corinthians 1–6* (AGJU 18; Leiden: Brill, 1993); David W. J. Gill, "In Search of the Social Elite in the Corinthian Church," *TynBul* 44 (1993): 323–37; Niels Hyldahl, "Paul and Hellenistic Judaism in Corinth," in *The New Testament and Hellenistic Judaism* (ed. Peder Borgen and Søren Giverson; Peabody, Mass.: Hendrickson, 1995), 204–16; Ben Witherington, *Conflict and Community in Corinth: A Socio-rhetorical Commentary on 1 and 2 Corinthians* (Grand Rapids: Eerdmans, 1995), 22–28; Christopher D. Stanley, " 'Neither Jew Nor Greek': Ethnic Conflict in Graeco-Roman Society," *JSNT* 64 (1996): 101–24; Braxton, *Tyranny of Resolution*, 71–105; Thiselton, *Corinthians*, 23–29; Wayne A. Meeks, "Corinthian Christians as Artificial Aliens," in *Paul beyond the Judaism/Hellenism Divide* (ed. Troels Engberg-Pedersen; Louisville: Westminster John Knox, 2001), 129–38; John M. G. Barclay, "Matching Theory and Practice: Josephus's Constitutional Ideal and Paul's Strategy in Corinth," in Engberg-Pedersen, *Paul beyond the Judaism/Hellenism Divide*, 149–63. For a treatment of society and religion in Roman Corinth, see Donald Engels, *Roman Corinth: An Alternative Model for the Classical City* (Chicago: University of Chicago Press, 1990), 66–120; Richard M. Rothaus, *Corinth, the First City of Greece: An Urban History of Late Antique Cult and Religion* (Religions in the Greco-Roman World 139; Leiden: Brill, 2000); Robert M. Grant, *Paul in the Roman World: The Conflict at Corinth* (Louisville: Westminster John Knox, 2001). On the economic location of the Pauline churches,

competence of the implied audience, which includes Gentile converts (6:9–11; 8:7; 12:2), to understand and appreciate Paul's OT quotations and references. Although individuals within the audience, especially recent pagan converts, may not all have this competence, Paul assumes that his implied audience, with its presumed common Jewish heritage (cf. 10:1–11), as a whole and in general shares his knowledge of Jewish scriptural traditions.[18]

Although Paul presumes that his implied audience knows OT traditions, what about the actual, first-century audience at Corinth? How would those Gentile converts with no prior connection to Judaism or the synagogue acquire enough scriptural knowledge to follow and appreciate Paul's scriptural quotes and references in 1 Corinthians?[19] Most of the Christian traditions to which Paul refers his audience in 1 Corinthians have an OT basis (8:6, 11b; 10:16; 11:23–25; 12:3, 13; 15:3–5; 16:22).[20] Presumably Paul and his coworkers would have instructed these Gentiles in at least a rudimentary christological interpretation of the OT when they first preached

---

see Justin J. Meggitt, *Paul, Poverty, and Survival* (Edinburgh: Clark, 1998), 97–153; Gerd Theissen, "Social Conflicts in the Corinthian Community: Further Remarks on J. J. Meggitt, *Paul, Poverty, and Survival*," *JSNT* 25, no. 3 (2003): 371–91. For an examination of the situation in Corinth and Paul's response to it by utilizing principles and imagery from systems thinking, see C. K. Robertson, *Conflict in Corinth: Redefining the System* (Studies in Biblical Literature 42; New York: Lang, 2001). For the religious and sociological attraction of Jews and Gentiles to Paul's mission at Corinth, see Margaret E. Thrall, "The Initial Attraction of Paul's Mission in Corinth and of the Church He Founded There," in *Paul, Luke, and the Graeco-Roman World: Essays in Honour of Alexander J. M. Wedderburn* (ed. Alf Christophersen et al.; JSNTSup 217; London: Sheffield Academic Press, 2002), 59–73. On the economic and social disparity within the Corinthian community, see John H. Elliott, "The Jesus Movement Was Not Egalitarian but Family-Oriented," *BibInt* 11 (2003): 193–95. On the Corinthian "house churches" as home-based gatherings of the local church under the direction not of the wealthy or socially elite but of gifted leaders and teachers, see M. Bruce Button and Fika J. van Rensburg, "The 'House Churches' in Corinth," *Neot* 37 (2003): 1–28; see also David G. Horrell, "Domestic Space and Christian Meetings at Corinth: Imagining New Contexts and the Buildings East of the Theatre," *NTS* 50 (2004): 349–69.

18. For a somewhat related distinction between the particular and universal audience, see James D. Hester, "Speaker, Audience, and Situations: A Modified Interactional Model," *Neot* 32 (1998): 75–94. For a typology of audiences in 1 Corinthians that includes the empirical, the fictive or implied, and the universal audience, see Wuellner, "Paul as Pastor," 54–60. On the implied audience's presumed knowledge of Jewish scriptural traditions, see Tomson, *Paul and the Jewish Law*, 82–85; Rosner, *Paul, Scripture, and Ethics*, 183–85; Williams, *Wisdom*, 18–19.

19. On Gentile Christians with no prior link to Judasim at Corinth, see Witherington, *Conflict and Community in Corinth*, 28. For the view that many in the actual audience would not have understood Paul's scriptural references, see Dewey, "Textuality," 37–61; Christopher D. Stanley, "'Pearls before Swine': Did Paul's Audiences Understand His Biblical Quotations?" *NovT* 41 (1999): 124–44; Tuckett, "Paul, Scripture, and Ethics," 403–24.

20. Eriksson, *Traditions*, 73–134. On OT background to other teachings in 1 Corinthians, see Tomson, *Paul and the Jewish Law*; Rosner, *Paul, Scripture, and Ethics*.

the gospel to them. According to Luke, christological explanations of the scriptures played a key role in the preaching of the gospel (Luke 24:27, 44–45; Acts 8:32, 35; 13:27, 29; 17:2, 11–12; 18:24, 28).[21]

Since Paul spent a year and six months "teaching" the "word of God" in Corinth among the many Gentile Corinthians who believed and were baptized (Acts 18:5–11), he would have had ample time to instruct these Gentiles in the OT scriptures needed to understand the "word of God" (18:11) about Jesus Christ. In the preaching of Paul directed to both Jews and God-fearing Gentiles at Pisidian Antioch, "the word of God/the Lord" (13:44, 46, 48, 49) that the Jews contradicted but that the Gentiles (not just "God-fearers" but Gentiles in general, cf. 13:46–48) delighted in and glorified contained numerous allusions to and quotes from the OT (13:16–41).

Furthermore, Christian liturgies at Corinth most likely included the reading and exposition of scripture on analogy with the Jewish synagogues.[22] But even before their conversion to Christianity, the Gentiles at Corinth would most probably have been well informed about Judaism and the Jewish scriptures through the synagogue (cf. Acts 18:4, 7).[23] If Gentile converts were considered to be "proselytes to an Israel reconfigured around Christ," they would presumably be instructed in the scriptures of Israel.[24]

---

21. Christoph W. Stenschke, *Luke's Portrait of Gentiles Prior to Their Coming to Faith* (WUNT 108; Tübingen: Mohr Siebeck, 1999), 339: "Luke emphasises the fact that Gentiles coming to faith need systematic and comprehensive catechesis right away . . . to know and to follow the word of God which these Gentiles lacked previously."

22. Dewey ("Textuality," 52) disputes this, but according to Meeks (*First Urban Christians*, 146): "[T]he rich allusions to and arguments from scripture that Paul sometimes includes in his letters . . . presuppose *some* means for learning both text and traditions of interpretation. Regular readings and homilies in the assemblies are the most probable" (his emphasis). See also Bart J. Koet, "As Close to the Synagogue as Can Be: Paul in Corinth (Acts 18,1–18)," *Corinthian Correspondence*, 397–415; Donald D. Binder, *Into the Temple Courts: The Place of the Synagogues in the Second Temple Period* (SBLDS 169; Atlanta: Society of Biblical Literature, 1999), 295–97, 399–404; Martin Hengel, *The Four Gospels and the One Gospel of Jesus Christ: An Investigation of the Collection and Origin of the Canonical Gospels* (Harrisburg, Pa.: Trinity Press International, 2000), 117–18.

23. On the Galatian Gentile Christians' previous familiarity with the Jewish scriptures, see Roy E. Ciampa, *The Presence and Function of Scripture in Galatians 1 and 2* (WUNT 102; Tübingen: Mohr Siebeck, 1998), 261. What Ciampa suggests about the Galatian Gentile converts would also apply to the Corinthians: "[E]ven those who are described as former idolaters who converted to Christ may actually have been quite familiar with Scripture and Judaism through extended exposure to and involvement with the synagogue prior to their conversion to Christ. The penetration of Jewish culture and traditions into the communities where they lived was quite substantial in some cases and Jewish synagogues were evidently quite eager to disseminate the teachings of Scripture to as wide an audience as possible" (266).

24. Terence L. Donaldson, *Paul and the Gentiles: Remapping the Apostle's Convictional World* (Minneapolis: Fortress, 1997), 236–47. See also Hays, "Conversion of the Imagination," 395–97.

An analysis of Paul's rhetorical strategy in explicitly using scripture compels us to consider whether Paul has included, modified, or ignored the original context of those scriptural references. But it is another question whether or to what extent Paul expects his implied audience to be familiar with the original context. We will have to determine that by examining the new epistolary context of each rhetorical use of scripture. It may vary from case to case. We will be concerned then with both the background and the new rhetorical foreground of each explicit use of scripture. From both Paul's and his audience's point of view, what role does the scriptural background play in the new rhetorical use of scripture in 1 Corinthians? And in this new rhetorical use, this "recontextualization" of scripture, what role does each explicit scriptural quote and allusion play in its respective new context within the Letter?

Preliminary Analysis and Overview

For the purposes of this investigation we are adopting a framework that divides the body of 1 Corinthians into six rhetorical demonstrations, each of which is further divided into smaller rhetorical units.[25] The goal of our investigation is an analysis of the impact of the explicit uses of scripture on Paul's implied audience in each of these demonstrations. Noteworthy at the outset is that scripture plays a role in each of the six rhetorical demonstrations in 1 Corinthians.

First Rhetorical Demonstration: 1 Corinthians 1:18–4:21

There are six explicit references to the OT in the first rhetorical demonstration in 1 Cor 1:18–4:21. The first two scriptural references frame the first unit in 1:18–31. The first explicit reference to scripture, introduced with the words "for it is written," occurs near the beginning of the first unit and quotes from Isa 29:14b: "I will destroy the wisdom of the wise and the intelligence of the intelligent I will set aside" (1 Cor 1:19). The second

---

25. For an outline of the six rhetorical demonstrations with their respective smaller units, see Raymond F. Collins, *First Corinthians* (SP 7; Collegeville, Minn.: Liturgical Press, 1999), 29–31. For slightly different configurations of the rhetoric in 1 Corinthians, see Mitchell, *Rhetoric of Reconciliation*, 184–85; Witherington, *Conflict and Community*, vi–viii, 76. Mitchell has four main sections of rhetorical proof, while Witherington sees nine distinct rhetorical arguments. With regard to modern attempts to apply categories of ancient rhetoric to Paul, Collins (*First Corinthians*, 86–87) perceptively notes: "Recourse to ancient rhetoric is useful. It provides us with a way of looking at Paul's letter that offers a different and insightful vantage point, but it must not be pushed to the extreme. The somewhat artificial categories of the manuals must not be superimposed on Paul's living communication to the Corinthians. . . . [T]his commentary will simply identify the major units in the body of Paul's letter as 'rhetorical demonstrations.'"

explicit reference to scripture, introduced with the words "so that as it is written," serves as the climactic conclusion of the first unit and quotes apparently from Jer 9:23 and/or 1 Kgdms 2:10: "If anyone is to boast, *in the Lord* let him boast" (1 Cor 1:31).

The first rhetorical demonstration's third unit in 2:6–16 contains the next two explicit references to scripture. Toward the middle of the unit there is a quotation, introduced by the words "but as it is written," based on a number of possible references to scripture (Isa 64:3; 52:15; 65:16; Jer 3:16; Sir 1:10): "What things eye has not seen and ear has not heard and has not arisen in the heart of a human being, what things God has prepared for those who love him" (1 Cor 2:9). At the conclusion of the unit there is an explicit reference to Isa 40:13 introduced simply by the word "for" (γάρ): "Who has known the mind of the Lord, that he will instruct him?" (1 Cor 2:16a).[26]

In the midst of the sixth unit (3:18–23) of the first rhetorical demonstration, introduced by the words "for it is written," there is a quotation of Job 5:13: "He is the one who catches the wise in their cleverness" (1 Cor 3:19b). This scriptural quote is closely coupled with the next, introduced by the words "and again," which cites from Ps 93:11 (LXX): "The Lord knows the thoughts of the wise that they are futile" (1 Cor 3:20). The joining of these two scriptural citations by the word "wise" that they have in common exemplifies the Jewish exegetical procedure known as *gezera shava*.[27]

Second Rhetorical Demonstration: 1 Corinthians 5:1–7:40

Although not explicitly introduced as a quote, the next scriptural reference, "Drive out the evil one from out of your very midst" (5:13b), is clearly based on a formulaic refrain repeated throughout several closely related passages in Deut 13:(5) 6; 17:7, 12; 19:13, 19; 21:9, 21; 22:21, 22, 24; 24:7. That this refrain would presumably be very familiar to the implied audience may be why it needs no introductory formula. At any rate, we include it in our investigation as an explicit scriptural "reference" even if it is not technically a formally introduced "quotation." It serves as the climactic

---

26. By considering explicit scriptural references in addition to quotations, we are being more inclusive than Stanley (*Paul*, 189 n. 21) who excludes 1 Cor 2:16; 5:13; 10:26; 11:7–12; 14:25; 15:25, 32 "in accordance with strict guidelines that limit the investigation to passages that offer explicit indication to the reader that a citation is being offered (introductory formula, interpretive comments, etc.)."

27. David Instone Brewer, *Techniques and Assumptions in Jewish Exegesis before 70 CE* (TSAJ 30; Tübingen: Mohr Siebeck, 1992), 18; Christoph Plag, "Paulus und die *Gezera schawa*: Zur Übernahme rabbinischer Auslegungskunst," *Jud* 50 (1994): 138–39.

conclusion to the second unit (1 Cor 5:9–13) within the second rhetorical demonstration in 5:1–7:40.

In the midst of the fourth unit (6:12–20) there occurs another scriptural reference within the second rhetorical demonstration. Introduced by the words "for, it says," it quotes from Gen 2:24: "The two will become one flesh" (1 Cor 6:16b).

Third Rhetorical Demonstration: 1 Corinthians 8:1–11:1

There are four explicit references to scripture in the third rhetorical demonstration in 8:1–11:1. The first two occur together in the midst of the fourth unit (9:1–14). The words "for in the law of Moses it is written" introduce the first reference, which quotes from Deut 25:4: "You shall not muzzle a threshing ox" (1 Cor 9:9). The words "for our sake indeed it was written that" introduce the second reference, whose origin is not immediately evident. It may be based on Isa 28:24, 28; 45:9; and/or Sir 6:19: "The one plowing ought to plow in hope and the one threshing in hope of sharing" (1 Cor 9:10). The word that these two scriptural references have in common, "threshing," links them closely together for mutual interpretation in accord with the Jewish exegetical procedure of *gezera shava*.

The next scriptural reference occurs in the midst of the eighth unit (10:1–13) of the third rhetorical demonstration. Introduced by the words "just as it is written," it quotes from Exod 32:6: "The people sat down to eat and drink and stood up to play" (1 Cor 10:7b).

The fourth and final scriptural reference in the third rhetorical demonstration occurs in the midst of the tenth and final unit (10:23–11:1). Although introduced simply by the word "for" (γάρ), it quotes verbatim from Ps 23:1 (LXX): "To the Lord are the earth and its fullness" (1 Cor 10:26).

Fourth Rhetorical Demonstration: 1 Corinthians 11:2–34

Rather than being formally introduced as quotations, the scriptural references in the first unit (11:2–16) of the fourth rhetorical demonstration in 11:2–34 are embedded within the rhetorical argumentation. Although not usually considered in treatments of scripture in 1 Corinthians, these verses are included because one of our goals is to demonstrate the importance of explicit scriptural references in Paul's rhetorical strategy in this Letter. These verses are obviously dependent upon the biblical creation traditions in Gen 1:27; 2:18, 21–24; 3:16, which would presumably be quite familiar to Paul's implied Corinthian audience: "For man, on the one hand, should not have his head covered, being the image and glory of God, the woman, on the other hand, is the glory of man. For man is not from woman but woman from man. For indeed man was not created on account of the woman but woman on account of the man. For this reason the woman should have authority over her head, on account of the angels. But neither is woman apart from man nor man apart from woman in the Lord. For just as the woman is from the man, so also the man is through the woman; but all things are from God" (1 Cor 11:7–12).

Fifth Rhetorical Demonstration: 1 Corinthians 12:1–14:40

There are two scriptural references in the fifth rhetorical demonstration in 12:1–14:40, both of which occur in the eleventh (14:20–25) of twelve units. Near the beginning of the unit, introduced by the words "in the law it is written that," the first scriptural reference quotes primarily from Isa 28:11–12: "In foreign tongues and in lips of foreigners I will speak to this people, and not even thus will they listen to me, says the Lord" (1 Cor 14:21). But it is also related to Deut 28:49 and Jer 5:15. The unit concludes with a second scriptural reference, introduced by the words "he will worship God announcing." It appears to be based on Isa 45:14; Zech 8:23; Dan 2:46–47; 1 Kgs 18:39: "God is really among you!" (1 Cor 14:25).

Sixth Rhetorical Demonstration: 1 Corinthians 15:1–58

The sixth rhetorical demonstration in 15:1–58 contains six explicit references to the OT. The first two occur toward the conclusion of the third unit (15:20–28). Introduced by the words "for it is necessary that" (δεῖ γάρ), the first scriptural reference is adapted from Ps 109:1 (LXX): "He reign until He places all the enemies under his feet" (1 Cor 15:25). The second scriptural reference, introduced simply by the word "for" (γάρ), quotes from Ps 8:7b (LXX): "He subjected all things under his feet" (1 Cor 15:27a). Since these two scriptural references are linked together for mutual interpretation by the words "all" and "under his feet," which they have in common, they provide yet another illustration of the Jewish exegetical procedure of *gezera shava*.

The third scriptural reference within the sixth rhetorical demonstration occurs in the midst of the fourth unit (15:29–34). Introduced by the words "if the dead are not raised," it quotes from Isa 22:13b: "Let us eat and drink, for tomorrow we die" (1 Cor 15:32b).

The sixth rhetorical demonstration's fourth scriptural reference occurs near the beginning of the sixth unit (15:44b–49). The words "so also it is written" introduce it, and it quotes from Gen 2:7: "The first human, Adam, became a living being" (1 Cor 15:45a).

The final two scriptural references in the sixth rhetorical demonstration occur in the midst of the seventh and final unit (15:50–58). They are both introduced by: "Then will come to be the word that is written." The first quotes from Isa 25:8a—"Death is swallowed up in victory" (1 Cor 15:54b)—and the second from Hos 13:14b: "Where, O death, is *your* victory? Where, O death, is *your* sting?" (1 Cor 15:55). These final two OT quotes in 1 Corinthians form yet another *gezera shava*, linked together for mutual interpretation by the words "death" and "victory," which they have in common.

Outline of Scriptural References in 1 Corinthians

1. First Rhetorical Demonstration (1:18–4:21)
   a. 1:19: "For it is written, 'I will destroy the wisdom of the wise and the intelligence of the intelligent I will set aside'" (Isa 29:14b)
   b. 1:31: "So that as it is written, 'If anyone is to boast, *in the Lord* let him boast'" (Jer 9:23; 1 Kgdms 2:10)
   c. 2:9: "But as it is written, 'What things eye has not seen and ear has not heard and have not arisen in the heart of a human being, what things God has prepared for those who love him'" (Isa 64:3; 52:15; 65:16; Jer 3:16; Sir 1:10)
   d. 2:16a: "For, 'Who has known the mind of the Lord, that he will instruct him?'" (Isa 40:13)
   e. 3:19b: "For it is written, 'He is the one who catches the wise in their cleverness'" (Job 5:13)
   f. 3:20: "And again, 'The Lord knows the thoughts of the wise that they are futile'" (LXX Ps 93:11)

2. Second Rhetorical Demonstration (5:1–7:40)
   a. 5:13b: "Drive out the evil one from out of your very midst" (Deut 13:6; 17:7, 12; 19:13, 19; 21:9, 21; 22:21, 22, 24; 24:7)
   b. 6:16b: "For, it says, 'The two will become one flesh'" (Gen 2:24)

3. Third Rhetorical Demonstration (8:1–11:1)
   a. 9:9: "For in the law of Moses it is written, 'You shall not muzzle a threshing ox'" (Deut 25:4)
   b. 9:10: "For our sake indeed it was written that, 'In hope ought the one plowing to plow and the one threshing in hope of receiving a share'" (Isa 28:24, 28; 45:9; Sir 6:19)
   c. 10:7b: "Just as it is written, 'The people sat down to eat and drink and stood up to play'" (Exod 32:6)
   d. 10:26: "For, 'To the Lord are the earth and its fullness'" (LXX Ps 23:1)

4. Fourth Rhetorical Demonstration (11:2–34)
   a. 11:7–12: "For man, on the one hand, should not have his head covered, being the image and glory of God, the woman, on the other hand, is the glory of man. For man is not from woman but woman from man. For indeed man was not created on account of the woman but woman on account of the man. For this reason the woman should have authority over her head, on account of the angels. But neither is woman apart from man nor man apart from woman in the Lord. For just as the woman is from the man, so also the man is through the woman; but all things are from God" (Gen 1:27; 2:18, 21–24; 3:16)

5. Fifth Rhetorical Demonstration (12:1–14:40)
   a. 14:21: "In the law it is written that, 'In foreign tongues and in lips of foreigners I will speak to this people, and not even thus will they listen to me, says the Lord'" (Isa 28:11–12; Deut 28:45–49; Jer 5:13–15)
   b. 14:25: "He will worship God announcing, 'God is really among you!'" (Isa 45:14; Zech 8:23; Dan 2:46–47; 1 Kgs 18:39)

6. Sixth Rhetorical Demonstration (15:1–58)
   a. 15:25: "For it is necessary that 'He reign until He places all the enemies under his feet'" (LXX Ps 109:1)
   b. 15:27a: "For, 'He subjected all things under his feet'" (LXX Ps 8:7b)
   c. 15:32b: "If the dead are not raised, 'Let us eat and drink, for tomorrow we die'" (Isa 22:13b)
   d. 15:45a: "So also it is written, 'The first human, Adam, became a living being'" (Gen 2:7)
   e. 15:54b: "Then will come to be the word that is written, 'Death is swallowed up in victory'" (Isa 25:8a)
   f. 15:55: "Where, O death, is your victory? Where, O death, is your sting?" (Hos 13:14b)

CHAPTER 2

1 Corinthians 1:19

*I will destroy the wisdom of the wise
and the intelligence of the intelligent I will set aside.*

Old Testament Background

The scriptural quotation in 1 Cor 1:19 is identical to LXX Isa 29:14b except that Paul has replaced the LXX κρύψω (I will hide) with ἀθετήσω (I will set aside) as the emphatic conclusion.[1] Paul's alteration enhances the linguistic artistry and poetic power of the chiastically arranged synonymous parallelism of the quotation.[2] But there are also other considerations from the OT background for Paul's preference.

LXX Ps 88:35 provides an impressive precedent for Paul's preference of ἀθετήσω in the final emphatic position of a chiastically constructed synonymous parallelism: (A) "Nor will I violate (B) my covenant and (B′) the things going forth from my lips (A′) I will never set aside (ἀθετήσω)."[3] This powerful pronouncement of a promise of God stands as an antithetical counterpart to Isa 29:14b. The God who emphatically promises never to violate or set aside God's own covenant or words in LXX Ps 88:35 just as

---

1. For the reasons why Paul himself made this change rather than taking it over from a pre-Pauline source (the MT also has the verb "hide" in the third person rather than "set aside"), see Koch, *Schrift*, 152–53; Stanley, *Paul*, 185–86; Wilk, *Bedeutung*, 44–45; Hans-Christian Kammler, *Kreuz und Weisheit: Eine exegetische Untersuchung zu 1 Kor 1,10–3,4* (WUNT 159; Tübingen: Mohr Siebeck, 2003), 71.

2. Stanley, *Paul*, 186: "By substituting the stronger ἀθετήσω, Paul creates a chiastic parallel with the preceding ἀπολῶ that serves to drive this point home to his hearers." See also Kammler, *Kreuz*, 71.

3. Whereas in 1 Cor 1:19 ἀθετήσω is a future indicative, in LXX Ps 88:35—its only occurrence in the LXX—it is an identical aorist subjunctive; see Gregory J. Lockwood, *1 Corinthians* (Concordia Commentary; St. Louis: Concordia, 2000), 62. The influence of LXX Ps 88:35 on 1 Cor 1:19 is neglected by Williams, *Wisdom*, 48–49.

emphatically promises to destroy and set aside the highest wisdom and intelligence of the world in the Pauline version of Isa 29:14b.

Paul's preference for ἀθετήσω finds additional basis in LXX Ps 32:10, which similarly expresses God's destructive power over the thinking and reasoning of the world: "The Lord disperses the plans of nations; he sets aside (ἀθετεῖ) the thoughts of peoples and sets aside (ἀθετεῖ) the plans of rulers."[4] LXX Ps 32:10 is linked to LXX Ps 88:35 by the catchword they have in common, "set aside," with God as subject in both cases.[5] In turn, LXX Ps 32:10 is linked to Isa 29:14b-15 by a similar theme and by the catchword βουλή (plan or counsel).[6] In the Psalm verse "the Lord disperses the plans (βουλάς) of nations . . . and sets aside the plans (βουλάς) of rulers" (see also the reference to "the plan [βουλή] of the Lord" in the following verse [LXX Ps 32:11]), whereas in Isa 29:15, "Woe to those profoundly making a plan (βουλήν) but not through the Lord; woe to those making a plan (βουλήν) in secret."

By altering the Isaian text with ἀθετήσω in the final emphatic position, Paul evokes for an implied audience thoroughly familiar with the scriptures more than just this particular Isaian text and its immediate context. Indeed, the Isaian text is too limited for Paul's purposes in 1 Corinthians. It refers to the wisdom and intelligence of the people of Israel (cf. "this people," ὁ λαὸς οὗτος and τὸν λαὸν τοῦτον in Isa 29:13–14).[7] The use of ἀθετήσω, a verb that is twice used in LXX Ps 32:10 in a context that speaks not only of God dispersing the plans of the *nations*, but of God "setting aside" (ἀθετεῖ) the thoughts of *peoples* and the plans of *rulers*, helps Paul to universalize the Isaian text to fit the context in 1 Corinthians, where Paul is concerned with the wisdom of the whole world (cf. 1 Cor 1:20).[8]

---

4. In contrast to the MT of this Psalm verse, LXX Ps 32:10 adds "sets aside (ἀθετεῖ) the plans of rulers," thus doubling and so reinforcing the use of the verb ἀθετέω. On the possible influence of LXX Ps 32:10 on 1 Cor 1:19, see Neil Richardson, *Paul's Language about God* (JSNTSup 99; Sheffield: Sheffield Academic Press, 1994), 124.

5. There is a further catchword connection between these two texts provided by "disperses" (διασκεδάζει) in LXX Ps 32:10 and "I will (never) disperse" (διασκεδάσω) spoken by God in LXX Ps 88:34. A further fact linking these two Psalm texts is that they are the only two places in the LXX where the verbs "disperse" (διασκεδάννυμι) and "set aside" (ἀθετέω) with God as subject follow one another in the same immediate context.

6. According to Wilk (*Bedeutung*, 45 n. 21), "Ps 32:10 . . . bietet eine einzigartige Parallele zu Jes 29:14b."

7. Because of the critical connotation of the term "this people" in reference to Israel, Wilk (*Bedeutung*, 246) maintains that Paul sees the people of Israel here as representing "die Gott fernstehende Welt."

8. That God "sets aside the plans of rulers (ἀρχόντων)" in LXX Ps 32:10 coheres with what Paul says in 1 Cor 2:6–8 about the wisdom of the "rulers" (ἀρχόντων) of this age (cf. 2:6, 8) not recognizing the wisdom of God.

Paul's use of the general introductory formula "it is written" (1 Cor 1:19), rather than a more specific "it is written in Isaiah," allows for a reference to more than Isa 29:14b and its immediate context. The Pauline version of the Isaian text evokes for the audience not just the text and context of Isa 29:14b but all of the other texts in the scriptures that speak of a similar theme and that are often interrelated by catchword connections (such as LXX Ps 32:10). This is not to say that the Pauline quote is necessarily a mixed quotation of Isa 29:14b and LXX Ps 32:10, or that the audience recognizes a reference to this particular Psalm text.[9] Rather, the Pauline alteration of the Isaian text coincides with and evokes in a metonymic way what the audience has heard not only in this Isaian text but elsewhere in the scriptures (especially in LXX Ps 32:10) about God's destructive power over the human wisdom and intelligence of the world.[10]

Literary-Rhetorical Analysis

The formula, "for it is written" (γέγραπται γάρ), introduces this first explicit quotation from scripture in 1 Corinthians.[11] The perfect passive form of the verb projects a meaning of what has been written in the past and still stands written for the present. What was written as authoritative scripture in the past still has validity for the present situation of Paul and the Corinthians.[12]

Let us analyze the structure, content, and oral pattern of the quotation, as considered in itself, to determine its rhetorical effects on its audience. The quotation presents its audience with a very concisely constructed, poetically patterned chiasm consisting of synonymously parallel pairs:

A ἀπολῶ—I will destroy
B τὴν σοφίαν τῶν σοφῶν—the wisdom of the wise

---

9. Wilk, *Bedeutung*, 45 n. 21: "[A]nders als bei dem vergleichbaren Mischzitat in Röm 11:8 liegt in 1 Kor 1:19 der etwaige Bezug auf Ps 32:10 (𝔊) allein im Sprachgebrauch des Paulus begründet."

10. On the "metonymic" function of quotations according to which they serve as brief references or abbreviations that represent or refer to a larger whole (in our case not just Isaiah but the scriptures in general), see John Miles Foley, *Immanent Art: From Structure to Meaning in Traditional Oral Epic* (Bloomington: Indiana University Press, 1991), 1–60; Warren Carter, *Matthew and Empire: Initial Explorations* (Harrisburg, Pa.: Trinity, 2001), 83, 95–96.

11. Collins, *First Corinthians*, 95: "In 1 Corinthians Paul introduces most of his scriptural citations in a formal and traditional Jewish fashion, using a characteristic lemma, γέγραπται, 'it is written' (1:19, 31; 2:9; 3:19; 9:9; 10:7; 14:21; 15:45)."

12. Thiselton (*Corinthians*, 160) refers here to "the force of the perfect tense of γράφω as expressing the present, lasting, effects which result from a past action." See also Andreas Lindemann, *Der erste Korintherbrief* (HNT 9; Tübingen: Mohr Siebeck, 2000), 44.

B´ καὶ τὴν σύνεσιν τῶν συνετῶν—and the intelligence of the intelligent
A´ ἀθετήσω—I will set aside

Initially (A) the audience hears a first-person singular speaker (God) authoritatively proclaiming with the future tense the promise that "I will destroy" (ἀπολῶ). An alliterated, intensified phrase, "the wisdom of the wise" (B), expresses the direct object of the destruction. The genitive construction, "of the wise" (τῶν σοφῶν) maximizes the meaning of the noun, "the wisdom" (τὴν σοφίαν). God will destroy the wisdom not just of ordinary people but the highest form of wisdom, the wisdom of those deemed to be "the wise ones." The annihilation of their wisdom will obliterate the very foundation of their high status as the wise of the world.

The second half of the chiasm begins with a synonymously parallel repetition of the direct object in the form of another alliterated, intensified phrase, "the intelligence of the intelligent" (B´). Again, the genitive construction, "of the intelligent" (τῶν συνετῶν), maximizes the meaning of the noun, "the intelligence" (τὴν σύνεσιν), to express the highest form of human intelligence. This second phrase, "the intelligence of the intelligent," serves as the direct object of the first-person singular verb in the future tense, "I will set aside" (ἀθετήσω), that emphatically concludes the chiasm (A´). God powerfully promises to "set aside," "reject," or "nullify" the very intelligence upon which the intelligent rely for their high status in the world.[13]

The second half of the chiasm inversely repeats and thus reinforces the verbal impact of the first half. The more-or-less synonymous, alliterated verbs—I will destroy (ἀπολῶ) and I will set aside (ἀθετήσω)—occur at opposite ends of the chiasm (A and A´) to function as a literary inclusion that structurally surrounds and encloses, thus predominating over, the more-or-less synonymous noun phrases—the wisdom of the wise and the intelligence of the intelligent (B and B´)—that are pulled together to form the center of the chiasm.[14] In and through the chiasm God has the first authoritative and powerful word, "I will destroy," and the last authoritative and powerful word, "I will set aside," over the highest forms of human wisdom and intelligence.

The highly artistic oral and poetic patterning within the chiasm coincides with its structural form and content to produce a rather striking

---

13. BDAG, 24; Meinrad Limbeck, "ἀθετέω," *EDNT* 1:35.
14. "Wisdom" (σοφία) and "intelligence" or "understanding" (σύνεσις) are frequently paired as synonymous or closely related equivalents throughout the LXX.

rhetorical effect on the audience. Each of the parallel pair of alliterated verbs begins with the short vowel "α"—alpha, the first letter of the alphabet—and ends with the long vowel "ω"—omega, the last letter of the alphabet. Both verbs thus project a kind of microcosmic inclusion or representative summary of the entire Greek alphabet to bolster their powerful impact. In both verbs the vowels predominate over the consonants—three vowels and two consonants in ἀπολῶ (A) and four vowels and three consonants in ἀθετήσω (A′).

Conversely, each word in the parallel pair of alliterated noun phrases begins with a consonant—"τ" or "σ" respectively. And each ends with the same consonant, "ν." In both noun phrases the consonants predominate over the vowels—ten consonants and seven vowels in τὴν σοφίαν τῶν σοφῶν (B) and twelve consonants and eight vowels in τὴν σύνεσιν τῶν συνετῶν (B′). Whereas in the noun phrases the consonants surround and enclose the vowels, in the verbs the vowels surround and enclose the consonants.

The audience hears the vowel-dominant verbs predominating over the consonant-dominant noun phrases that serve as their direct objects as follows: The sound of the last stressed open syllable, "τή," in the final emphatic verb, ἀθετήσω, in accord with the meaning of this verb, "sets aside," "rejects" or "nullifies" the sound of the first stressed closed syllable, "τὴν," that begins each noun phrase. In other words, the final verb leaves in the ears of the audience the last "τή" sound that thus predominates over the two previous "τὴν" sounds in the chiasm. Likewise, the sound of the very last syllable with a long vowel, "σω," in the final emphatic verb, ἀθετήσω, predominates as the last sound of the chiasm over the similar-sounding syllables with short vowels, σο-σο-σύ-συ, in the alliterated noun phrases. Finally, the sound of the long vowel in the final open syllable of each verb, "ω," chiastically predominates over the sounds of the same long vowel in the closed final syllables, τῶν σοφῶν–τῶν συνετῶν, in the alliterated noun phrases at the center of the chiasm. The dynamics of the oral patterning thus coincide with the meaning that God will both destroy and set aside both the wisdom of the wise and the intelligence of the intelligent.

There is a slight progression in sound that heightens the rhetorical impact from the first to the second half of the chiasm. The sound of the total of six "ν" consonants, as well as the number of three syllables in the final word, συνετῶν, in the second noun phrase (B′) amplifies the sound of the total of four "ν" consonants, as well as the number of two syllables in the final word, σοφῶν, in the first noun phrase (B). Similarly, the four syllables of the final verb, ἀθετήσω (A′), augment the three syllables of the first verb, ἀπολῶ (A). This coincides with a slight progression in nuance from simple and complete "destruction" without further ado to a "setting aside" or "rejection" of human wisdom and intelligence in favor of something new and different.[15]

This highly artistic, poetic, and concise chiasm makes the quotation memorable—not only easy to memorize but having lasting ramifications in the ears and on the mind. It sharpens the contrast between the destructive power of God and the wisdom of the world. It emphasizes God's final setting aside for something else of the human wisdom and intelligence God will destroy. In and of itself, then, this chiastically constructed quotation potently and poetically persuades its audience to turn away from worldly wisdom to the power of God.[16]

Relation to the Antecedent Context in 1 Corinthians 1:1–18

In this section we consider how the scriptural quotation in 1:19 as the authoritative word of God promising God's destruction and setting aside of the wisdom and intelligence of the world relates rhetorically to what the implied Corinthian audience has heard from Paul as the epistolary author in 1:1–18.

Opening Address in 1 Corinthians 1:1–3

Paul has pointedly included his audience among those currently "being saved" (σῳζομένοις) by God (divine passive), namely, "us" (1:18). What does the scriptural quote in 1:19 as an expression of the "power of God" (δύναμις θεοῦ, 1:18) mean for the audience whom Paul initially addressed as "the church of God" (τῇ ἐκκλησίᾳ τοῦ θεοῦ) that is existing in Corinth (1:2)? Recalling the biblical description of Israel as the "assembly" or "church" of the Lord, their characterization as "the church of God" indicates that God has elected and determined them "to be the center and

---

15. Wilk, *Bedeutung*, 161 n. 4: "Weit stärker als ἀπόλλυμι weist ἀθετέω im paulinischen Sprachgebrauch auf eine bestehende Alternative hin." This nuance of meaning for ἀθετήσω in 1 Cor 1:19 is recognized by James A. Davis, *Wisdom and Spirit: An Investigation of 1 Corinthians 1.18–3.20 against the Background of Jewish Sapiential Traditions in the Greco-Roman Period* (Lanham, Md.: University Press of America, 1984), 71–72. But Davis then unfortunately wants to give the same meaning to ἀπολῶ, thus eliminating the subtle development of meaning in the verbs.

16. Harvey, *Listening to the Text*, 287. On chiasm and the dynamics of biblical parallelism, see also Charles H. Talbert, *Reading Corinthians: A Literary and Theological Commentary on 1 and 2 Corinthians* (New York: Crossroad, 1987), xv; Robert Alter, *The Art of Biblical Poetry* (New York: Basic, 1985), 3–84.

crystallization-point of the eschatological Israel now being called into existence by him."[17] In a transition from the collective singular "church of God" to a plural form, Paul further characterizes his addressees as "those who have been and still are being consecrated" (ἡγιασμένοις) by God (perfect passive participle as divine passive) through their union with Christ Jesus (1:2).[18] The scriptural quote that expresses the power of God thus has particular relevance for Paul's audience as the eschatological Israel christologically reconfigured by God.[19]

As Paul was called (κλητὸς) to be an apostle of Christ Jesus through the will of God (1:1), so the Corinthians are called (κλητοῖ) by God to be holy.[20] They are thus to continue their consecration in Christ Jesus (1:2) by keep-

---

17. Jürgen Roloff, "ἐκκλησία," *EDNT* 1:412. "The church of God" is here, according to Collins (*First Corinthians*, 52), "an epithet that evokes the memory of the nation gathered together in the wilderness during the time of the Exodus, Israel's preeminent experience of redemption and salvation (Deut 23:1–8; Judg 20:2, etc.)." Gordon D. Fee, *The First Epistle to the Corinthians* (NICNT; Grand Rapids: Eerdmans, 1987), 31–32, states: "It already had been used in the LXX to refer to Israel as a gathered people (see Deut. 4:10 and scores of other references), and in the Greek world it was used especially of the body politic, assembled to conduct the affairs of state.... In its use as a term for the local community of believers the emphasis still often lay on their being a gathered community (cf. 5:1–5; 11:18; 14:23), but it also came to serve as the primary designation for themselves as the newly constituted, eschatological people of God." According to BDAG, 303, "the term ἐκκλησία apparently became popular among Christians in Greek-speaking areas for chiefy two reasons: to affirm continuity with Israel through use of a term found in Gk. translations of the Hebrew Scriptures, and to allay any suspicion, esp. in political circles, that Christians were a disorderly group." See also Robertson, *Conflict in Corinth*, 126–35.

18. Thiselton, *Corinthians*, 76–77: "The change from the singular to the plural is noteworthy. The singular stresses the solidarity of the readers as one united corporate entity; the plural calls attention to the individual responsibility of each member to live out his or her consecrated status in Christ." On "consecrated" here, Fee (*Corinthians*, 32 n. 21) states: "The verb has a rich OT background, whereby what was formerly profane or ordinary had been consecrated, and thus set apart, strictly for divine purposes." Hans Conzelmann, *1 Corinthians* (Hermeneia; Philadelphia: Fortress, 1975), 21: "[I]t gives expression to the character of sanctification as being a matter of grace. Holiness is received, not achieved." See also BDAG, 10; Lockwood, *1 Corinthians*, 26; Thiselton, *Corinthians*, 76.

19. Donaldson, *Paul and the Gentiles*, 236–48.

20. On "Sosthenes the brother" (1:1) as Paul's co-sender of the letter, see Eduard Verhoef, "The Senders of the Letters to the Corinthians and the Use of 'I' and 'We,'" in *The Corinthian Correspondence* (ed. Reimund Bieringer; BETL 125; Louvain: Louvain University Press, 1996), 421: "Paul may have had a rhetorical reason for mentioning Sosthenes: the appearance of that name in the prescript would give his argument more persuasive force and reliability in the eyes of the Corinthians."

ing themselves separate from the surrounding pagan society as God's new holy people, eschatological Israel.[21] The Corinthians are called to be holy "along with all those who call upon the name of our Lord (cf. Joel 3:5) Jesus Christ in every place, their (Lord) and ours" (1:2). And so all other Christians are included together with Paul's Corinthian audience in the "us" (1:18) for whom the scriptural quote in 1:19 expresses the power of God that is presently saving them.[22]

Thanksgiving in 1 Corinthians 1:4–9

In the thanksgiving section of the letter (1:4–9), Paul continues to characterize his audience's special relationship to God in Christ Jesus. He thanks his God (θεῷ) always for them for the grace of God (θεοῦ) given them in Christ Jesus (1:4). The God through whom the testimony of Christ was confirmed (ἐβεβαιώθη) among them (1:6) is the God who also will confirm (βεβαιώσει) them until the end blameless on the day of our Lord Jesus Christ (1:8).[23] Indeed, as Paul reinforces the promise, *faithful* is God (θεός) through whom they have been called into fellowship with his Son Jesus Christ our Lord (1:9).[24] Thus, the word of the cross that is the power of God

---

21. Horst Balz, "ἅγιος," *EDNT* 1:17: "[B]elievers themselves are regarded as holy, i.e., called out of the world about them into the presence of God as a *holy* people." Collins, *First Corinthians*, 52: "In Paul's biblical tradition the epithet 'holy' was especially used of Israel (Lev 11:44; 20:26), a people in a special covenanted relationship with YHWH, a nation set apart to be holy as YHWH was holy (Lev 19:2)." On the phrase "called to be holy," Thiselton (*Corinthians*, 77) points out that "believers are *called* to a lifestyle which reflects their *already* given status. Hence the theological and ethical make contact in this phrase in 1:2." See also Fee, *Corinthians*, 32–33; David E. Garland, *1 Corinthians* (BECNT; Grand Rapids: Baker, 2003), 27–28.

22. Lockwood, *1 Corinthians*, 26: "The NT applies ἐπικαλέομαι (call upon) to believers who, prompted by their hearing the Gospel in faith . . . call on the name of Jesus Christ and thus receive his rich mercy and salvation." The LXX of Joel 3:5 reads "all who call upon the name of the Lord will be saved (σωθήσεται)" (cf. Rom 10:13; Acts 2:21). See also Thiselton, *Corinthians*, 78.

23. David W. Kuck, *Judgment and Community Conflict: Paul's Use of Apocalyptic Judgment Language in 1 Corinthians 3:5–4:5* (NovTSup 66; Leiden: Brill, 1992), 241: "The function of the eschatological language in 1 Cor 1:7-8, therefore, is to shore up their confidence in their identity as a unique community because of their distinctive destiny in the final judgment. . . .The eschatological language of 1:7-8 is evidence that the Corinthians had accepted, at least formally, Paul's preaching of the final saving judgment of God for those who are in Christ."

24. We understand "God" rather than the immediately antecedent "Jesus Christ" as the subject of the relative pronoun ὅς in 1:8 for the following reasons: (1) the thanksgiving section begins and ends with a reference to God (1:4, 9); (2) God is the implied subject of all the passive verbs in the section; (3) these passives include "was confirmed" (1:6), where it is God who confirmed the testimony of Christ and thus God who *also* (note the καί) "will confirm" (1:8)

(θεοῦ) by which, in accord with the scriptural promise in 1:19, "I will destroy the wisdom of the wise and the intelligence of the intelligent I will set aside," is one of the ways God "will confirm" as blameless until the end the Corinthians together with all other Christians—"us," who are currently being saved by God (1:18).[25]

Theme and Occasion of the Letter in 1 Corinthians 1:10-18

Introduced by the Greek conjunction γάρ "for (γάρ) it is written," the scriptural quote in 1:19 further explains the preceding statement in 1:18:[26] "For the word of the cross to those who are being destroyed is foolishness, but to those who are being saved—us, it is the power of God."[27] Within the statement's strong antithetical parallelism, "those being destroyed" finds not only a contrast but an emphatic addition of the first-person plural pronoun embracing the audience in "those being saved—us" and "foolishness" is contrasted not with an expected single noun, "wisdom," but with an emphatic noun phrase, "power of God."[28] Paul employs the word "power" rather than "wisdom" here in accord with his use of the scriptural quote, which serves as an emphatic expression of God's power to destroy wisdom.[29]

---

the Corinthians to the end; and (4) that God is "faithful" reinforces the promise that God will confirm them to the end. See also Fee, *Corinthians*, 44; Lockwood, *1 Corinthians*, 33.

25. Brad Eastman, *The Significance of Grace in the Letters of Paul* (Studies in Biblical Literature 11; New York: Lang, 1999), 37: "The one who will strengthen the believers 'to the end' (1:8) has already shown his faithfulness in his call. The Corinthians can be certain of God's future help, since the present reality of their existence as believers is grounded in his sovereign call."

26. On γάρ as a conjunction used to express cause, reason, clarification, or inference, see BDAG, 189.

27. For a discussion of the message about the suffering servant of God in Isaiah 53 as the background of 1 Cor 1:18, which, however, neglects the quotation from Isa 29:14 in 1:19, see Otto Betz, "Der gekreuzigte Christus, unsere Weisheit und Gerechtigkeit (Der alttestamentliche Hintergrund von 1.Korinther 1-2)," in *Tradition and Interpretation in the New Testament: Essays in Honor of E. Earle Ellis for His Sixtieth Birthday* (ed. Gerald F. Hawthorne and Otto Betz; Grand Rapids: Eerdmans, 1987), 195-99.

28. Collins, *First Corinthians*, 102: "Paul underscores the power of God, which is emphatically placed at the end of his sentence in Greek. The parallelism between the two members of the antithesis is further broken by the use of 'us.'" See also Brown, *Cross*, 75; Lindemann, *Erste Korintherbrief*, 43-44; Petrus J. Gräbe, *The Power of God in Paul's Letters* (WUNT 123; Tübingen: Mohr Siebeck, 2000), 54-55. On the force of the present participles here, Raymond Pickett, *The Cross in Corinth: The Social Significance of the Death of Jesus* (JSNTSup 143; Sheffield: Sheffield Academic Press, 1997), 61: "By using present participles in drawing the distinction between these two categories of people Paul contemporizes the initial effect of his preaching of the cross in order to stress its continued significance for the life of the community."

29. The LXX background of the word for "power" (δύναμις) here is explored by Romano Penna, "The Gospel as 'Power of God' according to 1 Corinthians 1:18-25," in *Paul the Apos-*

Although the word of the cross is the power of God for those being saved (us), the scriptural quote expresses the negative side of that saving power, thus further explaining and intensifying the negative side of the antithetical parallelism.[30] Those for whom the word of the cross is foolishness are now being destroyed (ἀπολλυμένοις) by God (divine passive) (1:18) because in the authoritative scriptures God has promised to destroy (ἀπολῶ) the wisdom of the wise (1:19).[31] Through the scriptural quote Paul places the wise of the world along with their wisdom and the intelligent of the world along with their intelligence into the category of those on their way to eschatological destruction in the final judgment. The scriptural quote is thus persuading the Corinthian audience, as among those who by the power of God are on their way to eschatological salvation, away from the "wisdom of the wise and the intelligence of the intelligent."[32]

The scriptural quote in 1:19 further relates to what Paul says about his mission in 1:17: "For Christ did not send me to baptize but to evangelize,

---

tle: *Jew and Greek Alike* (Theological and Exegetical Study 1; Collegeville, Minn.: Liturgical Press, 1996), 172–73. He states: "It is always a matter of the δύναμις of God manifesting itself in victory over the enemies, and thus it comes to be always the saving presence of God in favor of the one for whom it is put into action" (172).

30. Helmut Merklein, *Der erste Brief an die Korinther: Kapitel 1–4* (ÖTK 7; Gütersloh: Gütersloher Verlagshaus, 1992), 178: "Daß Paulus von 'Kraft Gottes' spricht, erklärt sich wohl aus der Verbindung mit 'retten.' "

31. Hays, "Conversion of the Imagination," 403: "Paul's choice of the expression τοῖς ἀπολλυμένοις in 1 Cor 1.18 anticipates the strong verb ἀπολῶ in the Isaiah quotation. For this reason, we should read the participle as a true passive voice construction: those who regard the cross as foolishness are not just 'perishing' but actually 'being destroyed' *by God*. God's eschatological judgment is taking effect precisely in their incomprehension of God's saving action" (his emphasis). See also Collins, *First Corinthians*, 101; Lockwood, *1 Corinthians*, 61; Gräbe, *Power of God*, 55; Jeffrey S. Lamp, *First Corinthians 1–4 in Light of Jewish Wisdom Traditions: Christ, Wisdom, and Spirituality* (Studies in Bible and Early Christianity 42; Lewiston, N.Y.: Mellen, 2000), 136–37.

32. For a provocative argument that through wordplay "those being destroyed" (ἀπολλυμένοις) in 1:18 allude to the adherents of Apollos, the "Apollinists," and that "I will destroy" (ἀπολῶ) in 1:19 alludes to the name of Apollos, as Paul's main target in 1:12, see Joop F. M. Smit, " 'What Is Apollos? What Is Paul?': In Search for the Coherence of First Corinthians 1:10–4:21," *NovT* 44 (2002): 243–44. For another argument that in 1 Cor 1–4 Paul is enhancing himself in comparison to Apollos and thus undermining Apollos as his primary target, see D. P. Ker, "Paul and Apollos—Colleagues or Rivals?" *JSNT* 77 (2000): 75–97. But, for the view that it is not Apollos himself but his adherents who are the problem in Corinth, see Matthias Konradt, "Die korinthische Weisheit und das Wort vom Kreuz: Erwägungen zur korinthischen Problemkonstellation und paulinischen Intention in 1 Kor 1–4," *ZNW* 94 (2003): 181–214. And for more on the relation between Paul and Apollos, see Paul Barnett, "Paul, Apologist to the Corinthians," in *Paul and the Corinthians: Studies on a Community in Conflict. Essays in Honour of Margaret Thrall* (ed. Trevor J. Burke and J. Keith Elliott; NovTSup 109; Leiden: Brill, 2003), 316–19.

not in wisdom of word, so that the cross of Christ might not be emptied." Rather than evangelizing "in wisdom of word" (ἐν σοφίᾳ λόγου), Paul evangelizes with the "word" (λόγος) of the cross of Christ, which is the power of God (1:18) that in accord with the authoritative scriptures destroys the "wisdom" (σοφίαν) of the wise (1:19). Through the scriptural quote Paul places "wisdom of word" among the "wisdom of the wise" and the "intelligence of the intelligent" that the power of God operative in the "word" of the cross destroys and sets aside. The scriptural quote thus helps to attract the audience away from a preoccupation with "wisdom of word" in favor of the "power of God" in the "word" of the cross.

The key, enigmatic phrase "wisdom of word" (σοφίᾳ λόγου) is extremely rich and complex in meaning. In the biblical tradition the noun "wisdom" and the closely related adjective "wise" have several layers or nuances of meaning that often cannot be sharply separated.[33] In 1:17 "wisdom" denotes a spiritual or intellectual capacity synonymous with such terms as "understanding," "intelligence," "knowledge," "learning." But at the same time it refers to practical knowledge and technical skill synonymous with such terms as "skillfulness," "cleverness," "craftiness," "experience."[34] The Greek term for "word" (λόγος) likewise embraces a range of different meanings.[35] In 1:17 "word" refers to external speech or verbal expression as well as to internal reasoning or thought process.[36] Thus, the phrase "wisdom of word" refers to the rhetorical skill and eloquence involved in public proclamation as well as to the wisdom or understanding arrived at through clever and persuasive reasoning. It includes both the form and content of wise or sophisticated speech.[37]

---

33. Harald Hegermann, "σοφία," *EDNT* 3:258: "In the NT σοφία has a uniquely colorful spectrum of meanings whose elements cannot always be sharply distinguished."

34. On both "wisdom" (σοφία) and "wise" (σοφός), see BDAG, 934–35; Harald Hegermann, "σοφός," *EDNT* 3:261–62; idem, "σοφία," 258–61.

35. See BDAG, 598–601.

36. See the helpful note on 1:17 in the NAB. The English word "discourse" may come close to expressing this double sense of the Greek term.

37. Fee, *Corinthians*, 65; Pogoloff, *Logos and Sophia*, 108–13; Thiselton, *Corinthians*, 143–45. Bullmore (*Rhetorical Style*, 219) refers to the phrase "wisdom of word" as "a purposeful combination of . . . two terms designed to represent the complex of 'philosophy' and rhetoric which was endangering the Corinthian church. As it faithfully represents both sides of this complex, the translation 'eloquent wisdom' is a good one." For the view that "wisdom of word" also introduces a theme of "theological wisdom" in 1 Cor 1:17–3:4, see Angela Standhartinger, "Weisheit in *Joseph und Aseneth* und den paulinischen Briefen," *NTS* 47 (2001): 493–98. For an interpretation of "wisdom of word" in which "wisdom" is equated with the Jewish way of life, the torah, and "word" with a particular ruling by a Jewish sage, all of which is linked exclusively to the "Petrines," that is, the party of Cephas at Corinth (cf. 1:12), see Michael D. Goulder, *Paul and the Competing Mission in Corinth* (Peabody, Mass.: Hendrick-

Paul's reference to "wisdom of word" plays a significant role in the letter's overall rhetorical strategy. That Paul refuses to evangelize "in wisdom of word" (1:17) implies that his audience's attraction to popular sophistic rhetoric and eloquence—sophisticated speech—that involves keen competition for social status lies behind the rivalries among them that have been reported to him (1:11–13).[38] It is against such divisions that the thesis statement for the entire letter in 1:10 is directed: "I urge you, brothers, through the name of our Lord Jesus Christ, that you all say the same thing and there be no divisions among you, but that you be united in the same mind and the same conviction."[39] With its powerful promise of God's destruction of the "wisdom of the wise" and thus of the "wisdom of word" (1:17) through the word of the cross (1:18), the scriptural quote in 1:19 plays an important part in the letter's overall strategy to eliminate divisiveness and factionalism in the church at Corinth.[40]

That Christ sent (ἀπέστειλέν) Paul to evangelize (1:17) recalls and

---

son, 2001), 47–63. For the view that "word" (λόγος) in 1:17 refers exclusively to "reason," so that the phrase "not with wisdom of word" actually means "not with rational, reasoning, logical wisdom," see Smit, "'What Is Apollos?'" 245–46.

38. Peter Marshall, *Enmity in Corinth: Social Conventions in Paul's Relations with the Corinthians* (WUNT 2; Tübingen: Mohr, 1987); Timothy H. Lim, "'Not in Persuasive Words of Wisdom, but in the Demonstration of the Spirit and Power' (I Cor. 2:4)," *NovT* 29 (1987): 137–49; Pogoloff, *Logos and Sophia*; Litfin, *Paul's Theology of Proclamation*; Bruce W. Winter, *Philo and Paul among the Sophists: Alexandrian and Corinthian Responses to a Julio-Claudian Movement* (2d ed.; Grand Rapids: Eerdmans, 2002), 172–202; idem, *After Paul Left Corinth: The Influence of Secular Ethics and Social Change* (Grand Rapids: Eerdmans, 2001).

39. On 1:10 as the thesis statement for the entire letter, see Margaret M. Mitchell, "Rhetorical Shorthand in Pauline Argumentation: The Functions of 'the Gospel' in the Corinthian Correspondence," in *Gospel in Paul: Studies on Corinthians, Galatians and Romans for Richard N. Longenecker* (ed. L. Ann Jervis and Peter Richardson; JSNTSup 108; Sheffield: Sheffield Academic Press, 1994), 69; idem, *Paul*, 65–66, 184. On the audience of 1 Corinthians as a community divided over its leaders, see Andrew D. Clarke, *Serve the Community of the Church: Christians as Leaders and Ministers* (Grand Rapids: Eerdmans, 2000), 174–85. On Paul's addressing of his audience as "brothers," indicating that they are the family of God in a spiritual "sibling" relationship with him, Bruce W. Winter, "The 'Underlays' of Conflict and Compromise in 1 Corinthians," in *Paul and the Corinthians: Studies on a Community in Conflict: Essays in Honour of Margaret Thrall* (ed. Trevor J. Burke and J. Keith Elliott; NovTSup 109; Leiden: Brill, 2003), 154 n. 44: "Paul addressed them on 20 occasions as 'brothers' and 'sisters' in 1 Cor. and uses the term in another 17 instances as he appeals to them in their relationship with each other, himself and others. It appears to be part of his argument in seeking to resolve the pastoral issues. He uses it more in 1 Cor. than in any other of his letters."

40. On the divisions in the church at Corinth, see Charles K. Barrett, "Sectarian Diversity at Corinth," in *Paul and the Corinthians: Studies on a Community in Conflict. Essays in Honour of Margaret Thrall* (ed. Trevor J. Burke and J. Keith Elliott; NovTSup 109; Leiden: Brill, 2003), 287–302.

develops Paul's introductory presentation of himself to his audience: "Paul called to be an apostle (ἀπόστολος) of Christ Jesus through the will of God" (1:1).[41] The very voice of God in the scriptural quote in 1:19 expresses the power of God (δύναμις θεοῦ) through whose will (διὰ θελήματος θεοῦ) Paul was called to be an apostle of Christ. The rivalries reported to Paul "by those of Chloe" (1:11) involve a misunderstanding of Paul's apostleship to the point that Paul provocatively asks: "Surely Paul was not crucified (ἐσταυρώθη) for you, was he?" (1:13).[42] The scriptural quote in 1:19, in which God promises to destroy the "wisdom of the wise" and thus the "wisdom of word" (1:17) as an expression of the power of God that is "the word of the cross (σταυροῦ)" (1:18), plays a crucial role in Paul's persuasion of his audience away from an inappropriate preoccupation with the "wisdom of word" of various apostles that lies behind the rivalries (cf. 1:12) and misunderstanding of his apostleship.[43] Indeed, Paul's apostolate is to evangelize not "in wisdom of word, so that the cross (σταυρὸς) of Christ might not be emptied" (1:17).[44]

The future promise of the exercise of God's power in the scriptural quote of 1:19, "I will destroy the wisdom of the wise and the intelligence of the intelligent I will set aside," has already to a certain extent been fulfilled in the past event of Jesus' crucifixion. But the scriptural expression of the

---

41. Sosthenes is a co-sender of the letter (1:1). His characterization as "the brother" (ὁ ἀδελφὸς) rather than "my" or "our" brother designates him as an intermediary figure between Paul and the Corinthians. He is the brotherly coworker of Paul as well as the brotherly fellow believer of the Corinthian audience. As a co-sender of the letter he strengthens the bond of receptivity between Paul and the Corinthians. On Sosthenes as a coworker and co-sender, see Wolf-Henning Ollrog, *Paulus und seine Mitarbeiter: Untersuchungen zu Theorie und Praxis der paulinischen Mission* (WMANT 50; Neukirchen-Vluyn: Neukirchener Verlag, 1979), 30–31, 78, 183. On the probability that this is the same Sosthenes mentioned in Acts 18:7, see 31 n. 135. For the suggestion that Sosthenes' role as coauthor is evident in the "we" of 1 Cor 1:18–31 and 2:6–16, see Jerome Murphy-O'Connor, "Co-Authorship in the Corinthian Correspondence," *RB* 100 (1993): 562–79. The "we" in these passages, however, seems to include more than Sosthenes, rhetorically drawing in other coworkers and especially the audience.

42. On Chloe as a presumably well-to-do woman and "those of Chloe" as more likely slaves or freedmen than family members, see Andreas J. Köstenberger, "Women in the Pauline Mission," in *The Gospel to the Nations: Perspectives on Paul's Mission* (ed. Peter Bolt and Mark Thompson; Downers Grove, Ill.: InterVarsity, 2000), 227.

43. For an argument that these rivalries involve "preferences" rather than "parties," see Christof W. Strüder, "Preferences Not Parties: The Background of 1 Cor 1,12," *ETL* 79 (2003): 431–55.

44. For a recent discussion of 1 Cor 1:10–17, see Clive Marsh, "'Who Are You For?': 1 Corinthians 1:10–17 as Christian Scripture in the Context of Diverse Methods of Reading," in *Paul and the Corinthians: Studies on a Community in Conflict. Essays in Honour of Margaret Thrall* (ed. Trevor J. Burke and J. Keith Elliott; NovTSup 109; Leiden: Brill, 2003), 157–76.

power of God was not exhausted in that event. The scriptural promise of God's power still has a future dimension that continues to be activated and fulfilled in the very proclamation about the cross of Christ. Not just the content of the event of the cross in itself but the form in which it is communicated, the very "word" (λόγος), the external verbal proclamation with its connotations of internal reasoning, *is* presently the power of God by which the scriptural promise to destroy and set aside "the wisdom of the world" and thus "the wisdom of word" becomes a reality (1:18). This reality will be fully realized at the last judgment. Paul was sent to evangelize, to proclaim the "word" of the cross, so that the original event of the crucifixion, the cross of Christ, is not "emptied" of this scripturally promised power of God (1:17).[45]

Relation to the Subsequent Context in 1 Corinthians 1:20–4:21

Since the word of the cross is the power of God promising, in accord with the scriptural quote in 1:19, to destroy "the wisdom of the wise (σοφῶν)," Paul begins to draw out the meaning of the scriptural quote by provocatively posing to his Corinthian audience enamored with "wisdom (σοφίᾳ) of word" (1:17) a rhetorical triplet of questions:[46] "Where is the wise one (σοφός)? Where is the scribe (γραμματεύς)?[47] Where is the debater

---

45. Litfin, *Paul's Theology of Proclamation*, 193–201; Pickett, *Cross*, 61; Hays, "Conversion of the Imagination," 404; Michael J. Gorman, *Cruciformity: Paul's Narrative Spirituality of the Cross* (Grand Rapids: Eerdmans, 2001), 277–78.

46. Pogoloff, *Logos and Sophia*, 158: "Paul employs an *expolitio* of 1:19 in 1:20, repeating the sense of the citation in phrases redolent with more language from Isaiah, but now expanding the term σοφός with the list σοφός, γραμματεύς, and συζητητής. Taken in this universalized sense, σοφός becomes a generic term for a person, whether Greek or Jew, who claims to be humanly wise. This is borne out by the following terms which refer to scholars of both the Jewish and Hellenistic worlds." On both the Jewish and Hellenistic connotations of the three terms, see also Loveday Alexander, "IPSE DIXIT: Citation of Authority in Paul and in the Jewish and Hellenistic Schools," in *Paul beyond the Judaism/Hellenism Divide* (ed. Troels Engberg-Pedersen; Louisville: Westminster John Knox, 2001), 125–27. Goulder (*Paul and the Competing Mission*, 57–58), however, maintains an exclusively Jewish reference for all three terms. On the rhetorical use of *repetitio* or *expolitio* here with anaphora (repetition of "where"), see Collins, *First Corinthians*, 103–4; Kammler, *Kreuz*, 73.

47. On "scribe" as a term for a Jewish scholar, Pogoloff (*Logos and Sophia*, 171) states: "Jewish scribes, then, fit into the Hellenistic world. They competed with others who boasted of the superiority of their wisdom. Their competition was inevitably shaped by the dominant Hellenistic culture.... The scribes, like sophists and rhetors, ran schools, asserted their authority, sought to be perceived as wise, gained status if they were so perceived, and were thus able to enjoy the benefits of a cultured life. Thus, it should not surprise us that a Jewish scribe can

(συζητητής) of this age?" (1:20a).⁴⁸ Although the three subjects introduced by the interrogative "where" (ποῦ; cf. LXX Isa 33:18 for a similar rhetorical triplet) are more-or-less synonymous terms for educated intellectual leaders as representative of the wisdom of the world, there is a progression in the length of the words within the series ending in a climax embracing the entire triplet.⁴⁹ From the two-syllable word σοφός (wise one), the catchword with the quote in 1:19, the audience hears the four-syllable word γραμματεύς (scribe) followed by the ten-syllable phrase συζητητὴς τοῦ αἰῶνος τούτου (the debater of this age). The climactic phrase, "of this age," which, as an apocalyptic term, implies a contrast with "the age to come," modifies each of the subjects in the series.⁵⁰

The answer that the rhetorical triplet of questions bluntly provokes from the audience is "Nowhere!" The wise one, scribe, and debater of "this age" have no position in the new age inaugurated by the crucifixion of Christ. In view of the scriptural quote promising God's destruction and setting aside of the wisdom of the wise and the intelligence of the intelligent (1:19), the intellectual elite of "this age," those involved with the "wisdom

---

be called either a σοφός or a συζητητής. The titles would have been particularly fitting in the ears of a cosmopolitan resident of Corinth, who witnessed a steady stream of Hellenized wise men of various nationalities whose social rôles were all constrained by Hellenistic cultural expectations." On the translation of γραμματεύς here, Thiselton (*Corinthians*, 164) suggests: "Hence, if we allow for a blend of Graeco-Roman and Jewish nuances, we might translate *person of letters*, to preserve the connection with word history, or, perhaps less controversially, *expert*. Today we might well use some such term as '*the professional*.' "

48. As Pogoloff (*Logos and Sophia*) remarks, the term συζητητής "is easily understood as a 'disputant,' i.e., one who jointly inquires into a matter. Such a dispute (ζήτημα) may be a philosophical investigation or an official or judicial inquiry, i.e., a rhetorical exercise by a philosopher or rhetor. Thus, 'debater' is a good translation for the disputant familiar in Corinth, from law courts to lecture halls to dining rooms." On "debater" as a nonpejorative term for the Greek philosopher, see Markus Lautenschlager, "Abschied vom Disputierer: Zur Bedeutung von συζητητής in 1 Kor 1,20," *ZNW* 83 (1992): 276–85; Kammler, *Kreuz*, 74–76.

49. Wolfgang Schrage, *Der erste Brief an die Korinther (1 Kor 1,1–6,11)* (EKKNT 7/1; Zürich: Benziger, 1991), 176: "Paulus durch die drei Beispiele rhetorisch-pleonastisch alle Formen menschlicher Weisheit treffen will." See also Lamp, *First Corinthians 1–4*, 137.

50. Conzelmann, *1 Corinthians*, 43: "The length of the third member provides a climax to the threefold anaphora. . . . No subtle distinctions are to be sought between the three concepts. The qualification τοῦ αἰῶνος τούτου, 'of this world,' stands, for rhetorical reasons, only in the third member, but applies in content to all three. . . . The expression 'this aeon' derives from apocalyptic; it has its counterpart in the expectation of the 'coming aeon.' " See also Christian Wolff, *Der erste Brief des Paulus an die Korinther* (2d ed.; THKNT 7; Leipzig: Evangelische Verlagsanstalt, 2000), 37; Kammler, *Kreuz*, 73.

of word" (1:17) causing the rivalries at Corinth (1:10–13), do not have the high status the audience might think they have.[51]

The foundation that the world's intellectual elite stand on for their high social status has disintegrated. With an interrogative expecting an affirmative answer (οὐχὶ), Paul asks his Corinthian audience, "Has not God made foolish the wisdom of the world?" (1:20b). That God has made foolish the wisdom of the world (τὴν σοφίαν τοῦ κόσμου) expresses an actualization of the scriptural promise in 1:19 that "I will destroy the wisdom of the wise (τὴν σοφίαν τῶν σοφῶν)."[52] God has "destroyed" the wisdom "of the world," represented by the wise one, scribe, and debater "of this age" (1:20a), by rendering it foolish. Although the word of the cross is foolishness (μωρία) to the world's intellectual elite, the human wisdom at the heart of their sophistication God has made foolish (ἐμώρανεν), so that they are "being destroyed"(1:18), that is, on their way to eschatological destruction by God in the final judgment.[53]

The scriptural promise in 1:19 implies God's destructive setting aside of the intelligence and wisdom of the world in favor of something else. That alternative begins to become explicit in terms of the "wisdom of God" in 1:21. As Paul explains, "in the wisdom of God" the world did not through wisdom come to know or acknowledge God.[54] God was thus pleased

---

51. Fee, *Corinthians*, 71: "The various wise ones all belong to this present age that has been judged by God and is on its way out."

52. In 1 Cor 1:19-20 Paul may be inspired by LXX Isa 19:11-12: "The leaders of Tanis will be fools (μωροὶ); as for the wise (σοφοὶ, cf. σοφῶν in 1:19) counselors of the king, their counsel will be made foolish (μωρανθήσεται, divine passive, cf. ἐμώρανεν ὁ θεὸς in 1:20; cf. LXX Isa 44:25). How will you say to the king, 'We are sons of the intelligent (συνετῶν, cf. συνετῶν in 1:19), sons of the kings of old'? Where (ποῦ) are now your wise ones (σοφοὶ)? (cf. ποῦ σοφός in 1:20a)."

53. Edward Adams, *Constructing the World: A Study in Paul's Cosmological Language* (Edinburgh: Clark, 2000), 112: "The genitive τοῦ κόσμου indicates belonging: God has nullified the wisdom which is *possessed* by the world. . . . With ἐμώρανεν Paul indicates that God has actively *made* the wisdom of the world to appear as foolishness. God has turned the world's wisdom into its very antithesis, foolishness. . . . God's mockery of the world and its wisdom corresponds to the destruction (ἀπολῶ) of the wisdom of the wise, as predicted by Isaiah. The thought is thoroughly apocalyptic. In the event of the cross, God has initiated the change of the ages. The old world/age, the κόσμος, has been judged and condemned. Its wisdom has been destroyed, cast aside and ridiculed."

54. For discussions of whether the prepositional phrase "in the wisdom of God" is temporal, spatial, adverbial, or circumstantial, see A. J. M. Wedderburn, "ἐν τῇ σοφίᾳ τοῦ θεοῦ—1 Kor 1.21," *ZNW* 64 (1973): 132–34; Lamp, *First Corinthians 1–4*, 138–40. Lamp concludes: "The adverbial or circumstantial understanding best attributes the failure of the world to know God through its own wisdom to the proactive will of God. The phrase is then best rendered in the sense of 'providentially' or 'in the wise counsel of God'" (140).

through the foolishness (μωρίας) of the preaching—the preaching of the word of the cross that is foolishness (μωρία) for those being destroyed (1:18a)—to save (σῶσαι) those who believe, that is, "us," Paul and his audience, those being saved (σῳζομένοις) by the power of God (1:18b) and thus on their way to eschatological salvation by God in the final judgment.[55]

The positive counterpart to the wisdom (σοφίαν) of the wise of the world that God promises in the scriptural quote of 1:19 to destroy and set aside becomes fully explicit in Paul's statement in 1:24 that Christ—a Christ who has been and still is "crucified" (perfect passive participle in 1:23), the Christ of "the word of the cross" (1:18)—is "power of God and wisdom (σοφίαν) of God."[56] Paradoxically this power and wisdom of God, by which God is saving the believing audience of Paul, is the foolishness and weakness that is wiser and stronger than human beings (1:25). It is stronger and wiser than human beings because, in accord with the scriptural promise of 1:19, God will destroy human wisdom and replace it with the wisdom of God.

The scriptural quote of 1:19 finds further actualization and development as it contributes to Paul's rhetorical strategy in 1:26–28. Paul directs his audience to consider their "calling" (κλῆσιν, 1:26), that is, their being part of those called (κλητοῖς), both Jews and Greeks, for whom Christ is power of God and wisdom of God (1:24) to save those who believe (1:21), namely, "us," who are being saved by the power of God (1:18) expressed in the scriptural quote of 1:19.[57] By the human standards of this world, not

---

55. Adams, *Constructing the World*, 112–13: "The knowledge of God which Paul has in view here is thus what might be called a 'saving' knowledge of God. Paul insists that the world has not come to know God in a saving way. . . . It will not do, therefore, in the light of vv. 20–21, merely to say that the wisdom of the world has been superseded or transcended by a fuller revelation. The world's wisdom and the word of the cross are here set in complete antithesis."

56. Lindemann, *Erste Korintherbrief*, 46–47: "Das Part. Perf. χριστὸς ἐσταυρωμένος zeigt an, daß Christus der Gekreuzigte *bleibt*, d. h. es geht nicht um ein vergangenes (und damit womöglich durch Ostern 'überholtes') Geschehen, sondern das Kerygma spricht von der Gegenwart des *gekreuzigten* Christus" (his emphasis). Lamp, *First Corinthians 1–4*, 143: "[I]dentifying Christ as θεοῦ δύναμις presents no real surprise, for Paul began his discussion in v. 18 by designating the word of the cross as δύναμις θεοῦ. The significant advance in this argument is found in the identification of Christ as θεοῦ σοφία. This ascription stands as the crescendo of his argument."

57. Lockwood (*1 Corinthians*, 73) notes "the close link between κλῆσις in 1:26 and κλητοῖς in 1:24." In 1:2 Paul designated his Corinthian audience as "those called (κλητοῖς) (by God) to be holy." As Eastman (*Significance of Grace*, 38) notes, "[T]he Corinthians' background made it readily apparent that their present standing among the people of God was due entirely to God's grace." See also Mark J. Goodwin, *Paul, Apostle of the Living God: Kerygma and Conversion in 2 Corinthians* (Harrisburg, Pa.: Trinity Press International, 2001), 143.

many of Paul's audience were of high social status in Greco-Roman Corinth.[58] Not many were "wise" (the educated, intellectual elite), not many were "powerful" (those with political and social influence based upon their wealth), and not many were "of noble birth" (those entitled to social esteem and distinction based on their pedigree) (1:26).[59] Nevertheless, God chose them to actualize and expand God's promise as expressed in the scriptural quote of 1:19.

In 1:27a, Paul states that it is "the foolish things of the world" (τὰ μωρὰ τοῦ κοσμου)—those things (such as the cross) and those people the world considers to be foolish, including the not many who are wise (σοφοὶ) among the Corinthian audience (1:26)—that God chose in order to shame the wise (σοφούς).[60] This develops his assertion in 1:20b that God has made foolish the wisdom of the world (τὴν σοφίαν τοῦ κόσμου) as an actualization of God's scriptural promise in 1:19 to destroy the wisdom of the wise (τὴν σοφίαν τῶν σοφῶν). That God will "shame" the wise in his choosing of the foolish will become fully evident in the final judgment, when those who are foolish in the eyes of the world will be saved by the power of God, while those who are wise, those with whom the Corinthian audience is enamored because of their "wisdom of word" (1:17), but those for whom the word of the cross is foolishness, will be destroyed (1:18) in accord with God's scriptural promise to destroy the wisdom of the wise (1:19).[61]

---

58. Fee, *Corinthians*, 79–80: "The prepositional phrase 'by human standards,' which qualifies 'wise,' is intended for all three terms (cf. 'of this age' in v. 20) and reflects the perspective of their current thinking." On the prepositional phrase κατὰ σάρκα ("by human standards") here, Adams (*Constructing the World*, 114) states: "The word σάρξ here carries apocalyptic associations and signifies the sphere of opposition of God. κατὰ σάρκα is the point of view which is characteristic of this sphere. The prized social distinctions of the Hellenistic world are thus consigned by Paul to the old world/age."

59. Conzelmann, *1 Corinthians*, 50; Dieter Sänger, "Die δυνατοί in I Kor 1:26," *ZNW* 76 (1985): 285–91; Lamp, *First Corinthians 1–4*, 147; Winter, *Philo and Paul*, 190–95. After a survey of possible OT allusions in 1:26, Williams (*Wisdom*, 108–10) opts for Jer 9:22, but concludes: "It is, however, quite likely that many Gentile readers would not have grasped such an allusion." See also O'Day, "Jeremiah 9:22–23," 262–66. For a refutation of the assertion that 1:26b should be read as a question—"are not many of you wise, powerful, and of noble birth?"—see Collins, *First Corinthians*, 110.

60. "Of the world" (τοῦ κοσμου) does not have the possessive sense of "belonging to," as in 1:20, "but has the sense of 'in the estimation of' or 'from the perspective of,'" according to Adams, *Constructing the World*, 114–15. For the suggestion that the role of the "fool" taken by Paul and the Corinthians, as well as that the message of the cross is foolishness (1:18), is best understood from the background of the popular theater and the fool's role in mime, see Laurence L. Welborn, "Μωρὸς γένεσθω: Paul's Appropriation of the Role of the Fool in 1 Corinthians 1–4," *BibInt* 10 (2002): 420–35.

61. As Fee (*Corinthians*, 83) notes, by the term "shame" (καταισχύνη) here "Paul does not mean something subjective, the 'feelings of shame' that the wise are now to feel. Rather, he has

Although not many of the called Corinthians are powerful (1:26), those considered weak in the world God nevertheless chose to shame the strong (1:27b).⁶² And although not many of the called Corinthians are of noble birth (1:26), those considered of lowly birth and despised in the world—those who are nothing—God nevertheless chose to reduce to nothing those who are something (1:28). From God's scriptural promise to destroy (ἀπολῶ) the wisdom of the wise (1:19), Paul's rhetorical strategy has progressed to God's making foolish (ἐμώρανεν) the wisdom of the world (1:20) to God's choosing of the Corinthian audience not only to shame (καταισχύνῃ) the wise and strong of the world (1:27), but to reduce to nothing (καταργήσῃ), and thus utterly destroy, the entire social value system of this world (1:28).⁶³

The scriptural quote of 1:19, which expresses the negative side of the "power of God" (δύναμις θεοῦ) to save those who believe while destroying those for whom the "word" (λόγος) of the cross is foolishness (1:18), reverberates throughout the remainder of Paul's rhetorical demonstration in 1:18–4:21. In 2:4–5 Paul insists that his "word" (λόγος) and his preaching were not with a persuasion of wisdom (σοφίας) but with a demonstration of spirit and power (δυνάμεως), so that the faith of his Corinthian audience might be not in human wisdom (σοφίᾳ ἀνθρώπων) but in the power of God (δυνάμει θεοῦ). And in 4:19–20 at the climactic conclusion of this first rhetorical demonstration, Paul states that when he returns to Corinth he will know not the "word" (λόγον) of those who are inflated but the power (δύναμιν), for the kingdom of God is not a matter of "word" (λόγῳ) but of power (δυνάμει). The scriptural quote of 1:19 thus plays a major role in Paul's persuasion of his implied audience not to place their faith in the "wisdom of word" (συφίᾳ λόγου, 1:17) causing the rivalries among them (1:10–13) but in the *power* of God that is the *word* of the cross (1:18).⁶⁴

---

here picked up an OT theme that expresses the vindication of God over his enemies (or over the enemies of the righteous), a vindication that is related to God's righteous judgments (e.g., Ps. 6:10; 31:17; 35:4, 26–27). With Paul this vindication has become eschatological; in choosing the Corinthians God has already begun the final vindication over his enemies." On "shame" as a corporate, social, and public phenomenon in an "honor-shame" culture, see Thiselton, *Corinthians*, 186–87.

62. On the concept of "weakness" in 1 Cor 1:25, 27, see David Alan Black, *Paul, Apostle of Weakness: Astheneia and Its Cognates in the Pauline Literature* (New York: Lang, 1984), 93–100.

63. Adams, *Constructing the World*, 115: "The verb καταργέω is employed by Paul with reference to final eschatological destruction.... God's overturning of the values of the κόσμος is part and parcel of an apocalyptic judgement on the κόσμος which will culminate in its total destruction."

64. Charles A. Wanamaker, "A Rhetoric of Power: Ideology and 1 Corinthians 1–4," in *Paul and the Corinthians: Studies on a Community in Conflict. Essays in Honour of Margaret*

Summary on 1 Corinthians 1:19

1. The Pauline alteration of Isa 29:14 in 1 Cor 1:19 coincides with and evokes what the audience has heard not only in this Isaian text but elsewhere in the scriptures about God's destructive power over the human wisdom and intelligence of the world.

2. By not only sharpening the contrast between the destructive power of God and the wisdom of the world, but emphasizing God's final setting aside for something else of the human wisdom and intelligence God will destroy, the chiastically constructed scriptural quotation in 1 Cor 1:19 aims to turn its audience away from worldly wisdom to the power of God.

3. As an expression of the power of God, the scriptural quote in 1:19 has particular relevance for Paul's audience as the eschatological Israel christologically reconfigured by God (1:1–3). This power of God is one of the ways God will confirm as blameless until the end the Corinthians together with all other Christians, who are currently being saved by God (1:4–9). God's scriptural promise in 1:19 to destroy the "wisdom of the wise" and thus the "wisdom of word" (1:17) as an expression of the power of God that is "the word of the cross" (1:18) plays a crucial role in Paul's persuasion of his audience away from an inappropriate preoccupation with the "wisdom of word" of various apostles that lies behind the Corinthian rivalries and misunderstanding of his apostleship (1:10–18).

4. From God's scriptural promise to "destroy" the wisdom of the wise (1:19), Paul's rhetorical strategy progresses to God's "making foolish" the wisdom of the world (1:20) to God's choosing of the Corinthian audience not only to "shame" the wise and strong of the world (1:27), but to "reduce to nothing," and thus utterly destroy, the entire social value system of this world (1:28) by the power of God that is the word of the cross (1:20–4:21).

Thrall (ed. Trevor J. Burke and J. Keith Elliott; NovTSup 109; Leiden: Brill, 2003), 136–37: "Without any means of physical coercion he [Paul] engaged in the one strategy available to him for reclaiming the church from the grips of factionalism, the construction of a rhetoric of persuasion that could reestablish and sustain his authority while re-unifying the community. It is this which gives 1 Cor. 1:10–4:21 its strongly ideological character as Paul uses meaning encoded in language and rhetoric in order to achieve his goals."

CHAPTER 3

1 Corinthians 1:31

If anyone is to boast, in the Lord *let him boast.*

Old Testament Background

Most maintain that in 1 Cor 1:31 Paul is referring primarily if not exclusively to LXX Jer 9:23: "But rather in this (ἐν τούτῳ) let boast (καυχάσθω) the one who boasts (ὁ καυχώμενος), to understand and know that I am Lord (κύριος)."[1] But some point out the possibility that Paul may also be referring to 1 Kgdms 2:10: "but rather in this (ἐν τούτῳ) let boast (καυχάσθω) the one who boasts (ὁ καυχώμενος), to understand and know the Lord (κύριον)."[2] The Jeremiah text might be the primary allusion because Jer 9:22 uses the words "wise one" (σοφός) and "strong one" (ἰσχυρός), which also occur in 1 Cor 1:26–27. First Kingdoms 2:10, however, uses the words "powerful one" (δυνατός) and "intelligent one" (φρόνιμος), which also occur in 1 Cor 1:26 and 4:10 respectively.[3] But with regard to the quo-

---

1. Conzelmann, *1 Corinthians*, 52; Fee, *Corinthians*, 87; O'Day, "Jeremiah 9:22-23," 259-67; Stanley, *Paul*, 186-88; Witherington, *Conflict and Community*, 118; Collins, *First Corinthians*, 113; Lindemann, *Erste Korintherbrief*, 52; Lockwood, *1 Corinthians*, 80; Thiselton, *Corinthians*, 195; Williams, *Wisdom*, 103-12; Kammler, *Kreuz*, 141-42.

2. Koch, *Schrift*, 35-36; Schrage, *Erste Brief*, 1:205-6; Hays, *First Corinthians*, 34-35; idem, "Conversion of the Imagination," 404-6; J. Ross Wagner, " 'Not beyond the Things Which Are Written': A Call to Boast Only in the Lord (1 Cor 4.6)," *NTS* 44 (1998): 283-86; Tuckett, "Paul, Scripture, and Ethics," 416-22. In addition to Jer 9:22-23 and 1 Kgdms 2:10, Williams (*Wisdom*, 113-14) refers to LXX Ode 3:10, which is, however, not relevant as OT background for Paul. Karen H. Jobes and Moisés Silva, *Invitation to the Septuagint* (Grand Rapids: Baker Academic, 2000), 78 n. 22: "The Odes, which are appended to the Psalms in a few manuscripts, form part of the liturgical services in the Eastern Orthodox Church. This book consists of a series of prayers taken from both the Old and New Testaments; it is therefore somewhat misleading to include it within the corpus of the Septuagint."

3. Schrage, *Erste Brief*, 1:205 n. 615: "[J]e einmal steht Paulus näher dem Text von 1Sam 2,10 LXX (φρόνιμος, δύνατος) und einmal dem von Jer 9,23 (σοφός, ἰσχυρός)."

tation itself, the main words—"the one who boasts," "Lord," and "let him boast"—could come from either 1 Kgdms 2:10 or LXX Jer 9:23.[4] Is Paul referring to one or the other or both of these scriptural texts?

We would like to argue that, whatever may have been Paul's primary source for the scriptural quote in 1:31, he does not expect his implied Corinthian audience necessarily to recognize that the quote comes from either 1 Kdgms 2:10 or LXX Jer 9:23, but that it evokes in a metonymic way any and all of the scriptural texts that refer to "boasting" or placing one's total trust in God alone. The rhetorical function and effect of the scriptural quote in its new context in 1 Corinthians, then, does not depend upon its audience's recall of any particular OT text or context, whether those of 1 Kgdms 2:10 or LXX Jer 9:23, but simply upon its origin and authority from scripture in general.

We offer the following considerations as confirmation of this argument: First, in introducing the scriptural quote of 1:31 to his audience, Paul employs the general formula "so that as it is written" rather than a more specific formula such as "in Jeremiah it is written" or "Jeremiah says" or "David says."[5] This general formula allows the audience to recall 1 Kgdms 2:10 and/or LXX Jer 9:23 and/or any other places in the scriptures that speak of boasting in God alone rather than in human beings.

Second, although bearing striking similarities to both 1 Kgdms 2:10 and LXX Jer 9:23, Paul's version of the scriptural quote is not an exact, verbatim citation of either of these texts.[6] Rather than having the one who would boast to boast in "understanding and knowing" the Lord as in these two OT texts, Paul has the one who would boast to boast simply "in the Lord," thus placing more emphasis on the Lord as the immediate object of

---

4. Lim, *Scripture*, 174: "The Pauline verse appears to resemble a summary statement of Jeremiah 9:23-4 more than a quotation of one of its phrases."

5. For examples of such specific Pauline scriptural introductions in other contexts, see Rom 4:6; 11:9 ("David says"); 9:25 ("in Hosea it says"); 9:27 ("Isaiah cries out"); 9:29 ("Isaiah has foretold"); 1 Cor 9:9 ("for in the law of Moses it is written"); etc. For a complete list of the various ways that Paul introduces scriptural quotations, see E. Earle Ellis, *Paul's Use of the Old Testament* (Edinburgh: Oliver and Boyd, 1957), 156-85. In 2 Cor 10:17, Paul employs the same scriptural quote as in 1 Cor 1:31, but without any introductory formula.

6. For a treatment of the differences, but only with LXX Jer 9:23 to the neglect of 1 Kgdms 2:10, see Stanley, *Paul*, 186-88. The differences have led Koch (*Schrift*, 35-36, 42) to the conclusion that Paul is not quoting directly from the OT but from Jewish or Christian oral tradition. Whatever may be Paul's source for the quote, he gives it the rhetorical authority of what is written in the scriptures in 1 Cor 1:31. The Pauline version of the quote derives from the key concept of boasting found throughout the OT, according to Christian Wolff, *Jeremia im Frühjudentum und Urchristentum* (TU 118; Berlin: Akademie, 1976), 137-41. See also Williams, *Wisdom*, 104-8.

the boasting. This allows for the audience more easily to evoke other places in scripture where God is directly the object of boasting.

Third, the content of the quotation in 1:31 that one should "boast" or place complete reliance only in God is certainly a very common one throughout the OT. Although the particular expressions for "boasting" in 1:31 recall primarily and especially 1 Kgdms 2:10 and/or LXX Jer 9:23, there are other occurrences and forms of the same Greek word for "boasting" with God as the object in the OT.[7] Thus, Paul's scriptural quote in 1 Cor 1:31, "If anyone is to boast, *in the Lord* let him boast," carries with it the authority and rhetorical force not necessarily of any particular OT text or context but of the OT scriptures as a whole and in general.[8]

Literary-Rhetorical Analysis

The formula "so that as it is written" introduces the scriptural quotation in 1 Cor 1:31. The conjunction "so that" (ἵνα) indicates that the citation "if anyone is to boast, *in the Lord* let him boast" serves as the result or consequence of what Paul has previously asserted, especially in 1:29-30. And "as it is written" (καθὼς γέγραπται) indicates that this result or consequence corresponds to what has been and still stands as authoritatively written (perfect passive) scripture.[9]

The audience experiences the quotation in itself as a pithy, alliterated, and potent imperatival construction, "instructing what should be the content of any legitimate boasting."[10] It begins with a present participle, ὁ καυχώμενος, serving as a verbal noun with a conditional nuance, "whoever boasts" or "if anyone is to boast."[11] This is followed by a prepositional

---

7. See, e.g., LXX Deut 10:21; 1 Chr 16:35; 29:11; Jer 17:14; Sir 1:11; 9:16; 10:22; 25:6; 39:8; 50:20; Ps 5:12; 31:11; 88:18; 149:5. See also Josef Schreiner, "Jeremia 9,22.23 als Hintergrund des paulinischen 'Sich-Rühmens,'" in *Neues Testament und Kirche: Für Rudolf Schnackenburg* (ed. Joachim Gnilka; Freiburg: Herder, 1974), 530-42.

8. Winter, *Philo and Paul*, 195: "He (Paul) cites without further comment at this stage the universal proscription from the OT that the only legitimate boasting is that which glories in the Lord's accomplishments."

9. Lockwood, *1 Corinthians*, 75: "There is an ellipsis in the clause. Paul has omitted a verb like γένηται, 'in order that *it might come about* as has been written.'" See also Fee, *Corinthians*, 87 n. 41; Schrage, *Erste Brief*, 1:217.

10. Kenneth L. McKay, "Aspect in Imperatival Constructions in New Testament Greek," *NovT* 27 (1985): 216.

11. On this as a "conditional participle," see Charles K. Barrett, *A Commentary on the First Epistle to the Corinthians* (HNTC; New York: Harper & Row, 1968), 61. The conditional nuance is confirmed by the context as the participle follows what Paul stated in 1:29: "so that no human being might boast before God." Since the participle follows a statement denying the

phrase, ἐν κυρίῳ, "in the Lord," placed in an emphatic position before the third-person singular imperative καυχάσθω, "let him boast," that concludes the quotation.[12] In an A-B-A pattern, the two expressions of boasting (A) surround the phrase "in the Lord" (B) at the emphatic center of the construction.[13] Within the alliteration of initial "k" sounds that closely link the three main words, the single "k" sound in the phrase "in the Lord" distinguishes it from the duplicated "k" sounds in the expressions of boasting, further enhancing its central, emphatic position. The final "o" sound of the emphatic "in the Lord" links it alliteratively with the final "o" sound of the concluding "let him boast" as the apodosis of this conditional imperatival expression: "If anyone is to boast (ὁ καυχώμενος), *in the Lord* (ἐν κυρίῳ) let him boast (καυχάσθω)."

The richly connotative Pauline concept of "boasting" refers not only to a socio-psychological "bragging," "taking pride in," or "glorying in" that evokes honor and status in society, but also serves as a quasi-technical theological and apocalyptic-eschatological term to express what one places a deep trust and reliance upon as the basis and support for one's life.[14] It often includes or implies what one can rely upon for salvation and eternal life in and after the last judgment. "Boasting," then, has both a present and future orientation. The concise scriptural quote of 1:31 powerfully persuades its audience away from "boasting," from putting a total trust and reliance in anything other than the Lord. They are to "boast" or "glory" and thus seek honor and status not in the qualities or accomplishments of themselves or

---

legitimacy of boasting, it seems best to translate it in a conditional sense—"there is no boasting before God" (1:29) but "if anyone is to boast . . ." (1:31).

12. On the "emphatic character" of the phrase "in the Lord" here, see Stanley, *Paul*, 187–88; Lindemann, *Erste Korintherbrief*, 52.

13. Rollin A. Ramsaran, *Liberating Words: Paul's Use of Rhetorical Maxims in 1 Corinthians 1–10* (Valley Forge, Pa.: Trinity Press International, 1996), 32: "Paul has reformulated the LXX form of this wisdom, shaping it into a tight, memorable maxim that places a form of καυχάομαι (to boast) around each side of the substituted phrase ἐν κυρίῳ."

14. Josef Zmijewski, "καυχάομαι," *EDNT* 2:278: "As is the case already in the LXX (cf. e.g., Ps 48:7) the motif of trust is inherent in Paul's use of the term 'boast.' In boasting the individual declares what he relies on and what is his support in life, i.e., what his life is built on." Fee, *Corinthians*, 84: "We 'boast' in that in which we have risked everything in order to secure ourselves." See also Charles K. Barrett, "Boasting (καυχᾶσθαι, κτλ.) in the Pauline Epistles," in *L'Apôtre Paul: Personnalité, style et conception du ministère* (ed. Albert Vanhoye; BETL 73; Louvain: Louvain University Press, 1986), 363–68. For a recent treatment of Pauline "boasting," focused primarily on Romans, and its relation to Jewish "boasting," see Simon J. Gathercole, *Where Is Boasting? Early Jewish Soteriology and Paul's Response in Romans 1–5* (Grand Rapids: Eerdmans, 2002). See also Duane F. Watson, "Paul and Boasting," in *Paul in the Greco-Roman World: A Handbook* (ed. J. Paul Sampley; Harrisburg, Pa.: Trinity Press International, 2003), 77–100.

any other human beings, but directly and solely in the Lord as the only legitimate basis for boasting.

Relation to the Antecedent Context in 1 Corinthians 1:1–30

Within this scriptural quote's new context in 1 Corinthians, to whom do the emphatic words "in the Lord" refer—to the Lord God or to the Lord Jesus Christ? There are good reasons for the implied audience to identify the object of the boasting as the Lord God. First, in its original OT context the quote, explicitly introduced here by "as it is written," is certainly referring to God as the "Lord."[15] And second, the immediately preceding epistolary context of the scriptural quote in 1:31 contains five explicit references to God as the acting subject of salvific activity and therefore as the appropriate object of one's boasting.

Thus, anyone who boasts is to boast in the Lord God, since "God chose" (ἐξελέξατο ὁ θεός, stated three times in 1:27–28) the Corinthians as among the foolish, the weak, and the nothings of the world to shame the wise and the strong and to destroy those who are something. Furthermore, it is "because of him" (ἐξ αὐτοῦ, 1:30a), that is, because of the God before whom (ἐνώπιον τοῦ θεοῦ) no human being can boast (1:29), that "you," the Corinthians, are in Christ Jesus (1:30a).[16] And it is "from God" (ἀπὸ θεοῦ) that Christ Jesus became wisdom for us with the implication that it is also from God that Christ Jesus became "righteousness and holiness and redemption" for us (1:30b).[17]

---

15. When Paul utilizes a scriptural quote containing "Lord," he normally retains its reference to God. There is at least one clear exception, however, in the quotation of LXX Joel 3:5 in Rom 10:13, "For everyone who calls upon the name of the Lord will be saved." Here "Lord" undoubtedly refers to the Lord Jesus rather than the Lord God, since Rom 10:9 states: "If you confess with your mouth that Jesus is Lord and believe in your heart that God raised him from the dead, you will be saved." But of course the implied audience of 1 Corinthians at this point of the letter does not necessarily know of Paul's normal usage in this regard. Furthermore, whereas "God" is the object of our boasting "through our Lord Jesus Christ" in Rom 5:11, "Christ Jesus" is the object of our boasting in Phil 3:3, while "the cross of our Lord Jesus Christ" is the object of Paul's boasting in Gal 6:14. God is the reference for boasting in the "Lord" in 1 Cor 1:31 according to Witherington, *Conflict and Community*, 118; Thiselton, *Corinthians*, 195.

16. On the meaning of "in Christ" in 1:30, Lamp (*First Corinthians 1–4*, 150) concludes: "This verse may be summarized to state that to be in Christ is to be within the sphere of God's wisdom, which is understood as the full scope of God's redemptive activity." On the various dimensions of the Pauline phrase "in Christ," see A. J. M. Wedderburn, "Some Observations on Paul's Use of the Phrases 'in Christ' and 'with Christ,'" *JSNT* 25 (1985): 83–97.

17. Schrage, *Erste Brief*, 1:216: "Ausschlaggebend für das rechte Verständnis ist, daß man ἡμῖν ἀπὸ θεοῦ bei der Charakterisierung von σοφία auch bei den übrigen Begriffen mithört. Gott ist der alleinige Urheber auch von Gerechtigkeit, Heiligung und Erlösung." See also Lindemann,

But there are also good reasons for the implied audience to identify the object of the boasting as the Lord Jesus Christ. Thus, anyone who boasts is to boast "in the Lord" (ἐν κυρίῳ, 1:31) as those who are "in Christ Jesus" (ἐν χριστῷ Ἰησοῦ), who became wisdom for us from God as well as righteousness and holiness and redemption (1:30), and who has been referred to as "our Lord (κύριος) Jesus Christ" six times previously in the letter (1:2, 3, 7, 8, 9, 10).[18] Indeed, the implied audience could well consider "in Christ Jesus" in 1:30 to be an abbreviated variation of "in our Lord Jesus Christ."

For the function of the scriptural quote of 1:31 in Paul's rhetorical strategy it does not seem to matter whether the audience understands "Lord" as God or Jesus Christ. In the context, boasting in the Lord God means trusting or relying in the God who is not only the source of the Corinthian audience's being "in Christ Jesus," but the God who made Christ Jesus for all of "us" believers God's wisdom as well as God's righteousness and holiness and redemption (1:30). And boasting in the Lord Jesus Christ means trusting or relying in Jesus Christ not only as the Lord "in whom" the Corinthian audience finds themselves due solely to the grace of God, but as the Lord whom God has made for all believers God's wisdom as well as God's righteousness and holiness and redemption (1:30). In either case the boasting is ultimately in God rather than human beings or human accomplishments.[19]

Although "all flesh" may not boast (καυχήσηται) in human wisdom, power, or social status (cf. 1:26–28) "before" (ἐνώπιον) God (1:29), anyone in the Corinthian audience who boasts (καυχώμενος) may boast (καυχάσθω), but solely and directly "in" (ἐν) the Lord (God/Jesus Christ) (1:31), as those who by God are "in" (ἐν) Christ Jesus (1:30). Through the scriptural quote

---

Erste Korintherbrief, 52. For a translation of 1:30 that takes "in Christ" instrumentally and the final clause as expressing what the Corinthians (rather than Christ) have become through this instrumentality, see Wilhelm Bender, "Bemerkungen zur Übersetzung von 1 Korinther 1:30," *ZNW* 71 (1980): 263–68: "From him (God) you are through Jesus Christ—who has been made into wisdom for us by God—righteousness and holiness and redemption." But against Bender and for the view that "righteousness and holiness and redemption" stand in apposition to and further explain Christ's becoming "wisdom" for us, see Schrage, *Erste Brief*, 1:215 n. 666; Lamp, *First Corinthians 1–4*, 149–50; Lockwood, *1 Corinthians*, 75.

18. Because the addressees of the letter are ἐν χριστῷ (1:30), "deshalb sollen sie sich ἐν κυρίῳ sogar rühmen" (1:31), according to Lindemann, *Erste Korintherbrief*, 51; see also Wolff, *Erste Brief*, 46 n. 132. Christ is the reference for "Lord" in 1:31 also according to Merklein, *Erste Brief*, 1.203; Fee, *Corinthians*, 87; Collins, *First Corinthians*, 113; Gräbe, *Power of God*, 61; Lockwood, *1 Corinthians*, 79–80.

19. After noting the possibility of understanding "Lord" in 1:31 as either God or Jesus Christ, Schrage (*Erste Brief*, 1:217) concludes that in either case it amounts to eliminating all boasting in human beings: "Wer ernst nimmt, daß er sein Christ-Sein allein Gottes Gnade verdankt, kann sich nicht wieder an andere Autoritäten und Instanzen binden."

in 1:31 Paul is thus exhorting his implied Corinthian audience, "you" (ὑμεῖς) who are in Christ Jesus due solely to God (1:30), that they may boast, only if they boast *in the Lord* (God/Jesus Christ). By doing so they are realizing that they are part of and thus joining "us" (ἡμῖν), all believers, for whom Christ Jesus has become wisdom from God, as well as righteousness and holiness and redemption (1:30), so that *all* believers may boast only if they boast exclusively *in the Lord* (God/Jesus Christ).[20]

Paul's scriptural exhortation that the audience may boast if they boast *in the Lord* (1:31) means that they may have a triumphant trust, a delightful dependence, and a rigorous reliance in the Lord as believers who are already being and will be finally saved in the future, final judgment, because Christ Jesus has become "wisdom for us from God" (1:30). "Boasting" in and thus proudly relying upon this wisdom (σοφία) for us from God for our eschatological salvation follows from and reinforces Paul's previous assertion that Christ crucified is the power of God and the wisdom (σοφίαν) of God for us, the audience, as those called to be believers, whether Jews or Greeks (1:23–24). The scriptural quote thus enjoins the audience to "boast" not in the eloquent and prestigious "wisdom (σοφίᾳ) of word" (1:17), the "wisdom (σοφίαν) of the wise" that God promises to destroy (1:19), and the "wisdom (σοφίαν) of the world" that God has made foolish (1:20), but in the paradoxical "wisdom (σοφίᾳ) of God" (1:21) evident in the word of the cross of Christ as the power of God to save those who believe (1:17–21).

With a rhetorical triplet of synonymous expressions for eschatological salvation, Paul further elaborates upon this "wisdom for us from God" (1:30) as the basis for the scriptural injunction that the audience may boast if they boast *in the Lord* (1:31). Christ Jesus has become "wisdom for us from God—as well as righteousness and holiness and redemption" (1:30). Although more-or-less synonymous, these three terms each express a slightly different nuance of eschatological salvation, and each exerts, in light of the antecedent context, a slightly different rhetorical effect upon the audience.[21]

---

20. Fee, *Corinthians*, 85 n. 36: "The shift from 'you' to 'us' is significant here. The sentence begins as a direct word to the Corinthians, as to their existence in Christ Jesus over against the wise of the world. But at this point the perspective broadens to include all who are Christ's."

21. According to Collins (*First Corinthians*, 112): "The accumulation of terms, the rhetorical device of *repetitio*, implies that the entirety of God's salvific beneficence has been mediated to his people 'in Christ Jesus.'" But without further explanation or foundation, Collins (113) goes on to assert: "The location of 'redemption' as the third of the series may represent an instance of the rhetorical device of *gradatio*, in which the emphasis falls on the final element of a series arranged in ascending order." But we find no evidence for an "ascending order" to this triplet of synonymous salvific terms, and, as we will see, each relates differently yet significantly to the preceding context. As Fee (*Corinthians*, 86) notes: "These are not three different steps in the saving process; they are rather three different metaphors for the same event (our salvation

That Christ Jesus has become "righteousness" (δικαιοσύνη) for us from God (1:30) means that God himself has freely and graciously established those who are "in Christ Jesus" in a right and proper juridical and forensic relationship with God within the sphere of God's covenantal relationship with all of its various demands, obligations, and commandments. That Christ Jesus is "righteousness" for us from God expresses eschatological salvation in terms of our being acquitted and upheld as innocent of transgressions and failures within our covenantal relationship with God now and in the future, final judgment.[22] This "righteousness" for us from God develops Paul's previous assertion of the hope that God will confirm the audience until the end "blameless" (ἀνεγκλήτους) with regard to judgment on the day of our Lord Jesus Christ (1:8), because "faithful is God, through whom you have been called into fellowship with his Son Jesus Christ our Lord" (1:9).[23] Therefore, the audience, who "by God are in Christ Jesus" (1:30), may "boast" *in the Lord* (1:31) in light of the eschatological salvation that is theirs in Christ as "righteousness" for us from God.

That Christ Jesus has become "holiness" (ἁγιασμὸς) for us from God means that God has set apart from the world and dedicated or consecrated to himself those who are "in Christ Jesus" (1:30). Indeed, Paul has already addressed his Corinthian audience as those who have been and still are "consecrated" or "made holy" (ἡγιασμένοις) in Christ Jesus, and thus who are called to be "holy" (ἁγίοις), that is, to live in accord with the holiness they have received rather than achieved from God (1:2).[24] God will confirm those who are consecrated and holy as blameless in the final judgment on the day of our Lord Jesus Christ (1:8), since faithful is the God through

---

that was effected in Christ), each taken from a different sphere and each emphasizing a different aspect of the one reality."

22. Schrage, *Erste Brief*, 1:216: "Ist Gott aber Ursprung und Subjekt der Gerechtigkeit, dann ist δικαιοσύνη nicht *unsere* Gerechtigkeit, sondern *Gottes* Gerechtigkeit für uns, die in Christus Wirklichkeit geworden ist." Fee, *Corinthians*, 86: " 'Righteousness,' therefore, is not so much an ethical term here as it is forensic, and highlights the believer's undeserved stance of right standing before God, despite his/her guilt from having broken his law." See also Thiselton, *Corinthians*, 193; Karl Kertelge, "δικαιοσύνη," EDNT 1:326–28.

23. According to Fee (*Corinthians*, 43), "blameless" (ἀνεγκλήτους) in 1:8 "carries the sense of their being guiltless (with reference to the law) when appearing before God at the final judgment because Christ's righteousness has been given to them." Thiselton, *Corinthians*, 101–2: "The Greek carries a range of meanings: *blameless, irreproachable*, and *unimpeachable*. . . . This well exemplifies the meaning that no charge can be brought by way of accusation. This applies to the time which leads up to the day of the Lord as well as to being presented free from any charge on the day itself." See also Kuck, *Judgment*, 240–41.

24. According to Balz ("ἅγιος," 18), those who are holy "live primarily not from the demand but from the gift of holiness." See also Schrage, *Erste Brief*, 1:216; Thiselton, *Corinthians*, 193; Lindemann, *Erste Korintherbrief*, 52.

whom the audience has been called into fellowship with his Son Jesus Christ our Lord (1:9). Therefore, the audience, as those consecrated in Christ Jesus and called to be holy, may "boast" *in the Lord* (1:31) for the eschatological salvation that is theirs in Christ as "holiness" for us from God.

That Christ Jesus has become "redemption" (ἀπολύτρωσις) for us from God (1:30) means that God has made Jesus Christ our "redeemer" or "deliverer" or "savior," the one through whom we are being "saved" (σῳζομένοις) eschatologically (1:18) because of God's decision "to save" (σῶσαι) those who believe (1:21).[25] Therefore, the audience, who "by God are in Christ Jesus" (1:30), may "boast" *in the Lord* (1:31) in light of the eschatological salvation that is theirs in Christ as "redemption" for us from God.

Relation to the Subsequent Context
in 1 Corinthians 2:1–4:21

The scriptural exhortation in 1:31, "If anyone is to boast, *in the Lord* let him boast (καυχάσθω)," reverberates in its negative counterpart in 3:21, "So let no one boast (καυχάσθω) in human beings." No one in the Corinthian audience is to boast in "human beings" (ἀνθρώποις) because "the foolishness of God is wiser than human beings (ἀνθρώπων) and the weakness of God is stronger than human beings (ἀνθρώπων)" (1:25); because "your faith is not in the wisdom of human beings (ἀνθρώπων)" (2:5); because "what God has prepared for those who love him has not arisen in the heart of a human being (ἀνθρώπου)" (2:9); because "we speak of the things freely given to us by God not with words taught by human (ἀνθρωπίνης) wisdom" (2:12–13); because "a natural human being (ἄνθρωπος) does not receive the things of the Spirit of God" (2:14); and because the Corinthians are not to live in a "human" (κατὰ ἄνθρωπον) way, as if they are merely human beings (ἄνθρωποί) (3:3–4).

---

25. Karl Kertelge, "ἀπολύτρωσις," *EDNT* 1:138–39: "[H]ere [1 Cor 1:30] ἀπολύτρωσις . . . designates Jesus Christ as the redeemer himself (*abstractum pro concreto*) in view of the salvation of believers established by him. . . . Jesus' giving of his own life points to the redeeming work of God and effectively mediates it. . . . The believer now attains 'redemption'—God's decisive eschatological act of salvation (cf. *1 Enoch* 51:2; Luke 21:28)—through and in Christ." Collins, *First Corinthians*, 113: " 'Redemption' basically signifies the manumission of slaves (cf. 7:23), but Paul uses the term as a theological metaphor. Paul's idea is at once theological, soteriological, and christological (see Rom 3:23–26). In redemption the emphasis lies on the divine initiative. What God initiated is experienced as a remission of sins. God's agent in redemption, the mediator of redemption, is Jesus Christ . . . who effects redemption through his salvific death and resurrection." See also BDAG, 117; Schrage, *Erste Brief*, 1:216–17; Thiselton, *Corinthians*, 194–95.

That no one is to boast in human beings implies that the audience is to boast in God instead. This follows from Paul's statement that the wisdom of the human beings of this world is foolishness with God, as confirmed by a linked pair of scriptural quotes expressing the vast superiority of the Lord God over "wise" human beings (3:19–20). The audience need not boast in human beings, "for everything is yours" (3:21b).[26]

The "everything" that belongs to the audience begins to be delineated with three examples of human beings they should not boast in—"whether Paul or Apollos or Cephas" (3:22). This recalls and reverses for the audience their rivalries based on boasting in these individual human beings by claiming, "I belong to Paul, or I belong to Apollos, or I belong to Cephas" (1:12). By this kind of factious rivalry, especially with regard to Paul and Apollos, they are not only behaving in a "human" way and demonstrating that they are merely "human beings" themselves (3:3–4)—"fleshly" rather than "spiritual" people who have received the Spirit that is from God (2:12–3:1)—but they are thus also boasting in "human beings" (3:21) rather than in the Lord (1:31).

Instead of the audience aligning themselves into rivalries based on their allegiance to one or other of these three human beings, they are to realize that Paul, Apollos, and Cephas together are part of the "everything" that belongs to them, not as individual members of the audience, not as "I," but as "you" (cf. the plural ὑμῶν in 3:21, 22), as a whole, united community. Paul, Apollos, and Cephas belong to the audience as servants (διάκονοι) through whom they believed, as servants who are themselves dependent upon the Lord for the appointment and fulfillment of their particular service (3:5).[27] Although Paul's service was to "plant" and that of Apollos to "water," in themselves they are nothing, since the "growth" came from God (3:6–7). Since they are merely God's coworkers, whereas the audience is God's "field," God's "building" (3:9), and God's "temple" in whom the Spirit of God dwells (3:16), the audience must not boast in these mere human beings (3:21) but only in the Lord (1:31).

Next in the series of realities included in the "everything" that belongs

---

26. On "everything is yours" as a Stoic maxim that Paul plays upon but redefines, see Fee, *Corinthians*, 154–55 n. 17; Schrage, *Erste Brief*, 1:314; Lockwood, *1 Corinthians*, 127 n. 13; Collins, *First Corinthians*, 166; Lindemann, *Erste Korintherbrief*, 93; Thiselton, *Corinthians*, 325–26.

27. On the meaning of "servants" here, see Alfons Weiser, "διακονέω," *EDNT* 1:303; Thiselton, *Corinthians*, 299–301; Fee, *Corinthians*, 130–31; Schrage, *Erste Brief*, 1:290–91; Lindemann, *Erste Korintherbrief*, 80; Collins, *First Corinthians*, 145: " 'Servant' connotes a relationship with a lord and master.... The Lord not only assigns the task, but also enables the task to be fulfilled."

to the audience is the "world" (κόσμος, 3:22). This is the world whose wisdom (σοφία τοῦ κόσμου), although attractive to the audience and its social environment, God has rendered as foolishness (3:19; 1:20). It is the world (κόσμος) that did not know God through wisdom (1:21). It is the world whose foolish (τὰ μωρὰ τοῦ κόσμου) and whose weak (τὰ ἀσθενῆ τοῦ κόσμου) God chose to shame its wise and strong (1:27). It is the world whose lowly born (τὰ ἀγενῆ τοῦ κόσμου) God chose to reduce to nothing those who are something (1:28). Because the audience (and the authors, "we") have received not the spirit of the world (τὸ πνεῦμα τοῦ κόσμου) but the Spirit that comes from God, so that they can understand the things freely given them by God (2:12), the "world" with its wisdom inferior to God is subordinate to, subservient to, and thus "belongs to" the audience. That is why the audience must not boast in the human beings of this world (3:21) but only in the Lord (1:31).[28]

The next two items included in the "everything" that belongs to the audience, "whether life or death" (3:22), go together as a rhetorical merism—a pair of opposites embracing a totality. In this case the whole of human existence as defined by its limits of life and death belongs to the audience as a gift from God (2:12). This is followed by another merism, "whether the present or the future" (3:22), embracing the total temporal spectrum that determines ongoing human existence (cf. Rom 8:38). This also belongs to the audience as a gift from God and serves as the final delineation in the rhetorical series that begins with "for everything is yours" (3:21) and progresses to an emphatically reiterated "everything is yours!" (3:22).[29] Because "everything belongs to you"—to the audience as a unified whole, individuals in the audience ought not to be causing rivalry and disunity by claiming, "I belong to Paul, Apollos, Cephas" (1:12), and thus boasting in human beings (3:21) rather than in the Lord (1:31).

The rhetorical series climactically concludes with a catchword connection that dramatically reverses the direction of the possession—"everything

---

28. On Paul's use of "world" in 1 Corinthians, Adams (*Constructing the World*, 147–48) concludes: "Paul uses κόσμος in a predominantly negative way. For the most part, κόσμος bears the negative apocalyptic sense 'this world.' . . . κόσμος is the main negative term of the epistle. . . . Paul challenges the world-view linked with κόσμος (= world/universe). The κόσμος is no longer the well-ordered, beautiful, praiseworthy and ever-enduring world, to which human beings are microcosmically linked. It is now the anti-godly, hostile world which is under God's judgement and doomed to destruction."

29. Fee, *Corinthians*, 154: "Because in Christ Jesus both 'life' itself and therefore 'the future' are ours, 'death' is ours as well, as is 'the present.' We die, but 'life' cannot be taken from us; we live the life of the future in the present age, and therefore the present has become our own possession." See also Thiselton, *Corinthians*, 326–27.

is yours (ὑμῶν), and you (ὑμεῖς) are Christ's, and Christ is God's" (3:23).[30] Everything belongs to the audience only because the audience belongs to Christ and ultimately to God. Thus the entire audience as a unified whole, "you" (ὑμεῖς), belongs to Christ, not just individual members of a factional party within the audience whose slogan is "I (ἐγώ) belong to Christ" (1:12).[31] That everything belongs to the audience because they belong to Christ who in turn belongs to God is why the audience must not boast in human beings (3:21) but in the Lord (1:31). That Christ belongs to God confirms that whether the audience boasts in the "Lord" Christ or in the "Lord" God, they are ultimately boasting in the God through whom they belong to Christ (1:30) rather than in human beings.[32]

"These things" (ταῦτα), referring to all that Paul has said and implied since 1:10 but especially to the agricultural and architectural images and metaphors in 3:5–4:5, Paul has "applied" figuratively and allusively (μετεσχημάτισα) to himself and Apollos as examples for the benefit of the audience (4:6a).[33] From Paul and Apollos they are to learn to practice the maxim, "Not beyond the things that are written (γέγραπται)!" (4:6b), which refers not only to the explicit scriptural quotations previously introduced by "it is written" (γέγραπται in 1:19, 31; 2:9; 3:19), but to the whole

---

30. Fee, *Corinthians*, 154 n. 16: "The two δέ's in this and the next clause are consecutive, not adversative, and thus correctly translated 'and.' " See also Schrage, *Erste Brief*, 1:316.

31. Wolff, *Erste Brief*, 78: "Damit nimmt Paulus wohl vor allem auf das Selbstverständnis der Christusgruppe (1,12) Bezug; indem er es auf *alle* bezieht, korrigiert er die Exklusivität." On the Christ party's false view of Christ, see Richardson, *Paul's Language about God*, 114–15. According to Collins (*First Corinthians*, 166), "Contrasted with the simple mention of Paul, Apollos, and Cephas in v. 22, the wording, 'you are Christ's,' confirms the suggestion that the slogan in 1:12 is a product of Paul's own rhetoric."

32. On the reversal of boasting in 1 Cor 3:18–23, see Winter, *Philo and Paul*, 195–96.

33. "These things" refer exclusively to 3:5–4:5 according to Kuck, *Judgment*, 210–11; Johan S. Vos, "Der ΜΕΤΑΣΧΗΜΑΤΙΣΜΟΣ in 1 Kor 4,6," *ZNW* 86 (1995): 154–72; Wolff, *Erste Brief*, 84. On the meaning and reference of μετεσχημάτισα, see also Benjamin Fiore, " 'Covert Allusion' in 1 Corinthians 1–4," *CBQ* 47 (1985): 85–102; idem, *The Function of Personal Example in the Socratic and Pastoral Epistles* (AnBib 105; Rome: Biblical Institute, 1986), 168–75; David R. Hall, "A Disguise for the Wise: μετασχηματισμός in 1 Corinthians 4.6," *NTS* 40 (1994): 143–49. For a summary of the discussion, including the theories that it refers to a rhetorical device of "disguised form" or "covert allusion" in which Paul and Apollos are fictional disguises for anonymous teachers at Corinth, see Thiselton, *Corinthians*, 348–51. He translates μετεσχημάτισα in 4:6 as "I have allusively applied" in order "to convey precisely the balance between the probability and openness latent in the Greek. Clearly the examples are *allusive* to those whom Paul does not mention by name; but it goes beyond the evidence to claim that Paul and Apollos themselves are necessarily only *ciphers of rhetorical fiction* whom Paul himself exempts from his own warnings. Indeed, his reference to his own self-knowlege or conscience (4:4) suggests the opposite. Mere *example* undertranslates; *covert* rhetoric overtranslates" (351; Thiselton's emphases).

plurality of "things" (ἅ) written in scripture that similarly speak of shunning human wisdom in favor of God's vastly superior wisdom by relying or "boasting" in the Lord.[34] Thus, the individuals in the audience are to learn not to be "puffed up" or "inflated" (φυσιοῦσθε) with pride or conceit in favor of one (such as Apollos) against the other (such as Paul) (4:6c).[35]

As "ministers of Christ and stewards of the mysteries of God" (4:1), Paul and Apollos have not gone beyond what is written in the scriptures by boasting in themselves or in their own accomplishments as human beings. It was the Lord who gave each of them their respective roles as the "servants" through whom the audience came to believe (3:5). Since it was God who caused the "growth" of faith in the audience, Paul, who "planted," and Apollos, who "watered," are "nothing" in themselves (3:6–7). Neither "boasts" nor "is puffed up" in himself as superior to the other. Rather, they are "one" in their work, with each to receive his own reward for his own labor (3:8), united as coworkers of God (3:9). The audience is to learn from them likewise not to go beyond what is written in the scriptures by boasting or being puffed up in favor of one of them against the other (4:6).

With its second-person singular object the rhetorical question, "Who makes you (σε) distinctive?" (4:7a), is aimed directly at the individual "I"

---

34. For a summary and critique of seven possible interpretations of "the things that are written" in 4:6, see Thiselton, *Corinthians*, 352–55. For interpretations involving nonscriptural references for the phrase, see Laurence L. Welborn, "A Conciliatory Principle in 1 Cor. 4:6," *NovT* 29 (1987): 320–46; James C. Hanges, "1 Corinthians 4:6 and the Possibility of Written Bylaws in the Corinthian Church," *JBL* 117 (1998): 275–98; Ronald L. Tyler, "First Corinthians 4:6 and Hellenistic Pedagogy," *CBQ* 60 (1998): 97–103. For refutations of the non-scriptural interpretations, see Hays, "Conversion of the Imagination," 407 n. 40; Lockwood, *1 Corinthians*, 140 n. 15. As Wagner ("Not Beyond," 279–87) argues, the primary scriptural reference may well be to 1:31, but the plural "things" that is written indicates additional references, not only to the other previous scriptural quotes in the letter but to the same general theme as found throughout the OT scriptures. Indeed, as we maintain above, the quote in 1:31 itself is not limited to a single OT reference. We would agree in general with Thiselton's (*Corinthians*, 355) conclusion: "It is perfectly possible, and indeed broadly convincing, to combine the thrust of (iv) *(what Paul has quoted from scripture)*, with the two broader principles of (ii), i.e., the regular *appeal to the* OT as Christian scripture, and (v), that this has assumed the *status of a maxim*" (Thiselton's emphases). (The "maxim," however, may be Paul's rhetorical invention.) See also Ronald L. Tyler, "The History of the Interpretation of τὸ μὴ ὑπὲρ ἃ γέγραπται in 1 Corinthians 4:6," *ResQ* 43 (2001): 243–52.

35. On the meaning of φυσιόω in 4:6 as being "puffed up" with pride or conceit regarding Paul and Apollos, see *EDNT* 3:444; BDAG, 1069. According to Mitchell (*Reconciliation*, 95), "φυσιοῦσθαι, 'being puffed up,' a term found throughout 1 Corinthians, is almost synonymous with καυχᾶσθαι. In fact, the two images, boasting and being puffed up, are often used in tandem in ancient Greek texts, as by Paul in 1 Cor 4:6–7."

who claims, "I belong to Paul or I belong to Apollos" (3:4; 1:12).³⁶ The question forces these individuals to realize that there is no basis for them to distinguish themselves either from one another by their allegiance to Paul or Apollos, or from Paul and Apollos, who do not make such distinctions between themselves, as they are both equally dependent upon and subordinate to God rather than human wisdom in their service to the Corinthians (3:5–9).

The next rhetorical questions, "What do you have (ἔχεις) that you have not received (ἔλαβες)? But if you have received (ἔλαβες), why do you boast as if not receiving (λαβών)?" (4:7b), cause the individuals within the audience to realize that each of them, like Paul and Apollos, is dependent upon and subordinate to God for all that they have and are. That each of them has received what they have and are from God recalls how Paul thanked God for the grace "given" them in Christ Jesus (1:4), how God "chose" them as the foolish, weak, and lowly of the world (1:27–28), how we have "received" (ἐλάβομεν) the Spirit of God, so that we might know the things "given" us by God (2:12), how we "have" (ἔχομεν) (from God) the mind of Christ (2:16), how "you are" God's field, God's building (3:9), and God's temple (3:16), and how "everything is yours" who belong to Christ and God (3:21–23). Since none of them can boast (καυχᾶσαι) as if not receiving (4:7b), they are not to boast (καυχάσθω) in human beings (3:21). Indeed, in accord with the scriptural quote, "If anyone is to boast (καυχώμενος), *in the Lord* let him boast (καυχάσθω)" (1:31).³⁷

Summary on 1 Corinthians 1:31

1. Although the particular expressions for "boasting" in 1:31 recall primarily and especially 1 Kgdms 2:10 and/or LXX Jer 9:23, Paul's scriptural quote in 1:31 carries with it the authority and rhetorical force not necessarily of any one particular OT text or context but of the OT scriptures as a whole and in general.

2. The concise scriptural quote of 1:31 powerfully persuades its audience away from "boasting," from putting a total trust and reliance, in

---

36. On the meaning of διακρίνει here as "make distinctive" or "make different," see BDAG, 231; Gerhard Dautzenberg, "διακρίνω," *EDNT* 1:305.

37. For a treatment of 1:31 as a "gnomic maxim," see Ramsaran, *Liberating Words*, 33: "The maxim drives the point home and calls for consideration and response: coming-to-faith was all God's doing—maintain your weakness, allow the power of God to work through you, give up your attempts to gain strength through alignment into divisions, and (implicitly) do not boast in human beings."

anything other than the Lord. They are to "boast" or "glory" and thus seek honor in this life and for the life to come directly and solely in the Lord as the only legitimate basis for boasting.

3. For the function of the scriptural quote of 1:31 in Paul's rhetorical strategy it does not matter whether the audience understands "Lord" as God or Jesus Christ; in either case the "boasting" is ultimately in God rather than human beings or human accomplishments.

4. The scriptural quote enjoins the audience to "boast" not in the eloquent and prestigious "wisdom of word" (1:17), the "wisdom of the wise" that God promises to destroy (1:19) and the "wisdom of the world" that God has made foolish (1:20), but in the paradoxical "wisdom of God" (1:21) evident in the word of the cross of Christ as the power of God to save those who believe (1:17–21).

5. As among those for whom Christ Jesus has become "wisdom for us from God—as well as righteousness and holiness and redemption" (1:30)—three more-or-less synonymous terms, each expressing a slightly different nuance of eschatological salvation and each exerting, in light of the antecedent context, a slightly different rhetorical effect—the audience joins *all* believers, who may boast only if they boast exclusively *in the Lord*.

6. Because "everything" belongs to the audience as a unified whole, individuals in the audience ought not to be causing rivalry and disunity by claiming, "I belong to Paul, Apollos, Cephas" (1:12), and thus boasting in human beings (3:21) rather than in the Lord (1:31).

7. Since none in the Corinthian audience can "boast" as if not receiving (4:7b) everything they have and are from God, they are not to boast in human beings (3:21)—either themselves, Paul, or Apollos. Rather, in accord with the scriptural quote, "If anyone is to boast, *in the Lord* let him boast" (1:31).

CHAPTER 4

1 Corinthians 2:9

*What things eye has not seen and ear has not heard
and have not arisen in the heart of a human being,
what things God has prepared for those who love him*

Old Testament Background

Many consider the scriptural citation in 1 Cor 2:9, although introduced by the very general formula "but as it is written," to be based primarily, if loosely, on LXX Isa 64:3: "From eternity we have not heard nor have our eyes seen a God but you and your works which you will do for those who wait for mercy."[1] First Corinthians 2:9 refers to what things "eye has not seen" (ὀφθαλμὸς οὐκ εἶδεν) and what things ear "has not heard" (οὐκ ἤκουσεν). Similarly, LXX Isa 64:3 refers to what "we have not heard" (οὐκ ἠκούσαμεν) and what "our eyes have not seen" (οὐδὲ οἱ ὀφθαλμοὶ ἡμῶν εἶδον).

But the thoughts being expressed in these two texts are quite different. Whereas 1 Cor 2:9 refers to what an eye has never seen and what an ear has never heard, LXX Isa 64:3 refers to our never hearing nor seeing with our eyes any God but the one God and the works of that God. So, LXX Isa 64:3 is actually referring to what we have heard and seen—God and the works of God, whereas 1 Cor 2:9 is referring to what has never been

---

1. Stanley, *Paul*, 188: "The presence of the standard Pauline introductory formula καθὼς γέγραπται tells the reader that a citation is intended, but the wording that follows agrees with no known verse in the Greek or Hebrew Bibles. The closest would appear to be Isa 64.3, but even here the resemblance is quite loose, and extends only to the first line of the quotation." See also Hervé Ponsot, "D'Isaïe LXIV, 3 à I Corinthiens II, 9," *RB* 90 (1983): 229–42; Koch, *Schrift*, 36–41; Williams, *Wisdom*, 161–64; Thiselton, *Corinthians*, 251; Fee, *Corinthians*, 108; Wolff, *Erste Brief*, 57; Kammler, *Kreuz*, 217–18; Garland, *1 Corinthians*, 103: "Paul loosely quotes from the LXX version of Isa. 64:3 . . . and Paul may be thinking of it in a loose association with elements of a medley of other passages (Job 28:12–28; Isa. 48:6; 52:15; 65:17; Jer. 3:16; Sir. 1:10)."

humanly seen or heard. Furthermore, "what things (ἅ) you will do for those who wait for mercy" in LXX Isa 64:3 differs notably from "what things (ἅ) God has prepared for those who love him" in 1 Cor 2:9.[2]

Somewhat closer to the thought if not the precise language of the first part of the quote in 1 Cor 2:9, which speaks of what things have not been seen, heard, or perceived, may be LXX Isa 52:15: "Thus many nations will be amazed at him and kings will close their mouth, for those to whom it has not been reported concerning him will see and those who have not heard will understand." To the implied Corinthian audience "what things eye has not seen (εἶδεν) and ear has not heard (ἤκουσεν) and have not arisen in the heart of a human being" (1 Cor 2:9a) but what things God has now revealed to us (2:10a) concerning Jesus Christ who was crucified by the rulers of this age, despite being the "Lord of glory (δόξης)" (2:8), serves as a fulfillment of the prediction concerning the Isaian suffering servant of God. Despite the promise that he would be glorified (δοξασθήσεται, Isa 52:13) by God (divine passive), his appearance will be without glory (ἀδοξήσει) from human beings and his glory (δόξα) away from human beings (52:14). Those to whom it has not been reported concerning him will see (ὄψονται) and those who have not heard (ἀκηκόασιν) will understand (52:15).

Furthermore, that what things have not been seen, heard, or perceived by human beings (1 Cor 2:9a) but God has now revealed (ἀπεκάλυψεν) to us (2:10a) serves as an answer to the question in the next Isaian verse about the report concerning the suffering servant of God in Isa 53:1b: "To whom has the arm of the Lord been revealed (ἀπεκαλύφθη)?" The "arm" (βραχίων) of the Lord is an "anthropomorphic symbol of God's power."[3] And the "wisdom of God" in 1 Cor 2:6–7 concerning the crucified Christ that has now been revealed to us by God was previously coordinated with the

---

2. For various attempts to locate the scriptural quote in 1 Cor 2:9 in an apocryphal writing, see Eckard von Nordheim, "Das Zitat des Paulus in 1 Kor 2,9 und seine Beziehung zum koptischen Testament Jakobs," *ZNW* 65 (1974): 112–20; Otfried Hofius, "Das Zitat 1 Kor 2,9 und das koptische Testament des Jakob," *ZNW* 66 (1975): 140–42; Hedley Frederick Davis Sparks, "1 Kor 2,9: A Quotation from the Coptic Testament of Jacob?" *ZNW* 67 (1976): 269–76; Klaus Berger, "Zur Diskussion über die Herkunft von I Kor. ii. 9," *NTS* 24 (1978): 270–83; Michael E. Stone and John Strugnell, *The Books of Elijah, Parts 1–2* (SBLTT 18; Missoula, Mont.: Scholars Press, 1979); Joseph Verheyden, "Origen on the Origin of 1 Cor 2,9," in *The Corinthian Correspondence* (ed. Reimund Bieringer; BETL 125; Louvain: Louvain University Press, 1996), 491–511. For summaries of the various proposals and their problems, see Thiselton, *Corinthians*, 251; Lindemann, *Erste Korintherbrief*, 67; Collins, *First Corinthians*, 131–32; Fee, *Corinthians*, 108–9; Schrage, *Erste Brief*, 1:246; Koch, *Schrift*, 36–39.

3. BDAG, 183.

"power of God" in 1:24, which was then contrasted to the "wisdom of human beings" in 2:5.

But there are other OT texts about what human beings have not seen, heard, and perceived with their eyes, ears, and heart that 1 Cor 2:9a may recall for the audience. That God has now revealed to us (2:10a) "what things eye (ὀφθαλμὸς) has not seen (εἶδεν) and ear (οὖς) has not heard (ἤκουσεν) and have not arisen in the heart (καρδίαν) of a human being" (2:9a) reverses what is stated in LXX Deut 29:3: "Yet the Lord God has not given you a heart (καρδίαν) to know and eyes to see (ὀφθαλμοὺς βλέπειν) and ears to hear (ὦτα ἀκούειν) to this day." Whereas God did not give Israel an understanding of his plan of salvation as evident in the Exodus events (Deut 29:1–3), "God has now revealed to us" (1 Cor 2:10a) an understanding of the hidden and mysterious wisdom of God (2:1, 7) regarding his plan of salvation (1:18, 21) through Christ crucified (2:2, 8).

That God has now revealed to us (1 Cor 2:10a) "what things eye (ὀφθαλμὸς) has not seen (εἶδεν) and ear (οὖς) has not heard (ἤκουσεν) and have not arisen in the heart (καρδίαν) of a human being" (2:9a) also reverses the prophetic message God gave to Isaiah for Israel in LXX Isa 6:9–10: "You shall indeed hear (ἀκοῇ ἀκούσετε) but you shall not understand; and you shall indeed see (βλέποντες βλέψετε), but you shall not perceive. For the heart (καρδία) of this people has become dull, and with their ears (ὠσὶν) they hear (ἤκουσαν) with difficulty, and they have closed their eyes (ὀφθαλμοὺς) lest they should see (ἴδωσιν) with their eyes (ὀφθαλμοῖς), and with their ears (ὠσὶν) hear (ἀκούσωσιν), and with their heart (καρδίᾳ) understand, and turn around, and I should heal them."

And that God has now revealed to us (1 Cor 2:10a) "what things eye (ὀφθαλμὸς) has not seen (εἶδεν) and ear (οὖς) has not heard (ἤκουσεν) and have not arisen in the heart (καρδίαν) of a human being" (2:9a) may also recall for the Corinthian audience what God revealed to Ezekiel in LXX Ezek 40:4—"with your eyes (ὀφθαλμοῖς) see (ἰδέ) and with your ears (ὠσίν) hear (ἄκουε) and place into your heart (καρδίαν) all that I show you"—and in LXX Ezek 44:5: "place into your heart (καρδίαν) and see (ἰδέ) with your eyes (ὀφθαλμοῖς) and with your ears (ὠσίν) hear (ἄκουε) all that I speak with you." There are a number of OT texts, then, concerned with eyes seeing, ears hearing, and hearts imagining or understanding, that 1 Cor 2:9a may evoke for its implied Corinthian audience.[4]

---

4. The expression in 1 Cor 2:9a of what "has not arisen in the heart" reflects the Hebrew idiom "go up into the heart" (see Thiselton, *Corinthians*, 249; Lindemann, *Erste Korintherbrief*, 66) and occurs in its Greek form in the LXX to refer to something that has been experienced in the past and has or will or will not be remembered or thought of, "arise in the heart," again in Isa 65:17; Jer 3:16; 51:21; 4 Kgdms 12:5. In LXX Jer 39:35, however, it is used to refer to some-

One of the main OT texts that the second part of the quote in 1 Cor 2:9, "what things God has prepared for those who love him (τοῖς ἀγαπῶσιν αὐτόν)," recalls for its implied audience is Sir 1:10b: "and he [God] provided her [wisdom] for those who love him (τοῖς ἀγαπῶσιν αὐτόν)." Indeed, Sir 1:10 and its preceding context in 1:1–9 resonate remarkably well not only with both parts of the scriptural quote in 1 Cor 2:9 but also with its immediate context.[5]

Paul's description of God's wisdom (θεοῦ σοφίαν) as "hidden in mystery" in 1 Cor 2:7a and the first part of the quote in 2:9a, "what things eye has not seen and ear has not heard and have not arisen in the heart of a human being," recall how "all wisdom (σοφία) is from the Lord" in Sir 1:1a and resonate with the question in 1:3b: "Who will search out wisdom (σοφίαν)?" That God predetermined wisdom "before the ages (πρὸ τῶν αἰώνων) for our glory" in 1 Cor 2:7b recalls how wisdom is with God "for ever" (εἰς τὸν αἰῶνα) in Sir 1:1b, how "wisdom was created before all things (προτέρα πάντων) and prudent understanding from eternity (ἐξ αἰῶνος)" in 1:4, and how "the Lord himself created her" in 1:9a. That none of the rulers of this age knew (ἔγνωκεν) God's wisdom in 1 Cor 2:8 recalls the question of who knows (ἔγνω) wisdom's great deeds in Sir 1:6b. The wisdom that a human eye has not seen (εἶδεν) in 1 Cor 2:9a God has seen (εἶδεν) in Sir 1:9. And that God has revealed (ἀπεκάλυψεν) to us his wisdom in 1 Cor 2:10a answers the question in Sir 1:6a: "To whom has the root of wisdom been revealed (ἀπεκαλύφθη)?"

"What things God has prepared for those who love him (τοῖς ἀγαπῶσιν αὐτόν)" in 1 Cor 2:9b evokes for the implied audience yet other scriptural texts that speak of what God does for those who love him. In LXX Deut 7:9 God is described as "a faithful God who keeps covenant and mercy for those who love him (τοῖς ἀγαπῶσιν αὐτόν)." Similarly, in LXX Neh 5:1 God "keeps the covenant and the mercy for those who love him (τοῖς ἀγαπῶσιν αὐτὸν)." In LXX Ps 145:20, God "preserves all who love him (τοὺς ἀγαπῶντας αὐτὸν)." This theme continues in *Pss. Sol.* 6:6, which speaks of God "providing mercy for those who love him (τοῖς ἀγαπῶσίν αὐτὸν) in

---

thing God had never imagined—the idolatrous abominations that "did not arise in my heart" (οὐκ ἀνέβη ἐπὶ καρδίαν μου). This comes close to the way this idiom is used in 1 Cor 2:9a to express what human beings have never imagined—what things "did not arise in the heart of a human being" (ἐπὶ καρδίαν ἀνθρώπου οὐκ ἀνέβη).

5. We cannot agree with Lindemann's (*Erste Korintherbrief*, 67) assessment that the influence of Sir 1:10 upon 1 Cor 2:9 is questionable, since the context is very different. As we will see, there are significant similarities between the contexts of both of these texts revolving around the theme of God's wisdom.

truth." In *Pss. Sol.* 14:1, God is "faithful to those who love him (τοῖς ἀγαπῶσίν αὐτὸν) in truth" (cf. *Pss. Sol.* 4:25).[6]

There are other texts that express various things that God has "prepared" (ἡτοίμασεν in 1 Cor 2:9b) for his chosen people and members of them, who implicitly love God. In LXX Exod 15:17, God is invoked to bring in his people Israel and "plant them on the mountain of your inheritance, on your prepared (ἕτοιμον) inheritance, which you, Lord, made ready, the sanctuary, Lord, which your hands prepared (ἡτοίμασαν)." In LXX Exod 23:20, God will send his angel to go before his chosen people of Israel "to bring you into the land which I have prepared (ἡτοίμασα) for you" (see also LXX Ezek 20:6).

In LXX Ps 22:5, God has "prepared" (ἡτοίμασας) a table for the psalmist in the presence of those who afflict him. In LXX Ps 131:17, God has "prepared" (ἡτοίμασα) a "lamp for my anointed." And there are various expressions of the kingdom/kingship God has "prepared" for individuals in 1 Kgdms 2:3; 13:13; 2 Kgdms 5:12; 7:12; 1 Chr 14:2; 17:11. These specific things that God has "prepared" for those who implicitly love him condition the Corinthian audience for the unseen, unheard, and inconceivable things God has prepared for those who love him in 1 Cor 2:9b.

In conclusion, although Sir 1:10 (more than Isa 64:3) with its wisdom theme and context provides significant background for 1 Cor 2:9 and its context, the scriptural quote in 2:9 is not meant to evoke any single text from the OT. It is introduced very generally and simply by "as it is written," without further specifying where it is written. The wording of the quote itself as a whole and in this form occurs nowhere in the OT. Rather, it has brought together various formulations and concepts found in a number of different places in the OT. Thus, Paul's scriptural quote in 1 Cor 2:9, "What things eye has not seen and ear has not heard and have not arisen in the heart of a human being, what things God has prepared for those who love him," carries with it the persuasive authority and rhetorical force not necessarily of any particular OT text or context but of the OT scriptures as a whole and in general.[7]

---

6. For texts that speak of what God does for those who love "me" (God or divine wisdom), see LXX Exod 20:6; Deut 5:10; Prov 8:21. On "loving God" in Paul, see also Oda Wischmeyer, "ΘΕΟΝ ΑΓΑΠΑΝ bei Paulus: Eine traditionsgeschichtliche Miszelle," *ZNW* 78 (1987): 141–44.

7. A saying similar to 1 Cor 2:9 is attributed to Jesus in the *Gospel of Thomas* 17. It "represents a secondary development of the tradition compared with the version which Paul gives in 1 Cor 2:9," according to Christopher M. Tuckett, "Paul and Jesus Tradition: The Evidence of 1 Corinthians 2:9 and Gospel of Thomas 17," in *Paul and the Corinthians: Studies on a Commu-*

Literary-Rhetorical Analysis

The formula "but as it is written" introduces the scripture quotation in 1 Cor 2:9. The conjunction "but" (ἀλλά) indicates that the citation, "what things eye has not seen and ear has not heard and have not arisen in the heart of a human being, what things God has prepared for those who love him," plus the rest of the sentence in 2:10a, "God has revealed to us through the Spirit," stands in contrast to what Paul has just stated about God's unknown wisdom in 2:8: "which none of the rulers of this age knew, for if they had known it, they would not have crucified the Lord of glory."[8] Furthermore, the "but as it is written" in 2:9 continues the contrast, introduced by the "but (ἀλλά) we speak" in 2:7, between "God's wisdom hidden in mystery, which God predetermined before the ages for our glory" and "the wisdom of this age or of the rulers of this age who are passing away" in 2:6.[9] And "as it is written" (καθὼς γέγραπται, perfect passive) indicates that this contrast corresponds to what has been and still stands as authoritatively written scripture.

The quotation presents the audience with a pair of coordinate relative clauses, each introduced by the neuter plural relative pronoun ἅ, "what things," which in turn coordinate with a previous pair of relative clauses in 2:7b–8, each introduced by the feminine singular relative pronoun ἥν, "which," referring to the "wisdom (σοφίαν) of God hidden in mystery" that "we speak" (2:7a).[10] The pair of relative clauses in the quotation of 2:9,

---

nity in Conflict. Essays in Honour of Margaret Thrall (ed. Trevor J. Burke and J. Keith Elliott; NovTSup 109; Leiden: Brill, 2003), 73.

8. The quotation thus functions as the object of the verb "revealed" in 2:10a. Fee (*Corinthians*, 107 n. 40) objects to this: "But this destroys Paul's syntax altogether by missing the adversative force of ἀλλά in v. 9 and running roughshod over the explanatory γάρ that begins v. 10." We are maintaining an adversative force between what God has revealed to us in 2:9–10a and the wisdom of this age mentioned in 2:6, 8. Furthermore, we opt for the variant reading of δέ rather than γάρ in 2:10a. For the text-critical evidence and reasoning, see Bruce M. Metzger, *A Textual Commentary on the Greek New Testament* (New York: United Bible Societies, 1971), 546; Collins, *First Corinthians*, 132; Thiselton, *Corinthians*, 254–55.

9. For more on what the ἀλλά in 2:9 contrasts, see Bo Frid, "The Enigmatic ΑΛΛΑ in 1 Corinthians 2.9," NTS 31 (1985): 603–11; Fee, *Corinthians*, 107–8; Schrage, *Erste Brief*, 1:255–56; Lindemann, *Erste Korintherbrief*, 65; Wolff, *Erste Brief*, 57; Thiselton, *Corinthians*, 248–49. We do not agree with Frid that 2:9 is an ellipsis lacking the words "these things we have come to know." Lindemann also disagrees with Frid, but denies the contrast with 2:8, only seeing ἀλλά in 2:9 as parallel to the one in 2:7.

10. Archibald Robertson and Alfred Plummer, *A Critical and Exegetical Commentary on the First Epistle of St Paul to the Corinthians* (ICC; Edinburgh: Clark, 1914), 40. Fee (*Corinthians*, 108) thinks the second ἅ (2:9b) functions as ταῦτα, "these things," which would then be the referent for the first ἅ and thus form a complete sentence rather than two coordinate relative

then, elaborate on this wisdom of God that stands in contrast to the wisdom of this age (2:6, 8).

The quotation's first relative pronoun, "what things," in 2:9 introduces a triplet of clauses that moves the audience through a progression of expressions of what things lie beyond our human capacities. In the first two clauses, the relative pronoun functions as the object—"what things eye has not seen and ear has not heard." But in the third and climactic clause of the triplet, the relative pronoun functions as the subject—"what things have not arisen in the heart of a human being." With this third clause the audience has thus progressed from the incapacity of the visual and auditory sense organs—eye and ear—to the incapacity of the "heart" (καρδίαν) as the center and source of human thinking, feeling, and volition.[11] The audience has advanced from what things cannot be seen or heard implicitly by a human being to what things cannot even be thought, imagined, or conceived explicitly by any human being (ἀνθρώπου).

The quotation's second clause, introduced by the relative pronoun "what things" in 2:9, stands in apposition to the first, further elaborating upon it—"what things God has prepared for those who love him." As things that God has prepared for those human beings who love him, what things lie beyond the human capacity to see, hear, or even imagine, and thus beyond the human wisdom of the leaders of this age (2:5-6, 8), would be things extremely valuable and desirable for the audience. And that is what God has revealed to "us" (ἡμῖν, 2:10a), Paul and his Corinthian audience, those who have been favored by (1:2-9) and thus love God.[12]

---

clauses. Similarly, Thiselton (*Corinthians*, 248–50) thinks the second ἅ (2:9b) functions as ὅσα, for which there is a variant reading, and should be translated as "how very much," in which case "God prepared" becomes the main verb of a complete sentence. But Thiselton admits that most view ἅ in 2:9b as a relative pronoun, meaning "what things" God prepared (248).

11. BDAG, 508; Thiselton, *Corinthians*, 249; Alexander Sand, "καρδία," *EDNT* 2:250: "Καρδία refers thus to the *inner person*, the seat of understanding, knowledge, and will."

12. The emphatic position of "us" in 2:10a places it in immediate juxtaposition with "those who love him" in 2:9. See Fee, *Corinthians*, 109 n. 51; Thiselton, *Corinthians*, 255; Joachim Theis, *Paulus als Weisheitslehrer: Der Gekreuzigte und die Weisheit Gottes in 1 Kor 1–4* (Biblische Untersuchungen 22; Regensburg, Germany: Pustet, 1991), 243; Sigurd Grindheim, "Wisdom for the Perfect: Paul's Challenge to the Corinthian Church (1 Corinthians 2:6–16)," *JBL* 121 (2002): 705.

Relation to the Antecedent Context in 1 Corinthians 2:1–8

In 1 Cor 2:1, Paul tells his Corinthian audience that he came to them proclaiming "the mystery of God,"[13] that is, a divine secret plan that is otherwise hidden and unknown to human comprehension and conception.[14] An integral element of this mystery of God is Jesus Christ as crucified (2:2).[15] In 2:6 there is a shift in the rhetorical dynamics from Paul in the first-person singular addressing the Corinthians in the second-person plural (2:1–5) to Paul speaking in the first-person plural—a strategy tending to draw his Corinthian audience to himself as fellow believers, as those whose faith is not in the wisdom of human beings but in the power of God (2:5).[16]

The mystery (μυστήριον) of God that Paul proclaims "to you," the Corinthians (2:1), thus becomes the wisdom of God hidden in mystery (μυστηρίῳ) that "we [Paul and potentially the Corinthians and all believers] speak" (2:7).[17] This is the wisdom of God that is authoritatively attested by

---

13. For the text-critical preference of the reading "mystery" (μυστήριον) rather than "witness" (μαρτύριον) here, see Metzger, *Textual Commentary*, 545; Thiselton, *Corinthians*, 207. But note the argument in favor of μαρτύριον as the original by Grindheim, "Wisdom," 695 n. 22.

14. BDAG, 662, defines μυστήριον here as "the secret thoughts, plans, and dispensations of God which are hidden from human reason, as well as from all other comprehension below the divine level, and await either fulfillment or revelation to those for whom they are intended." See also Helmut Krämer, "μυστήριον," *EDNT* 2:446–49.

15. Note the explanatory γάρ at the beginning of 2:2. On 1 Cor 2:2 and christology, see Wiard Popkes, "1 Kor 2,2 und die Anfänge der Christologie," *ZNW* 95 (2004): 64–83.

16. The I-you dynamics in 2:1–5 is characterized by emphatic double uses of the first-person singular pronoun, "as for me" (κἀγώ in 2:1, 3), and the first-person singular possessive adjective, "my (μου) word and my (μου) proclamation" (2:4), to refer to Paul. This enhances the contrast between Paul and other preachers at Corinth, but also allows his Corinthian audience, whom he continually reminds of what happened when "I" came to "you" (πρὸς ὑμᾶς, ὑμῖν in 2:1; ἐν ὑμῖν in 2:2; πρὸς ὑμᾶς in 2:3; ὑμῶν in 2:5), to verify what he is saying through their shared experience. See Thiselton, *Corinthians*, 208, 217–18; Smit, "'What Is Apollos?'" 236–37. For the debate on how continuous or discontinuous 2:6–16 is within its context, including whether or not it is a non-Pauline interpolation, see William O. Walker, *Interpolations in the Pauline Letters* (JSNTSup 213; Sheffield: Sheffield Academic Press, 2001), 127–46; Johan S. Vos, *Die Kunst der Argumentation bei Paulus: Studien zur antiken Rhetorik* (WUNT 149; Tübingen: Mohr Siebeck, 2002), 50–51.

17. That "we speak"(λαλοῦμεν) in 2:6–7 refers at least potentially to all believers is confirmed by 2:7b, which describes the wisdom of God that "we speak" as that "which God predetermined before the ages for our (ἡμῶν) glory." This glory is surely not just for Paul and his associate preachers but for all believers—all whose faith is not in the wisdom of human beings (2:5) and who thus speak the wisdom of God. See Kuck, *Judgment*, 193. Furthermore, as Lamp (*First Corinthians 1–4*, 160) notes: "As for identifying private conversation in the use of the verb λαλέω . . . If Paul had meant something along the lines of private instruction, certainly he could have chosen a more precise verb than λαλέω, a verb that commonly means 'utter.'"

the scriptures as "what things eye has not seen and ear has not heard and have not arisen in the heart of a human being" (2:9a), but which God has revealed "to us"—Paul, his Corinthian audience, and all believers (2:10a).[18]

In 2:5, Paul tells his Corinthian audience that their faith is not in the wisdom of human beings but in the power of God. This wisdom of "human beings" (ἀνθρώπων) in general is then specified and exemplified as the wisdom that is of this age and the rulers of this age who are passing away (2:6).[19] This human wisdom stands in contrast to God's wisdom, which is hidden in mystery (2:7). In their wisdom as mere human beings the rulers of this age did not know this wisdom of God (2:8). But this hidden and humanly unknown wisdom of God, characterized by the authoritative scriptures as "what things have not arisen in the heart of a human being (ἀνθρώπου)" (2:9), God has now revealed "to us"—Paul, his Corinthian audience, and all Christians—through the Spirit (2:10a).[20]

In 2:7b, Paul describes God's wisdom as that which "God (ὁ θεὸς) predetermined before the ages for our glory," that is, for the glory of all believers. The scriptural quote in 2:9 then develops this idea of the benefit of God's wisdom for the audience by describing God's wisdom as "what things God (ὁ θεὸς) has prepared for those who love him," that is, for all believers—"for us" (ἡμῖν) for whom God revealed these things (2:10a) concerning God's wisdom which God predetermined for "our" (ἡμῶν) glory (2:7b).[21]

---

18. Selby, "Paul, the Seer," 369-70: "Paul's language reflects a deliberate attempt to place himself in the apocalyptic tradition. He has assumed the *persona* of the 'inspired seer' who receives a divine revelation and who faithfully—yet also in weakness, fear and trembling—transmits the mysterious, secret wisdom of God to God's people." See also Kammler, *Kreuz*, 216.

19. For a recent addition to the many who see "the rulers of this age" in 2:6 as demonic rather than human rulers, see M. E. Adeyemi, "The Rulers of This Age in First Corinthians 2:6-8: An Exegetical Exposition," *Deltion Biblikon Meleton* 28 (1999): 38-45. But for the more likely interpretation that they are human rulers, see Wesley A. Carr, "The Rulers of This Age—I Corinthians II.6-8," *NTS* 23 (1976): 20-35; Fee, *Corinthians*, 103-4; Lamp, *First Corinthians 1-4*, 163-64; Wolff, *Erste Brief*, 53-54. For an extensive discussion and bibliography on the issue, see Thiselton, *Corinthians*, 228 (bibliography), 233-39, who leans toward the interpretation that they are human rulers, but notes: "Even if Paul's language *denotes* human leaders, *connotations* remain of a structural power either by cumulative inbuilt fallenness or by association with still stronger cosmic forces" (238). See also Grindheim, "Wisdom," 694-95 n. 20.

20. For the suggestion that 2:8-10 reflects, at least indirectly, Paul's Damascus Christophany experience, see Seyoon Kim, *Paul and the New Perspective: Second Thoughts on the Origin of Paul's Gospel* (Grand Rapids: Eerdmans, 2002), 116-17.

21. Fee, *Corinthians*, 106: "'For our glory' is eschatological language, referring to the final goal of salvation, namely that God's people should share in his own glory. Hence the crucified one is in this context also called 'the Lord of glory' (v. 8)." See also Collins, *First Corinthians*, 130; Thiselton, *Corinthians*, 242-45.

The scriptural quote's double use of the neuter plural relative pronoun ἅ, "what things," to refer to God's wisdom (2:9) develops the previous double use of the feminine singular relative pronoun ἥν, "which," to refer to God's wisdom (2:7b–8a). This rhetorical movement from the singular to the plural indicates the multifaceted dimension of God's wisdom and arouses in the audience an awareness of the multiplicity of things involved in God's wisdom that God, in Christ crucified (2:2) and through the Spirit, has now revealed to us (2:10a).[22]

Relation to the Subsequent Context in 1 Corinthians 2:10–15

With its double use of the neuter plural relative pronoun ἅ, "what things," to describe the wisdom of God (2:7–8) involved in the mystery of Christ crucified (2:1–2), the scriptural quote in 2:9 provides specific elaboration for the audience's understanding of the content of the otherwise somewhat vague and general series of further neuter plural expressions referring to this same wisdom of God in the subsequent context.[23] This series of neuter plurals can be conveniently viewed in the following list:

2:9: "what things"(ἅ) . . . "what things . . ." (ἅ)
2:10: "all things" (πάντα) . . . "the deep things (τὰ βάθη) of God"
2:11: "the things (τὰ) of God"
2:12: "the things freely given (τὰ . . . χαρισθέντα) by God to us"
2:13: "what things (ἅ) we speak" . . . "spiritual things" (πνευματικὰ)
2:14: "the things (τὰ) of the Spirit of God"
2:15: "all things" (πάντα)

The neuter plural, "the depths" or "the deep things" (τὰ βάθη) of God, is part of the comprehensive neuter plural, "all things" (πάντα), that the Spirit searches (2:10b). "The deep things" refers to "something nonphysical perceived to be so remote that it is difficult to assess."[24] These "deep things" of God have been very aptly described for the audience by the scriptural

---

22. With regard to the difference in relative pronouns here, Lamp (*First Corinthians 1–4*, 166) remarks: "In each case the relative pronoun takes as its antecedent a reference to God's redemptive plan; ἥν recalls θεοῦ σοφίαν while the neuter ἅ appears to take as its antecedent the collective elements of salvation encapsulated in θεοῦ σοφία." And according to Davis (*Wisdom and Spirit*, 96), "So the referent or antecedent of the relative in 1 Co 2.9 need be nothing other than the collective elements of θεοῦ σοφία, the details of the divine plan."

23. Although Lamp (*First Corinthians 1–4*, 171–72) points out the references of many (but not all) of these neuter plural expressions to the wisdom of God, he fails to connect them with the neuter plural relative pronouns in the scriptural quote of 2:9.

24. BDAG, 162.

quote's neuter plural expressions of what has been humanly unseen, unheard, and unimagined, yet destined for those who love God: "What things (ἅ) eye has not seen and ear has not heard and have not arisen in the heart of a human being, what things (ἅ) God has prepared for those who love him"(2:9). These "deep things" God has now, as the wisdom of God (2:7) mysteriously hidden in Christ crucified (2:2), revealed to "us," Paul, his Corinthian audience, and all believers, through the Spirit (2:10a).

The neuter plural, "the deep things of God" (τὰ βάθη τοῦ θεοῦ), in 2:10 is abbreviated as the neuter plural, "the things of God" (τὰ τοῦ θεοῦ), that no one knows except the Spirit of God in 2:11. And this neuter plural, "the things of God," then expands into yet another neuter plural, "the things freely given by God to us" (τὰ ὑπὸ τοῦ θεοῦ χαρισθέντα ἡμῖν), which "we," Paul and his Corinthian audience, may understand because we have received not "the spirit of the world" but "the Spirit that comes from God" in 2:12.[25] Because we have received the Spirit "that comes *from* God" (ἐκ τοῦ θεοῦ), we may understand the things freely given to us "*by* God" (ὑπὸ τοῦ θεοῦ).

The "things freely given" (χαρισθέντα) by God to us (2:12) pluralizes the singular "grace" (χάρις) from God with which Paul greeted his audience (1:3) and the singular "grace" (χάριτι) of God given to them in Christ Jesus for which Paul thanks God (1:4). This "grace" was then delineated in terms of "every speech or discourse (λόγῳ) and every knowledge" with which the Corinthians were enriched in every way in Christ (1:5). Indeed, they lack no "gift" (χαρίσματι) as they await the revelation of our Lord Jesus Christ (1:7). The neuter plural, "things freely given by God" (2:12), then, includes all of these "gifts" (1:7) with which the Corinthians have been specifically enriched, as well as those that have been generally given to "us" (ἡμῖν, 2:12)—Paul, the Corinthians, and all believers, the same "us" (ἡμῖν, 2:10) to whom God revealed the neuter plural contents of the scriptural quote in 2:9.[26] "The things freely given by God to us" thus develops the scriptural

---

25. According to Adams (*Constructing the World*, 117), "[T]he effect of his [Paul's] remark in 2:12 is to reinforce the disjunction between the Corinthians and the κόσμος. He is making the point, once again, that his readers do not belong to the world and the present age. Their reception of God's Spirit sets them apart from the κόσμος."

26. According to Eastman (*Significance of Grace*, 46), " '[G]ifts bestowed' (τὰ χαρισθέντα) is most probably a deliberate allusion to God's grace. The plural form seems to be a comprehensive expression, going beyond the 'gift' of salvation (cf. Rom 6:23) to include the other benefits of salvation such as sanctification, as well as 'gifts' of the Spirit given to believers (cf. 1:4; 12:1–31)." According to Vos (*Kunst der Argumentation*, 54), "Statt über die Tiefen Gottes spricht Paulus in V. 12 jedoch über die Gnadengaben Gottes. Ruft die Formulierung von V. 10 beim Leser zunächst das Bild besonderer göttlicher Geheimnisse hervor, so kann man in V. 12 auch an

quote by expressing what humanly unseen, unheard, and inconceivable things God has prepared for those who love him, which "we," who love and are loved by God, may now understand.[27]

The neuter plural relative pronoun, "which things" (ἅ), at the beginning of 2:13 refers to the neuter plural, "the things freely given by God to us," at the end of 2:12. Not only may we understand these things (2:12b), but "we also speak of these things not in words taught by human wisdom but in [words] taught by the Spirit" (2:13a). That we also speak (λαλοῦμεν) of "these things" develops for the audience Paul's previous assertion that "we speak (λαλοῦμεν) a wisdom among the mature, but a wisdom not of this age nor of the rulers of this age who are passing away. Rather we speak (λαλοῦμεν) God's wisdom hidden in mystery" (2:6–7a). It is the scriptural quote in 2:9 that specified this wisdom of God with neuter plurals as "what things (ἅ) eye has not seen and ear has not heard and have not arisen in the heart of a human being, what things (ἅ) God has prepared for those who love him," which now include the neuter plural, "the things freely given by God to us" (2:12), "which things" (ἅ) we also speak not in words taught by human wisdom but as God's wisdom revealed (2:10) and taught to us by the Spirit (2:13a).

The neuter plural, "which things" (ἅ), in 2:13a receives another referent in the neuter plural, "things of the Spirit" (πνευματικὰ), in 2:13b: "Which things we also speak not in words taught by human wisdom but in (words) taught by the Spirit, interpreting to people of the Spirit things of the Spirit."[28] The neuter plural "things of the Spirit" thus continues to charac-

---

die elementare Heilserkenntnis denken. Die Undeutlichkeit in der Formulierung dürfte damit zusammenhängen, daß es Paulus weniger auf den genauen Inhalt als auf den geheimnisvollen und übernatürlichen Charakter der Erkenntnis ankommt."

27. The first-person dative plural "us" (ἡμῖν), the recipients of the things freely given by God, at the end of 2:12 forms an inclusion with the first-person dative plural "us" (ἡμῖν), the recipients of God's revelation of the contents of the scriptural quote, at the beginning of 2:10 as an expression of how God loves "us" as among those who love him (2:9).

28. Thiselton (*Corinthians*, 265) notes that "in the previous verse Paul has underlined the transcendence and otherness of God's Spirit as *issuing from God* (τὸ πνεῦμα τὸ ἐκ τοῦ θεοῦ). We believe that this is a decisive indication that Paul wishes the adjectival form πνευματικός to be understood as meaning *of the Spirit* (of God), and not as the more bland *spiritual*, which allows for the very misunderstanding which Paul wishes to exclude." Thiselton's translation is perhaps a better rendering of the paronomasia noted by Collins (*First Corinthians*, 135): "Paul's qualifying participial clause is linked to the antithesis by means of paronomasia, three uses of πνεῦμα-, following immediately after one another, πνεύματος πνευματικοῖς πνευματικά." To expect (as do Fee, *Corinthians*, 115 n. 75; Schrage, *Erste Brief*, 1:261) the definite article τοῖς with πνευματικοῖς to justify a reference to persons here would diminish the paronomasia. Furthermore, πνευματικοῖς occurs without the article in a reference to persons in 3:1. As Lockwood (*1 Corinthians*, 98; see also Wolff, *Erste Brief*, 60) notes, the context supports the reference to

terize for the audience the neuter plural expressions of the humanly unseen, unheard, and inconceivable things God has prepared for those who love him in the scriptural quote of 2:9. They are "things of the Spirit" because God has revealed them to us through the Spirit (πνεύματος)—the Spirit (πνεῦμα) that searches everything, even the deep things of God (2:10).[29] They are "things of the Spirit" because they are the things of God that the Spirit (πνεῦμα) of God alone knows (2:11). And they are "things of the Spirit" because we speak of them in words taught by the Spirit (πνεύματος) (2:13).

"We," that is, Paul and potentially all believers, especially his Corinthian audience, "interpret" or "explain" (συγκρίνοντες) these "things of the Spirit" (πνευματικά), which have been expressed in the scriptural quote of 2:9, by speaking of them in words taught by the Spirit (πνεύματος) to "people of the Spirit" (πνευματικοῖς)— the people who are included in the "we," all believers, who have received the Spirit (πνεῦμα) that comes from God (2:12–13).[30] These "people of the Spirit" are thus included in the "mature" (τελείοις), that is, all believers, among whom "we," Paul and potentially all believers, speak God's wisdom (2:6–7)—the wisdom, the "things of the Spirit," expressed in the scriptural quote of 2:9.[31]

The neuter plural expressions in the scriptural quote of 2:9 continue to be described by yet another neuter plural, "the things of the Spirit of God" (τὰ τοῦ πνεύματος τοῦ θεοῦ), which the merely "physical" or "natural" (ψυχικὸς) person does not receive, for they are foolishness to him and he is not able to know them, because only by means of the Spirit (πνευματικῶς)

---

persons for πνευματικοῖς in 2:13: "In 2:15, Paul speaks of 'the spiritual person' (ὁ πνευματικός), who is contrasted with the 'unspiritual person' of 2:14 (ψυχικὸς ἄνθρωπος). Even more decisive is 3:1, where we find the dative plural πνευματικοῖς referring to 'spiritual' people in contrast to 'fleshly' people." For the justification of the interpretation we have adopted as well as the other possibilities for interpreting the participial clause, πνευματικοῖς πνευματικὰ συγκρίνοντες, in 2:13b, see Thiselton, *Corinthians*, 264–67; Lockwood, *1 Corinthians*, 98; Collins, *First Corinthians*, 135; Wolff, *Erste Brief*, 60–61; Lindemann, *Erste Korintherbrief*, 71; Schrage, *Erste Brief*, 1:261–62.

29. Collins, *First Corinthians*, 135: "What are interpreted are πνευματικά, that is, the things God has revealed through the Spirit (v. 9)."

30. Thiselton (*Corinthians*, 266) makes a (too fine?) distinction between "interpreting" and "explaining" here: "Since *interpreting* may entail opening the understanding through *life experience* and *stance* as well as simply intellectual *explanation*, *interpret* is preferable to *explain*." Kuck, *Judgment*, 194: "[T]he first-person plural form used throughout 2:6–16 and the term πνευματικός refer to all Christians."

31. On "the mature" in 2:6 as referring to all believers, who have received the Spirit, see Thiselton, *Corinthians*, 231–33; Fee, *Corinthians*, 102; Kuck, *Judgment*, 193; Collins, *First Corinthians*, 122, 128–29; Lindemann, *Erste Korintherbrief*, 61–63; Wolff, *Erste Brief*, 54; Schrage, *Erste Brief*, 1:249; Grindheim, "Wisdom," 702–9.

can they be examined (2:14).³² The person of the Spirit (πνευματικὸς), that is, every believer, who has received the Spirit that comes from God (2:12), examines all things, but he himself can be examined by no one (2:15).³³

As the final neuter plural in the series, "all things" (πάντα) forms an inclusion with the "all things" (πάντα) that began the series following the scriptural quote of 2:9. Just as the Spirit searches "all things," even "the deep things of God" (2:10), so the person of the Spirit examines "all things," including "the things of the Spirit of God" (2:14), which "we," Paul and all believers, not only understand but speak, namely, the things expressed in the scriptural quote of 2:9: "What things eye has not seen and ear has not heard and have not arisen in the heart of a human being, what things God has prepared for those who love him."³⁴

Summary on 1 Corinthians 2:9

1. Although the wisdom theme and context of Sir 1:10 provides more relevant background for 1 Cor 2:9 and its context than other suggested OT texts, such as Isa 64:3, the scriptural quote in 2:9 is not meant to evoke any single text from the OT. It is introduced very generally and without indication of its OT location simply by "as it is written." Taken as a whole, the citation itself occurs nowhere in the OT. Rather, it has brought together various formulations and concepts found in a number of different places in the OT. Thus, Paul's scriptural quote in 2:9 carries with it the persuasive authority and rhetorical force not of any particular OT text or context but of the OT scriptures as a whole and in general.

2. With its scriptural expression of what things God has prepared for

---

32. Kuck, *Judgment*, 194 n. 225: "ψυχικός refers not to a class of Christians inferior to the πνευματικοί but rather to all who have not accepted God's revelation." Stephen J. Chester, *Conversion at Corinth: Perspectives on Conversion in Paul's Theology and the Corinthian Church* (London: Clark, 2003), 289: "The πνευματικός–ψυχικός terminology thus functions to assert the Corinthians' sense of their superlative personal religious distinction. They are different from the rest of humanity, who languish as mere ψυχικοί."

33. On the meaning of ἀνακρίνω in 2:14–15 as "examine," "evaluate," "judge," "discern," and so on, see Mathias Rissi, "κρίνω," *EDNT* 2:321; BDAG, 66. According to Vos (*Kunst der Argumentation*, 56), "Man kann ἀνακρίνειν in 15b, wie es für 15a naheliegt, als synonym mit ἐρευνᾶν und γινώσκειν betrachten.... Im Begriff ἀνακρίνειν verschiebt sich dann der Akzent vom Kognitiven zum Forensischen." See also Wilk, *Bedeutung*, 289–90 n. 17; Fee, *Corinthians*, 117. By translating ἀνακρίνειν as "examine" here we are attempting to preserve both its cognitive and forensic connotations.

34. For a comparison of 1 Cor 2:6–3:4 with Philo's exegetical treatments of creation, see Gregory E. Sterling, "'Wisdom among the Perfect': Creation Traditions in Alexandrian Judaism and Corinthian Christianity," *NovT* 37 (1995): 367–76.

those who love him, what things lie beyond the human capacity to see, hear, or even imagine, the citation of 2:9 prompts its audience to an awareness of their privileged position as among those to whom God has now revealed these things through the Spirit.

3. In contrast to the human wisdom of this age and the rulers of this age (2:5–8), God's hidden, mysterious, and humanly unknown wisdom, characterized by the authoritative scriptures as "what things have not arisen in the heart of a human being" (2:9), God has now revealed "to us"—Paul, his Corinthian audience, and all believers—through the Spirit (2:10a).

4. The scriptural quote in 2:9 expresses the benefit of God's wisdom for the audience by describing God's wisdom as "what things God has prepared for those who love him," that is, for all believers—"for us" for whom God revealed these things (2:10a) concerning God's wisdom which God predetermined for "our" glory (2:7b).

5. The movement from the singular references to God's wisdom in 2:7b–8a to the plural in the scriptural quote of 2:9 indicates the multifaceted dimension of God's wisdom and arouses in the audience an awareness of the multiplicity of things involved in God's wisdom that God, in Christ crucified (2:2) and through the Spirit, has now revealed to us (2:10a).

6. "The things freely given by God to us" in 2:12 develops the scriptural quote in 2:9 by expressing what humanly unseen, unheard, and inconceivable things God has prepared for those who love him, which "we," Paul and his audience who love and are loved by God, may now understand.

7. Just as the Spirit searches "all things," even "the deep things of God" (2:10), so the person of the Spirit examines "all things," including "the things of the Spirit of God" (2:13–14), which "we," Paul, his Corinthian audience, and all believers who have received the Spirit that comes from God (2:12), not only understand but speak, namely, the things authoritatively expressed in the scriptural quote of 2:9: "What things eye has not seen and ear has not heard and have not arisen in the heart of a human being, what things God has prepared for those who love him."

Chapter 5

1 Corinthians 2:16a

Who has known the mind of the Lord,
that he will instruct him?

Old Testament Background

Although not explicitly introduced as a scriptural quotation, the rhetorical question in 1 Cor 2:16a, "Who has known (ἔγνω) the mind (νοῦν) of the Lord, that he will instruct (συμβιβάσει) him?" clearly comes from Isa 40:13.[1] Indeed, it is an apparent abbreviation of LXX Isa 40:13: "Who has known (ἔγνω) the mind (νοῦν) of the Lord and who has become his counselor, that he will instruct (συμβιβᾷ) him?"[2] Paul has left out the second interrogative clause, "who has become his counselor," evidently for the sake of his rhetorical strategy.[3]

But there are several other OT texts similar in both form and content to the rhetorical question that Paul utilizes from Isa 40:13 in 1 Cor 2:16a. In Jdt 8:14 it is asked, "How will you search out God, who has made all these things, and know (ἐπιγνώσεσθε) his mind (νοῦν), and comprehend his

---

1. Against an idea that the question in 2:16a is not a scriptural reference but simply Pauline language, Wilk (*Bedeutung*, 287–88 n. 1) points out that the reference to the "mind of the Lord" (νοῦς κυρίου) after a domination in 2:5–10 of references to the "Spirit" (πνεῦμα) of God is very striking and that Paul has not elsewhere used the verb "instruct" (συμβιβάζειν).

2. Paul also employs a different form of the future indicative verb (συμβιβάσει) than the LXX (συμβιβᾷ); on the different forms, see Koch, *Schrift*, 49 n. 7. Lockwood (*1 Corinthians*, 100) incorrectly identifies συμβιβᾷ as a present, rather than a variant form of the future, tense.

3. Thiselton, *Corinthians*, 275: "The quotation thus begins exactly as Paul quotes it (with his addition of *for*), but the middle clause is omitted, since 'Who has become his adviser?' (σύμβουλος) is less pointed than the dynamic barb 'Who *should instruct him?*'" Collins, *First Corinthians*, 137: "Paul has sharpened the rhetorical impact of the prophetic cry by omitting the ... question, 'who has become his counselor?' (Isa 40:13b)." Note that in his quotation of Isa 40:13 in Rom 11:34 Paul includes "who has become his counselor?" but omits "that he will instruct him." Cf. Lim, *Scripture*, 158–60.

thought?" In Wis 9:13 it is asked, "For what human will know (γνώσεται) the plan of God or who will conceive what the Lord wills?" In Wis 9:17 it is asked, "Who has known (ἔγνω) your plan, unless you have given wisdom (σοφίαν; cf. 1 Cor 1:17–2:13) and sent your holy spirit (πνεῦμα; cf. 1 Cor 2:4–14) from on high?" In LXX Job 15:8 it is asked, "Or have you heard the doctrine of the Lord such that wisdom (σοφία) reached you?" And in LXX Jer 23:18 it is asked, "For who has stood in the council of the Lord and seen his word? Who has heeded and heard?"

That there are so many other scriptural rhetorical questions that, like Isa 40:13, express the human incomprehension of God's mind and way of thinking strengthens the probability that Paul's implied Corinthian audience recognizes his rhetorical question in 1 Cor 2:16a, which is also notably distinct in vocabulary from what precedes it, as a scriptural reference. Nevertheless, since Paul does not call explicit attention to its origin in scripture, it would appear not to matter greatly for his rhetorical strategy if his audience recognizes it as scriptural or not. Paul employs this scriptural rhetorical question not only for its implicit scriptural authority but for its rhetorical power. Or, to put it in other terms, in the case of 1 Cor 2:16a the authority of the scriptural reference lies in its rhetorical appropriateness and potency.[4]

Literary-Rhetorical Analysis

The scriptural reference in 2:16a begins with the question, "Who has known the mind of the Lord?" The "mind (νοῦν) of the Lord" refers to God's mind-set, to the way or result of God's thinking—God's thoughts, ideas, or plans.[5] The relative pronoun (ὅς) that follows introduces a result

---

4. Williams (*Wisdom*, 209–35) limits his treatment of the scriptural origin and background of 2:16a to Isa 40:13, its context, and its relation to early Jewish literature. Except for a mention of Jdt 8:14 he largely neglects the many other OT texts indicated above as similar to Isa 40:13 in form and content.

5. Thiselton, *Corinthians*, 275: "[T]he word *mind* (νοῦς) constitutes 'not an instrument of thought' but 'a mode of thought' or 'mind-set.' " It denotes "a constellation of thoughts and beliefs which provides the criteria for judgments and actions," according to Robert Jewett, *Paul's Anthropological Terms: A Study of Their Use in Conflict Sayings* (AGJU 10; Leiden: Brill, 1971), 361. See also Collins, *First Corinthians*, 138. Wolff (*Erste Brief*, 62) refers to it as "das planende Denken Gottes as solches." Based on its Isaian origin and context, Williams (*Wisdom*, 226–27) argues that it signifies "God's plan of salvation." Against A. Sand, "νοῦς," EDNT 2:479; BDAG, 680; Vos, *Kunst*, 56, Paul is not identifying "mind" with "spirit" (πνεῦμα) here. In the preceding context Paul states that only the Spirit knows "the things of God," which includes the thoughts or mind of God (2:11). The Spirit thus knows, but is not identical to, the mind of God. And subsequently Paul explicitly contrasts the "mind" with the

clause that concludes the question: "that he will instruct [or "teach" or "advise"—συμβιβάσει] him?"[6] In itself the question expresses the human impossibility (without divine assistance) of understanding the thoughts and ways of God, as well as the absurdity of a human instructing or advising God, with the implication that it is rather God who instructs and advises us. It thus is clearly intended as a rhetorical question demanding from its audience an implicit but obvious answer, "No one."[7] The scripture reference's rhetorical question is immediately contradicted, however, by the remainder of the verse: "But *we* have the mind (νοῦν) of Christ!" (2:16b).[8]

Relation to the Antecedent Context in 1 Corinthians 1:21–2:15

In 1:21, Paul stated that the world did not "know" (ἔγνω) God through wisdom. In 2:7-8 he went on to say that none of the rulers of this age "has known" (ἔγνωκεν) the wisdom of God hidden in mystery, for if they "had known" (ἔγνωσαν) it, they would not have crucified the Lord of glory. Indeed, only the Spirit of God, and thus not the spirit of a human being, "has known" (ἔγνωκεν) "the things of God" (2:11)—elements included within the wisdom of God. And the natural human being does not receive "the things of the Spirit of God," the elements included within the wisdom of God, for they are foolishness to him and he cannot "know" (γνῶναι) them (2:14). These various expressions of the human impossibility of "knowing" the wisdom of God and what it includes reach their climactic summation in the scriptural reference's rhetorical question, "For who has known (ἔγνω) the mind of the Lord, that he will instruct him?" in 2:16a.

"spirit" (14:14-15). See also Schrage, *Erste Brief*, 1:267; Wolff, *Erste Brief*, 62 n. 220; Mehrdad Fatehi, *The Spirit's Relation to the Risen Lord in Paul: An Examination of Its Christological Implications* (WUNT 128; Tübingen: Mohr Siebeck, 2000), 189.

6. Thiselton, *Corinthians*, 274: "The grammar and syntax of the relative pronoun ὅς requires comment: the relative *who* both picks up the LXX and functions in effect as a consecutive to express result, or more accurately, 'contemplated result.'"

7. Fee (*Corinthians*, 119) paraphrases: "Who is the person who wants to match wits with God?"

8. Lindemann (*Erste Korintherbrief*, 73) claims that although the scriptural reference originally functioned as a rhetorical question to be answered by "no one," it no longer has that function in 1 Cor 2:16a, evidently because of the statement in 2:16b that "we have the mind of Christ," which Lindemann considers "uneingeschränkt als positive Aussage zu verstehen." Although the "positive" statement in 2:16b contradicts the expected negative answer of the rhetorical question in the scriptural reference, it does not lessen or eliminate its effect on the audience as a rhetorical question. As Fee (*Corinthians*, 119) affirms: "Thus Paul reworks Isa. 40:13 in such a way that in its present form it serves as a rhetorical question, demanding the answer 'No one.'"

The "wisdom" of God included within the "mind" or "thoughts" of the Lord was delineated by the scriptural quote in 2:9 as "what things eye has not seen and ear has not heard and have not arisen in the heart of a human being, what things God has prepared for those who love him." What is included in God's wisdom was then further described as "the deep things of God" (2:10b), "the things of God" (2:11b), "the things freely given to us by God" (2:12b), "spiritual things" (2:13b), and "the things of the Spirit of God" (2:14a). The scriptural reference in 2:16a thus sums up the "wisdom of God" (θεοῦ σοφίαν, 2:7a) and all of the various thoughts and things included within it by the "mind of the Lord" (νοῦν κυρίου) that no mere human can comprehend.[9]

That no one has known the mind of the Lord God so as to instruct him (2:16a) explains why the person who has the Spirit that has known the things of God (2:11) can be examined, criticized, scrutinized, or judged (ἀνακρίνεται) by no purely natural human being who does not have this Spirit (2:15b). But that *we* have the mind of Christ (2:16b) explains why *we*, as persons who have the Spirit that has known the things and thus the mind of the Lord God, can examine, criticize, scrutinize, or judge (ἀνακρίνει) all things (2:15a).

The implication for the audience is that Paul and his fellow believers cannot be examined or judged by those who are informed and enamored with merely human wisdom rather than the wisdom of God in Christ crucified (1:13, 17, 23; 2:2, 8). Paul's Corinthian audience, then, ought to be able to examine and judge the "wisdom of word," which has so infatuated some of them that it has caused divisions among them (1:10–17), for what it is—the wisdom of human beings rather that the wisdom of God, which they are privileged to know and possess.[10]

---

9. Although there is a reference to Christ as the crucified "Lord" of glory in 2:8b, the audience understands the "mind of the Lord" in 2:16a as the mind of God. First, being within a scriptural reference or allusion, "Lord" would naturally refer to God. And second, the immediately preceding context after the reference to Christ as Lord in 2:8b refers repeatedly to God and things related to the mind or thoughts of God, rather than to Christ: "what things *God* has prepared" (2:9b), "*God* revealed ... the deep things of *God*" (2:10), "the things of *God* ... the Spirit of *God*" (2:11), "the Spirit that comes from *God* ... the things freely given to us by *God*" (2:12), and "the things of the Spirit of *God*" (2:14a).

10. Fee, *Corinthians*, 119: "Who among his detractors, now enamored with human wisdom and passing judgment on Paul, is so capable of knowing the mind of the Lord that he/she can bypass the very wisdom of God itself as it is revealed in the cross?" See also Thiselton, *Corinthians*, 274.

Relation to the Subsequent Context in 1 Corinthians 2:16b

As already noted above, the scriptural reference's rhetorical question in 2:16a is immediately contradicted by Paul's exclamation in 2:16b: "But *we* have the mind of Christ!" Although no purely natural human being can know the mind of the Lord God, nevertheless, *we*, Paul, his Corinthian audience, and all believers, are privileged not just to "know" but to "have" or "possess" the very mind of Christ the Lord (cf. 2:8).[11]

The emphatic use of the first-person plural pronoun "we"—"But *we* (ἡμεῖς) have the mind of Christ!"—climaxes the previous emphatic uses of the first-person plural pronoun in expressions of what we believers have been privileged to receive from God. The scriptural quote's reference in 2:9 to "what things God has prepared for those who love him" is immediately followed by an emphatic use of the first-person plural pronoun—"*to us* (ἡμῖν) God has revealed through the Spirit" (2:10a). Emphatic uses of the first-person plural pronoun frame the statement of what we believers have been privileged to receive from God in 2:12: "*We* (ἡμεῖς) have not received the spirit of the world, but the Spirit that comes from God, so that we might understand the things freely given by God *to us* (ἡμῖν)."

Because we believers have "received" (ἐλάβομεν) the Spirit that comes from God (2:12a), the Spirit that has "known" (ἔγνωκεν) "the things of God" (2:11b) included in the "wisdom of God" (2:7), we, despite the scriptural reference's rhetorical question expressing the unknowability of God's mind, not only "have known" (ἔγνω) the mind of the Lord (2:16a), but we "have" or "possess" (ἔχομεν) the mind of Christ (2:16b).[12] That we have "received" and thus "have" the Spirit makes us "Spiritual people"—people of the Spirit of God (2:13, 15)—capable of knowing and having the mind of Christ the Lord (2:8) as the mind of the Lord God (2:16a).[13]

---

11. Lindemann, *Erste Korintherbrief*, 74: "ἡμεῖς ἔχομεν bezieht sich weder speziell auf Paulus noch sind lediglich die Pneumatiker als besondere Gruppe gemeint; sondern es sind einfach 'wir' Christen." See also Williams, *Wisdom*, 228–32. Collins, *First Corinthians*, 137: "Unlike other instances in which his scriptural hermeneutic leads to an implicit christological appropriation of the biblical text, Paul specifically redefines 'the mind of the Lord' as 'the mind of Christ.'" See also Fee, *Corinthians*, 119 n. 87.

12. On the relation between "having" and "receiving," see Paul's question in 1 Cor 4:7: "[W]hat do you have (ἔχεις) that you have not received (ἔλαβες)?"

13. Grindheim, "Wisdom," 708: "In 1 Cor 2:14–16 the Corinthians are challenged to show themselves as spiritual. This does not mean that Paul wants them to reach a state previously completely unknown to them. Rather, they are urged to make use of the gift they received when they came to faith in Christ. They received the spirit of God and became spiritual. Let them now show themselves as such." R. Timothy McLay, *The Use of the Septuagint in New Testament Research* (Grand Rapids: Eerdmans, 2003), 151: "[H]is [Paul's] generous inclusion

By asserting that we have the mind of *Christ*, Paul reminds and sums up for his audience that the wisdom of God (2:7) included in the scriptural reference's "mind of the Lord" is the paradoxical wisdom involved in the "mind" or way of thinking that God has revealed in Christ as crucified (1:13, 17, 23; 2:2)—the crucified "Lord of glory" (2:8).[14] That we believers have the "mind" of Christ crucified means that we not only know but possess the Spiritual thoughts, realities, and benefits included in the wisdom of God that is mysteriously hidden in the crucifixion of Christ (2:1-2, 7) and conceived by "the mind of the Lord" (2:16a).[15] The Corinthians can thus eliminate the divisions among them and be united in the same "mind" (νοΐ, 1:10), because they know and have the "mind" (νοῦν) of Christ—God's paradoxical way of thinking and wisdom hidden to the world but revealed to the Corinthians and all believers in Christ crucified.[16]

Summary on 1 Corinthians 2:16a

1. That the scriptural reference's rhetorical question in 2:16a clearly comes from Isa 40:13 but is reminiscent of many other OT texts with a similar form and content heightens the likeliness that the implied audience rec-

---

of his readers in the declaration *we have the mind of Christ* is a subtle suggestion that they should be exercising their Christ-given intellect with respect to the matters at hand. While Paul may have his tongue firmly planted in his cheek regarding who in fact does have the mind of Christ, he stakes a claim at least for himself, if not also for his readers."

14. Schrage, *Erste Brief*, 1:267: "Χριστός heißt für Paulus gerade der Gekreuzigte." Thiselton, *Corinthians*, 275: "[U]p to this point all of the major references to *Christ* have been to *a Christ crucified*." Collins, *First Corinthians*, 137: "'Christ' is a christological epithet by means of which Paul customarily refers to the death and resurrection of Jesus. By redesignating the mind of the Lord as 'the mind of Christ' Paul alludes to the revelation of divine wisdom in the crucifixion, albeit noting that it must be understood in otherwordly terms." See also Kammler, *Kreuz*, 234.

15. Lamp, *First Corinthians 1-4*, 174: "This assertion extends the implications of believers possessing τὸ πνεῦμα τοῦ θεοῦ by affirming that believers have access to the very mind of God and are thus able to perceive θεοῦ σοφία as there conceived." Kuck, *Judgment*, 194: "In the climactic v. 16, the expected answer to the Biblical question is negative—no one can know the Lord's mind. However, by God's revelation through the Spirit 'we'—as opposed to the worldly rulers, the outsiders, the ψυχικοί—do have the mind of Christ, that is, the saving knowledge of God's purpose in the crucified Christ."

16. Wendell Lee Willis, "The 'Mind of Christ' in 1 Corinthians 2,16," *Bib* 70 (1989): 121: "The mind of Christ, then, is an ethical outlook formed around this message [the word of the cross], which is manifest in the proper attitudes and conduct among believers." Lamp, *First Corinthians 1-4*, 174: "In 1:10 Paul is urging the abolition of divisions by urging a common perceptual frame of reference. The mention of νοῦν χριστοῦ appears to recall this admonition in 1:10."

ognizes it as an allusion to scripture. It impresses its audience, then, not only with its implicit scriptural authority but most especially with its appropriateness as a provocative and potent rhetorical question.

2. In itself the scriptural reference's rhetorical question in 2:16a expresses the human impossibility of understanding the thoughts and ways of God, as well as the absurdity of a human instructing or advising God, with the implication that it is rather God who instructs and advises us.

3. The scriptural reference's rhetorical question in 2:16a not only climaxes the various expressions of the human impossibility of "knowing" the "wisdom of God" (2:7a) and what it includes in 2:7–14, but sums up all of the various thoughts and things included within the wisdom of God (2:9–14) by the "mind of the Lord" that no mere human can comprehend.

4. That no one has known the mind of the Lord God so as to instruct him (2:16a) explains why the person who has the Spirit that has known the things of God (2:11) can only be examined, criticized, scrutinized, or judged by someone who has this Spirit (2:15b). Hence, Paul and his fellow believers cannot be examined or judged by those who are informed and enamored with merely human wisdom rather than the wisdom of God in Christ crucified (1:13, 17, 23; 2:2, 8). Paul's audience, then, ought to be able to examine and judge the "wisdom of word," which has so infatuated some of them that it has caused divisions among them (1:10–17), for what it is—human wisdom rather that the wisdom of God, which they are privileged to know and possess.

5. Paul's exclamation in 2:16b, "But *we* have the mind of Christ!" not only contradicts the scriptural reference's expression of the human unknowability of the thoughts of God's mind in 2:16a, but also climaxes the previous emphatic uses of the first-person plural pronoun in expressions of what "*we*" believers have been privileged to receive from God in 2:9–12.

6. That we believers have the "mind" of Christ, the crucified "Lord" of glory (2:8), means that we not only know but possess the Spiritual thoughts, realities, and benefits included in the wisdom of God that is mysteriously hidden in the crucifixion of Christ (2:1–2, 7) and conceived by the "mind" of the "Lord" God (2:16a). The audience is thus to eliminate the divisions among them and be united in the same "mind" (1:10), because they know and have the "mind" of Christ—God's paradoxical way of thinking and wisdom hidden to the world but revealed to all believers in Christ crucified.

CHAPTER 6

1 Corinthians 3:19b–20

He is the one who catches the wise in their cleverness.
The Lord knows the thoughts of the wise
that they are futile.

Old Testament Background

Because they are linked for mutual interpretation by the words "the wise," which they have in common, thus exemplifying the Jewish exegetical device that came to be known as *gezera shava*, we treat the next two scripture quotations in 1 Cor 3:19b–20 together.[1] The first, introduced by "for it is written," quotes a version of Job 5:13a: "He is the one who catches the wise in their cleverness" (3:19b).[2] The second, introduced by the words

---

1. With reference to *gezera shava*, Stockhausen ("2 Corinthians 3," 156) explains: "In Jewish exegetical texts the verbal linkage between two or more texts is often performed for the sake of interpretation. What one text lacks in detail, or in clarity, is supplied from the other, or others, with which it shares specific verbal affinity.... The texts, now related through specific verbal links, may be further related through any of their themes. They become mutually explanatory as a whole." Brewer (*Techniques*, 18) explains this type of *gezera shava* as "the interpretation of one text in the light of another text to which it is related by a shared word or phrase. The two texts are often concerned with the same subject, but the existence of the same word or phrase in two texts can suggest a relationship between them even if they are concerned with completely unrelated subjects." As Stockhausen (*Moses' Veil*, 27) further points out: "The unity of the word of God as preserved in the books of Moses and the prophets, in content and so also in verbal expression, based on their divine authorship, is the necessary presupposition of the *gezera shava* as an exegetical technique."

2. The Pauline version of Job 5:13a differs from both the LXX—"He is the one who catches (καταλαμβάνων) the wise in understanding (φρονήσει)"—and the MT: "He is the one who takes (לֹכֵד) the wise in their craftiness (בְּעָרְמָם)." The Pauline quote of Job 5:13a has close affinities with the MT and probably comes from a revised version of the LXX of Job that no longer exists, acccording to Berndt Schaller, "Zum Textcharakter der Hiobzitate im paulinischen Schrifttum," *ZNW* 71 (1980): 21–26. According to Stanley (*Paul*, 191), LXX Job 5:13a and 1 Cor 3:19b "might represent wholly independent translations of the Hebrew text of Job."

"and again," quotes a modification of LXX Ps 93:11: "The Lord knows the thoughts of the wise that they are futile" (3:20). Paul has altered the original "thoughts of human beings (τῶν ἀνθρώπων)" in the Psalm text by substituting "of the wise" (τῶν σοφῶν), so that in this case the *gezera shava* between Job 5:13a and LXX Ps 93:11 is a Pauline creation.³

Although the quotation in 3:19b comes from Job 5:13a, Paul does not precisely locate its origin for his audience but simply introduces it vaguely and generally with the formula "for it is written" (γέγραπται γάρ). Thus, the basic idea expressed is not limited by its identification with this particular passage from Job but resonates with other OT passages that speak similarly of God's thwarting of human wisdom. That God catches or traps the wise (σοφούς) in their cleverness or craftiness in Paul's quote of Job 5:13a is similarly expressed, for example, in LXX Jer 8:9: "The wise (σοφοί) have been shamed and terrified and taken (ἑάλωσαν) [by God; divine passives]; because they have rejected the word of the Lord, what wisdom (σοφία) is there in them?"

Furthermore, one of the key words in Paul's quote of Job 5:13a, the "cleverness" or "craftiness" or "cunning" (πανουργία) of the wise confounded by God, recalls for the audience familiar with what "is written" in the scriptures the use of this same word with similar negative connotations with regard to wisdom in several passages from the wisdom tradition in the book of Sirach:⁴ "There is a cleverness (πανουργία) that is an abomination, and there is a fool lacking wisdom (σοφία)" (Sir 19:23); "there is a cleverness (πανουργία) that is exact but unjust" (Sir 19:25a); and "one who is not clever (πανοῦργος) cannot be taught, but there is a cleverness (πανουργία) that increases bitterness" (Sir 21:12).

Nor does Paul precisely locate for his audience the origin of the quote

---

See also Koch, *Schrift*, 71–72; Williams, *Wisdom*, 302–3; Thiselton, *Corinthians*, 322–23; Garland, *1 Corinthians*, 129.

3. Stanley, *Paul*, 194–95: "The verbal link that such a substitution creates between vv. 19 and 20 (τοὺς σοφούς/τῶν σοφῶν) is thoroughly typical of contemporary Jewish exegesis. All in all, there is little reason to doubt that the present modification goes back to Paul himself." See also Koch, *Schrift*, 153; Williams, *Wisdom*, 303.

4. On the meaning of πανουργία, see *EDNT* 3:10. BDAG, 754: "quite predominately, and in our literature exclusively, in an unfavorable sense (rascally, evil) *cunning, craftiness, trickery*, literally 'readiness to do anything.'" Robertson and Plummer, *Corinthians*, 71: "'Versatile cleverness,' 'readiness for anything' in order to gain one's own ends." Thiselton, *Corinthians*, 322: "The Greek πανουργία derives from the notion of being ready to turn one's hand to anything or everything (παν-), but regularly denotes the negative quality of *cunning, knavery*, or *craftiness*." Lockwood, *1 Corinthians*, 123: "In the LXX context of Paul's quotation from Job 5:13, the noun πανοῦργοι, which is related to πανουργία, is used in Job 5:12 as a synonym for σοφοί (Job 5:13)."

in 3:20 from LXX Ps 93:11. He simply introduces it with the words "and again" (καὶ πάλιν) in continuation of the vague and general formula, "it is written," that introduced the quote with which it is coupled in 3:19b. The quote in 3:20, then, likewise resonates with other OT passages with similar expressions referring to the vast superiority of God's wisdom in relation to the vain or futile thoughts involved in human wisdom.

One of the key words in Paul's quote in 3:20 is that for "thoughts" (διαλογισμοὺς). That God, in the vast superiority of his wisdom, knows the "thoughts" of the humanly wise and that they are vain or futile resonates for the audience with such OT texts as "You [God] understand my thoughts (διαλογισμούς) from afar" (LXX Ps 138:2b); "his [mankind's] breath will go forth and he will return to his earth; on that day all their thoughts (διαλογισμοὶ) will perish" (LXX Ps 145:4); "a wheel of a wagon is the heart of a fool and his thought (διαλογισμὸς) turning like an axle" (Sir 33:5); "their [the wicked's] thoughts (διαλογισμοὶ) are thoughts (διαλογισμοὶ) of fools" (LXX Isa 59:7b).

Another key word in Paul's quote in 3:20 is that for "futile" or "vain" (μάταιοι), describing the thoughts of the humanly wise. This idea resonates for his scripturally informed audience with such OT texts as "For you will say for [the wicked's] thought (εἰς διαλογισμόν) that they will take your cities for futility (εἰς ματαιότητα)" (LXX Ps 138:20); "for there is no truth in their [enemies of the psalmist] mouth; their heart is futile (ματαία)" (LXX Ps 5:10a); "everyone has spoken futilities (μάταια) to his neighbor; with deceitful lips and a double heart they have spoken" (LXX Ps 11:3); "but human beings are futile (μάταιοι); human beings are false, in being unjust with the balances; they together are of futility (ματαιότητος)" (LXX Ps 61:10); "for the fool will speak foolish things and his heart will ponder futilities (μάταια)" (Isa 32:6a).

But the most important words, the words that unite the two quotations in a *gezera shava*, are those for "the wise" (τοὺς σοφοὺς in 3:19b; τῶν σοφῶν in 3:20).[5] Together both quotations express God's total superiority, control, and mastery over the wisdom of human beings and thus resonate in the ears of the scripturally knowledgeable audience with other similar OT expressions: "As for the wise (σοφοὶ) counselors of the king, their counsel will be

---

5. That Paul has created this *gezera shava* by substituting "thoughts of the wise (τῶν σοφῶν)" for "thoughts of human beings (τῶν ἀνθρώπων)" in LXX Ps 93:11 underscores the importance of the term "wise" here, as it enables the Psalm text to resonate with not only Job 5:13a but other OT texts referring to God's superiority over the humanly wise. And that Paul's alteration of LXX Ps 93:11 remains in general accord with its original meaning is indicated in the next verse in 1 Cor 3:21a, "Let no one boast in human beings (ἀνθρώποις)," in which "human beings" refers to "the wise" in the scripture quotes in 3:19b–20.

made foolish [by God; divine passive] . . . where are now your wise ones (σοφοί)?" (Isa 19:11–12); "I will destroy the wisdom of the wise (τὴν σοφίαν τῶν σοφῶν)" (Isa 29:14b; cf. 1 Cor 1:19); "how will you say that we are wise (σοφοί) and the law of the Lord is with us? A false pen has resulted in futility (μάτην) for the scribes" (Jer 8:8); "thus says the Lord: 'Let not the wise one (σοφὸς) boast in his wisdom (σοφίᾳ)' " (Jer 9:22).

To sum up, then, although the two quotations in 3:19b–20 come from Pauline versions of Job 5:13a and LXX Ps 93:11, their rhetorical power and authority derive from more than just these two particular texts. Their introduction with the indefinite formula "for it is written" enables them to evoke for Paul's scripturally astute implied audience similar OT passages expressing the general idea of God's vast superiority and total domination over the merely humanly wise.[6]

Literary-Rhetorical Analysis

Considered in itself, the first quote from Job 5:13a in 1 Cor 3:19b expresses the action of one who is grasping with his hands, laying hold of, seizing, catching, trapping, or ensnaring (δρασσόμενος).[7] The objects of this action are "the wise" (τοὺς σοφοὺς), who are thus portrayed as cunning wild animals in a hunt or clever, slippery contestants in a competition. The one who catches them outwits them, ironically ensnaring them "in" or "by" (ἐν) their own evil and deceptive cleverness, cunning, or craftiness (πανουργίᾳ).[8]

The first quote in 3:19b is closely linked to the second quote from LXX

---

6. Hays, *First Corinthians*, 59: "Paul once again appeals to Scripture in verses 19–20 to demonstrate the futility of human wisdom. This time, however, rather than repeating any of the texts he cited earlier (1:19; 1:31; 2:9; 2:16) he adduces two completely different texts (Job 5:12–13 and Ps. 94:11)—thereby heightening the impact of his assault on wisdom by suggesting the wider range of Scripture's witness in support of his case." With reference to both 1:19 and 3:19b–20, Kuck (*Judgment*, 193) states: "These OT citations are not isolated texts plucked out arbitrarily by Paul. They are part of a rich OT and Jewish tradition that asserts God's sovereignty as creator over human pretensions."

7. For the meaning of δρασσόμενος, a *hapax legomenon* in the NT, see BDAG, 261; *EDNT* 1:353; Robertson and Plummer, *Corinthians*, 70–71; Lockwood, *1 Corinthians*, 123; Collins, *First Corinthians*, 165; Thiselton, *Corinthians*, 322.

8. Conzelmann, *1 Corinthians*, 80; Barrett, *Corinthians*, 94: "The *wise* are like cunning beasts, for whom the hunter is nevertheless too clever." Fee, *Corinthians*, 152: "The first text is expressed in the imagery of hunting, in which the hunter uses the very craftiness, or cunning, of the prey as the means of capture." Adams, *Constructing the World*, 119: "The image is that of the hunter and his prey. God, the hunter, uses the cunning of the wise as the means of their entrapment."

Ps 93:11 in 3:20 by the words "and again," "and also," or "and furthermore" (καὶ πάλιν).⁹ This indicates to the audience that the second quote will continue or advance the thought of the first. Indeed, the combination of these two scriptural quotes through the device of *gezera shava* brings them together for a mutually interpretive result revolving around the term they have in common—"the wise."

The implicit subject of the action of catching the wise in the first quote advances to the explicit expression of the subject of the action in the second scriptural quote—the "Lord" (κύριος). The "cleverness" of the wise in the first quote is interpreted as or exemplified in the "thoughts," "reasonings," or "plots" (διαλογισμοὺς) of the wise, which the Lord knows are "futile," "vain," or "ineffective" (μάταιοι) in the second quote.¹⁰ And so the combination of quotes through *gezera shava* results in a scripturally authoritative assertion of God's prevailing superiority over the humanly wise in "catching" or "seizing" them precisely in their devious and deceptive "cleverness" because that "cleverness" consists of thoughts that the Lord God in his superior wisdom "knows" are ultimately futile. Making the audience wary of the attractive and seductive "cleverness" or "craftiness" of the humanly wise, the combination of quotes thus persuades them to value rather the superior wisdom of the God who knows that the clever thoughts of the humanly wise are futile, amounting to nothing.

Relation to the Antecedent Context in 1 Corinthians 1:17–3:19a

Paul stated that Christ sent him to evangelize not with the "wisdom of word" (σοφίᾳ λόγου, 1:17), which seems to have enamored his audience and caused divisions and rivalries among them (1:10–13), but with the "word of the cross" (1:18) of Christ, which is the power of God by which God in the first scriptural quote in the letter in 1:19 promises to prevail over the

---

9. On the meaning of πάλιν, see *EDNT* 3:9; BDAG, 752: "marker of a discourse or narrative item added to items of a related nature, *also, again, furthermore, thereupon* . . . very often in a series of quotations from scripture."

10. On the meaning of διαλογισμός, see BDAG, 232; Gerd Petzke, "διαλογισμός," *EDNT* 1:308: "Both the verb and the noun are technical terms for a reckoning. In the LXX this calculating motif of consideration frequently takes on the meaning 'consider evil' or 'plot.' In the NT these concepts are employed almost exclusively with a negative connotation." On the meaning of μάταιος, see BDAG, 621: "idle, empty, fruitless, useless, powerless, lacking truth." Horst Balz, "μάταιος," *EDNT* 2:396: "μάταιος also has (as already in the Greek linguistic realm), esp. from its biblical tradition, the meaning *vain/futile/deceitful* and refers to a senseless understanding of reality in contrast to the only valid reality of God or to skeptical resignation in the face of God's distance from this world."

wisdom of the wise of this world and age: "I will destroy the wisdom of the wise (τὴν σοφίαν τῶν σοφῶν) and the intelligence of the intelligent I will set aside."[11] When the powerful word of the cross of Christ is proclaimed, God's promise to prevail over the wise of this world is fulfilled by rendering their wisdom as foolishness: "Has not God made foolish the wisdom (σοφίαν) of the world?" (1:20b).

Although not many in Paul's Corinthian audience are wise (σοφοὶ) "according to flesh" (κατὰ σάρκα), that is, in the estimation of the social world (1:26), nevertheless God chose "the foolish things of the world," such as the cross of Christ (1:18) or Christ crucified (1:23) and those Christians not considered "wise" according to the world, to shame "the wise" (τοὺς σοφούς) of the world (1:27)—thus furthering the fulfillment of the scriptural promise that God will prevail over the wise (1:19).[12] Although not many in the Corinthian audience are wise in the eyes of the world (1:26), Paul exhorts anyone among them who thinks he is wise in this age to become foolish in the eyes of the world in order to become truly wise before God (3:18).[13] The reason for this—"for the wisdom of this world is foolishness with God" (3:19a)—recalls and reinforces for the audience the previous indication of the fulfillment of God's scriptural promise to prevail over the wise (1:19) in terms of making the wisdom of the wise of this world foolish (1:20b).[14]

Then occurs our combined quotation in 3:19b–20 as the scriptural foundation for the fulfillment of God's promise to prevail over the wisdom of the wise in terms of the wisdom of this world being foolishness with God (3:19a): "For it is written, 'He is the one who catches the wise (τοὺς σοφοὺς) in their cleverness.' And again, 'The Lord knows the thoughts of the wise

---

11. For a full discussion of the scriptural quote in 1:19, see ch. 2.

12. Adams, *Constructing the World*, 114: "The word σάρξ here carries apocalyptic associations and signifies the sphere of opposition to God. κατὰ σάρκα is the point of view which is characteristic of this sphere. The prized social distinctions of the Hellenistic world are thus consigned by Paul to the old world/age." Thiselton, *Corinthians*, 183: "[W]e have translated κατὰ σάρκα not simply as *by human standards* (NRSV et al.), but in conjunction with σοφοί *as the world counts cleverness*, which is more value-laden, as Paul intends."

13. Adams, *Constructing the World*, 118: "The Corinthians had indeed considered themselves to be wise (the formula used by Paul here, εἴ τις, is generally taken as pointing to claims which were actually being made by the Corinthians; cf. 8:2; 11:16; 14:37). But, says Paul, they are deceiving themselves because they are judging wisdom by the wrong criteria. The wisdom to which they have latched on belongs to the old, out-going age (ὁ αἰὼν ὅυτος, 1:20, 27–29; 2:6–8). Paul urges his readers to adopt a stance which is a complete reversal of worldly standards, a perspective consonant with God's new age."

14. On 3:19a, Adams (*Constructing the World*, 119) points out: "In 1:20, Paul stated that God 'made foolish' the wisdom of the world. Here he expresses the foolishness of the world in God's sight as a settled fact."

(τῶν σοφῶν) that they are futile.' " That the wisdom or "cleverness" of the wise includes thoughts that God knows are "futile" or "vain" indicates to the implied audience that these thoughts are ultimately foolish—that the wisdom of the wise of this world is foolishness with God. With this combined quote, then, Paul further persuades his audience away from the "wisdom of word" (1:17; 2:1) causing rivalries among them (1:10–13) and toward the superior "wisdom of God" hidden in the mystery (2:7) of God that is Jesus Christ crucified (2:1–2), as proclaimed in the "word of the cross" of Christ (1:17–18).

The double scriptural quotation in 3:19b–20 advances for the audience the rhetorical strategy inherent in each of the previous scriptural quotes in 1 Corinthians. The powerful promise proclaimed by God in the first person, "*I will destroy* the wisdom of the wise and the intelligence of the intelligent *I will set aside*," in the first scriptural quote in 1:19 progresses to a third-person report in 3:19b–20 confirming with scriptural authority how God is indeed fulfilling that promise: " '*He is the one who catches* the wise in their cleverness.' And again, '*The Lord knows* the thoughts of the wise that they are futile.' " God will destroy the wisdom of the wise and set aside the intelligence of the intelligent because of God's vastly superior wisdom and intelligence, as expressed scripturally in 3:19b–20. God is wiser than the wise of the world, outsmarting them by catching or trapping them in the cleverness of their wisdom with a higher knowledge or intelligence that the thoughts of the wise are futile and thus ultimately foolish in light of the greater wisdom of God hidden in the phenomenon of Christ crucified.

Since it is because of God that Paul and his audience of believers are in Christ Jesus, who became wisdom for us from God (1:29–30), the only legitimate "boasting" is in the Lord God according to the second scriptural quote in 1:31: "If anyone is to boast, *in the Lord* (κυρίῳ) let him boast."[15] A further basis for this scriptural exhortation is provided for the audience by the scriptural assertion in 3:20 that "the Lord (κύριος) knows the thoughts of the wise that they are futile." With strong rhetorical emphasis the quote in 1:31 insists that it is "*in the Lord*" (and not human beings) that one should boast. There is a similar rhetorical emphasis on the Lord in the combined quote in 3:19b–20, which identifies the initially anonymous "he is the one who catches the wise" with the pointed assertion that it is "*the Lord*" who knows the thoughts of the wise that they are futile.[16]

The next scriptural quote in 2:9 plays its rhetorical role in expressing

---

15. For a full discussion of the scriptural quote in 1:31, see ch. 3.
16. That "boasting" is an underlying implication of the quote is indicated by what immediately follows in 3:21a: "So let no one boast in human beings."

the humanly unseen, unheard, and unknown things—"the things that have not arisen in the heart of a human being, the things God has prepared for those who love him"—that God has now revealed to us (2:10), Paul and his audience of believers.[17] This revelation privileges us with a divine knowledge and wisdom that surpasses the wisdom of the world. The scriptural quote in 3:19b–20 then makes us realize that to us has been revealed the superior wisdom of the God who "catches the wise in their cleverness" and "knows the thoughts of the wise that they are futile." We believers are privileged to have received the humanly unknown things of the divine wisdom inherent in Christ crucified that God has prepared for those who love him, while the humanly conceived but divinely known clever thoughts of the wise of this world are futile.

As we indicated previously, the various expressions of the human impossibility of "knowing" the wisdom of God and what it includes (1:21; 2:7–8, 11, 14) reach a climactic summation in the next scriptural quote's rhetorical question in 2:16a: "For who has *known* (ἔγνω) the mind of the Lord, that he will instruct him?"[18] But Paul immediately assures his audience that we, however, have the mind of Christ (2:16b). The scriptural quote in 3:20 further delineates what is in the mind of the Lord—"the Lord *knows* (γινώσκει) the thoughts of the wise that they are futile." Since we have the mind of Christ, which enables us to "know" the mind of the Lord, then we have the superior knowledge of God that the thoughts of the humanly wise of this world are futile and ultimately foolish in light of the wisdom of God inherent in the word of the cross. The realization on the part of the audience that they possess this superior divine knowledge further persuades them away from the wisdom of the wise of this world and toward the wisdom of God in Christ crucified.

Relation to the Subsequent Context in 1 Corinthians 3:21–4:21

In 3:21a, Paul immediately draws out for each individual in his audience the consequences of the scriptural quote's double expression in 3:19b–20 of God's higher knowledge over the wisdom of the wise of this world—"so let no one boast in human beings." The progression from God catching the wise (σοφούς) and knowing the futile thoughts of the wise (σοφῶν) in the combined scriptural quote to no one boasting in human beings (ἀνθρώποις)

---

17. For a full discussion of the scriptural quote in 2:9, see ch. 4.
18. For a full discussion of the scriptural quote in 2:16a, see ch. 5.

underscores the mere humanness of the wisdom of the wise of this world in comparison with the vast superiority of God's wisdom.[19] And no one is to boast in human beings because, according to the scriptural quote in 1:31, there is only one legitimate type of boasting: "If anyone is to boast, *in the Lord* let him boast."[20] Rather than boasting in human beings, then, one is to boast in the Lord God, who knows the futile and therefore foolish thoughts of those who are merely humanly wise in this world.

That no one among them is to boast in human beings (ἀνθρώποις, 3:21a) recalls for the audience how Paul accused them of behaving in a merely human way (κατὰ ἄνθρωπον, 3:3) and as mere human beings (ἄνθρωποί, 3:4), rather than as those who possess the Spirit that is from God (2:12), giving them the mind of Christ (2:16) and enabling them to speak in words not taught by human (ἀνθρωπίνης) wisdom but by the Spirit (2:13).[21] There is jealousy and rivalry among them, because they are acting as mere human beings in claiming, on the basis of human wisdom, the allegiance of belonging to such human beings as Paul, Apollos, or Cephas (3:3–4; 1:11–12).[22]

As individuals they need not claim allegiance to or boast in such human beings, since such human beings, as well as everything else, belong to them as a community: "For all belongs to you, whether Paul or Apollos or Cephas or the world or life or death or the present or the future, all belongs to you, and you to Christ, and Christ to God" (3:21b–23).[23] Belonging to

---

19. As we already indicated, that Paul has altered "the thoughts of human beings (τῶν ἀνθρώπων)" in LXX Ps 93:11 to "the thoughts of the wise" (τῶν σοφῶν) in 1 Cor 3:20 facilitates this rhetorical progression.

20. Wolff, *Erste Brief*, 77: "Es gibt nur *ein* legitimes christliches καυχᾶσθαι: sich dessen zu rühmen, was man durch den gekreuzigten Christus ist (1,31)."

21. On ἐν ἀνθρώποις in 3:21, Lockwood (*1 Corinthians*, 123) comments: "Paul speaks of natural, fallen 'human beings' in the same way that he used ἄνθρωπος in 3:3–4." Litfin, *Paul's Theology of Proclamation*, 219: "[T]o him [Paul] the phrases ἐλάβομεν τὸ πνεῦμα τὸ ἐκ τοῦ θεοῦ (2.12) and ἡμεῖς νοῦν Χριστοῦ ἔχομεν (2.16) were synonymous."

22. Jerry L. Sumney, *"Servants of Satan," "False Brothers," and Other Opponents of Paul* (JSNTSup 188; Sheffield: Sheffield Academic Press, 1999), 40–41: "The command not to boast about humans in 3.21 can be identified as an explicit reference to the opposition Paul faces because Paul supports the command in v. 22 by mentioning himself, Apollos and Cephas.... Verse 21 begins with another interpretation of the Corinthians' behavior with respect to leaders or teachers: they boast about them. This criticism indicates that they claim some superiority on the basis of the teacher they cite as most authoritative. Verse 22 reveals this as the content of their boast when it returns to those teachers mentioned in 1.12."

23. Adams, *Constructing the World*, 120: "The genitive of possession in these verses ... is clearly intended to pick up the genitives of 1:12 and 3:4. Paul is deliberately inverting the Corinthian slogans 'I belong to Paul', and so on, into 'they belong to you.' The rest of the items on the list are also things which may dominate or possess the Corinthians: the world with its shaping influence, life with its concerns, death, present circumstances and future uncertainties.

Christ, the audience has the mind of Christ enabling them to know the mind of and thus to share in the knowledge of the Lord God (2:16).[24] The Lord God's vastly superior knowledge that the clever thoughts of the wise are futile, as expressed in the scriptural quote of 3:19b–20, gives the audience, who shares this knowledge, a dominance over not only the humanly wise but everything else that concerns their existence.

From Paul and Apollos (cf. 3:5–4:5) the Corinthian audience is to learn to practice the maxim, "Not beyond the things that are written (γέγραπται)!" (4:6b), which refers not only to the explicit scriptural quotations previously introduced by "it is written" (γέγραπται in 1:19, 31; 2:9; 3:19), but to the whole plurality of "things" written in scripture that similarly speak of God's vastly superior knowledge and wisdom over the humanly wise and eloquent of this world.[25] As it applies to what is written in the combined scriptural quote in 3:19b–20, the maxim not to go beyond the things that are written urges the audience not to go beyond or against the knowledge they share with the Lord God that the clever thoughts of the wise of this world are futile in comparison with the divine wisdom inherent in Christ crucified. The audience would be going beyond or against this scripturally recorded knowledge if they are "puffed up" with pride (4:6c) and boast (3:21a) in one wise human being (such as Apollos) over against another (such as Paul) (4:6c).

Summary on 1 Corinthians 3:19b–20

1. Although the double quotation in 3:19b–20 comes from Pauline versions of Job 5:13a and LXX Ps 93:11, its rhetorical power and authority derive from more than just these two particular texts. The introduction with the indefinite formula "for it is written" enables this scriptural combination to evoke for the audience similar OT passages expressing the general idea of God's vast superiority and total domination over the merely humanly wise.

2. Making the audience wary of the attractive and seductive "clever-

---

Paul's point is that their standing in Christ places them above all dominations. The leaders in whom they boast, and all the things which currently determine their lives belong to the Corinthians, not the Corinthians to them." For a discussion of 3:21-23 as a rhetorical maxim about proper freedom, see Ramsaran, *Liberating Words*, 33–35. See also Collins, *First Corinthians*, 166–67; Fee, *Corinthians*, 153–55; Thiselton, *Corinthians*, 325–29.

24. Kuck, *Judgment*, 195–96: "Paul can agree that all things are theirs, because God has through the Spirit revealed his wisdom in Christ."

25. For a fuller discussion of the maxim in 4:6, see the comments and notes on this verse in ch. 3.

ness" of the humanly wise, the combination of quotes in 3:19b–20 persuades them to value rather the superior wisdom of the Lord God, who knows that the clever thoughts of the humanly wise are futile and thus ultimately foolish.

3. With the combined quote in 3:19b–20 Paul further persuades his audience away from the "wisdom of word" (1:17; 2:1) causing rivalries among them (1:10–13) and toward the superior "wisdom of God" hidden in the mystery (2:7) of God that is Jesus Christ crucified (2:1–2), as proclaimed in the "word of the cross" of Christ (1:17–18).

4. The double scriptural quotation in 3:19b–20 advances for the audience the rhetorical strategy inherent in each of the previous scriptural quotes in 1 Corinthians:

a. God will destroy the wisdom of the wise and set aside the intelligence of the intelligent, as promised in the first scriptural quote in the letter in 1:19, because of God's vastly superior wisdom and intelligence over the clever but futile thoughts of the humanly wise, as expressed scripturally in 3:19b–20.

b. A further basis for the scriptural exhortation in the letter's second quote in 1:31, "If anyone is to boast, *in the Lord* let him boast," is provided for the audience by the scriptural assertion in 3:20 that "the *Lord* knows the thoughts of the wise that they are futile."

c. We believers are privileged to have received the humanly unknown things of the divine wisdom inherent in Christ crucified that God has prepared for those who love him, as expressed in the letter's third scriptural quote in 2:9, while the humanly conceived but divinely known clever thoughts of the wise of this world are futile, as expressed in the pair of scriptural quotes in 3:19b–20.

d. The letter's fourth scriptural quote in 2:16a asks, "For who has *known* the mind of the Lord, that he will instruct him?" The scriptural quote in 3:20 further delineates what is in the mind of the Lord that we who have the mind of Christ are able to know (2:16b)—"the Lord *knows* the thoughts of the wise that they are futile."

5. The progression from God catching the *wise* and knowing the futile thoughts of the *wise* in the combined scriptural quote in 3:19b–20 to no

one boasting in *human beings* in 3:21a underscores the mere humanness of the wisdom of the wise of this world in comparison with the vast superiority of God's wisdom.

6. The Lord God's vastly superior knowledge that the clever thoughts of the wise are futile, as expressed in the scriptural quote of 3:19b–20, gives the audience, who shares this knowledge, a dominance over not only the humanly wise but everything else that concerns their existence (3:21b–23).

7. As it applies to what is *written* in the combined scriptural quote in 3:19b–20, the maxim not to go beyond the things that are *written* (4:6b) urges the audience not to go beyond or against—by boasting in the humanly wise (3:21a; 4:6c)—the knowledge they share with the Lord God that the clever thoughts of the wise of this world are futile in comparison with the divine wisdom inherent in Christ crucified.

CHAPTER 7

1 Corinthians 5:13b

Drive out the evil one from out of your very midst.

Old Testament Background

Paul's climactic command in 1 Cor 5:13b, "Drive out (ἐξάρατε) the evil one (τὸν πονηρὸν) from out of your very midst (ἐξ ὑμῶν αὐτῶν)," closely corresponds to a formulaic refrain emphatically commanding the expulsion of evil and/or evil persons from within the community of Israel, which recurs no less than eleven times in various formulations within Deut 13–24. There are four variations of this formula of Deuteronomic law in the MT, all of which employ the second-person singular Piel form of the verb בער, "to burn," and thus "to exterminate or purge":[1]

וּבִעַרְתָּ הָרָע מִקִּרְבֶּךָ: So you shall purge the evil from your midst (Deut 13:6; 17:7; 19:19; 21:21; 22:21, 24; 24:7)

וּבִעַרְתָּ הָרָע מִיִּשְׂרָאֵל: So you shall purge the evil from Israel (Deut 17:12; 22:22)

וּבִעַרְתָּ דַם־הַנָּקִי מִיִּשְׂרָאֵל: So you shall purge the guilt of innocent blood from Israel (Deut 19:13)

וְאַתָּה תְּבַעֵר הַדָּם הַנָּקִי מִקִּרְבֶּךָ: But you shall purge the guilt of innocent blood from your midst (Deut 21:9)

There are five variations of the formula in the LXX correspondences to the MT, three of which, occurring a total of nine times, employ ἐξαρεῖς, the second-person singular indicative future active of the verb ἐξαίρω, "to

---

1. Deuteronomy uses the singular address in such laws to support its theology of the responsibility of the people as such (rather than of a king) to keep the Torah, according to J. Gordon McConville, "Singular Address in the Deuteronomic Law and the Politics of Legal Adminstration," *JSOT* 97 (2002): 19–36.

remove, get rid of, obliterate, expel, or drive out"[2]—the same verb that Paul employs in the second-person plural imperative aorist active (ἐξάρατε) in his use of the formula in 1 Cor 5:13b:

ἀφανιεῖς τὸν πονηρὸν ἐξ ὑμῶν αὐτῶν: You shall destroy the evil one from your very midst (Deut 13:6)
ἐξαρεῖς τὸν πονηρὸν ἐξ ὑμῶν αὐτῶν: You shall drive out the evil one from out of your very midst (Deut 17:7; 19:19; 21:21; 22:21, 24; 24:7)
ἐξαρεῖς τὸν πονηρὸν ἐξ Ισραηλ: You shall drive out the evil one from out of Israel (Deut 17:12; 22:22)
καθαριεῖς τὸ αἷμα τὸ ἀναίτιον ἐξ Ισραηλ: You shall cleanse the guilt of innocent blood from out of Israel (Deut 19:13)
σὺ δὲ ἐξαρεῖς τὸ αἷμα τὸ ἀναίτιον ἐξ ὑμῶν αὐτῶν: But you shall drive out the guilt of innocent blood from out of your very midst (Deut 21:9)[3]

Except for the change to the plural aorist imperative verb form to fit his epistolary context, Paul's version of the formula in 1 Cor 5:13b is identical in wording to the seven occurrences in LXX Deut 13:6; 17:7; 19:19; 21:21; 22:21, 24; 24:7 and very close in thought to the two occurrences in LXX Deut 17:12; 22:22. That this formula recurs as a refrain concentrated within these particular chapters of Deuteronomy makes it familiar and recognizable as a scriptural injunction to the audience Paul has in mind—his implied, ideal audience knowledgeable at least in a general way of the OT scriptures.[4]

---

2. Takamitsu Muraoka, *A Greek-English Lexicon of the Septuagint: Chiefly of the Pentateuch and the Twelve Prophets* (Louvain: Peeters, 2002), 191–92.

3. On the relation of the formula as it occurs in LXX Deut 13:6 to the Hebrew version, John William Wevers, *Notes on the Greek Text of Deuteronomy* (SBLSCS 39; Atlanta: Scholars Press, 1995), 230–31: "The verse concludes with a typical Deut demand for the removal of evil from ὑμῶν αὐτῶν. The verb used is, however, unique in this formula which otherwise usually uses ἐξαρεῖς, not ἀφανιεῖς. In all cases of the formula the Hebrew uses the root בער 'to burn,' hence to purge. In any event, the notion of removal is central to the formula. The community must excise the evil one from itself. It should be noted that מקרבך is rendered by the emphatic plural form in which αὐτῶν is added to ὑμῶν. Whenever the formula occurs in second person the Hebrew has the singular מקרבך, whereas LXX always has ἐξ ὑμῶν αὐτῶν. The point that LXX makes is that the community (σύ [see Deut 21:9]) must officially remove . . . from among you (i.e. from the Israelites as individuals). . . . It should also be noted that הרע is ambiguous; it can be understood as the abstract 'evil' or as the concrete 'the evil one.' LXX always makes it refer to the person: τὸν πονηρόν. To the translator it was the evildoer who had to be removed, made to disappear, from the community."

4. It is another question as to the extent actual individuals within Paul's historical audience may have been familiar with the OT scriptures. But to suppose that a majority within Paul's historical audience did not recognize and appreciate his scriptural references would mean that the Paul who himself founded the Corinthian community greatly underestimated the capabilities of his audience in this regard and was thus a rather inept author indeed.

For this reason Paul does not need to introduce it explicitly as a scriptural quotation.⁵

There are additional considerations as to why the audience would not need an explicit introduction to recognize 1 Cor 5:13b as a scriptural quotation. The unusual and distinctive, non-Pauline character of every element of the quotation alerts and further confirms for the audience its scriptural origin. The verb, "drive out" (ἐξάρατε), occurs only here in all of Paul's letters (and in the NT); the object, "the evil one" (τὸν πονηρόν), occurs only here in 1 Corinthians; and the prepositional phrase, "from out of your very midst" (ἐξ ὑμῶν αὐτῶν), contains a use of the second-person plural reflexive pronoun (cf. 5:2) that occurs only here in the NT.⁶ But perhaps the best explanation for the lack of an explicit scriptural introduction is Paul's rhetorical strategy of immediately, emphatically, and climactically quoting the scriptural command without further ado to exploit its optimal authoritative impact for reinforcing the main thrust of 5:1–13.⁷

To conclude, because of its multiple recurrences in Deuteronomy and its noteworthy, non-Pauline vocabulary, 1 Cor 5:13b can be expected to be recognized and appreciated as a scriptural quotation by Paul's implied audience. But that it is not explicitly introduced and located in any particular text of Deuteronomy, or of the OT for that matter, means that the audience need not necessarily recall any of the variety of specific original contexts in which this scriptural formula was employed. It is a scriptural formula used in a number of related but different situations. The implied audience need only recognize it as an authoritative quotation that they have heard more than once from somewhere in the OT scriptures and that Paul has now applied to their situation.⁸

---

5. Despite the obvious scriptural origin of 1 Cor 5:13b, Stanley (*Paul*, 195 n. 44), in accord with a (overly?) rigid methodolgy, omits it from his study of explicitly introduced scriptural citations in Paul. Although Koch (*Schrift*, 17–18) with caution admits that 1 Cor 5:13b can be considered a scriptural quotation, he does not fully treat it as such.

6. Collins, *First Corinthians*, 224; BDF, 150 § 288 (1); Maximilian Zerwick, *Biblical Greek* (Rome: Biblical Institute, 1963), 66–67.

7. Rosner, "Function of Scripture," 514: "[T]he lack of an introductory formula, such as γέγραπται, to signal a quotation in v. 13b can be explained in terms of asyndeton suiting the chapter's emotionally charged atmosphere; in some instances no introduction can serve as an introduction." Garland, *1 Corinthians*, 191: "Omitting an introductory formula for the quotation heightens its force as a command."

8. Rosner (*Paul*, 61–93) and Hays ("Conversion," 409–12) overinterpret the significance of the original Deuteronomic contexts of the scriptural formula quoted in 1 Cor 5:13b. As noted by Tuckett, "Paul," 416: "The OT legislation of Deuteronomy does *not* seem to be an important factor in Paul's argument. Such legislation *may* have been in the background of Paul's thinking. But it is hard to see that this would have been picked up in any way by Paul's

Literary-Rhetorical Analysis

Beginning abruptly with the second-person plural aorist imperative verb, ἐξάρατε, the scriptural injunction in 1 Cor 5:13b commands the audience as a group or community "to remove, get rid of, obliterate, expel, root out, banish, or drive out" the evil one (τὸν πονηρὸν).[9] The aorist imperative as well as the indefinite designation, "the evil one," allow for a reference both to a specific individual in the given context and to any such evil person as a general principle. Reinforcing the ἐξ that prefixes the verb, "drive *out*," the ἐξ that introduces the prepositional phrase, "from *out* of your very midst," intensifies the separation commanded as an absolute necessity. The audience must drive the evil one *from out of and away from* the midst of themselves.[10] The addition of the reflexive αὐτῶν to the second-person plural pronoun ὑμῶν underscores the responsibility for the urgent expulsion of the evil one by and for the benefit of the audience as individual members of the community.

In sum, Paul employs the bluntly authoritative scriptural mandate in 1 Cor 5:13b to impose upon his Corinthian audience a very urgent, strict, and unconditional obligation to expel the evil person from out of the very midst of themselves.

Relation to the Antecedent Context in 1 Corinthians 5:1–13a

First Corinthians 5:1–13 subdivides into four units—5:1–2 (first unit), 5:3–5 (second unit), 5:6–8 (third unit), and 5:9–13 (fourth unit)—each of which contains an expression or expressions in one form or another of Paul's command to the Corinthian community to discontinue fellowship with an erring member.[11] As we shall see, the scriptural injunction in 1 Cor 5:13b rhetorically reinforces and/or develops all of the various expressions of this repeated command in each of the four units.

---

audience on the basis of what Paul actually says in vv. 1–12 at least. V. 13 may simply represent a use of at most biblical terminology or phraseology with no further overtones detectable, at least to the readers. It thus seems very improbable that Paul's language here would have led his readers to any wider context of Deuteronomy." See also Pascuzzi, *Ethics*, 139–44.

9. For the differences in aspect between the present and aorist imperative, see Zerwick, *Biblical Greek*, 78–81; Stanley E. Porter, *Verbal Aspect in the Greek of the New Testament, with Reference to Tense and Mood* (Studies in Biblical Greek 1; New York: Lang, 1993), 336–47.

10. Thiselton, *Corinthians*, 417: "The double use of ἐκ (ἐξ) intensifies the injunction."

11. Kathleen Callow, "Patterns of Thematic Development in 1 Corinthians 5:1–13," in *Linguistics and New Testament Interpretation: Essays on Discourse Analysis* (ed. David Alan Black, Katherine Barnwell, and Stephen Levinsohn; Nashville: Broadman, 1992), 194–206.

In the first unit (5:1–2), Paul's exclamation to his Corinthian audience that "you are puffed up (πεφυσιωμένοι)" with arrogance (5:2a) and the accompanying rhetorical question, "should you not rather have mourned?" (5:2b), follow his announcement that it is widely reported that there is sexual immorality (πορνεία) among them, a sexual immorality not found even among the pagans, namely, that a certain member of the community is living with (literally, "having" [ἔχειν]) the wife of his father (5:1).[12] Paul continues his rhetorical question of rebuke with a clause implicitly commanding that "the one who has done this deed should be removed from out of your midst" (5:2c).[13]

Paul's implicit command that the sinful individual "should be removed" (ἀρθῇ) in 5:2c employs the third-person singular aorist subjunctive passive of αἴρω without an expressed agent of the action and therefore leaves it rather vague as to the one who is to perform the necessary removal. The scriptural injunction in 5:13b employs the same verbal root, αἴρω, but with an intensifying prepositional prefix (ἐξ), in the second-person plural aorist imperative active to directly address Paul's Corinthian audience—"you drive out" (ἐξάρατε). The Corinthian community members themselves are the ones who should not only "remove" but "drive out" the deviant member from among them.[14]

---

12. Callow, "Patterns," 201: "[T]he use of καί rather than δέ in verse 2a makes it more likely that they were already puffed up: no specific connection is claimed between verses 1 and 2." See also Kathleen Callow, "The Disappearing Δέ in 1 Corinthians," in *Linguistics and New Testament Interpretation: Essays on Discourse Analysis* (ed. David Alan Black, Katherine Barnwell, and Stephen Levinsohn; Nashville: Broadman, 1992), 183–93, especially 188. For the view that the Corinthians ought to "mourn" in the biblical sense of confessing the sin of the erring member as if it were their own, because it is imperative to protect the well-being of the community before God, see Brian S. Rosner, "'Οὐχὶ μᾶλλον ἐπενθήσατε'—Corporate Responsibility in 1 Corinthians 5," *NTS* 38 (1992): 470–73. For a discussion of the social and legal consequences of a sexual relationship with one's stepmother, or perhaps with the concubine of one's late father, as unusual but not illegal according to Roman law, see Craig Steven de Vos, "Stepmothers, Concubines, and the Case of Πορνεία in 1 Corinthians 5," *NTS* 44 (1998): 104–14. On Paul's Christianity as being partially Jewish and partially Gentile, see Jack T. Sanders, "Paul between Jews and Gentiles in Corinth," *JSNT* 65 (1997): 67–83.

13. On the ἵνα clause in 5:2c as imperative, see Zerwick, *Biblical Greek*, 142; Maximilian Zerwick and Mary Grosvenor, *A Grammatical Analysis of the Greek New Testament* (Rome: Biblical Institute, 1979), 505. Callow, "Patterns," 201: "The special prominence in verse 2a (exclamation) and 2b (rhetorical question conveying rebuke) thus highlights both the complacent attitude of the Corinthians and their failure to respond appropriately to the πορνεία situation. These, combined with the implied command in verse 2c, provide evidence for a thematic contribution of *motivation by rebuke*, the rebuke being both for inappropriate attitudes, and for failure to act."

14. As Thiselton (*Corinthians*, 388) notes, the intensive compound form of the verb, "drive out from" (ἐξάρατε), in the scriptural injunction in 5:13b "is even stronger, perhaps

Since it is widely reported that the sexual immorality is within the Corinthian community—"among you" (ἐν ὑμῖν, 5:1)—the one responsible for it must be removed "from out of your midst" (ἐκ μέσου ὑμῶν, 5:2c). The ἐξ ("from out of") that introduces the prepositional phrase (ἐξ ὑμῶν αὐτῶν) in the scriptural injunction in 5:13b reinforces the ἐξ that prefixes the verb, ἐξ-άρατε ("drive out from"), to underline that the removal of the culprit among them must be from out of and away from the midst of the community. The use of the reflexive αὐτῶν in the prepositional phrase in the scriptural injunction further conveys to the audience that they themselves are responsible for removing this sinful member that is among them and thus right before their eyes—"from out of your very midst" (5:13b). The scriptural injunction in 5:13b further develops this first unit's implicit command in 5:2c by labeling and thus condemning "the one who has done this deed" of sexual immorality (πορνεία) as "the evil one" (τὸν πονηρὸν).[15]

In the second unit (5:3–5) the command to dissociate with the sexually immoral man is expressed in terms of the assembly, gathered together with Paul present in spirit and in the name and power of the Lord Jesus, carrying out the judgment that Paul, though physically absent, has already made on the man in question (5:3–4). They are to "hand over," "deliver," or "consign" (παραδοῦναι, as imperatival infinitive) "this man to Satan for the destruction of the flesh, so that the spirit may be saved on the Day of the Lord" (5:5).[16] The hope for Paul and his audience then is that the man will come to his senses, repent, and be restored to the community.[17] Thus, the

---

because in the first instance the community's stance *implicitly* leaves him in the cold so that he departs, whereas the more formal act *explicitly* enacts a formal pronouncement as a speech-act of verdict and directive."

15. For the possibility of a wordplay between the "evil one" (πονηρόν) in 5:13b and "sexual immorality" (πορνεία) in 5:1 (2x) as well as "sexually immoral one" (πόρνος) in 5:9, 10, 11, see Zaas, "Cast Out," 259–61.

16. For recent discussions of 1 Cor 5:5, see Adela Yarbro Collins, "The Function of 'Excommunication' in Paul," *HTR* 73 (1980): 251–63; Gerald Harris, "The Beginnings of Church Discipline: 1 Corinthians 5," *NTS* 37 (1991): 1–21; Brian S. Rosner, "Temple and Holiness in 1 Corinthians 5," *TynBul* 42 (1991): 137–45; Simon J. Kistemaker, " 'Deliver This Man to Satan' (1 Cor 5:5): A Case Study in Church Discipline," *Master's Seminary Journal* 3 (1992): 33–46; James T. South, "A Critique of the 'Curse/Death' Interpretation of 1 Corinthians 5.1–8," *NTS* 39 (1993): 539–61; Barth Campbell, "Flesh and Spirit in 1 Cor 5:5: An Exercise in Rhetorical Criticism of the NT," *JETS* 36 (1993): 331–42; Lyle D. Vander Broek, "Discipline and Community: Another Look at 1 Corinthians 5," *RefR* 48 (1994): 5–13; Dale B. Martin, *The Corinthian Body* (New Haven: Yale University Press, 1995), 168–69; V. George Shillington, "Atonement Texture in 1 Corinthians 5.5," *JSNT* 71 (1998): 29–50.

17. On "the destruction of the flesh" in 5:5 as not referring to death, see Thiselton, *Corinthians*, 399–400: "[N]otions that Paul and the congregation have *consigned* the man to a process which *causally* leads on to death have no necessary connection with a proper under-

scriptural injunction reinforcing Paul's authority, "drive out the evil one from out of your very midst" (5:13b), is not only for the welfare, holiness, and salvation of the community, but also for the eventual and ultimate salvation of the sexually immoral and evil man.

In the third unit (5:6–8), Paul's rhetorical question in 5:6b, "Do you not know that a little leaven leavens the [whole] batch of dough?" (cf. Gal 5:9), relies upon the audience's common knowledge of the penetrating and influential effects of leaven upon a batch of dough as a metaphor to address the problem of the sexually immoral man in their midst.[18] The "little leaven" (μικρὰ ζύμη), with emphasis upon the "little," characterizes the sexually immoral man as one who, though only one member ("a little") of the community, can detrimentally influence the entire community ("batch of dough") if his sexually immoral relationship with his father's wife is tolerated.[19]

Therefore, Paul commands his audience to clean out (ἐκκαθάρατε) the "old leaven," the sexually immoral man and thus the improper relationship, so that they may be a "new batch of dough," inasmuch as they already are actually "unleavened."[20] The transition of the leaven metaphor to a context

---

standing of the judicial verdictive and directive illocutions which expel him from the congregation. Since Paul explicitly states that the whole purpose is ἵνα τὸ πνεῦμα σωθῇ, unless we restrict this *saving act* to the congregation's purification without reference to the offender at all (which the syntax hardly suggests), no grounds remain for assuming that Paul does not still hope that the offender will abandon his illicit relationship and return to the congregation. . . . What Paul hopes will be destroyed is his attitude of self-congratulation, which deprivation from the respect and support of the church is likely to bring about." See also Fee, *Corinthians*, 208–13.

18. Paul uses the rhetorical question in 5:6b, introduced by "do you not know that" (οὐκ οἴδατε ὅτι; see also 1 Cor 3:16; 6:2, 3, 9, 15, 16, 19; 9:13, 24), to "signal a contradiction between what is and what ought to be, between what Corinth knows and does," according to Roy A. Harrisville, *I Corinthians* (ACNT; Minneapolis: Augsburg, 1987), 84. On "leaven" (ζύμη), Fee (*Corinthians*, 216) notes: "What is in view is not 'yeast' (as in the NIV), which was not plentiful in antiquity, and which in any case is fresh and wholesome. 'Leaven' was not so. It consisted of keeping back a 'little' portion of last week's dough, allowing it to ferment, then adding it to this week's dough, which in turn was thoroughly fermented to give it lightness (= sourdough bread)." See also Lockwood, *1 Corinthians*, 171; Thiselton, *Corinthians*, 401.

19. Thiselton, *Corinthians*, 402: "[N]ote the emphatic position of μικρά, *little*. Paul calls attention to the unstoppable, spreading, disastrous influence on the nature and identity of the whole community which is out of all proportion to what those who were *self-satisfied* evidently imagined could spring from a 'little' case of one immoral relationship, even if one of an utterly outrageous nature."

20. Michael Newton, *The Concept of Purity at Qumran and in the Letters of Paul* (SNTSMS 53; Cambridge: Cambridge University Press, 1985), 91–92: "The use of the verb ἐκκαθαίρω indicates the presence of something unclean which needs to be removed and here Paul is clearly pointing to the fornicator who must be excluded so that the community as the

of the feast of Passover and Unleavened Bread then becomes explicit: "For, indeed, our Passover lamb, Christ, has been sacrificed" (5:7).[21] Paul then exhorts that "we celebrate the [Passover] feast"—a metaphor for living joyfully and behaving well morally—not with the "old leaven," the sexually immoral man.[22] For this individual is a "leaven" that ferments "wickedness and evil," but we are to celebrate with the "unleavened bread" which is "purity and truth" (5:8).[23]

With the scriptural injunction in 5:13b, "Drive out the evil one from out of your very midst," Paul parallels and rhetorically reinforces his command in 5:7a, "Clean out the old leaven that you may be a new batch of dough, inasmuch as you are unleavened." The verb "drive out" (ἐξάρατε)

'new lump' and 'unleavened' can function as intended." Pickett, *Cross*, 109–10: "The operative image of the church in this portion of the letter is that of God's holy temple (3.16–17), which suggests that what was ultimately at issue was the purity of the community. The man who was living with his father's wife must be expelled in order to maintain this purity. This concern is further expressed by the imagery of the leaven which has to be cleansed out (5.6–7)."

21. Newton, *Purity*, 92: "What Paul is, in effect, saying here is that the Christians are living, as it were, during the festival of Unleavened Bread which follows the slaughter of the paschal lamb, who in this case is Christ. Just as Jewish homes during the festival remained cleansed of leaven so must the community of believers (God's building, 1 Cor. 3:9) during the time that remains until the *eschaton* be likewise cleansed." Pickett, *Cross*, 110: "The eschatological significance of Christ's death is in view in this context in the sense that it is the new reality wrought by that event that is invoked. Paul urges the Corinthians to become what they already are in Christ, a 'new batch of dough.'"

22. Fee, *Corinthians*, 218–19: "Still keeping the imagery of the Feast ('let us keep the Festival'), Paul broadens the application of the death of Christ to Christian life as a whole.... [O]n the basis of the crucifixion of Christ, God's people are to keep an ongoing feast of the celebration of God's forgiveness by holy living.... They are to celebrate their new life in Christ minus the 'old leaven,' a command that ties the present broader imperative to the earlier specific one. This at least includes an elimination of the kinds of sexual immorality represented by the excluded man." Newton, *Purity*, 93: "The Church now, by virtue of celebrating its own Passover, exists in a covenantal relationship with God. Christ, its own paschal lamb, has been sacrificed and it lives as if during the festival. Its members, in Paul's words, are the new dough, the unleavened bread untainted by the old, the presence of which would prevent the proper celebration of the festival."

23. On "wickedness and evil" (κακίας καὶ πονηρίας), Conzelmann (*1 Corinthians*, 99) notes: "The two words are synonymous (already in the LXX): the duplication is rhetorical." On "purity and truth" (εἰλικρινείας καὶ ἀληθείας), Thiselton (*Corinthians*, 407) explains: "The word εἰλικρινείας is rare. εἰλικρίνεια occurs in 2 Cor 2:17 to denote *purity* or *transparency* of motive on Paul's part.... This coheres well with the meaning of ἀλήθεια, *truth*, here ... *truth* relates to being true to the Christian's *identity* as sharing in the afflictions of Christ and a *Christian lifestyle*. Hence, here, *purity and truth* means the living out of a Christian life in actions which reflect the identity and reality of the new creation, as against that which is tainted by the self-interest and moral degeneracy, which must be *cleaned out*."

alliterates with "clean out" (ἐκκαθάρατε), and each employs the prefixed preposition ἐκ to express both intensity and movement away from. Both are abrupt, direct, and urgent commands to Paul's audience.[24]

The scriptural injunction further characterizes explicitly as "the evil one" (πονηρὸν) the "old leaven" (and "little leaven" in 5:6), the "leaven of wickedness and evil (πονηρίας)" (5:8), which refers to the sexually immoral man. And the scriptural injunction to drive out the evil one "from out of your very midst" for the benefit of the community and the individual members of it complements the purpose of the command to clean out the old leaven—"that you may be a new batch of dough, inasmuch as you are unleavened"—as an action necessary for the community to be what it should be—"the unleavened bread of purity and truth" (5:8). The audience, then, must "drive out" and "clean out" the evil one in order to rid itself of the detrimental influence of the sexually immoral relationship (πορνεία) among them (5:1), and thus of the reason for their being "puffed up" with arrogance (5:2a) and "boasting" inappropriately (5:6a).[25]

In the fourth unit (5:9–13), Paul expands the audience's focus both beyond the sexually immoral man to others like him and beyond the sexually immoral behavior of this man to other kinds of immoral behavior. In 5:9, Paul reminds his audience that he wrote to them previously not to associate with sexually immoral persons. He quickly adds in 5:10 that he did not mean for them not to associate with the sexually immoral persons "of this world," or other types of immoral persons, such as the greedy and robbers or idolaters, otherwise they would have to leave "the world."[26] Rather he wrote to them not to associate with any member of their community who is a sexually immoral person, such as the man living with his father's

---

24. What Thiselton (*Corinthians*, 405) says about "clean out" in 5:7a applies to "drive out" in 5:13b as well: "The imperative ἐκκαθάρατε is the first aorist active imperative of ἐκκαθαίρω, in which the compound ἐκ signifies both motion and intensity, and the effective aorist signifies the summons to perform a specific act. It is not too much to perceive in the Greek compound and syntax an implicit urgency about effectively completing this action with thoroughness, expecially in its ritualistic context."

25. For the relationship between the reference to Satan in 1 Cor 5:5 and to the Passover feast in 1 Cor 5:6–8, as well as the view that Paul's hope that the sexually immoral man will repent and be restored to the community fits well with the Passover motif, see Karl-Heinrich Ostmeyer, "Satan und Passa in 1.Korinther 5," *Zeitschrift für Neues Testament* 9 (2002): 38–45.

26. Adams, *Constructing the World*, 125: "ὁ κόσμος οὗτος in 5:10a [and κόσμος in 5:10b] obviously bears the negative apocalyptic sense of 'this world.' The genitive indicates belonging: Paul is speaking of the sexually immoral, greedy, and so on, *who belong to* this world.... The κόσμος is a world which is populated by immoral and corrupt people, so numerous that believers cannot avoid contact with them."

wife (5:1), or who is greedy or an idolater or a reviler or a drunkard or a robber.²⁷ Indeed, they are not even to eat and thus share the communal intimacy of meal fellowship, with any such member (5:11).²⁸

With its bold and authoritative command, the scriptural injunction in 5:13b reinforces and develops Paul's directives to the audience in 5:9–11. Paul's audience is not only, negatively, "not to associate with" (μὴ συναναμίγνυσθαι in 5:9, 11) and "not to eat with" (μηδὲ συνεσθίειν in 5:11) the sexually immoral man and those who are like him or those who are guilty of other types of evil behavior, but they must, positively, "drive out" (ἐξάρατε) "the evil one"—the sexually immoral man and other immoral persons—from their very midst (5:13b). The generic "evil one" in the scriptural injunction thus includes not only the sexually immoral man but all other types of "evil" individuals within the Corinthian community.

With a rhetorical question Paul indicates that he, and by implication his audience as well, does not have the competence or responsibility to judge those outside of their community, "Why am I to judge those outside?" (5:12a).²⁹ He then provokes his audience's affirmation that they themselves are the ones who have both the competence and responsibility to judge those, like the sexually immoral man, inside of their community: "Is it not those inside that *you* [emphatic ὑμεῖς] are to judge?" (5:12b). As an aside Paul adds that "as for those outside God will judge" (5:13a).³⁰

---

27. On the catalog of vices in 5:10–11, which extends Paul's prior instruction beyond sexually immoral behavior, see Peter S. Zaas, "Catalogues and Context: 1 Corinthians 5 and 6," *NTS* 34 (1988): 622–29. Pascuzzi, *Ethics*, 132–33: "By classing the 'one calling himself a brother' with the other perpetrators of evil mentioned in the vice list, Paul is, in effect, arguing that the incestuous man is a rank sinner, identifiable with those sinners mentioned elsewhere cf. 6,9–10, who will not inherit the kingdom."

28. Collins, *First Corinthians*, 223: "Paul wishes that the community not have social interaction, of which the common meal is a most important sign, with someone whose behavior egregiously violates social mores. Such a ban includes but is not restricted to exclusion from eucharistic fellowship." Dennis E. Smith, *From Symposium to Eucharist: The Banquet in the Early Christian World* (Minneapolis: Fortress, 2002), 203: "[T]he meeting described in 1 Corinthians 5 may have included a meal, but this is not certain. Nevertheless, it is striking that the imagery of the communal meal provides a basis for the definition of the community even in this context. Indeed, as practiced by various Greco-Roman clubs and as exemplified in the regulations of the Qumran community, exclusion from the community was especially effective when it was carried out at the communal banquet."

29. Fee, *Corinthians*, 226: "Paul is not dealing with himself personally, but with himself as he represents the Christian community."

30. On 5:13a as an aside, Callow ("Patterns," 205) notes that "comparison with other verses in 1 Corinthians shows that verse 13a exhibits a pattern commonly found in asides: something which has just been mentioned is repeated at the beginning of the clause with δέ. Then something new is said about it, which is not mentioned again thereafter.... We thus

The scriptural injunction to drive out the evil one "from out of your very midst (ἐξ ὑμῶν αὐτῶν)" in 5:13b emphatically and authoritatively urges the audience to carry out their responsibility to judge "those inside (τοὺς ἔσω)" (5:12b). The audience is to "judge" (κρίνετε, 5:12b) those inside and thus confirm the "judgment" Paul himself has already made (κέκρικα, 5:3) by "driving out" (ἐξάρατε, 5:13b) the sexually immoral man and those like him (5:1–11). By "driving *out* (ἐξ-)" the evil one "from out" (ἐξ) of their very midst (5:13b), the audience will place such persons in the realm of "those outside (τοὺς ἔξω)" (5:12a, 13a), where it is God who will ultimately judge them.[31]

Relation to the Subsequent Context in 1 Corinthians 6:1–7:2

Paul's subsequent statements in 6:1–7:2 regarding the sexually immoral and their behavior reinforce the scriptural injunction in 5:13b urging his audience to drive out from their very midst the "evil one" (πονηρὸν), that is, the sexually immoral one (πόρνος, 5:11) guilty of the sexual immorality (πορνεία) of living with his father's wife (5:1) and those of similar evil behavior. In 6:9, Paul commands his audience not to be deceived, for "sexually immoral ones" (πόρνοι) are among those who will not inherit the kingdom of God. In 6:13, Paul impresses upon his audience that the body is not meant for "sexual immorality" (πορνείᾳ) but for the Lord. In 6:18, Paul's bold and blunt command for his audience to literally "flee from" and thus shun "sexual immorality" (πορνείαν) echoes the scriptural bold and blunt command to drive out the evil one from out of their very midst. And in 7:2, Paul instructs his audience that it is because of cases of "sexual immorality" (πορνείας) that each man should have his own wife and each woman should have her own husband.[32]

---

interpret verse 13a as an aside, leaving verse 12 to carry the emotive thematic strand, and verse 13b as the main structural theme of the passage [5:9–13]."

31. Thiselton, *Corinthians*, 416–17: "The disclaimer about *outsiders* makes sense only as a way of underlining the importance of responsible household rules for *those inside*." Pascuzzi, *Ethics*, 145: "Paul's concern was to impress on the community the need to join him in what was ultimately the defense of its own well-being through appropriate and responsible action."

32. For an argument that 1 Cor 5–6 forms a unified response to the misdeeds of Paul's Corinthian audience, see Will Deming, "The Unity of 1 Corinthians 5–6," *JBL* 115 (1996): 289–312. For a contention that Paul's opponents in 1 Cor 5–6 were not libertines but ascetics who condoned the incestuous behavior of the sexually immoral man (5:1) because he was an important member of the church, see Michael D. Goulder, "Libertines? (1 Cor. 5–6)," *NovT* 41 (1999): 334–48.

Summary on 1 Corinthians 5:13b

1. The audience can be expected to recognize and appreciate 1 Cor 5:13b as a scriptural quotation because of its multiple recurrences in Deuteronomy and its noteworthy, non-Pauline vocabulary. But that it is not explicitly introduced and located in any particular OT text means that the audience need not necessarily recall any of the variety of specific original contexts in which this scriptural formula was employed. The implied audience need only recognize it as an authoritative quotation that they have heard more than once from somewhere in the OT scriptures and that Paul has now applied to their situation.

2. Paul employs the bluntly authoritative scriptural mandate in 1 Cor 5:13b to impose upon his Corinthian implied audience a very urgent, strict, and unconditional obligation to expel the evil person from out of the very midst of themselves.

3. The scriptural injunction in 1 Cor 5:13b rhetorically reinforces and/or develops all of the various expressions of the repeated command to discontinue fellowship with an erring member in each of the four units—5:1–2, 3–5, 6–8, and 9–13:

a. In 5:1–2 the Corinthian audience themselves are the ones commanded not only to "remove" (5:2c) but to "drive out" the deviant member, whom the scriptural injunction characterized as "the evil one," from out of their very midst (5:13b).

b. In 5:3–5 the scriptural injunction to "drive out" (5:13b) reinforces the command to "hand over" the evil man "to Satan for the destruction of the flesh, so that the spirit may be saved on the Day of the Lord" (5:5), not only for the welfare, holiness, and salvation of the community, but also for the eventual and ultimate salvation of the sexually immoral and evil man.

c. In 5:6–8 the scriptural injunction in 5:13b, "Drive out the evil one from out of your very midst," parallels and rhetorically reinforces Paul's command in 5:7a, "Clean out the old leaven that you may be a new batch of dough, inasmuch as you are unleavened." The audience, then, must "drive out" and "clean out" the evil one in order to rid itself of his detrimental influence among them (5:1), and thus of the reason for their being "puffed up" with arrogance (5:2a) and "boasting" inappropriately (5:6a).

d. In 5:9–13 the scriptural injunction to "drive out" the evil one (5:13b) reinforces and develops Paul's directives to the audience "not to associate with" (5:9, 11) and "not to eat with" (5:11) the sexually immoral man and those who are like him or those who are guilty of other types of evil behavior. The scriptural injunction to drive out the evil one "from out of your very midst" (5:13b) emphatically and authoritatively urges the audience to carry out their responsibility to judge "those inside" of their community (5:12b).

4. Paul's subsequent statements in 6:1–7:2 regarding the sexually immoral and their behavior echo and thus reinforce the scriptural injunction in 5:13b urging his audience to drive out from their very midst the "evil one," that is, the sexually immoral one (πόρνος, 5:11; cf. 6:9) guilty of the sexual immorality (πορνεία; cf. 6:13, 18; 7:2) of living with his father's wife (5:1) and those of similar evil behavior.

Chapter 8

1 Corinthians 6:16b

The two will become one flesh.

Old Testament Background

The words "the two will become one flesh," introduced by the interpretive aside "for, it says" in 1 Cor 6:16b, quote Gen 2:24c in accord with the LXX, which differs from the MT in expressing the subject as "the two," referring to man and wife, rather than simply as "they":[1]

    LXX Gen 2:24c: καὶ ἔσονται οἱ δύο εἰς σάρκα μίαν
                          and the two will become one flesh
    MT Gen 2:24c: וְהָיוּ לְבָשָׂר אֶחָד
                          and they will become one flesh
    1 Cor 6:16b: ἔσονται γάρ, φησίν, οἱ δύο εἰς σάρκα μίαν
                         for, it says, "the two will become one flesh"

Paul does not explicitly draw his implied audience's attention to the scriptural quote's unmistakable location in Genesis. He merely relies upon their familiarity with this very fundamental scriptural text regarding the origin of marriage from the biblical tradition of creation. However, the use of the verb "is united" both before the quote in 6:16a, "whoever is united (κολλώμενος) to the prostitute is one body,"[2] and after the quote in 6:17,

---

1. Stanley, *Paul*, 195: "[T]he quotation in 1 Cor 6.16 follows the unanimous wording of the LXX tradition for Gen 2.24." Thiselton, *Corinthians*, 467: "[T]he Hebrew MT does not include *the two* behind οἱ δύο, even if the words are found in the Samaritan Pentateuch and the Targum of Jonathan. The LXX's *two* does occur in the numerous quotations in Philo and in Mark 10:8, Matt 19:5, and Eph 5:31."

2. Although πόρνη for Paul can refer to any kind of extramarital sex, it refers primarily to the prostitute in 6:12–20. Renate Kirchhoff, *Die Sünde gegen den eigenen Leib: Studien zu πόρνη und πορνεία in 1 Kor 6,12–20 und dem sozio-kulturellen Kontext der paulinischen

"whoever is united (κολλώμενος) to the Lord is one spirit," further indicates and confirms for the audience the Genesis origin of the quote by recalling its preceding context in Gen 2:24ab: "Therefore a man shall leave his father and his mother and will be united (προσκολληθήσεται) with his wife, and the two will become one flesh."[3]

To sum up, although not explicitly introduced as such, 1 Cor 6:16b is a direct quotation of LXX Gen 2:24c, which relies upon the implied audience's knowledge of both the quoted words and their immediate context in Genesis as a reference to the fundamental unity established between a man and his wife by the institution of marriage as created by God.

Literary-Rhetorical Analysis

Rather than introducing the scriptural quote in 6:16b with the usual "for, it is written," Paul employs an explanatory conjunction plus an impersonal verb in the active voice to express not writing but speaking—"for, it says" (γάρ, φησίν).[4] This indicates to the audience that the scriptural quote from Gen 2:24c gives voice to a fundamental, universal authority about the reality of human marriage that holds even if this "saying" were not "written" in the scriptures. The authority of this "saying," then, transcends and thus enhances its authority as scripture. Furthermore, the use of the active,

---

Adressaten (SUNT 18; Göttingen: Vandenhoeck & Ruprecht, 1994), 196: "Πόρνη nennt Paulus nicht speziell eine Prostituierte, sondern jede Frau, mit der ein christlicher Mann nach Paulus' Meinung nach nicht sexuell verkehren darf, d.h. eine, die nicht die einzige Sexualpartnerin und also die Ehefrau ist. Faktisch waren es vor allem Prostituierte, zu denen die Adressaten von 1Kor 6,12–20 nichtehelichen Sexualkontakt aufnahmen bzw. unterhielten."

3. Referring to κολλώμενος, Collins (*First Corinthians*, 247) remarks: "Used three times by Paul (6:16, 17; Rom 12:9), its appearance here appears to be dictated by Paul's allusion to the text of Gen 2:24." According to Fee (*Corinthians*, 259 n. 44), Paul uses κολλώμενος rather than the compounded form with προς, as found in Genesis, because it would be more appropriate for its reference to the relationship with Christ in 6:17. For references to Gen 2:24 in extrabiblical Jewish literature, see Kirchhoff, *Sünde*, 160–64, who concludes: "Paulus knüpft mit seiner Rezeption von Gen 2,24 an die Tradition an, die Gen 2,24 als eine Grundordnung versteht. Die Grundordnung, die er aus dem Vers ableitet, gilt im Unterschied zur Interpretation in den angeführten Texten nicht nur für sexuelle Beziehungen" (165).

4. Lockwood, *1 Corinthians*, 211–12: "When introducing a quotation, φησίν (like λέγει) is used impersonally. In its only other occurrence in Paul (2 Cor 10:10), it is impersonal." Collins, *First Corinthians*, 248: "The location of the interpretive aside 'it is said' (φησίν) in the course of a biblical citation is a unique stylistic feature of this passage. Elsewhere Paul typically uses the classic lemma 'it is written' (γέγραπται) to introduce biblical citations." See also Koch, *Schrift*, 25 n. 5. Thiselton, *Corinthians*, 467: "The impersonal verbal form φησίν usually denotes oral speech rather than written texts but clearly refers to the quotation of Gen 2:24.... [I]n the LXX φημί chiefly translates נאם (na'am), which in its substantival form is regularly used in *oracle of Yahweh*, or *thus says the Lord*."

impersonal verb for speaking, "it says," underlines for the audience how this fundamental scriptural text "speaks" with divine authority immediately and directly to the situation at issue.[5]

The quotation itself "speaks" to the implied audience with a fundamental and divine scriptural authority about "the two" (οἱ δύο), that is, on the one hand, the man who leaves his father and mother (Gen 2:24a)—his family and home—and, on the other hand, the wife to whom he is united (Gen 2:24b) not only in the act of sexual intercourse but by living and associating closely with her. The audience is to realize and fully appreciate that these two divinely created human beings "will become" (ἔσονται . . . εἰς), by the fundamental divine authority of the Creator, "one flesh" (σάρκα μίαν), that is, a unity of persons at the level of their human, physical, and bodily existence.[6] The audience, therefore, must assent to this authoritative scriptural "saying" stating that the "two" persons by virtue of their intimate association in marriage become "one" physical or "fleshly" entity.[7]

In sum, the scriptural quotation of Gen 2:24c in 1 Cor 6:16b "speaks" to Paul's implied Corinthian audience with a fundamental and divine authority that requires their agreement that the two persons united by the bond of marriage actually become a single physical entity.

The Chiastic Structure in 1 Corinthians 6:12–20

Before looking at the antecedent (6:12–16a) and subsequent (6:17–20) contexts respectively of the scriptural quotation of Gen 2:24c in 1 Cor 6:16b, we need to consider and establish the following chiastic structure formed by both of those contexts in 6:12–20:[8]

---

5. On the universal implication that Gen 2:24 applies to both Jews and Gentiles according to Jewish law, see Tomson, *Paul and the Jewish Law*, 100.

6. Thiselton, *Corinthians*, 467: "[F]ollowing the Hebrew idiom behind the Greek, we translate ἔσονται with most English VSS as *shall become one flesh*, representing וְהָיוּ לְבָשָׂר אֶחָד (*wehayu lebasar 'echad*), where the Greek preposition εἰς represents the Heb ל (*le*) to qualify the verb's relation to the noun." Lockwood, *1 Corinthians*, 212: "[T]he two *become* and therefore now *are* one flesh."

7. Fee, *Corinthians*, 259: "While the union of man and wife as 'one flesh' implies far more than merely physical union, Paul's concern here is strictly with the physical aspects of the union."

8. The chiastic structure that we are proposing for 1 Cor 6:12–20 was inspired by, but differs considerably from, that delineated for 6:13c–20 by Kenneth E. Bailey, "Paul's Theological Foundation for Human Sexuality: I Cor. 6:9–20 in the Light of Rhetorical Criticism," *NETR* 3 (1980): 27–41. Bailey fails to follow closely the rigorous criteria for determining a true chiasm as listed by Craig L. Blomberg, "The Structure of 2 Corinthians 1–7," *CTR* 4

Superscription: 6:12

"All things are permitted for me" but not all things are beneficial!
"All things are permitted for me" but as for me I will not be dominated by anything!

Chiasm: 6:13–20

A   ¹³ "(a) <u>Food</u> (βρώματα) for the (b) <u>stomach</u> (κοιλίᾳ) and the (b´) <u>stomach</u> (κοιλία) for (a´) <u>food</u> (βρώμασιν), but God (θεὸς) will destroy both the one and the other." The (a) body (σῶμα) however is not for sexual immorality but for the (b) <u>Lord</u>, and the (b´) <u>Lord</u> for the (a´) body (σώματι). ¹⁴ God (θεὸς) <u>raised</u> the <u>Lord</u> and will also <u>raise</u> us through his power.

B   ¹⁵ Do you not know that your bodies (σώματα) are <u>members</u> of <u>Christ</u>? Shall I then take away the <u>members</u> of <u>Christ</u> and make (them) <u>members</u> of a prostitute (πόρνης)? May it never happen!

C   ¹⁶ª Or do you not know that <u>whoever is united</u> (<u>κολλώμενος</u>) to the prostitute is <u>one</u> (<u>ἓν</u>) body (<u>σῶμά</u>)?

(1989): 3–20: (1) There must be a problem in perceiving the structure of the text in question, which more conventional outlines fail to resolve; (2) there must be clear examples of parallelism between the two "halves" of the hypothesized chiasmus, to which commentators call attention even when they propose quite different outlines for the text overall; (3) verbal (or grammatical) parallelism as well as conceptual (or structural) parallelism should characterize most if not all of the corresponding pairs of subdivisions; (4) the verbal parallelism should involve central or dominant imagery or terminology, not peripheral or trivial language; (5) both verbal and conceptual parallelism should involve words and ideas not regularly found elsewhere within the proposed chiasmus; (6) multiple sets of correspondences between passages opposite each other in the chiasmus as well as multiple members of the chiasmus itself are desirable; (7) the outline should divide the text at natural breaks which would be agreed upon even by those proposing very different structures to account for the whole; (8) the center of the chiasmus, which forms its climax, should be a passage worthy of that position in light of its theological or ethical significance; (9) ruptures in the outline should be avoided if at all possible. See also Ian H. Thomson, *Chiasmus in the Pauline Letters* (JSNTSup 111; Sheffield: Sheffield Academic Press, 1995), 13–45; John W. Welch, "Criteria for Identifying and Evaluating the Presence of Chiasmus," in *Chiasmus Bibliography* (ed. John W. Welch and Daniel B. McKinlay; Provo, Utah: Research, 1999), 157–74; David E. Aune, *The Westminster Dictionary of New Testament and Early Christian Literature and Rhetoric* (Louisville: Westminster John Knox, 2003), 93–96. For an application of these rigorous linguistic criteria to one of Paul's other letters, see John Paul Heil, "The Chiastic Structure and Meaning of Paul's Letter to Philemon," *Bib* 82 (2001): 178–206.

D ¹⁶ᵇ For, it says, "The two (οἱ δύο) will become one flesh (σάρκα μίαν) (Gen 2:24c).

C′ ¹⁷ But whoever is united (κολλώμενος) to the Lord is one (ἓν) spirit (πνεῦμά).

B′ ¹⁸ Flee sexual immorality (πορνείαν)! Every sin that a person commits is outside of the body (σώματός). But the sexually immoral one (πορνεύων) sins against his own body (σῶμα).

A′ ¹⁹ Or do you not know that your body (σῶμα) is a temple of the Holy Spirit within you, which you have from God (θεοῦ), and that you are not your own? ²⁰ For you have been bought at a price. So glorify God (θεὸν) in your body (σώματι)![9]

Introductory superscription for the chiasm: 6:12. First Corinthians 6:12, " 'All things are permitted for me' but not all things are beneficial! 'All things are permitted for me' but as for me I will not be dominated by anything!" serves as the superscription for the chiasm that follows in 6:13–20.[10] The grammatical change from the second-person plural address in 6:11 to the first-person singular statements in 6:12 and the thematic change from the transformation that has happened to the addressees who have been washed, sanctified, and justified in 6:11 to the theme of modifying individual liberties in 6:12 indicate to the audience the beginning of a new section in 6:12–20. As a generalizing statement about "all things" (πάντα occurs 3x) that are permitted one but that may not be beneficial and about an indefinite "anything" (τινος) that must not dominate one, 6:12 is also set

---

9. The key terms establishing the integrity of each unit are underlined. The key Greek terms establishing the parallels between the respective units are in bold print. And the key unparalleled Greek terms of the central (D) and (CC′) units of the chiasm are in italicized bold print.

10. Whether or not "all things are permitted for me" is an exact quotation of a Corinthian slogan, in its epistolary context it functions as a rhetorical slogan in which Paul has inserted himself as the exemplary and representative "I" (note the emphatic ἐγώ, translated "but as for me") with whom the individual members of his Corinthian audience are to identify. See Jerome Murphy-O'Connor, "Corinthian Slogans in 1 Cor 6:12–20," *CBQ* 40 (1978): 391–96; Roger L. Omanson, "Acknowledging Paul's Quotations," *BT* 43 (1992): 201–13; Brian J. Dodd, "Paul's Paradigmatic 'I' and 1 Corinthians 6.12," *JSNT* 59 (1995): 39–58; Mitchell, *Paul*, 54: "Because the appeal to himself as example is the unifying rhetorical strategy of the letter, enumerating and describing Paul's self-references in 1 Corinthians almost amounts to a summary of the contents of the letter."

apart from what follows as an introductory superscription whose generalizations receive specification and development in the chiasm that follows in 6:13–20.[11]

The integrity of 6:12 as a literary-rhetorical unit is secured by the repetition of the slogan "all things are permitted to me," the threefold occurrence of the term "all" (πάντα), and the wordplay sequence in which the double occurrence of ἔξεστιν ("it is permitted") is followed by ἐξουσιασθήσομαι ("I will be dominated").[12] None of these key terms occurs in the immediately preceding or subsequent verses.

How 6:12 functions as a superscription is further indicated by the suspense aroused for the audience by the expression "but not all things are beneficial (συμφέρει)," which leaves open *what* things are not beneficial for *whom* and in *what* regard.[13] And the expression "but as for *me*, I will not be dominated by anything," which leaves indefinite what the individual for whom all things are permitted may be in danger of being dominated by, further arouses the suspense of the audience. This suspense aroused by the superscription in 6:12 begins to receive its resolution in the chiasm that fol-

---

11. On the historical background and setting of 6:12–20, see Bruce W. Winter, "Gluttony and Immorality at Elitist Banquets: The Background to 1 Corinthians 6:12–20," *Jian Dao* 7 (1997): 77–90; idem, *After Paul*, 86–93; Brian S. Rosner, "Temple Prostitution in 1 Corinthians 6:12–20," *NovT* 40 (1998): 336–51; Goulder, "Libertines?" 334–48. Winter argues for a background in private, elitist banquets, in which there was a close connection between gluttony, drunkedness, and sexual indulgence, and in which the maxim "all things are permitted" was related to the assumption of the *toga virilis* by male Roman adolescents. See also Robertson, *Conflict in Corinth*, 232–33.

12. Richard A. Horsley, *1 Corinthians* (Nashville: Abingdon, 1998), 90: "Paul's counter to his repetition of the Corinthians' slogan in 6:12b involves a play on the verb 'authorize/empower' that is difficult to replicate in English—literally, 'I am empowered for everything, but I will not be overpowered by anything.'"

13. Lindemann, *Erste Korintherbrief*, 145: "Paulus läßt den Bezugspunkt dessen, was 'nützlich' ist, offen." This openness will allow Paul to address what is beneficial both for the body of the individual and for the community that constitutes the body of Christ in the chiasm that follows the superscription in 6:13–20. Thiselton, *Corinthians*, 462: "The verb carries the nuance of bearing (φέρω) together (συν-) for good as a benefit. The issue for Paul is *what helps* and *what hinders* in constituting credible corporate Christian identity as a community in corporate solidarity with Christ." Mitchell, *Paul*, 35: "Within Paul's argumentation, when he first introduces the term [συμφέρει] in 6:12, it carries its usual sense of self-interest until Paul later redefines it within the course of his progressive argument. As we have noted, appealing to the audience's self-interest ... lies at the heart of deliberative rhetoric, and it is what Paul uses to persuade the Corinthians to work for a new standard of 'common advantage,' and dissuade them from selfish behavior." See also Timothy Radcliffe, "'Glorify God in Your Bodies': 1 Corinthians 6,12–20 as a Sexual Ethic," *NBf* 67 (1986): 306–14.

lows in 6:13–20. Indeed, each unit of the chiasm, in one way or another, addresses the suspense aroused by the generalizations of the superscription.[14]

In the first (A) unit of the chiasm (6:13–14) it becomes evident to the audience what precisely may "dominate" the individual for whom "all things are permitted," namely, sexual immorality: "The body however is not for sexual immorality (πορνεία) but for the Lord and the Lord for the body" (6:13b). In other words, no Christian should allow his body to be "dominated" (ἐξουσιασθήσομαι, 6:12b) by illicit sexual intercourse, because one's body is under the dominion or authority of the Lord ("the body is for the Lord") and, vice versa, the Lord has dominion or authority over one's body ("the Lord is for the body").[15] Thus, the sexual immorality one may think is permitted is not "beneficial" (6:12a) for one's body.

The theme of not being dominated by sexual immorality (πορνεία) in general (6:13) progresses to not being dominated specifically by a prostitute (πόρνης) in the B unit of the chiasm (6:15). Paul emphatically denies that he or anyone (representative "I") should make the bodies of the Corinthian believers, which are members of Christ, members of a prostitute and thus be "dominated" (6:13b) by the prostitute rather than Christ. This would not be "beneficial" (6:13a) either to one's individual body or to the communal body of Christ to which one's individual body belongs as a member.

The question of bodies in general becoming a member of a prostitute then progresses to the question of an individual being united to the prostitute in the C unit of the chiasm (6:16a). In this unit Paul makes his audience aware that anyone who unites himself to the prostitute actually forms one body with her, implying a "domination" (6:13b) by her that is not "beneficial" (6:13a). That the one uniting with the prostitute forms one body with her is then confirmed by the central D unit of the chiasm (6:16b), the scriptural quote from Gen 2:24c, "The two will become one flesh."

The C′ unit of the chiasm (6:17) then asserts that anyone united to the Lord forms one spirit with him, implying a spiritual, "beneficial" (6:13a) "domination" (6:13b) by the Lord that transcends the physical, bodily domination by the prostitute. The statement in the B′ unit of the chiasm (6:18) that the sexually immoral one sins against his own body then continues to express how sexual immorality in general involves a "domination" (6:13b) that is not "beneficial" (6:13a). Finally, the statement in the A′ unit

---

14. According to Mitchell, *Paul*, 35–36: "In 6:13–20 Paul begins to lay the groundwork for his redefinition of τὸ συμφέρον which is at the heart of the entire argument in 1 Corinthians, in his effort to demonstrate to the Corinthians what their true best interests are."

15. For an OT example of how the body can be "dominated" through sexual intercourse, see Sir 47:19: "You [Solomon] laid your loins beside women and you were dominated (ἐνεξουσιάσθης) through your body."

of the chiasm (6:19–20) that "your body" is a temple of the Holy Spirit which is from God, so that "you are not your own, for you have been bought at a price," implies a "beneficial" (6:13a) "domination" (6:13b) by God that calls for glorifying God in "your body" by not engaging in sexual immorality.

The seven units of the chiasm in 6:13–20. The literary integrity of 6:13–14 as the first (A) unit of the chiastic structure in 6:13–20 is secured by the references to actions of God in both verses—"God will destroy both the one and the other" in 6:13 and "God raised the Lord and will also raise us through his power" in 6:14. Each of these statements about God is preceded by a smaller chiasm—"(a) Food for the (b) stomach and the (b´) stomach for (a´) food" and "The (a) body however is not for sexual immorality but for the (b) Lord, and the (b´) Lord for the (a´) body." In addition to the repetition of the word "God," this unit is characterized by repetitions of the words "food," "stomach," "body," "Lord" (3x), and "raise." With the exception of "body" none of these repeated terms occurs in the preceding (6:12) or subsequent (6:15) units.

Repetitions of the words "members" (3x) and "Christ" confirm the literary integrity of the chiasm's second (B) unit in 6:15. Neither of these two terms occurs in the preceding A (6:13–14) or subsequent C (6:16a) units.

The terms "whoever is united" (κολλώμενος) and "one body" (ἓν σῶμά) define the integrity of the third (C) unit of the chiasm in 6:16a. Neither of these terms occurs in the preceding B (6:15) or subsequent D (6:16b) units.

The scriptural quotation of Gen 2:24c in 6:16b forms the central and pivotal fourth (D) unit of the entire chiasm. This is confirmed by the fact that the key terms defining this unit's integrity, "the two" (οἱ δύο) and "one flesh" (σάρκα μίαν), occur only here within the chiasm.

The terms "whoever is united" (κολλώμενος), "the Lord" (τῷ κυρίῳ), and "one spirit" (ἓν πνεῦμά) define the integrity of the fifth (C´) unit of the chiasm in 6:17. None of these terms occurs in the preceding D (6:16b) or subsequent B´ (6:18) units.

The two pairs of terms, "sexual immorality" (πορνείαν)–"sexually immoral one" (πορνεύων) and "sin" (ἁμάρτημα)–"sins" (ἁμαρτάνει), establish the unity of the sixth (B´) unit of the chiasm in 6:18. None of these terms is found in the preceding C´ (6:17) or subsequent A´ (6:19–20) units.

And finally, the second-person plural pronoun "your/you" (3x) and the repetition of the word "God" define the integrity of the seventh and final (A´) unit of the chiasm in 6:19–20. None of these terms occurs in the preceding B´ (6:18) unit.

The parallels and pivot of the chiasm in 6:13–20. The A (6:13–14) and A´ (6:19–20) units of the chiasm in 6:13–20 are parallel in that each contains two references respectively to both "God" and the "body." There is a chiastic sequence to the occurrence of these key terms in each unit: God-body-body-God in the A unit but body-God-God-body in the A´ unit. The B (6:15) and B´ (6:18) units are parallel in that each contains references to a term for "body" (2x in the B´ unit) and a term involving sexual immorality—"prostitute" (πόρνης) in the B unit and "sexual immorality" (πορνείαν) as well as "sexually immoral one" (πορνεύων) in the B´ unit. The key terms "whoever is united" (ὁ κολλώμενος) and "one" (ἕν) constitute the parallels between the C (6:16a) and C´ (6:17) units. And finally, the key terms "the two" (οἱ δύο) and "one flesh" (σάρκα μίαν) from the scriptural quote of Gen 2:24c, which are unparalleled throughout the entire chiasm, establish the D (6:16b) unit as the central and pivotal unit of the chiasm in 6:13–20.

Relation to the Antecedent Context in 1 Corinthians 6:12–16a

In the superscription in 6:12 that introduces the chiasm in 6:13–20, Paul modifies the repeated rhetorical slogan, "all things are permitted for me," by warning, "but not all things are beneficial" and "as for me I [Paul as the representative individual with whom every individual in the audience is to identify] will not be dominated by anything." This arouses suspense in the audience as to what might not be beneficial and what might dominate them as individuals for whom all things are permitted. Paul's intense determination that he, as the representative "I" (emphatic ἐγώ), will not allow anything permitted him to dominate him persuades the individuals in his Corinthian implied audience to likewise strongly resolve not to be dominated by anything unbeneficial.[16]

The first (A) unit of the chiasm (6:13–14) is introduced by another rhetorical slogan with which the Corinthian audience is to identify either as a quotation or reformulation of a viewpoint which they hold or with which they are well familiar: "Food for the stomach and the stomach for food, but God will destroy both the one and the other" (6:13ab).[17] According to the

---

16. Kirchhoff, *Sünde*, 109: "V. 12 hat dadurch die Funktion eines Proömiums, das die Aufmerksamkeit der Hörer und Hörerinnen weckt und richtet.... Er spricht seine Hörer und Hörerinnen als solche an, die von ihm lernen können und weckt Aufnahmebereitschaft und Spannung."

17. For the reasoning for including 6:13b, "but God will destroy both the one and the other," as part of the slogan, see Karl Olav Sandnes, *Belly and the Body in the Pauline Epistles*

slogan, since God will ultimately destroy both food and the stomach that digests it, these kinds of bodily functions are morally irrelevant.[18] This slogan thus further specifies the repeated slogan of the superscription in 6:12 that "all things are permitted to me." All things in the area of food and the stomach, and thus in the closely related area of sexuality, are permitted as they are merely physical and transitory.[19]

But Paul's audience is to realize that the body (σῶμα), which includes but transcends matters of the stomach, is not for sexual immorality (πορνεία) in the way that food is for the stomach and the stomach for food.[20] Paul then counters and surpasses the slogan's chiasm, food-stomach-

---

(STNSMS 120; New York: Cambridge University Press, 2002), 192-95; Thiselton, *Corinthians*, 462-63; Collins, *First Corinthians*, 245: "Since 'destroy' (καταργήσει) is a Pauline term, one frequently used in 1 Corinthians with an eschatological nuance (1:28; 2:6; 6:13; 13:8 [2x], 10, 11; 15:24, 26), it is tempting to read this phrase as if it were a Pauline qualification of the Corinthians' buzzword. It is, however, more likely that the phrase should be taken as part of their slogan that Paul then counters with the competitive slogan of v. 13c. The complete slogan presents something of an Epicurean idea of human corporeal existence or a kind of anthropology that considers the body as being somewhat independent of the spirit. Bodily existence is for this world only."

18. According to Thiselton (*Corinthians*, 463), the particular uses of "stomach" (κοιλία) in first-century Greek literature helps to explain the three-stage logic of this slogan: "(1) κοιλία often means *the digestive system* rather than a location within the body, i.e., to say '*food is for digestion*' means that it soon passes through and is disposed of; (2) in this respect it stands as a kind of metonym for all things physical and transient; (3) hence, supposedly, on this line of reasoning, God is concerned only with those aspects of selfhood which will survive disintegration at death, i.e., what pertains to the spirit or to the Spirit." For a comparison between Paul and Plutarch, see Benjamin Fiore, "Passion in Paul and Plutarch: 1 Corinthians 5–6 and the Polemic against Epicureans," in *Greeks, Romans, and Christians: Essays in Honor of Abraham J. Malherbe* (ed. David L. Balch et al.; Minneapolis: Fortress, 1990), 135-43.

19. Winter, *After Paul*, 88: "'All things are permitted,' the self-justifying aphorism for the notorious conduct of the Corinthian Christians at dinners, concerned the 'intimate and unholy trinity' of eating and drinking and sexual immorality. Gluttony and drunkenness were an accepted part of the social life in Corinth, as were the promiscuous 'after-dinners.'. . . The élite who gave private banquets to which they invited clients as well as other guests provided not only for their physical hunger but also for their sexual appetites." Sandes, *Belly*, 196: "Verses 13–14 make sense within a line of thought claiming that what one did with the body was morally irrelevant. Some Corinthians claimed that the body did not matter, and bodily activities could therefore affect neither themselves nor the body of believers. The appearance of food and sex in tandem is, therefore, due to the logic of the slogans. And certainly Paul knew all too well that if Christian freedom in food-matters was interpreted to imply freedom to attend all kinds of banquets, sex would naturally follow in its wake."

20. Wolfgang Schrage, *Der erste Brief an die Korinther (1 Kor 6,12–11,16)* (EKKNT 7/2; Düsseldorf: Benziger, 1995), 22: "Σῶμα ist entsprechend der Ort, wo der Mensch Leben und Tod erfährt, seine Naturhaftigkeit, Krankheit, Sexualität, u.ä. Σῶμα is kein Etwas, kein Teil und kein bloßes Attribut des Menschen, sondern der Mensch selbst. . . . Darum kann σῶμα für die Person bzw. das Ich des Menschen eintreten, wie der kennzeichnende Wechsel des Begriffes

stomach-food, with another, namely, body-Lord-Lord-body: "the body is . . . for the Lord and the Lord for the body" (6:13c). According to the slogan God will ultimately destroy both food and the stomach (6:13b). But Paul counters and surpasses this with his assertion that the God who raised the Lord, who is for the body, will also raise "us," that is, our bodies, through his power (6:14).[21] Paul thus makes his audience realize that our bodies have a permanent importance "for the Lord" that transcends the physical and transitory nature of the appetites of the stomach, which include food and sexuality.

The second (B) unit of the chiasm (6:15) begins with a rhetorical question expecting an affirmative response from the audience of something they surely do and must have knowledge—"Do you not know that" (οὐκ οἴδατε ὅτι; see also 3:16; 5:6; 6:2, 3, 9).[22] The audience is to affirm that "your bodies are members of Christ" (6:15a). The chiasm has thus progressed from a focus on "the body" in general in the A unit to "your bodies," the individual bodies of the Corinthian community, in particular in the B unit. The shift from "Lord" in the A unit to "Christ" in the B unit corresponds to the shift from the salvific past ("God raised the Lord") and future ("and will also raise us") to the present salvific status of the audience—your bodies, which God will raise as he raised the Lord (6:14), "are" (ἐστιν) *even*

σῶμα mit dem Personalpronomen anzeigt (vgl. V 13–15 oder auch 12,27 u.ö.). . . . Der Mensch *hat* nicht einen Leib, sondern *ist* Leib, von dem er sich nicht als etwas ihm Fremdes distanzieren kann."

21. Kirchhoff, *Sünde*, 122 n. 55: "Dadurch, daß Paulus die Auferweckung des Herrn mit ἐγείρω und die der Christen mit ἐξεγείρω ausdrückt, wird die Parallelität der Aussagen gestört, so daß die Aufmerksamkeit auf die letzte Aussage, die Auferweckung der Christen gezogen wird." On the role of God in 6:13–14, Richardson (*Paul's Language*, 215) states: "In the first half of the statement the relationship between the stomach and food is followed by an emphatic ὁ δὲ θεός and a future verb καταργήσει. In the first half of the second statement the relationship between the body and the Lord is mentioned, and followed again by an emphatic ὁ δὲ θεός (this time with two verbs ἤγειρεν and ἐξεγερεῖ). The two verses, therefore, comprise a striking example of the warranting function of θεός-language, and of the subordination of 'the Lord' to God."

22. Kirchhoff, *Sünde*, 111–12: "Die rhetorische Frage dient dazu, Tatsachen—wie Paulus sie sieht—mit besonderem Nachdruck auszusprechen. Mit der Anrede οὐκ οἴδατε chiffriert Paulus das getadelte Verhalten als Mangel an Belehrung, die er dann im folgenden bietet. Durch sie nimmt Paulus Kontakt mit Adressaten und Adressatinnen auf, erhöht die Aufmerksamkeit und die Spannung." According to Thiselton (*Corinthians*, 316), this interrogative formula, which occurs ten times in 1 Corinthians, "indicates both Paul's intensity of feeling (surely you know *this!*) and his belief that the principle at issue is axiomatic for the Christian and should not have escaped attention as a cardinal element in the community's thinking."

now members of Christ.²³ That the individual bodies of the audience are metaphorical "members" or "limbs and organs" (μέλη) of Christ implies that they are integrally and intimately joined to the communal, metaphorical "body" of Christ.²⁴

Paul then asks whether "I"—Paul as representative of every individual in the audience for whom "all things are permitted" (6:12)—shall forcibly "take away" the "members of Christ," that is, the individual bodies of the audience which are part of the communal body of Christ, and make them "members" of the body of a prostitute (6:15b).²⁵ The chiasm has thus progressed from a focus on "sexual immorality" (πορνεία) in general, which is not for "the body" in general in the A unit, to a "prostitute" (πόρνη) in particular, who should not be joined with the "members"—the bodies—of Paul's particular audience in the B unit. Paul's provocative rhetorical question thus presents his audience with an appalling contradiction. His own immediate and extremely emphatic answer, "May it never happen!" (μὴ γένοιτο, 6:15c), evokes the audience not only to agree with him that this is

---

23. Kirchhoff, *Sünde*, 113: "τὰ σώματα ὑμῶν sind die Adressaten, das hat Paulus durch die Anknüpfung an σῶμα durch ἡμᾶς in V. 14 gesagt." Collins, *First Corinthians*, 247: "The shift in christological titles, 'Christ' rather than 'Lord,' indicates a movement of Paul's thought away from the eschatological destiny of Christians to the present and their corporate existence in Christ."

24. According to Fee (*Corinthians*, 258 n. 40), "members" refers "specifically to the 'limbs' and 'organs' of the body. Once 'body' came to be used metaphorically, this word naturally followed." He goes on to state: "The word 'members' is a term for an integral part of the 'body' of Christ" (258); see also Kirchhoff, *Sünde*, 113. Thiselton (*Corinthians*, 465) translates "members" here as "limbs and organs" with the explanation: "For the double context of public action in the world and sexual intimacy belongs integrally to Paul's logic." Contra Gosnell L. O. R. Yorke, *The Church as the Body of Christ in the Pauline Corpus: A Re-examination* (Lanham, Md.: University Press of America, 1991), 33–34; Wolff, *Erste Brief*, 127; Lindemann, *Erste Korintherbrief*, 148; and others who maintain no implication to the communal "body" of Christ in the statement that "your bodies are members of Christ," see E. Earle Ellis, "Soma in First Corinthians," *Int* 44 (1990): 132–44; Schrage, *Erste Brief*, 2.25: "Sind die σώματα der Christen die μέλη Χριστοῦ, dann sind die Christen gerade mit ihren Leibern eingegliedert in den Heils- und Herrschaftsbereich Christi und dem Herrn zugehörig, auch wenn nicht ausdrücklich vom 'Leibe Christi' gesprochen ... wird. Μέλη Χριστοῦ kann nur von σῶμα Χριστοῦ her verstanden werden" (2.25 n. 316). As Barrett (*Corinthians*, 292) explains: "The genitive (Χριστοῦ) is not of identity but of possession and authority; not, the body which is Christ, of which Christ consists, but, the body that belongs to Christ, and over which he rules." See also David J. Williams, *Paul's Metaphors: Their Context and Character* (Peabody, Mass.: Hendrickson, 1999), 89–90; Sang-Won (Aaron) Son, *Corporate Elements in Pauline Anthropology: A Study of Selected Terms, Idioms, and Concepts in the Light of Paul's Usage and Background* (AnBib 148; Rome: Biblical Institute, 2001), 88.

25. Kirchhoff, *Sünde*, 114: "Denn es ist die Handlung dessen, der mit einer πόρνη verkehrt (ποιήσω), die im Mittelpunkt der Inklusion τὰ μέλη τοῦ Χριστοῦ–πόρνης μέλη steht, die Paulus durch die ungewöhnliche Wortstellung (πόρνης μέλη statt μέλη πόρνης) gebildet hat."

a repulsive contradiction but to refrain from being involved in such unthinkably contradictory behavior.²⁶

Repeating the rhetorical interrogative formula "Do you not know that" (οὐκ οἴδατε ὅτι), Paul begins the C unit of the chiasm (6:16a) by provoking his audience to acknowledge that whoever "is united" (κολλώμενος), not only through sexual intercourse but by close association, with the prostitute is "one body" (ἓν σῶμά).²⁷ The chiasm has thus progressed from a plural focus on the individual "bodies" of the audience becoming members of any particular prostitute ("a" prostitute—πόρνης) in the B unit to a singular focus on the individual who is united to a definite prostitute ("the" prostitute—τῇ πόρνῃ) in the C unit. That any individual member of the Corinthian audience who unites himself with the prostitute "is" (ἐστιν) "one body" with her (6:16a) implicitly contradicts the present salvific status of the entire community whose "bodies" now "are" (ἐστιν) members (of the body) of Christ (6:15a).²⁸

The quotation of Gen 2:24c in 6:16b, "For, it says, 'The two will become one flesh,' " functions as the central and pivotal D unit of the entire chiasm. In its original OT context the quote refers to "the two"—the man who "will be united" (προσκολληθήσεται) to his wife (Gen 2:24b)—so that these "two" will become "one flesh" (σάρκα μίαν), one single physical and bodily entity, in the marriage union. Paul thus shocks his audience into the realization that just as the man who is united to his wife becomes "one

---

26. Kirchhoff, *Sünde*, 113: "Da Paulus in diesem Vers den Sexualverkehr eines Christen mit einer πόρνη interpretiert, übertragen die Adressaten mit der Zustimmung zu seiner Antwort die Anstößigkeit der Vorstellung, die Paulus provoziert, auf ihr eigenes Handeln und bewerten es mit derselben Eindeutigkeit und Schärfe negativ, wie sie die Frage verneinen." Collins, *First Corinthians*, 247: "The use of 'never' (μὴ γένοιτο), without its being part of a longer sentence, is a feature of Paul's rhetorical style (see Rom 3:4, 6, 31; 6:2, 15; 7:7, 13; 9:14; 11:1, 11; Gal 2:17; 3:21; 6:14)." On the use of this same rhetorical formula in Epictetus, see Abraham J. Malherbe, "ΜΗ ΓΕΝΟΙΤΟ in the Diatribe and Paul," *HTR* 73 (1980): 231–40.

27. Thiselton, *Corinthians*, 466: "Some discussion has taken place about the appropriate translation of κολλώμενος, the present participle middle of κολλάω, *to join, to bond, to glue, to bind indissolubly*, for which we propose *the person who is united in intimacy*." A sexual connotation is wrongly denied by J. I. Miller, "A Fresh Look at I Corinthians 6.16f," *NTS* 27 (1980): 125–27. A translation of "the one who sells himself into bondage (i.e., obligates himself)," justified, unconvincingly in our opinion, by appeal to an economic subordination metaphor, is suggested by Stanley E. Porter, "How Should κολλώμενος in 1 Cor 6,16.17 Be Translated?" *ETL* 67 (1991): 105–6. "Sticking" is the translation employed by J. Duncan M. Derrett, "Right and Wrong Sticking (1 Cor 6,18)?" *EstBib* 55 (1997): 89–106. For a discussion and critique of these proposals, see Thiselton, *Corinthians*, 466–67; Garland, *1 Corinthians*, 241.

28. Kirchhoff, *Sünde*, 114: "Denn V. 16f. drücken wie V. 15 die Beziehung zu Χριστός bzw. zu κύριος und zur πόρνη mit Wörtern aus, die zur Sinnlinie Leib gehören."

flesh"—with rhetorical emphasis on the "one" (μίαν) as the final word of the scriptural quotation—and thus "one body" with her, so the one who is united to the prostitute becomes "one body" with her (6:16a, C unit).[29] This contradicts the unity established between the bodies of the audience as members (of the body) of Christ (6:15a, B unit) and the unity expressed in the assertion that "the body is for the Lord and the Lord for the body" (6:13c, A unit).[30]

With its scriptural principle of marital unity the central D unit of the chiasm (6:16b) thus provides the basis for the various unities expressed in each of the preceding units of the chiasm. That "the two will become one flesh" explains to the audience why (γάρ—"for") the two—the prostitute and the one united with her—are one body in the C unit (6:16a). The scriptural principle's marital unity of two into one also explains how the two—the bodies of the audience and Christ—are one entity as members (of the one body) of Christ in the B unit (6:15a). And it explains how the two—the body and the Lord—are united in a mutual relationship as expressed by the assertion that "the body is for the Lord and the Lord for the body" in the A unit (6:13c). Furthermore, the scriptural quotation in the central D unit of the chiasm implies that the union between the members of the audience and Christ/the Lord is analogous to the marital union.[31]

---

29. Martin, *Corinthian Body*, 177: "Not only marriage, according to Paul's view, but any sexual intercourse effects a blending of the man's and woman's body into one body." Bruce N. Fisk, "ΠΟΡΝΕΥΕΙΝ as Body Violation: The Unique Nature of Sexual Sin in 1 Corinthians 6.18," *NTS* 42 (1996): 556: "For Paul, sexual union, whether within the marriage covenant or not, points beyond itself to a deeper union of profoundest moral significance."

30. Fee, *Corinthians*, 259: "To have sexual intercourse with a prostitute involves an illicit sexual joining of one's body to that of another (literally). It is not the sexual union itself that is incompatible with union with Christ; it is such a union *with a prostitute*."

31. Collins, *First Corinthians*, 247: "The biblical citation not only serves as an argument against sexual relations with a prostitute; it may also allude to the idea that the believer is united with Christ in a nuptial relationship." Kirchhoff, *Sünde*, 116: "Auffällig ist, daß Paulus in V. 15-17 anders als in V. 13f. nicht mehr von πορνεία spricht, sondern von einer πόρνη. Dieser Wechsel im Wortgebrauch ist dadurch veranlaßt, daß Paulus in V. 15 von Leib Christi spricht. Die Rede von der πόρνη ermöglicht es zum einen, den Kontrast zwischen der Zugehörigkeit zu Christus und der Ausführung der verbotenen sexuellen Handlung mit der Leibterminologie auszudrücken und zum anderen, die Beziehung zu Christus mit der Terminologie, die traditionell für die eheliche Beziehung gebraucht wird, zu interpretieren." On the marital union as a metaphor for the church's union with Christ in 1 Cor 6:12-20, see Rosner, *Paul*, 130-37; Giuseppe Baldanza, "L'uso della metafora sponsale in 1 Cor 6,12-20: Riflessi sull'ecclesiologia," *RivB* 46 (1998): 317-40; A. Merz, "Why Did the Pure Bride of Christ (2 Cor. 11.2) Become a Wedded Wife (Eph. 5.22-33)? Theses about the Intertextual Transformation of an Ecclesiological Metaphor," *JSNT* 79 (2000): 131-47.

Relation to the Subsequent Context in 1 Corinthians 6:17–20

As indicated by the introductory adversative particle δέ, the C´ unit of the chiasm (6:17), "But whoever is united to the Lord is one spirit," contrasts the C unit. Whereas the one "united" (κολλώμενος) with the prostitute is "one body" (ἓν σῶμά) in the C unit (6:16a), the one "united" (κολλώμενος) with the Lord is "one spirit" (ἓν πνεῦμά) in the C´ unit. Whereas the audience was shocked into the realization that any one of them associating with a prostitute forms "one body" with her in the C unit, the audience is now further surprised to hear that the union of any one of them with the Lord means forming not only, as expected by the parallelism, "one body" with him, but also, beyond that, "one spirit" with him.[32]

Here is where the central or pivotal function of the scriptural quote in the D unit of the chiasm becomes evident. That "the two will become one flesh" provides the scriptural basis in the D unit for the assertion that the two—the prostitute and the one united with her—forms "one body," as in the marital union, in the C unit. But the quote in the D unit also provides the scriptural basis for the assertion that the two—the Lord and the one united with him—forms not only "one body" in analogy to the marital union's "one flesh" but also "one spirit." The scriptural quote in the D unit of the chiasm thus "pivots" the audience's focus from the bodily unity with the prostitute in the C unit to the contrastive bodily and spiritual unity with the Lord in the C´ unit. This causes the audience to realize that the bodily union of any of them with the prostitute contradicts and is incompatible with both the bodily and spiritual union of any of them with the Lord.[33]

The "one spirit" unity that any individual in the audience united with

---

32. Thiselton, *Corinthians*, 468: "Paul does not appeal to a superiority of the πμεῦμα over the σῶμα." Schrage, *Erste Brief*, 2.29: "Σῶμα und πνεῦμα sind keine Antithese, wie man in Korinth anzunehmen scheint. Gerade die Leiblichkeit ist vielmehr der Ort der Präsenz des πνεῦμα."

33. Collins, *First Corinthians*, 248: "The graphic realism of Paul's language is difficult for the modern reader to grasp. His clause contrasts union with the Lord and union with a whore, bodily existence and 'spiritual' existence. Paul typically contrasts 'flesh' (σάρξ) and 'spirit' (πνεῦμα). 'Flesh' describes humanity or the human in its weakness and proneness to sin; 'spirit' describes humanity or the human in its openness to God and its readiness for salvation. Paul's allusion to Gen 2:24 appears to have caused him to depart from his usual lexical usage. Since the Spirit is the power of the future eschaton and Lord is eschatological terminology one should understand by Paul's reference to union with the Lord a harbinger of ultimate salvation." Fee, *Corinthians*, 260: "Paul's point is that the physical union of a believer with a prostitute is not possible because the believer's body already belongs to the Lord, through whose resurrection one's body has become a 'member' of Christ by his Spirit." See also Kirchhoff, *Sünde*, 172–76; Son, *Corporate Elements*, 88.

the Lord forms with him in the C′ unit of the chiasm (6:17) includes but goes beyond the implication of the "one body" unity that the individual "bodies" of the audience form with him as members (of the one body) of Christ in the B unit (6:15a). That the one united with the Lord forms "one spirit" with him means that he is united not only bodily but spiritually with "the Lord who is for the body and the body for the Lord" (6:13c), "the Lord" who was raised from the dead by the God who will also raise "us"— the members of the audience united spiritually with the Lord—through his power, as expressed in the A unit of the chiasm (6:14). That the members of the audience are united to the Lord not only as "one body" but as "one spirit" thus reminds them that their bodies, which have been washed, sanctified, and justified "in the name of the Lord Jesus Christ and in the Spirit of our God" (6:11), are destined to be raised by the spiritual "power" (δυνάμεως), which implies "the Spirit," of God.[34]

The B′ unit of the chiasm (6:18) begins with an urgent command in the present plural imperative (thus, with an iterative nuance) directed to the audience as a corporate whole: "Flee [or "keep away from," Φεύγετε] sexual immorality!" (6:18a).[35] After a focus on the audience's bodies being united to an indefinite "prostitute" (πόρνης) in the B unit (6:15b) and a definite "the prostitute" (τῇ πόρνῃ) in the C unit (6:16a), the focus returns to avoiding "sexual immorality" (πορνείαν) in general, thus recalling from the A unit that "the body is not for sexual immorality (πορνείᾳ)" (6:13c).

The B′ unit continues as Paul begins his explanation of why the audience must flee sexual immorality: "Every [other] sin that a person commits is outside of the body" (6:18b)[36]—both the individual's body and the cor-

---

34. Gerhard Friedrich, "δύναμις," *EDNT* 1.358: "Spirit and power are connected with each other even more frequently than word and power (Isa 11:2; 1 Cor 2:4; 1 Thess 1:5). In parallel statements the two words are synonymous (cf. Luke 1:17; Acts 6:5,8; 10:38)." For a Pauline statement that makes more explicit what is implicit in 1 Cor 6:14, 17, see Rom 8:11: "If the Spirit of him who raised Jesus from the dead dwells in you, he who raised Christ from the dead will give life to your mortal bodies also through his Spirit dwelling within you."

35. Thiselton, *Corinthians*, 470: "The present imperative φεύγετε is best expressed in translation as *keep away from*." For possible extratextual allusions to Joseph's flight from Potiphar's wife in Gen 39 and to the *Testament of Reuben*, see Brian S. Rosner, "A Possible Quotation of *Test. Reuben* 5:5 in 1 Corinthians 6:18a," *JTS* 43 (1992): 123–27; idem, *Paul*, 137–40. But Paul does not seem to draw on these possible allusions nor expect his audience to recognize them for his rhetorical strategy.

36. For an implicit interpolation of "other" here, based on the Greek grammatical construction, see Fisk, "ΠΟΡΝΕΥΕΙΝ," 544. For the reasons not to take 6:18b as a Corinthian slogan, see Fisk, "ΠΟΡΝΕΥΕΙΝ," 540–58; Brendan Byrne, "Sinning against One's Own Body: Paul's Understanding of the Sexual Relationship in 1 Corinthians 6:18," *CBQ* 45 (1983): 608–16.

porate body of Christ, as confirmed by the parallel B unit of the chiasm in which it is implied that the individual "bodies" of the audience are members of the corporate or communal body of Christ (6:15a). That every (other) sin is "outside of the body" means that it does not defile the body's (either that of the individual or that of the corporate "body" of Christ) unitive capacity, the capacity of the body to form a union with another body, as indicated by the scriptural quote in the central D unit of the chiasm that "the two will become *one* flesh" (6:16b).

"But," as Paul continues, "the sexually immoral one sins against his own body" (6:18c)—both his own body as an individual and the communal body of Christ to which he belongs (6:15a). That any "sexually immoral one" (πορνεύων) in the audience, that is, one who unites himself to "the prostitute" (τῇ πόρνῃ) so that he forms "one body" with her (6:16a), sins against his own body means that he defiles his own individual body's "one spirit" unity with the Lord (6:17), who is "for the body and the body for the Lord" (6:13c), as reinforced by the scriptural quote in the central D unit of the chiasm that "the two will become *one* flesh" (6:16b).[37]

It also means that he defiles the communal unity of the body of Christ of which he is a member (6:15a) by uniting himself to form "one body" with "the prostitute" (6:16a), who is outside of and thus not part of the unity of the corporate body of Christ. The sin is thus both individual and communal. He sins against himself, his own individual body, and the communal "body" of Christ which is united in a "one spirit" unity (6:17) with each of the individual "bodies" that are members of (the one communal body of) Christ (6:15a). That the two—the "bodies" of the audience and Christ—form one communal body (6:15a) that is also "one spirit" (6:17) is confirmed by the analogy with the marital union, as enunciated in the scriptural quote in the central D unit of the chiasm that "the two will become *one* flesh" (6:16b).[38]

---

37. Byrne, "Sinning," 613: "The immoral person perverts precisely that faculty within himself that is meant to be the instrument of the most intimate bodily communication between persons. He sins against his unique power of bodily communication and in this sense sins in a particular way 'against his own body.' No other sin engages one's power of bodily personal communication in precisely so intimate a way. All other sins are in this respect by comparison 'outside' the body." Fisk, "ΠΟΡΝΕΥΕΙΝ," 556–57: "The body against which one sins sexually (18c) is the body that has been joined illicitly to another (16a). Sexual sin is uniquely body-defiling because it is inherently body-joining. Again, because Paul believes sexual immorality establishes a 'one body' union with the prostitute, he views that act as destructive self-violation.... Sexual sin, as a bodily act, establishes a relationship; it forges a bodily union. Inherent in this illicit bodily union is body defilement; to form 'one body' with the prostitute is to violate 'one's body.' " See also Collins, *First Corinthians*, 249.

38. Mitchell, *Paul*, 120: "This argument in 6:12–20, like the rest of chaps. 5 and 6, centers on relations between insiders and outsiders. The insiders are μέλη Χριστοῦ, but the pros-

With a third use within the chiasm in 6:13–20 of the rhetorical interrogative formula "Do you not know that" (οὐκ οἴδατε ὅτι; cf. 6:15a, 16a), Paul begins the final A′ unit of the chiasm (6:19) by prompting his audience to acknowledge that "your body is a temple of the Holy Spirit within you, which you have from God, and that you are not your own." The second-person plurals, "your (ὑμῶν) body" and "within you (ὑμῖν)," express a distributive sense—each of your individual bodies and within each of you—as well as a communal sense—"your" corporate "body" as a whole, that is, the body of Christ that their individual bodies belong to as members (6:15a). This double meaning of the singular "your body" (σῶμα ὑμῶν) here in 6:19 is confirmed by its contrast to the plural "your bodies" (τὰ σώματα ὑμῶν) in 6:15a, when Paul refers exclusively to their individual bodies as members of (the corporate body) of Christ.[39]

The audience's realization "that you are not your own" in the A′ unit (6:19), that is, that both your individual bodies and your communal body do not really belong to you, develops their realization in the preceding B′ unit about an individual member of the audience sinning against one's own body (6:18c). Any sexually immoral one in the audience, one who unites himself with the prostitute (6:16a), sins not just against "his own" individual and corporate body but against the individual and corporate body that belongs ultimately to God himself.

The audience's realization that their individual and communal body "is a temple of the Holy Spirit (πνεύματός)" in the A′ unit (6:19) deepens their realization in the preceding C′ unit (6:17) that each of them who is united to the Lord forms a "one spirit (πνεῦμα)" unity with him, as established by the analogy to the marital union expressed in the scriptural quote in the central D unit of the chiasm, "the two will become *one* flesh" (6:16b). Not only is each of them united to the Lord as "one spirit," but the Holy "Spirit" of God actually dwells within them presently, both individually and communally. In turn, this recalls and develops the audience's realization in 3:16:

---

titute clearly is not (6:15), and thus should not be mingled with. She is beyond the boundary and is indeed a threat to the health of the whole community. Sex with prostitutes, the sin of πορνεία, is to be avoided on the basis of the principle of communal identity and communal ethical responsibility (6:18–20)." And on p. 120 n. 338: "As the pun on τὸ ἴδιον σῶμα in 6:18, as both one's own body and the body which is the community, shows. Because the body of Christ imagery is a prevailing image of the letter, which is based upon prior instruction which Paul can count on the Corinthians to know (6:15), any time σῶμα is used by Paul in 1 Cor we cannot discount also a communal referent."

39. This double meaning of "your body," in which "body" has both a distributive and collective sense, is missed by Yorke, *Church*, 33–34. Lockwood (*1 Corinthians*, 212) also points out only the distributive sense of the singular noun "body."

"Do you not know that you are the temple of God, and that the Spirit of God dwells in you?"

"For you have been bought at a price," as the A′ unit continues (6:20a; cf. 7:23), explains why ("for," γάρ) the audience's individual and communal body is not their own but belongs ultimately to God.[40] This instills a sentiment in the audience of their indebtedness to the God who has saved and "bought" them in the Christ event and who will raise them as he raised the Lord (6:14), as it recalls 6:11: "But you were washed, but you were sanctified, but you were justified in the name of the Lord Jesus Christ and in the Spirit of our God."

Consequently, in bringing the chiasm in 6:13–20 to its climactic conclusion, Paul emphatically urges his audience to "glorify God in your body" (6:20b)—both their individual and their communal body. The chiasm thus begins in the A unit with two references to God (6:13b, 14) and concludes in the A′ unit with two references to God (6:19, 20b). But whereas God is the subject in the first three references, in the final, climactic reference God is the object of the audience's appreciation for what God has done for them. The audience may "glorify" God in their individual and communal "body" in fleeing from sexual immorality and not sinning against their "body" (B′ unit, 6:18) by associating with the prostitute to form "one body" with her (C unit, 6:16a), because this completely contradicts and is totally incompatible with the "one spirit" unity that each of them, in whom the Holy Spirit of God dwells (3:16; 6:19), has with the Lord (C′ unit, 6:17), as confirmed by the scriptural quote concerning the marital union in the central D unit of the chiasm, "the two will become *one* flesh" (6:16b).[41]

The chiasm in 6:13–20, then, focuses its audience's attention on their individual and communal "body." It brings them first to the realization in the A unit (6:13–14) that their "body is for the Lord and the Lord for the body," which "body" God will raise as he raised the Lord. The audience is then appalled in the B unit (6:15) by the thought of making their "bodies," which are members of (the body of) Christ, members of a prostitute. In the

---

40. Fee, *Corinthians*, 264–65: "[T]he imagery here is that of slavery; the verb 'bought' with its accompanying genitive of quantity, 'at a price,' places it squarely in the slave market." On the slavery metaphor here, see also Thiselton, *Corinthians*, 475–79. For a possible allusion to Hos 3:1–3 here, see George L. Klein, "Hos 3:1–3—Background to 1 Cor 6:19b-20," *CTR* 3 (1989): 373–75.

41. Collins, *First Corinthians*, 249–50: "Far from being irrelevant to ultimate salvation, the body is the means whereby God is glorified. Throughout the letter Paul demonstrates his adamant opposition to any anthropology that separates spirit from body. His is a holistic anthropology in which body and spirit constitute one embodied existence that for the Christian has been incorporated into the one body of Christ."

C unit (6:16a) they are then shocked into the realization that their association with the prostitute forms "one body" with her, as confirmed by the scriptural quote in the central D unit that "the two will become *one* flesh" (6:16b).

This central and pivotal D unit then also provides, by analogy to the marital union, the basis for pivoting the audience's attention in the C′ unit (6:17) to the "one spirit" unity that each of them has with the Lord as a contradiction to the "one body" unity with the prostitute.[42] In the B′ unit (6:18) the audience then realizes that this "one body" unity with the prostitute sins against their own individual and communal "body." Consequently, in the climactic A′ unit (6:19–20) the audience, brought to the realization that their individual and communal "body" is actually not their own but a temple of the Holy Spirit, are to glorify God in both their individual and communal "body" by staying away from sexual immorality. In doing so they will avoid being dominated by anything that is not beneficial (6:12) to their "body."[43]

Summary on 1 Corinthians 6:16b

1. Although not explicitly introduced as such, 1 Cor 6:16b is a direct quotation of LXX Gen 2:24c, which relies upon the implied audience's knowledge of both the quoted words and their immediate context in Genesis as a reference to the fundamental unity established between a man and his wife by the institution of marriage as created by God.

2. The scriptural quotation of Gen 2:24c in 1 Cor 6:16b "speaks" to Paul's implied Corinthian audience with a fundamental and divine authority that requires their agreement that the two persons united by the bond of marriage actually become a single physical entity.

---

42. Krichhoff, *Sünde*, 120: "Mit Gen 2,24b begründet er [Paulus] eine Parallelität zwischen der Relation eines Mannes zur πόρνη und zum κύριος, die er εἷς εἶναι nennt. Diese Entsprechung bedeutet, daß es sich um alternative Relationen handelt."

43. With reference to 6:12–20, Mitchell (*Paul*, 234) concludes: "With a nice *double entendre* Paul exhorts the Corinthians to cleave to the Lord (and thus *his* body, the church), instead of cleaving (sexually) with prostitutes. Because the Christian belongs not to her or himself (6:19), but rather to the Lord and thus to his body, the church, the claim that 'one can do anything' cannot be the sole standard of conduct. In this short passage Paul draws on still another image of the church, the building image, which was prepared for already in chap. 3. Here its application is simultaneously individualistic and corporate ('your body is the temple of the holy spirit in you'). Not individual advantage but God's glory should be the measuring-rod for Christian decision-making."

3. The antecedent context (6:13–16a) of the scriptural quote (6:16b) within the chiasm in 6:13–20 first brings its audience to the realization in the A unit (6:13–14) that their "body is for the Lord and the Lord for the body," which "body" God will raise as he raised the Lord. The audience is then appalled in the B unit (6:15) by the thought of making their "bodies," which are members of (the body of) Christ, members of a prostitute. In the C unit (6:16a) they are then shocked into the realization that their association with the prostitute forms "one body" with her, as confirmed by the scriptural quote in the central D unit that "the two will become *one* flesh" (6:16b).

4. With regard to the subsequent context (6:17–20) of the scriptural quote (6:16b), as the central and pivotal D unit of the chiasm, it provides, by analogy to the marital union, the basis for pivoting the audience's attention in the C′ unit (6:17) to the "one spirit" unity that each of them has with the Lord as a contradiction to the "one body" unity with the prostitute. In the B′ unit (6:18) the audience then realizes that this "one body" unity with the prostitute sins against their own individual and communal "body." Consequently, in the climactic A′ unit (6:19–20) the audience, brought to the realization that their individual and communal "body" is actually not their own but a temple of the Holy Spirit, are to glorify God in both their individual and communal "body" by staying away from sexual immorality. In doing so they will avoid being dominated by anything that is not beneficial (6:12) to their "body."

CHAPTER 9

1 Corinthians 9:9–10

You shall not muzzle a threshing ox
In hope ought the one plowing to plow
and the one threshing in hope of receiving a share.

Old Testament Background

Introduced by "for in the law of Moses it is written," the command that "you shall not muzzle a threshing ox" in 1 Cor 9:9b quotes Deut 25:4. The quotation in 1 Cor 9:9b substitutes the verb κημώσεις for the verb φιμώσεις that appears in LXX Deut 25:4. Both of these verbs mean "muzzle," but φιμοῦν can also be used more generally to mean "silence."[1] Κημοῦν does not occur in the LXX. The corresponding verb in MT Deut 25:4 is חָסַם, meaning "muzzle, stop up":

MT Deut 25:4: לֹא־תַחְסֹם שׁוֹר בְּדִישׁוֹ
LXX Deut 25:4: οὐ φιμώσεις βοῦν ἀλοῶντα
1 Cor 9:9b: οὐ κημώσεις βοῦν ἀλοῶντα

After an intervening double question, "Is it for oxen that God is concerned? Or surely for our sake that he speaks?" (1 Cor 9:9c–10a), the emphatic affirmation, "For our sake indeed it was written that" (9:10b), introduces a closely related second scriptural quotation in 9:10c: "In hope ought the one plowing to plow and the one threshing in hope of receiving

---

1. Stanley, *Paul*, 196: "Whether the substitution originated with Paul (whether intentionally or by memory error) or with an editor or copyist before or after him is impossible to say at this point." Koch, *Schrift*, 142 n. 20: "Κημοῦν stellt also für den in Dtn 25,4 gemeinten Vorgang die präzisere Ausdrucksweise dar, doch ermöglicht dies keine Entscheidung über die Herkunft der Änderung." First Timothy 5:18 also quotes Deut 25:4, altering the word order but employing the same verb as in the LXX: "A threshing ox you shall not muzzle (βοῦν ἀλοῶντα οὐ φιμώσεις)." See also Garland, *1 Corinthians*, 419–20.

a share." These two scriptural quotes in 9:9–10 are joined together by means of the Jewish exegetical technique that later came to be known as *gezera shava*, according to which scriptural texts can be united to one another for mutual interpretation or explication by a word or words they have in common. The common word that joins the two quotes in 9:9–10 is "threshing"—ἀλοῶντα (present active accusative masculine singular participle) in 9:9b and ἀλοῶν (present active nominative masculine singular participle) in 9:10c.[2]

It is disputed whether "For our sake indeed it was written that" (9:10b) actually introduces a second quotation or merely refers back to the previous quotation of Deut 25:4 in 9:9b, since what follows in 9:10c does not, as it stands, correspond to any one particular OT scriptural text. But in light of the *gezera shava* here, which is based on the unity of all of the scriptures, "it was written" in 9:10b can be considered to refer both back to the quotation of Deut 25:4 and forward to the quotation to which it is connected by the word "threshing" in 9:10c.[3] In other words, the second quotation is a scriptural extension of the first that further explicates or elaborates upon it.[4] By the *gezera shava*, then, these two separate quotes have been linked to form one compound scriptural unity regarding "threshing." They can be considered as no longer two but as one scriptural quotation.[5]

Besides being introduced by "it was written that" (ἐγράφη ὅτι), the

---

2. On the exegetical device of *gezera shava*, see above on 1 Cor 3:19b–20 in ch. 6. On the use of the *gezera shava* in 1 Cor 9:9–10 to strengthen what Paul wants to express, Plag ("Paulus," 139) states: "Die Bemühung um eine *Gezera schawa* lässt aber erkennen, dass Paulus es für wichtig gehalten hat, seine Aussage auf diese Weise noch zu verstärken."

3. Stockhausen, *Moses' Veil*, 26–27: "The Jewish scriptures were, already in the first century and long before, regarded as a unity as the word of God for Israel and its heirs. . . . The unity of the word of God as preserved in the books of Moses and the prophets, in content and so also in verbal expression, based on their divine authorship, is the necessary presupposition of the *gezera shava* as an exegetical technique."

4. Thus, in this case, the ὅτι can be considered both *recitativum*, as it introduces the scriptural quote, and *explicativum*, as the quote it introduces further explains the previous quote of Deut 25:4 in 1 Cor 9:9b. Cf. Smit, *About the Idol Offerings*, 105–6; Schrage, *Erste Brief*, 2.302.

5. That the second quotation is a scriptural extension of the first is also indicated by the use of the different tenses of the verb "write" (γράφω). The perfect tense, "it is written" (γέγραπται), that is, "it has been and still is written," is used to introduce the primary quote of Deut 25:4 from the law of Moses in 9:9, while the aorist tense, "it was written" (ἐγράφη), is used to extend the primary quote with a secondary quote of unspecified origin in 9:10. Fee's (*Corinthians*, 409 n. 68) objection against a scriptural quote in 9:10, "Nowhere else does Paul use the aorist passive as an introductory formula to a quotation," fails to recognize the *gezera shava* and that the aorist is merely extending the initial and primary scriptural quotation introduced, as normally in Paul, with the perfect. See also Wolf, *Erste Brief*, 194; Schrage, *Erste Brief*, 2.302; Smit, *About the Idol Offerings*, 105.

poetic form and vocabulary of 9:10c indicate that Paul expects his implied audience to understand it as a scriptural quotation. It has the ring of a proverbial saying expressed in a progressive chiastic parallelism with ellipsis and alliterative words:

(a) ὀφείλει	ought
(b) ἐπ' ἐλπίδι	in hope
(c) ὁ ἀροτριῶν ἀροτριᾶν	the one plowing to plow
(c') καὶ (ὀφείλει) ὁ ἀλοῶν (ἀλοᾶν)	and the one threshing (ought to thresh)
(b') ἐπ' ἐλπίδι	in hope
(a') τοῦ μετέχειν	of receiving a share

There is a parallel in the central "c" units of the chiasm between "the one plowing" (ὁ ἀροτριῶν) and "the one threshing" (ὁ ἀλοῶν). All of the words in the "c" units are joined alliteratively by the "a," "o," and "n" sounds. The ellipsis of "ought" (ὀφείλει) and "to thresh" (ἀλοᾶν) in the c' unit sharpens its focus on "threshing" (ἀλοῶν) as the key catchword with "threshing" (ἀλοῶντα) in the quote of Deut 25:4 in 1 Cor 9:9b to form the *gezera shava* with the scriptural quote in 9:10c. There is a parallel in the "b" units between the identical phrases "in hope" (ἐπ' ἐλπίδι). The overall parallelism progresses from the expression in the first half that the one plowing ought to plow in hope to the expression in the second half of the object of that hope both for the one plowing and the one threshing, namely, "receiving a share" (μετέχειν), as indicated in the climactic a' unit.[6]

The non-Pauline character of the agricultural verbs in the central "c" units of the chiasm further confirms 9:10c as a scriptural quotation. The verb "plow" (ἀροτριάω) occurs nowhere else in the Pauline corpus. The verb "thresh" (ἀλοάω) occurs elsewhere in the Pauline corpus only in quotations of Deut 25:4 (1 Cor 9:9; 1 Tim 5:18). Furthermore, in applying the quotation in 9:10c to his own situation in 9:11 Paul prefers the closely related

---

6. On the dynamics of parallelism in biblical poetry, see Alter, *Biblical Poetry*, 3–26. Smit (*About the Idol Offerings*, 105), however, denies a poetic character to 9:10c despite the evidence demonstrated above: "To me it seems exaggerated to attribute a poetic character to this verse." Stanley (*Paul*, 196–97) affirms both the poetic and scriptural character of the quote in 9:10: "Though its citation character is disputed by some, it is difficult to see how an early reader could have taken 1 Cor 9.10b as anything but an intentional quotation. . . . Its poetic structure and content likewise show it to be an independent, pre-formed unit of tradition." See also Koch, *Schrift*, 41; Schrage, *Erste Brief*, 302.

verbs for "sow" (σπείρω; see also 1 Cor 15:36–37, 42–44; 2 Cor 9:6, 10; Gal 6:7–8) and "harvest" (θερίζω; see also 2 Cor 9:6; Gal 6:7–9).[7]

If 9:10c is indeed a scriptural quotation, which OT text is Paul quoting here? As is the case with many of the scriptural quotes in 1 Corinthians, Paul is not quoting any one particular OT text. Rather, he is depending upon his implied audience's recall of several OT texts that resemble the distinctive vocabulary and proverb-like expression of Paul's version of the scriptural quotation in 9:10c. The distinctive vocabulary concerns double occurrences of the verbs "plow" and "thresh." And the proverbial expression is that those who plow and/or thresh always do so with a view to an expected final outcome or product in the harvest. The main OT texts that the quote in 9:10c most resembles, then, are Isa 28:24, 28; 45:9; and Sir 6:19.[8]

The distinctive double occurrence in the first half of the scriptural quote in 1 Cor 9:10c of the verb "plow," in which the present active infinitive immediately follows the present active nominative masculine singular participle—"in hope ought the one plowing to plow (ὁ ἀροτριῶν ἀροτριᾶν)"—recalls for the implied audience this identical occurrence in LXX Isa 28:24a: "Not all the day is the one plowing to plow (ὁ ἀροτριῶν ἀροτριᾶν), is he?" And the proverb-like expressions in both of these texts are similar. In 1 Cor 9:10c, the one plowing ought to plow in hope of receiving a share of the harvest to eat—one plows in view of the final outcome or product. Similarly, in LXX Isa 28:24a one does not plow all the day, but does other things beforehand, like preparing to sow such seeds as black cumin and cumin (28:24b–25), in view of the final outcome or product in terms of the harvesting and eating of it—"the black cumin is threshed with a rod and the cumin will be eaten with bread" (28:27–28a).

In LXX Isa 45:9b, this proverb-like expression with the distinctive double occurrence of the verb "plow" is found again but with a slight variation in the verbal form from that found in LXX Isa 28:24a and 1 Cor 9:10c. The present active infinitive immediately follows the future indicative active third-person singular—"it is not that the one plowing will plow (ἀροτριῶν ἀροτριάσει) the earth all day, is it?"[9] In this case the proverbial saying is inserted within a metaphorical expression of the creator God as the potter who fashions (plows) the clay of the earth into a final product, his creation. The "one plowing," that is, God as the potter, does not plow (mold) the

---

7. On the non-Pauline character of the verbs "plow" and "thresh" in 9:10c as indicative of a scriptural quote, see Stanley, *Paul*, 197 n. 52; Collins, *First Corinthians*, 340.

8. On the quote in 9:10c, Lindemann (*Erste Korintherbrief*, 205) states: "Bei diesem Zitat handelte es sich dann um einen offenbar aus mehreren AT-Texten zusammengefügten, sorgfältig stilisierten Weisheitssatz."

9. This question is not found in MT Isa 45:9.

earth (clay) all day, but finishes the completed product in accord with his sovereign plan. The plowing, then, again is oriented toward or has in view the final product or outcome.[10]

The second half of the scriptural quote in 1 Cor 9:10c, "and the one threshing (ὁ ἀλοῶν) in hope of receiving a share," in which "to thresh" (ἀλοᾶν), although expected in view of the parallelism with "the one plowing to plow" (ὁ ἀροτριῶν ἀροτριᾶν) in the first half, is left out, recalls for the implied audience an OT text within the immediate context of Isa 28:24 that continues the agricultural theme, namely, Isa 28:28. MT Isa 28:28b reads: "for he [the one threshing] does not forever thresh it [the black cumin]," in which "thresh it" renders the emphatic double occurrence of the verb with the infinitive absolute—אָדוֹשׁ יְדוּשֶׁנּוּ. Like plowing, threshing does not last forever. There is an eventual outcome or product.

LXX Isa 28:28b differs from the MT considerably, reading, "for not forever will I [God] be angry with you." But at Isa 28:28b both the Symmachus and Theodotion translations correspond closely to the MT with its double occurrence of the verb "thresh," as they read: "but not forever will the one threshing thresh (ἀλοῶν ἀλοήσει) it [the black cumin]."[11] The "one threshing" (ὁ ἀλοῶν) with the ellipsis of "to thresh" (ἀλοᾶν) in 1 Cor 9:10c thus closely resonates with these early Greek translations of Isa 28:28b. It appears that the scriptural quotation in 1 Cor 9:10c contains a combination of Isa 28:24a and 28:28b with considerable linguistic modification, but with a very similar proverb-like expression regarding plowing and threshing in view of the final outcome.

The scriptural quote in 1 Cor 9:10c also resonates with the language and thought of Sir 6:19, in which the agricultural metaphor is employed for an invitation to pursue wisdom with a view to the final outcome or product: "Like the one plowing (ὁ ἀροτριῶν; cf. 1 Cor 9:10c) and the one sowing (ὁ σπείρων; cf. ἐσπείραμεν in 1 Cor 9:11) come to her (wisdom) and await her good crops. For in cultivating her you will toil a little while and soon you will eat of her products."

As for the emphatic "in hope" (ἐπ' ἐλπίδι) phrases in the "b" units of the chiasm in the scriptural quote in 1 Cor 9:10c, which are oriented toward a future receiving of a share of the harvest, there are a couple of Psalms that employ the same phrase with a similar orientation toward the

---

10. The distinctive double occurrence of "plow" also occurs in LXX Isa 7:25, "and every mountain will be certainly plowed (ἀροτριώμενον ἀροτριαθήσεται)," but not with the same verbal form nor in a similar proverbial expression.

11. Koch, *Schrift*, 42 n. 33; Stanley, *Paul*, 197 n. 53; Lindemann, *Erste Korintherbrief*, 205. On the Symmachus and Theodotion translations, see Jobes and Silva, *Septuagint*, 40–42; Fernández Marcos, *Septuagint*, 123–54; McLay, *Septuagint*, 127–30.

future. LXX Ps 4:9 reads: "I will both lie down and sleep in peace; for you alone, O Lord, made me dwell in hope (ἐπ' ἐλπίδι)." And LXX Ps 15:9 reads: "Therefore my heart was glad, and my tongue rejoiced; moreover my flesh will tent in hope (ἐπ' ἐλπίδι)."[12]

In sum, its introduction by "it was written that" in 1 Cor 9:10b, its poetic parallelism with alliteration and ellipsis, and its character as a proverb-like wisdom saying indicate that 9:10c is to be understood by Paul's implied audience as an additional scriptural quotation that extends and elaborates upon the quotation of Deut 25:4 in 9:9b, to which it is connected by the word "thresh" in accord with the *gezera shava* technique that links two scriptural texts for mutual interpretation by words they have in common. Although not a literal quotation of any one OT text, 9:10c most closely resembles a combination, with considerable reshaping, of Isa 28:24, 28 with affinities to Isa 45:9 and Sir 6:19.[13]

Literary-Rhetorical Analysis

Introduced by "for in the law of Moses it is written," the quotation of Deut 25:4 in 1 Cor 9:9b expresses with the authority of God's law (cf. 9:8), as mediated through Moses, a command with a second-person singular future indicative active verb that "you," that is, any given individual, "shall not muzzle" (οὐ κημώσεις), that is, prevent from eating by covering the mouth of any "ox" (βοῦν) that is engaged in the work of harvesting crops by "threshing" (ἀλοῶντα). The implication is that anyone who muzzles a threshing ox deprives it not only of nourishment needed for the work of threshing but also of the enjoyment of some of the fruits of the harvest for which it is laboring. According to God's law even an animal employed in threshing the crops of the harvest deserves to eat a share of the fruits of its threshing.[14]

After an initial intervening question expecting a negative answer from

---

12. Koch, *Schrift*, 42 n. 33. Translations are from Albert Pietersma, *A New English Translation of the Septuagint: The Psalms* (New York: Oxford University Press, 2000), 3, 11. With regard to the quote in 1 Cor 9:10c, Koch (*Schrift*, 42) concludes: "[U]nd angesichts der biblischen Sprache des Zitats ist es nicht verwunderlich, daß Paulus es als Schriftwort anführt."

13. With reference to the scriptural tradition behind this quotation, Stanley (*Paul*, 197) states: "Whether that tradition circulated in oral or written form is impossible to say at this point, as the wording of v. 10b is not appreciably close to any single passage in the Jewish Scriptures." But, especially in view of how well it fits his rhetorical strategy (as we will see below), Paul himself may have combined and reshaped Isa 28:24, 28 to create or discover a new scriptural text for connection to Deut 25:4 by means of the *gezera shava*.

14. In 1 Cor 9:8–10, Paul preserved both the literal meaning and theological significance of Deut 25:4, according to W. C. Kaiser, "The Current Crisis in Exegesis and the Apostolic Use

his audience, "Is it for oxen that God is concerned?" (9:9c), Paul quickly adds a second question expecting his audience's affirmative response, "Or surely for our [Barnabas and Paul's; cf. 9:6] sake that he speaks?" (9:10a).[15] Paul then emphatically reinforces his audience's anticipated affirmation by asserting, "For our sake indeed it was written that" (9:10b) to extend the divinely authoritative scriptural quotation of Deut 25:4 about oxen with a second scriptural quotation to which it is connected by the word "threshing" in 9:10c to anyone who both plows and threshes: "In hope ought the one plowing to plow and the one threshing in hope of receiving a share."[16]

The opening word of the scriptural quotation in 9:10c transforms what is written with the divine authority of the law of Moses in Deut 25:4 from a negative command, "You shall not muzzle," to a positive obligation, "ought" or "it ought to be" (ὀφείλει), the "a" unit of the chiasm.[17] Rather than this verb being immediately followed by its subject, the prepositional phrase "in hope" (ἐπ' ἐλπίδι), the "b" unit of the chiasm, is inserted instead by way of emphasis.[18] Then follows the participial subject (ὁ ἀροτριῶν) with infinitive (ἀροτριᾶν), the "c" unit of the chiasm, so that the first half of the quotation is rendered, "*In hope* ought the one plowing to plow." This broadens the quotation of Deut 25:4 by adding the prior work of plowing to that of threshing.[19] And by not repeating the word "ox," the second quo-

---

of Deuteronomy 25:4 in 1 Corinthians 9:8–10," *JETS* 21 (1978): 3–18. See also Williams, *Paul's Metaphors*, 33; Garland, *1 Corinthians*, 410.

15. For the suggestion that Paul's audience may have a Stoic conception of God's care for human beings, see Eduard Lohse, " 'Kümmert sich Gott etwa um die Ochsen?': Zu 1 Kor 9,9," *ZNW* 88 (1997): 314–15.

16. David Instone Brewer, "1 Corinthians 9.9–11: A Literal Interpretation of 'Do Not Muzzle the Ox,'" *NTS* 38 (1992): 564: "[T]he understanding that 'ox' in Scripture implied all labouring species was already well established by the time of Paul." But what Paul says in 9:9c–10b seems to indicate that he is not relying upon this understanding of ox in Deut 25:4 on the part of his audience. Indeed, one of the main reasons for the second quotation in 9:10c is to extend what is said about a threshing ox to any laboring species, which Paul then applies specifically to himself and Baranbas.

17. Smit, *About the Idol Offerings*, 106: "In his explanation Paul transposes the prohibition of Deut 25:4: 'You shall not' into a positive obligation: ὀφείλει, the best rendering of which is: 'It ought to be so.' This obligation originates with Moses, the lawgiver."

18. Robertson and Plummer, *Corinthians*, 184: "ἐπ' ἐλπίδι is emphatic by position." Fee, *Corinthians*, 408 n. 65: "This phrase is in the emphatic position in the first instance."

19. Smit, *About the Idol Offerings*, 106: "The introduction of the plower is a well-considered move. By adding the plower to the thresher Paul enlarges the scope of the prohibition quoted. This is a logical step: if the thresher, who cooperates in the final stage of grain production, is entitled to a share in the yield, then this also holds for the plower, who begins the same process of production. This step is the more obvious for, together with threshing, plowing is among the regular tasks of oxen."

tation allows for an expansion of the one plowing to include human beings. But this first half of the quotation arouses suspense for its audience—in hope of what ought the plower to plow?

Before resolving the suspense, the second half of the quotation begins by adding the participle "the one threshing" (ὁ ἀλοῶν), the "c´" unit of the chiasm, to "the one plowing." The ellipsis of an expected "ought" (ὀφείλει) to begin the second half enhances the chiastic arrangement by allowing the "c" (ὁ ἀροτριῶν ἀροτριᾶν) and "c´" (καὶ ὁ ἀλοῶν) units to be joined closely together in alliteration as the center of the chiasm. The ambiguity of both participles, "plowing" and "threshing," in the central units of the chiasm allows for their application beyond oxen to human laborers.[20] The ellipsis of an expected "to thresh" (ἀλοᾶν) after "the one threshing" not only singles out "threshing" as the connective participle with the quote of Deut 25:4, but also hastens and thus adds emphasis to the prepositional phrase "in hope" (ἐπὶ ἐλπίδι) as the "b´" unit of the chiasm, which, by repeating it, reinforces the identical phrase from the "b" unit of the chiasm.[21]

The second half of the quotation concludes with the climax of the chiasm, which resolves the suspense by stating the object of the hope for both the plower and the thresher—"*In hope* ought the one plowing to plow and the one threshing *in hope* of receiving a share" (9:10c). "Receiving a share" (τοῦ μετέχειν) of the harvested crops, the "a´" unit of the chiasm, thus corresponds to the "a" unit that began the chiasm, "ought" (ὀφείλει), by expressing the final outcome of the obligation. Since both those who plow and those who thresh do so in hope of eating a share of the harvest, there is an obligation in accord with God's law—an obligation Paul expects his implied audience to acknowledge through this combination of authoritative scriptural quotations in 9:9–10—that they indeed receive that share to which they are entitled and for which they labored in hope.[22]

---

20. Smit, *About the Idol Offerings*, 107: "These participles are deliberately ambiguous. For, by means of this ambiguity, an imperceptible transition is made from the plowing and the threshing ox to the plowing and the threshing laborer. The wording Paul uses is intended to give the impression that his explication is nothing more than a rewritten version of Deut. 25:4 and therefore has the same authority."

21. With regard to the phrase "in hope" in 9:10c, Fee (*Corinthians* 408 n. 65) notes that "it appears again in the second clause about the one who threshes. Thus it is the emphatic phrase in the sentence. 'In hope' the one plows; and 'in hope' the other threshes."

22. Smit, *About the Idol Offerings*, 106: "The plower is not the one on whom the duty rests, but the one to whom the obligation is due. 'The hope of getting a share,' forms the content of the obligation. So, according to the Law of Moses, the plower just as the thresher has a right to his share of the yield, be it at a later date." The point of the scriptural combination in 9:9–10 "is not simply that one is recompensed for one's work. Rather, one is also recompensed from one's work, in the sense that one receives a share of that which one does. One is not sim-

Relation to the Antecedent Context in 1 Corinthians 8:1–9:8

In 8:9, Paul refers to what some in his Corinthian audience consider to be their "right" or "freedom of choice"—"this right (ἐξουσία) of yours"—to eat meat sacrificed to idols because of their knowledge that the absolute oneness of God renders idols meaningless (8:1–6).[23] But not all among them have this knowledge. Some have been so accustomed even until now of "the idol" that they eat this meat as though it were actually being sacrificed to the god. Consequently, their "conscience" or "moral consciousness" (συνείδησις),[24] being weak, is "defiled"; that is, they are led into the sin of idolatry (8:7).[25]

---

ply rewarded with an external reward. There is instead an intrinsic connection between one's activity and one's recompense," according to Harry P. Nasuti, "The Woes of the Prophets and the Rights of the Apostle: The Internal Dynamics of 1 Corinthians 9," *CBQ* 50 (1988): 250.

23. Joop F. M. Smit, "1 Cor 8,1–6: A Rhetorical *Partitio*. A Contribution to the Coherence of 1 Cor 8,1–11,1," in *The Corinthian Correspondence* (ed. Reimund Bieringer; BETL 125; Louvain: Louvain University Press, 1996), 577–91. On the background and issue in general of eating idol meat in Corinth, see Wendell Lee Willis, *Idol Meat in Corinth: The Pauline Argument in 1 Corinthians 8 and 10* (SBLDS 68; Chico, Calif.: Scholars Press, 1985); Bruce N. Fisk, "Eating Meat Offered to Idols: Corinthian Behavior and Pauline Repsonse in 1 Corinthians 8–10," *TJ* 10 (1989): 49–70; Peter David Gooch, *Dangerous Food: 1 Corinthians 8–10 in Its Context* (Studies in Christianity and Judaism 5; Waterloo, Ontario: Wilfrid Laurier University Press, 1993); Justin J. Meggitt, "Meat Consumption and Social Conflict in Corinth," *JTS* 45 (1994): 137–41; Bruce W. Winter, *Seek the Welfare of the City: Christians as Benefactors and Citizens* (Grand Rapids: Eerdmans, 1994), 165–77; B. J. Oropeza, "Laying to Rest the Midrash: Paul's Message on Meat Sacrificed to Idols in Light of the Deuteronomistic Tradition," *Bib* 79 (1998): 57–68; Derek Newton, *Deity and Diet: The Dilemma of Sacrificial Food at Corinth* (JSNTSup 169; Sheffield: Sheffield Academic Press, 1998); Alex T. Cheung, *Idol Food in Corinth: Jewish Background and Pauline Legacy* (JSNTSup 176; Sheffield: Sheffield Academic Press, 1999); John Fotopoulos, *Food Offered to Idols in Roman Corinth: A Social-Rhetorical Reconsideration of 1 Corinthians 8:1–11:1* (WUNT 151; Tübingen: Mohr Siebeck, 2003).

24. Fee, *Corinthians*, 381: "[I]n the present case the word seems to be closer to its root meaning of 'consciousness' as to one's own actions (cf. the verb in 4:4), with a decided moral overtone to that consciousness." Gregory W. Dawes, "The Danger of Idolatry: First Corinthians 8:7–13," *CBQ* 58 (1996): 96: "We may conclude that the term συνείδησις can be understood in the same sense in both 1 Corinthians 8 and 1 Corinthians 10, namely, as the internal judge of what is right and what is wrong." Cheung, *Idol Food*, 132: "I propose that συνείδησις as used in 1 Corinthians 8–10 refers to one's moral consciousness or awareness with regard to the nature of the food." See also Ernesto Borghi, "La notion de conscience dans le Nouveau Testament: Une proposition de lecture," *Filología Neotestamentaria* 10 (1997): 85–98.

25. Dawes, "Danger," 98: "In particular, the behavior of those 'having knowledge' is leading the 'weak' into the mistaken judgment that they may take part in cultic meals in pagan temples. Because the 'weak' lack a clear conviction regarding the nonexistence of pagan gods, this action is for them an act of idolatry." Fee, *Corinthians*, 381: "In this way their moral consciousness is being 'defiled,' that is, their past associations with idols mean that a return to the wor-

Therefore, Paul cautions those who have such knowledge to be sure that this "right" of theirs to eat meat sacrificed to idols in no way becomes a stumbling block to the "weak" (8:9), that is, that they do not, by exercising their supposed "right," lead one who is "weak," a fellow "brother" for whom Christ died, into the sin of idolatry, by which he would be destroyed.[26] They would thereby sin themselves against Christ (8:10–12).[27] Rather, they are invited to imitate Paul's own personal conviction that he asserts as a paradigm for his audience: "Therefore, if food causes my brother to sin, I will never ever eat meat again, so that I may not cause my brother to sin" (8:13).[28] Paul considers the matter so serious that he would, as should they, give up the "right" or "freedom of choice" to eat not only "the meat sacrificed to idols" (τὰ εἰδωλόθυτα) but any "meat" (κρέα) at all so as not to lead a fellow Christian into sin.[29]

---

ship of the god by eating in his/her honor causes them to defile their new relationship with Christ."

26. Fotopoulos, *Food*, 218: "Scholars have generally agreed that Paul in v 9 is in principle agreement with the Strong's freedom to participate in sacrificial meals, but only warns that they should be mindful of the Weak. However, this position is not convincing, since ἐξουσία seems to be a catchword of the Strong, Paul having criticized the Strong's freedom (6:12) which they couple with their rhetorical abilities and knowledge (1 Cor. 2–4). Paul employs the word ἐξουσία ironically in order to show the negative consequences of its use by the Strong, warning them with the admonition βλέπετε."

27. This is what could happen theoretically, not necessarily what is actually happening, according to Karl-Gustav Sandelin, "Drawing the Line: Paul on Idol Food and Idolatry in 1 Cor 8:1–11:1," in *Neotestamentica et Philonica: Studies in Honor of Peder Borgen* (ed. David E. Aune et al.; NovTSup 106; Leiden: Brill, 2003), 119: "[W]hether it is necessary to postulate that Paul in 1 Cor 8:1–11:1 reacts against actual attendance by Corinthian Christians at banquets in temple precincts, should be answered in the negative." But, according to Fotopoulos, *Food*, 207: "Paul's argumentation loses all force if the Strong and Weak are merely hypothetical, since, then, no spiritual destruction is done to the Weak by the Strong's consumption of sacrificial food, thus leading the Weak into idolatry."

28. Smit, *About the Idol Offerings*, 90: "The pronoun 'I' in this verse is a rhetorical 'I' presenting a general rule in a lively manner." Newton, *Deity and Diet*, 309: "Paul's use of extreme language is indicated again by his use of a double negative οὐ μή, compounded by the phrase εἰς τὸν αἰῶνα, to show that he would never ever again, under any circumstances, eat in a temple if it were the cause of the stumbling of a weak brother." But Paul is even more extreme than this. He is saying that he would never ever again eat any kind of meat, not just the meat sacrificed to idols, in any place, not just in a temple.

29. Εἰδωλόθυτον refers to any food sacrificed to idols and not just to food sacrificed in pagan worship and eaten within a temple, according to E. Coye Still, "The Meaning and Uses of ΕΙΔΩΛΟΘΥΤΟΝ in First-Century Non-Pauline Literature and 1 Cor 8:1–11:1: Toward Resolution of the Debate," *TJ* 23 (2002): 225–34. According to David E. Garland, "The Dispute Over Food Sacrificed to Idols (1 Cor 8:1–11:1)," *PRSt* 30 (2003): 183–84: "He [Paul] conveys his disapproval of idol food by the very term he uses for it—εἰδωλόθυτον. Idol worshipers normally used ἱερόθυτον (10:28) to refer to something 'offered in sacrifice to a deity,' and the term

Paul's opening question in 9:1a, "Am I not free?" introduced by the adverb οὐκ, expects an affirmative answer from his audience. They are to admit that Paul is "free" (ἐλεύθερος) not to exercise his "right" or "freedom of choice" (ἐξουσία) to eat not only the meat sacrificed to idols but any meat, in order not to lead a "brother" into sin (8:13).[30] By speaking representatively in the first person, Paul is persuading those in his audience who know that idols are nothing to likewise exercise their freedom by abstaining from their "right" to eat meat sacrificed to idols in order not to lead another into the sin of idolatry and for the sake of the love that "builds up" (8:1).

But this opening question also introduces a series of questions that establish Paul's broader "freedom" as an apostle. With the questions "Am I not an apostle?" and "Have I not seen Jesus our Lord?" (9:1bc), Paul forces his audience to admit that he has a further freedom based on his authority as an authentic apostle. With the question "Are *you* [emphatic ὑμεῖς] not my work in the Lord?" (9:1d), the audience remembers that Paul has apostolic authority especially over them. Indeed, although Paul may not be an apostle for others, he certainly is for the Corinthians, since "you" (emphatic ὑμεῖς) are the "seal" or confirmation of "my" (emphatic μου) apostleship in the Lord (9:2), as, indeed, Paul has "fathered" them (cf. 4:14–15). That they are his "work" or "product" (ἔργον) connotes his apostolic labor on their behalf with the help of and for "the Lord."[31] It places them in debt to Paul for the apostolic service he has rendered them.[32]

εἰδωλόθυτον does not appear in papyri or literature before 1 Corinthians. It has a caustic, polemical edge since the word εἴδωλα connoted to both Jews and most Christians something detestable (Deut 29:17), opposed to the living God (1 Thess 1:9; 2 Cor 6:16), lifeless and 'dumb' (1 Cor 12:2), and demonic (Rev 9:20)." Thiselton (*Corinthians*, 657) translates the collective plural noun κρέα as "meat in any form." Collins, *First Corinthians*, 327: "Paul's abrupt introduction of his own person into the argument provides a focus against which the following digression (1 Corinthians 9) must be read." B. J. Oropeza, *Paul and Apostasy: Eschatology, Perseverance, and Falling Away in the Corinthian Congregation* (WUNT 115; Tübingen: Mohr Siebeck, 2000), 58: "The unity of Paul's thought in chapters 8 and 9, however, seems linked together by Paul when he uses himself as an example beginning in 8:13." See also Fotopoulos, *Food*, 222–23.

30. Paul Douglas Gardner, *The Gifts of God and the Authentication of a Christian: An Exegetical Study of 1 Corinthians 8–11:1* (Lanham, Md.: University Press of America, 1994), 69: "Paul was making a positive affirmation that stood against the appearances of *what he has just said*" (Gardner's emphasis).

31. Fee, *Corinthians*, 395 n. 19: "Even though they are Paul's workmanship, the ultimate responsibility lies with the Lord." Thiselton, *Corinthians*, 669: "*[I]n the Lord* counterbalances any suggestion that Paul regards this work (τὸ ἔργον μου) as his own personal 'achievement' apart from God's grace in Christ."

32. Collins, *First Corinthians*, 335: "Although Paul often uses words derived from the root εργ- ('work') to refer to his and his coworkers' apostolic labors, this is the sole instance

Paul's ("my," ἐμή) defense to those "examining" (ἀνακρίνουσίν; cf. 4:3–4) "me" (ἐμέ), that is, those questioning and comparing "my" (μου) apostleship (9:2) to that of Apollos and Cephas (cf. 1:12; 3:4–6, 22; 4:6) is this (9:3):[33] Surely it is not (μή) the case that "we," that is, Paul and his apostolic coworkers (such as Barnabas, cf. 9:6) do not (οὐκ) have the right to eat and drink (9:4)?[34] By leading his audience to admit that he, as their founding apostle, certainly has the "right" (ἐξουσίαν) to "eat," Paul establishes a connection with the alleged "right" (ἐξουσία) of some of them to "eat" (8:7, 8, 10, 13) meat sacrificed to idols (8:9).[35] Whereas some in the audience suppose that their "knowledge" (8:1, 7, 10, 11) may give them a right to eat idol food, Paul forces all in his audience to affirm that his apostolic authority over them definitely gives him the right to their material support—the right to "eat and drink."[36]

---

in which he refers to the product of his labor as an ἔργον, a work. The implication is that the Corinthian Christian community exists as the church of God because of Paul's apostolic labor among them."

33. Robertson and Plummer, *Corinthians*, 179: "The ἐμή and ἐμέ look back to σφραγίς μου τῆς ἀποστολῆς." That Paul is defending his apostleship here is denied by Wendell Lee Willis, "An Apostolic Apologia? The Form and Function of 1 Corinthians 9," *JSNT* 24 (1985): 33–48; Garland, "Dispute," 188–90; Fotopoulos, *Food*, 223. But, as Fee (*Corinthians*, 401) notes: "The implication in both 4:3–4 and here is that the Corinthians are in process of 'examining' or 'investigating' him; the evidence of this context makes it certain that the 'examination' is related to his apostolic authority." And Newton (*Deity and Diet*, 317) adds: "The form ἀνακρίνουσίν is, however, a dative plural masculine participle present active and does suggest that the criticism/scrutinizing of Paul's apostleship was indeed an ongoing reality in the present." See also Cheung, *Idol Food*, 142. As Collins (*First Corinthians*, 335) points out: "Paul's 'defense' is an ἀπολογία, a technical term used to describe a juridical defense. The language adopted by Paul suggests an adversarial situation but the evocation of this rhetorical situation would appear to be a stratagem on the part of Paul." Mitchell, *Paul*, 246: "Paul calls it 'defense' to justify rhetorically his use of himself as the example for imitation."

34. Thiselton, *Corinthians*, 678: "The use of the double negative μὴ οὐκ ἔχομεν intensifies the rhetorical force of the question." Fee, *Corinthians*, 402 n. 27: "This is intensely rhetorical." Lockwood, *1 Corinthians*, 295: "It has the force of a positive affirmation: we *do* have a right to eat and drink." On the use of "we" here, Fee (*Corinthians*, 402 n. 28) points out: "Probably it reflects the fact that Paul and his traveling companions all took this stance toward support. Thus he includes them with himself in this defense. Yet the context, and especially the interchange of 'we' and 'I' for the same content in vv. 12b and 15, indicates that he is primarily concerned with his own ministry."

35. Cheung, *Idol Food*, 141: "[I]t is clear that Paul still has the subject of idol food in mind. It is no accident that he begins the defense of his apostolic rights with reference to 'the right to food and drink' (9.4)." Collins, *First Corinthians*, 335: "Paul's reference to his own eating constitutes yet another link between his digressive apology and the context to which it relates."

36. With regard to a "right" to eat idol food, Cheung (*Idol Food*, 140) points out: "[T]his right simply does not exist for Paul! Such a 'right' cannot be supported by apostolic behavior—Peter and James certainly do not eat idol food. Nor can it be substantiated by the Law—Scripture clearly condemns eating idol food. Justice does not require it. No word from the Lord

With a second pointed rhetorical question employing double negatives expecting an affirmative response, Paul continues to provoke his audience to acknowledge his apostolic rights: Surely it is not (μή) the case that "we," Paul and his fellow apostles, do not (οὐκ) have the "right" to take along a Christian wife, as do also the rest of the apostles and the brothers of the Lord and Cephas? (9:5). Paul thus leads his audience to link his authoritative apostolic "right" (ἐξουσίαν) to be accompanied by a wife to the alleged "right" (ἐξουσία, 8:9) of some to "eat" idol food, as it implies the material support for such a wife to likewise "eat and drink" (9:4).[37]

Whereas the first two rhetorical questions with double negatives in 9:4–5 expect a positive answer, the third expects a negative response: "Or is it only myself and Barnabas who do not (οὐκ) have the right not (μή) to work?" (9:6).[38] The audience must concede that Paul, as their founding apostle, like all of the other apostles, has the authoritative "right" (ἐξουσίαν), in contrast to the alleged "right" (ἐξουσία, 8:9) of some to eat idol food, not to work with his own hands at a trade in order to eat, but to have his food and drink supplied by them.[39] That the audience is Paul's

---

permits it. Israel's cultus, with the implied incompatibility between the altar of Yahweh and that of the idols, demands not eating but abstention. To eat idol food is thus not even an option, let alone a right, for Paul." That the "knowers" among the Corinthians do have a genuine right to eat idol food but that they should not exercise it is argued by E. Coye Still, "Paul's Aims Regarding Εἰδωλόθυτα: A New Proposal for Interpreting 1 Corinthians 8:1–11:1," *NovT* 44 (2002): 333–43; Seyoon Kim, "*Imitatio Christi* (1 Corinthians 11:1): How Paul Imitates Jesus Christ in Dealing with Idol Food (1 Corinthians 8–10)," *BBR* 13 (2003): 210–17. But they fail to distinguish between the "knowledge" and the "right" of the "knowers." Paul grants and shares with the "knowers" the genuine knowledge that idols are meaningless (8:1–6). But Paul does not grant that this knowledge gives them an authentic "right," as indicated in 8:9 where he refers sarcastically to "*this* right of *yours*" (ἡ ἐξουσία ὑμῶν αὕτη). As Gardner (*Gifts*, 55) points out: "The use of ὑμῶν suggests that Paul is not aligning himself with this 'right.' Αὕτη emphasizes the particular ἐξουσία being addressed, indicating that Paul was referring back to the Corinthian display of knowledge (8:7)." See also Fee, *Corinthians*, 385; Gooch, *Dangerous Food*, 92–93; Dawes, "Danger," 98; Thiselton, *Corinthians*, 650; Smit, *About the Idol Offerings*, 88–89; Fotopoulos, *Food*, 218.

37. Thiselton, *Corinthians*, 680: "The communities expect to support the married couple, on the assumption that the *wife* shares her husband's Christian concerns and will support him in turn in these concerns." Cheung, *Idol Food*, 141: "Even the somewhat enigmatic 9.5 is best understood as a reference to the churches' support of the apostles' wives who accompany them in ministry."

38. Lockwood, *1 Corinthians*, 295: "The questions in 9:4–5 had the force of positive affirmations, but this question, introduced with ἤ, which *contrasts* it to the questions in 9:4–5, expects the answer no."

39. Cheung, *Idol Food*, 141: "[T]he repeated mention of ἐξουσία—arguably the keyword in ch. 9—harks back to the sarcastic reference to the knowers' ἐξουσία to eat idol food in 1 Cor. 8.9."

"work" (ἔργον) in the Lord (9:1) means that Paul has the right not to "work" (ἐργάζεσθαι) for a living but to depend upon them to provide him with food to eat.

Paul bolsters his apostolic right to receive food to eat from his Corinthian audience with a triplet of gnomic maxims in the form of rhetorical questions, each expecting a negative answer in 9:7.[40] With regard to the first question, the audience must admit that no one ever serves as a soldier with his own "provisions" (9:7a). Those for whom a soldier works supply him with "provisions" (ὀψωνίοις), which include food to eat.[41] And so it is with Paul. As an apostle he is entitled, like a soldier, to be provided with food to eat. In contrast to the questionable "right" of some to "eat" meat sacrificed to idols (8:1–12), Paul has an apostolic right to "eat" from the provisions he has earned.

With regard to the second question, the audience must affirm that no one plants a vineyard and does not eat of its fruit (9:7b). The reference to one who "plants" (φυτεύει) reminds the audience that it was Paul who "planted" (ἐφύτευσα, 3:6; cf. 3:7–8) the "seed" of the gospel among them as their founding apostle and father (4:15). In contrast to the alleged "right" of some to "eat" (ἐσθίουσιν, 8:7; cf. 8:4, 8, 10) meat sacrificed to idols, Paul has an apostolic right to "eat" (ἐσθίει) of the fruit that he himself planted.

With regard to the third question, the audience must acknowledge that no one shepherds a flock and does not "eat" of the milk of that flock (9:7c). In contrast to the supposed "right" of some to "eat" (ἐσθίουσιν, 8:7; cf. 8:4, 8, 10) meat sacrificed to idols, Paul, as the implied "shepherd" of his Corinthian "flock," has an authoritative apostolic right to "eat" (ἐσθίει) of the produce of his labor. Paul's use of the word "eat" with milk, rather than "drink," as might be expected, reinforces the contrast between his apostolic right to "eat" and his audience's implied lack of a right to "eat" idol food.[42]

---

40. Ramsaran, *Liberating Words*, 53: "Paul uses self-evident examples that are agreeable to his hearers. The persuasion is not from prior argumentation but rather from ideas that are common to repeated observation (see 9:8a): Every kind of laborer is entitled to subsistence."

41. On the meaning of ὀψώνιον, *TLNT* 2.600–603 states: "A compound formed from ὄψον, 'cooked fish, fish,' hence 'food,' and ὠνέομαι, 'to buy, acquire.' . . . In fact, from its first occurrence, ὀψώνιον refers to a purchase of food and means provisions. . . . The emphasis is not so much on costs or expenditures as on food and provisions." Thiselton, *Corinthians*, 684: "[O]ften corn, meat, fruits, nuts, and salt were given to soldiers on active service in place of pay." See also Chrys C. Caragounis, "ΟΨΩΝΙΟΝ: A Reconsideration of Its Meaning," *NovT* 16 (1974): 35–57; Fee, *Corinthians*, 405; Collins, *First Corinthians*, 338.

42. Fee, *Corinthians*, 405 n. 45: "[M]ilk is thought of as food for nourishment, not a drink; hence it is 'eaten.'" Thiselton, *Corinthians*, 684: "In the third analogy, we might have expected *drinks* the milk, whereas the Greek has ἐσθίει, *eats*. This is because milk for a shepherd would include the combined product of the milk which today we call *dairy* produce (e.g., including cheeses)."

With yet another rhetorical question Paul makes his audience aware that he is not saying "these things," that is, everything he has just said in 9:4–7 about his apostolic right to eat, according to a human perspective or authority (9:8a). Rather, as the audience is to agree and Paul is to demonstrate, "the law," the Jewish scriptural torah with its divine authority, also speaks about and thus corroborates his apostolic authority to eat (9:8b).[43]

"For in the law of Moses it is written" (9:9a) then further specifies that the scriptural command to follow from Deut 25:4 has the authority of the law God gave to Moses, and thus deserves the audience's obedience: "You shall not muzzle a threshing ox" (9:9b), that is, no one should prevent an ox that is working on the harvest to eat from that harvest. But Paul quickly makes his audience realize that with this scriptural command God is concerned not just with oxen (9:9c). His audience is to agree that indeed in this scriptural command God is speaking for the sake of "us" (9:10a), that is, Paul and Barnabas (9:6), apostles figuratively "threshing" for the Corinthians (cf. 3:6–9). The Corinthians must not "muzzle" them from eating of the harvest to which they are entitled.

That it was indeed "for our sake written" (9:10b) transforms the negative scriptural command about a threshing ox (9:9b) to a positive scriptural obligation concerning both those who plow and thresh: "In hope ought the one plowing to plow and the one threshing in hope of receiving a share" (9:10c). The audience is to realize that as those who have not only "threshed" but "plowed" (cf. 3:6–9) in hope on their behalf, Paul and Barnabas have the right to have their hope fulfilled by receiving from the Corinthians a share of the harvest to eat.[44] With the divine authority of the law of Moses, the combination of scriptural quotations in 9:9–10, then,

---

43. Collins, *First Corinthians*, 338: "Having invited the Corinthians to think about the rights that he as an apostle had a right to exercise (vv. 4–6), and after a short lesson in which he makes use of well-known examples of three types of people who were able to eat as a result of their work, Paul turns from a rational argument to an argument from authority.... Paul adapts this twofold approach as he demonstrates for his putative audience that he has a right to receive support from the Corinthian community.... 'The law' (ὁ νόμος) is contrasted with 'human authority' (ἄνθρωπον), thereby implying that the law is an expression of God's authority." On Paul's use of νόμος in 1 Corinthians, see Harm W. Hollander, "The Meaning of the Term 'Law' (ΝΟΜΟΣ) in 1 Corinthians," *NovT* 40 (1998): 117–35.

44. On Paul's scriptural interpretation here, Smit (*About the Idol Offerings*, 119) comments: "From agricultural laborers in the literal sense, such as the plower and the thresher, he [Paul] switches to agricultural laborers in the figurative sense. Finally this brings him to the preachers of the gospel, some of whom—he himself and Barnabas—have sown, while others have only threshed." Newton, *Deity and Diet*, 319: "The agricultural metaphor continues as Paul explains that both plougher and thresher rightfully can expect a share in the final harvested crop."

reinforces the audience's acknowledgment that Paul, as their founding apostle, is entitled to their material support so that he certainly has an authoritative apostolic right to eat (9:1–7), in contrast to those who suppose they have a "right" to eat meat sacrificed to idols (8:1–13).

Relation to the Subsequent Context in 1 Corinthians 9:11–18

Paul then further exploits the agricultural metaphors of "plowing" and "threshing" from the combined scriptural quotations in 9:9–10 in terms of "sowing" and "harvesting." The audience is to affirm that if "we," Paul and Barnabas, have "sown" spiritual seed, that is, the gospel, for "you," then it is no great thing, but to be naturally expected, that these apostles will "harvest" material things from "you" (9:11). That "we have sown" corresponds to the "plowing" and "threshing" in the scriptural quotations. And that "we will harvest" material things corresponds to "receiving a share" of the harvest. The audience realizes that in return for the spiritual benefits they have received from Paul's "sowing" the gospel among them as their founding apostle the scriptural quotations with their divine authority in 9:9–10 give Paul the right to receive from them a "harvest" of material things, especially the right to eat.[45]

The audience must admit that if other apostles share in this "right over you" for material support, then Paul (and Barnabas), as their founding apostle, shares in it all the more (9:12a). Since the scriptural quote in 9:10 gives Paul, as the apostle who has both "plowed" and "threshed" among the Corinthians, the right of "sharing" or "receiving a share" (μετεχειν), Paul, even more than all others, "shares" (μετεχουσιν) in this right over them.[46] This apostolic "right over you" (τῆς ὑμῶν ἐξουσίας) reminds the audience of "your right" (ἡ ἐξουσία ὑμῶν), the "right" that some among them think they possess to eat meat sacrificed to idols based on their knowledge of the meaninglessness of idols, but that Paul urges them not to exercise so as not to become a stumbling block to "the weak," those who do not have this knowledge (8:9).[47]

---

45. Schrage, *Erste Brief*, 2.303–4: "Das Evangelium ist eine pneumatische Saat, in der sich das Pneuma auch darin kräftig erweist, daß es irdische Früchte hervorbringt und die Gemeinde dazu veranlaßt, den Apostel mit den nötigen Dingen wie Nahrung, Kleidung, Geld usw. zu versorgen ... da ist es nichts Großes (μέγα), sondern etwas Selbstverständliches, daß für den Lebensunterhalt der Evangelisten gesorgt wird."

46. Fee, *Corinthians*, 410: "The verb 'share' echoes the harvest metaphor at the conclusion of v. 10."

47. Whereas ὑμῶν in 8:9 is a possessive genitive, the context and word order indicate that ὑμῶν in 9:12a is an objective genitive. With regard to the context, Fee (*Corinthians*, 410) states:

Although Paul's right to receive material support from his Corinthian audience is authorized by God's scriptural law (9:9–10), he provocatively proclaims: "Yet we have not used this right!" (9:12b). That Paul (and Barnabas) have not used "this right" (τῇ ἐξουσίᾳ ταύτῃ) to eat the food to which they are authoritatively entitled as apostles further persuades the "knowers" among the Corinthians not to use their putative right—"this right of yours" (ἡ ἐξουσία ὑμῶν αὕτη)—to eat meat sacrificed to idols (8:9).

Paul has not used his right to eat the food to which he is entitled in order not to place an "obstacle" (ἐγκοπήν) to the gospel of Christ (9:12c); that is, Paul does not want belief in the gospel he preaches to be hindered in any way by his right to material support as an apostle. Paul's non-use of his apostolic right to eat reminds and reinforces for his audience his previous conviction that if food causes a fellow believer to sin, then Paul will never eat any meat whatsoever in order not to "cause to sin" (σκανδαλίσω) a fellow believer (8:13). The "knowers" in the audience are thus further persuaded not to use their supposed "right" to eat meat sacrificed to idols in order not to become a "stumbling block" (πρόσκομμα) to those in the audience who do not possess the knowledge that idols are meaningless (8:9).[48]

The example that those who perform the temple services are entitled to "eat" (ἐσθίουσιν) from the temple (9:13a) further establishes for the audience Paul's right to eat as an apostle. And that those who minister at the altar have the right to "share with" (συμμερίζονται) the altar (9:13b) coincides with the right that the scriptural quotes in 9:9–10 give Paul to "receive a share" (μετέχειν) of the harvest to eat.[49]

"What is not clear is the nuance of the pronoun 'your.' Although this may well be a subjective genitive (= 'share in the rights you bestow'), it is more likely objective (= 'share in rights over you,' i.e., 'reap the benefits of the rights that are theirs by virtue of their ministry among you'). 'Rights' is what the argument is all about, namely 'rights' to material support, which are his by virtue of his apostleship." With regard to the word order, Fee (*Corinthians*, 410 n. 75) states: "Elsewhere when Paul uses the possessive, or subjective genitive, with ἐξουσία it follows the noun (cf. 8:9); the enclosed genitive (as here) suggests a slightly different relationship to ἐξουσία."

48. Lockwood, *1 Corinthians*, 297: "In this context the noun ἐγκοπή ('hindrance') is a synonym of πρόσκομμα ('stumbling block') in 8:9 and σκανδαλίζω ('to cause to fall') in 8:13." See also Dale B. Martin, *Slavery as Salvation: The Metaphor of Slavery in Pauline Christianity* (New Haven: Yale University Press, 1990), 121. Paul thus uses ἐγκοπή in 9:12 in a context of not hindering anyone from coming to faith in the gospel of Christ, but πρόσκομμα in 8:9 in a context of not causing one who already believes to stumble into sin.

49. On Paul's belief "that the community is a metaphorical temple, and that the temple must be characterized by holiness and purity similar to that in the Temple in Jerusalem with its notions of priestly support," see Peter Richardson, "Temples, Altars, and Living from the Gospel (1 Cor. 9.12b–18)," in *Gospel in Paul: Studies on Corinthians, Galatians, and Romans*

Although the Lord himself authorized those preaching the gospel to live and thus "eat" by the gospel (9:14; cf. Matt 10:10; Luke 10:7), Paul would rather die than use any of these rights to eat (9:15).[50] Indeed, the "recompense" that Paul receives for fulfilling his obligation to preach the gospel is that he offers the gospel free of charge so as not to make full use of the legitimate "right" (ἐξουσία) he has to eat as a preacher of the gospel (9:16–18).[51] Thus, the "knowers" at Corinth are likewise not to use their alleged "right" (ἐξουσία) to eat meat sacrificed to idols for the sake of not causing a fellow believer to fall from faith in the gospel and back into idolatry (8:9).[52]

With their authority as God's law, the scriptural quotations in 9:9–10, then, give Paul, as an apostle, the right, reinforced by a command of the Lord Jesus himself (9:14), to eat. Since Paul does not exercise this legitimate and divinely authorized right to eat in order not to hinder faith in the gospel, so those in his audience who know that idols are nothing and thus think they may freely eat meat sacrificed to idols must not exercise their supposed right to eat, as it may cause a believer to lose faith in the gospel (8:9).

Summary on 1 Corinthians 9:9–10

1. Its introduction by "it was written that" in 1 Cor 9:10b, its poetic parallelism with alliteration and ellipsis, and its character as a proverbial saying indicate that 9:10c is to be understood by Paul's audience as an additional scriptural quotation that extends and elaborates upon the quotation of Deut 25:4 in 9:9b, to which it is connected by the word "thresh" in accord with the *gezera shava* technique that links two scriptural texts for

---

for Richard N. Longenecker (ed. L. Ann Jervis and Peter Richardson; JSNTSup 108; Sheffield: Sheffield Academic Press, 1994), 108.

50. For a formal, linguistic relation between the scriptural command not to muzzle in 9:9b and Paul's non-use of his right to eat in 9:15, see Joost Smit Sibinga, "The Composition of 1 Cor. 9 and Its Context," *NovT* 40 (1998): 150. On the issue of Paul not conforming to the manner of life that the Lord had instructed for apostles, see David G. Horrell, "'The Lord Commanded . . . but I Have Not Used . . .': Exegetical and Hermeneutical Reflections on 1 Cor 9.14–15," *NTS* 43 (1997): 587–603.

51. John Byron, "Slave of Christ or Willing Servant? Paul's Self-Description in 1 Corinthians 4:1–2 and 9:16–18," *Neot* 37 (2003): 179–98.

52. Cheung, *Idol Food*, 141: "By making so much of his renunciation of the right to food and drink in order not to put any hindrance to the gospel, Paul's aim is not to teach the Corinthians the nature of Christian freedom. The rhetorical purpose is rather this: 'Go and do likewise. Renounce (idol) food.'" Fotopoulos, *Food*, 250: "Paul never indicates that a Christian can knowingly eat sacrificial food at a meal . . . identifying such eating as idolatry. . . . Thus, the Corinthians are to imitate the *exemplum* of Paul." See also Still, "Paul's Aims," 333–43; Sandelin, "Drawing the Line," 108–25; Garland, "Dispute," 173–97.

mutual interpretation by words they have in common. Although not a literal quotation of any one OT text, 9:10c most closely resembles a combination of Isa 28:24, 28 with affinities to Isa 45:9 and Sir 6:19.

2. Since both those who plow and those who thresh do so in hope of eating a share of the harvest, there is an obligation in accord with God's scriptural law as recorded in Deut 25:4—an obligation Paul expects his audience to acknowledge through the combination of authoritative scriptural quotations in 9:9–10—that they indeed receive that share to which they are entitled and for which they labored in hope.

3. With the divine authority of the law of Moses, the combination of scriptural quotations in 9:9–10 reinforces the audience's acknowledgment that Paul, as their founding apostle, is entitled to their material support so that he certainly has an authoritative apostolic right to eat (9:1–7), in contrast to those who suppose they have a "right" to eat meat sacrificed to idols (8:1–13).

4. With their authority as God's law, the scriptural quotations in 9:9–10 give Paul, as an apostle, the right, reinforced by a command of the Lord Jesus himself (9:14), to eat. Since Paul does not exercise this divinely authorized right to eat in order not to hinder faith in the gospel, so those in his audience who know that idols are nothing and thus think they may freely eat meat sacrificed to idols must not exercise their supposed right to eat, as it may cause a believer to lose faith in the gospel (8:9).

CHAPTER 10

1 Corinthians 10:7b

*The people sat down to eat and drink
and stood up to play.*

Old Testament Background

Introduced by the formula "as it is written" (ὥσπερ γέγραπται), the statement that "the people sat down to eat and drink and stood up to play" in 1 Cor 10:7b quotes Exod 32:6b:

MT Exod 32:6b: וַיֵּשֶׁב הָעָם לֶאֱכֹל וְשָׁתוֹ וַיָּקֻמוּ לְצַחֵק
LXX Exod 32:6b: καὶ ἐκάθισεν ὁ λαὸς φαγεῖν καὶ πιεῖν καὶ ἀνέστησαν παίζειν
1 Cor 10:7b: ἐκάθισεν ὁ λαὸς φαγεῖν καὶ πεῖν καὶ ἀνέστησαν παίζειν

A very minor difference between the Pauline version and the LXX is that the aorist active infinitive πιεῖν, "to drink," which appears in the LXX, is contracted to πεῖν.

That "the people" (ὁ λαός), that is, the chosen people of Israel whom God brought up out of slavery from Egypt in the exodus event (cf. LXX Exod 32:4), "sat down to eat and drink" refers to their communal partaking in the "peace offering" that was sacrificed together with holocausts for the feast of the idolatrous golden calf that Aaron fashioned for them (32:1–6a).[1] That then "they stood up to play" is further described as "the

---

1. John William Wevers, *Notes on the Greek Text of Exodus* (SBLSCS 30; Atlanta: Scholars Press, 1990), 521: "[R]eference is made to the people eating and drinking, which must apply to the שלמים sacrifices since they, but not the holocausts, were communal sacrifices in which the worshippers shared." Hans-Jürgen van der Minde, "ἐσθίω," *EDNT* 2.60: "The activity of eating, drinking, and dancing, introduced from the Scripture citation, are [*sic*] seen not simply as purely this-worldly acts, but are rather to be understood from the OT background as idolatry."

sound of the people shouting" (32:17), which Joshua thinks is the sound of battle, but that Moses determines is "the sound of those making a beginning of wine" (32:18), which was accompanied by "the dances" for the revelry involved in the idolatrous worship of the golden calf (32:19). "To play" (παίζειν) has a wide range of connotations—"to play like a child," "to sport," "to dance," "to jest," "to joke," "to sing," "to amuse oneself"— including that of sexual, orgiastic playing relevant to this context of the riotous revelry involved in idolatrous worship.[2]

Literary-Rhetorical Analysis

The implied audience realizes that "the people" (ὁ λαός) who sat down to eat and drink in Exod 32:6b are not just any people but the people of Israel as the covenantal people of God, chosen to be God's special possession above and beyond all other peoples. This people of God is to obey God's voice and keep God's covenant, as indicated by the word of God in LXX Exod 19:5: "And now if you really heed my voice and keep my covenant, you will be to me a people (λαός) above and beyond all the nations, for mine is all the earth."[3]

That this special people of God "sat down" (ἐκάθισεν) to eat and drink indicates to the audience that they are not just satisfying their hunger and thirst as a group of individuals but that they have sat down for a full and formal meal. That the people "sat down to eat and drink" *as a people* indi-

---

2. Fee, *Corinthians*, 454: "Although the verb in the LXX often refers to cultic dancing, and in the Exodus narrative the revelry is further expressed in terms of 'shouting' (v. 17), 'singing' (v. 18), and 'dancing' (v. 19), nonetheless in this case (both in the LXX and in Paul) it almost certainly carries overtones of sexual play." Schrage, *Erste Brief*, 2.398: "Von den im Kontext (Ex 32,19) erwähnten Reigentänzen her wird παίζειν nicht nur ein allgemeines Lustigsein meinen, sondern kultisch-orgiastische Tänze vor dem Goldenen Kalb." Oropeza, *Paul and Apostasy*, 140: "[T]he notion of 'playing' (צחק/παίζειν)—though having a wide range of meanings—included cultic dancing (Judges 21:21; 1 Kings 18:26) and could denote erotic behaviour (cf. Gen 26:8). In the golden calf narrative, the 'playing' may have borne both these connotations." See also Gardner, *Gifts*, 151; Lockwood, *1 Corinthians*, 329; Thiselton, *Corinthians*, 734–35; Sandnes, *Belly*, 199; Garland, *1 Corinthians*, 461.

3. Wevers, *Exodus*, 294–95: "The covenantal status of Israel is defined in the apodosis: you will be to me λαὸς περιούσιος. This is accompanied with an ἀπό phrase. The term περιούσιος, an adjective from περιουσία, 'surplus, abundance,' has the notion of 'above and beyond' in it, and this with ἀπό probably has a comparative sense to it, 'above and beyond all peoples.'" Hubert Frankemölle, "λαός," *EDNT* 2.340–41: "Belief in Israel as the elect people of God (λαὸς τοῦ θεοῦ) is unquestioned. This corresponds to the usage of the LXX, where λαός occurs *ca.* 2000 times, predominantly as a religious t.t. [technical term]. In the NT this significance of the prior history is assured esp. by OT citations ... in Paul citations are present in every occurrence of the word!"

cates a meal uniting and bringing them all together to share meal fellowship.[4] And that the people sat down both "to eat and drink" (φαγεῖν καὶ πεῖν) indicates a complete meal or banquet of communal fellowship with festive and celebratory connotations.[5]

Furthermore, as the audience knows from the context, the people sat down to eat and drink not just any food but "peace offerings," that is, sacrificial food offered to the idolatrous golden calf (Exod 32:6a). The people's sitting down to eat and drink a fellowship banquet of idolatrous food thus in itself contradicts their status as God's specially chosen "people."

The people not only "sat down" to eat and drink but then "stood up" to play. The people's "standing up" follows naturally and consequentially from their "sitting down." This tells the audience that the people compounded or complemented their sitting down "to eat and drink" a banquet of idolatrous food with their standing up "to play" (παίζειν), that is, to further riotous, idolatrous behavior with orgiastic connotations. Their idolatrous eating and drinking as a "people" led to their idolatrous playing as a riotous group of individuals. The audience is to realize that although the people "sat down" (ἐκάθισεν; singular) as a single entity to eat and drink, they "stood up" (ἀνέστησαν; plural) as a disparate group of individuals to rebellious, idolatrous playing, further contradicting their status as "the people" of God.[6]

Relation to the Antecedent Context in 1 Corinthians 8:1–10:7a

1 Corinthians 8:1–10:5

The quotation of Exod 32:6b in 1 Cor 10:7b, which expresses the idolatrous behavior of the people of Israel before the golden calf and which accompanies Paul's command for his Corinthian audience not to become

---

4. Angela Palzkill, "πίνω," *EDNT* 3.88: "The expression 'eating and drinking' is frequently used as an expression for table fellowship."

5. On "eating and drinking" to connote a full festive meal or banquet, see LXX 2 Kgdms 11:11; 1 Esd 9:54; Neh 8:12; Jdt 12:11; Isa 23:18. For "sitting" to "eat and drink" a banquet with emphasis on the meal fellowship involved, see LXX Jer 16:8: "Do not enter a banquet house to sit together (συγκαθίσαι) with them to eat and drink (φαγεῖν καὶ πιεῖν)." According to Oropeza (*Paul and Apostasy*, 140): "The concept of sitting was often associated with moral degradation by the later Jewish writers so that it became common for some rabbis to affirm that where one finds 'sitting' one finds seduction."

6. Wevers, *Exodus*, 521: "In the last clause the verb changes to the plural; the subject is still ὁ λαός, but after the common eating and drinking in connection with the peace offering they now as individuals stood up παίζειν."

idolaters in 1 Cor 10:7a, reinforces Paul's warning that those who have the knowledge that idols are nothing (8:1–6) not lead those who do not have this knowledge into idolatry. When those who do not have this knowledge and who have been so accustomed to idolatry in the past "eat" (ἐσθίουσιν) meat sacrificed to idols, their weak conscience is defiled (8:7) and they are thus led back into idolatry. For if someone sees one who has this knowledge "reclining at table" (κατακείμενον) in the temple of an idol, his weak conscience may be provoked to lead him to likewise recline at table "to eat" (ἐσθίειν) the meat sacrificed to idols (8:10). Thus, the scriptural quote that the people "sat down" (ἐκάθισεν) or reclined at table to "eat" (φαγεῖν) and drink and stood up to idolatrous play would be reenacted, and these people would again become idolaters (10:7).[7]

But in 10:1–13 Paul's concern is that even those with the knowledge that idols are nothing, and whose consciences are thus strong, may, like those without this knowledge and whose consciences are weak, also fall into idolatry by eating the meat sacrificed to idols.[8]

Paul makes his Corinthian audience aware that "our fathers," that is, our Israelite ancestors in the exodus event, were all "baptized" (ἐβαπτίσθησαν) into Moses in the cloud and in the sea (10:1–2; cf. Exod 13:21–22; 14:29–31). They all ate the same "spiritual" (πνευματικὸν) food, and they all drank the same "spiritual" (πνευματικὸν) drink, for they were drinking from a "spiritual" (πνευματικῆς) rock following them, a rock which was the Christ (10:3–4; cf. Exod 16:4, 35; 17:6; Num 20:11; Neh 9:15, 20; Ps 78:15, 20, 23–25; Ps 105:40–41).[9]

The audience is to realize that this "spirituality" of the Israelites prefigures their own, as "you were baptized" (ἐβαπτίσθητε) into Christ (1:13; cf. 1:14–17; 12:13). The Corinthians were thus taught by the Spirit, so that they are able to explain "things of the Spirit" (πνευματικὰ) to "people of the Spirit" (πνευματικοῖς) (2:13), each of them being a "person of the Spirit"

---

7. Joël Delobel, "Coherence and Relevance of 1 Cor 8–10," in *The Corinthian Correspondence* (ed. Reimund Bieringer; BETL 125; Louvain: Louvain University Press, 1996), 190: "1 Cor 8–10 appears at first sight as an incoherent passage, which very soon lost its relevance. Upon a closer look, however, one discovers a coherent whole based on consistent reasoning concerning a complex and many-sided problem."

8. Oropeza, *Paul and Apostasy*, 143: "[T]he problem concerning idol meats in 1 Corinthians 8 is not necessarily a separate issue from the idolatry which is mentioned in 10:1–13. Paul brings out primarily in chapter 8 how the strong in Corinth could cause the weak to apostatise through idol meats; in 10:1–13 Paul builds up an argument that the strong themselves could apostatise through idolatry."

9. Larry Joseph Kreitzer, "1 Corinthians 10:4 and Philo's Flinty Rock," *CV* 35 (1993): 109–26; P. E. Enns, "The 'Movable Well' in 1 Corinthians 10:4: An Extra-biblical Tradition in an Apostolic Text," *BBR* 6 (1996): 23–38.

(πνευματικὸς) able to examine or evaluate everything (2:15), even though Paul could not talk to them as "people of the Spirit" (πνευματικοῖς) because of their divisiveness (3:1). Just as the Israelites experienced spiritual benefits from their baptism, so the Corinthians experienced spiritual benefits from their baptism.[10] But as God was displeased with most of the Israelites, so that they were "struck down" (κατεστρώθησαν) in the desert (10:5; LXX Num 14:16: God "struck down" [κατέστρωσεν] the people in the desert; cf. Num 11:33; 14:11–12, 28–35; 26:64–65), so the ominous implication for the audience is that God may likewise be displeased with the Corinthians despite their spiritual benefits.

The Chiastic Structure of 10:6–11

The scriptural quotation of Exod 32:6b in 10:7b functions within the following chiastic arrangement in 10:6–11:

A   ⁶ *These things* happened as *prefigurations* for *us*, that we might not be cravers of evil things, just as *they* indeed craved.

    B   ⁷ *Do not* become idolaters as some of them, as it is written, "the people sat down to eat and drink and stood up to play."

       C   ⁸ *Let us not* commit sexual immorality, as some of them committed sexual immorality and twenty-three thousand fell on one day.

       C´   ⁹ *Let us not* put Christ to the test, as some of them tested and were being destroyed by the serpents.

    B´   ¹⁰ *Do not* grumble, just as some of them grumbled and were destroyed by the destroyer.

A´   ¹¹ *These things* came about for *them* by way of *prefiguration*,

---

10. With regard to the word "spiritual" (πνευματικός) here, Oropeza (*Paul and Apostasy*, 113) remarks that "Paul uses the term in a broad sense to persuade the Corinthians that the spirituality they received from the Lord, the Israelites also received. If this is the case, then choosing between precise definitions for πνευματικός is not an issue. The elements of supernatural, eschatological, and Spirit-conveyance may all be implied because Paul is essentially saying that regardless of which ways the Corinthians thought of themselves *pneumatics*, the Israelites were like-

and were written for *our* warning, upon whom the end of the ages has come.[11]

This chiastic structure is constituted by the following parallels (italicized above): "These things" (Ταῦτα δὲ), "prefigurations" (τύποι), "us" (ἡμῶν), and "they" (κἀκεῖνοι) in the A unit (10:6) are paralleled by "these things" (ταῦτα δὲ), "them" (ἐκείνοις), "by way of prefiguration" (τυπικῶς), and "our" (ἡμῶν) in the A´ unit (10:11). The negative command in the second-person plural, "Do not become idolaters" (μηδὲ εἰδωλολάτραι γίνεσθε), in the B unit (10:7) is paralleled by the negative command in the second-person plural, "Do not grumble" (μηδὲ γογγύζετε), in the B´ unit (10:10). The negative exhortation in the first-person plural, "Let us not commit sexual immorality" (μηδὲ πορνεύωμεν), in the C unit (10:8) is paralleled by the negative exhortation in the first-person plural, "Let us not test" (μηδὲ ἐκπειράζωμεν), in the C´ unit (10:9).

"These things" in the A unit (10:6) refers to what was just reported in 10:1–5, namely, that God struck down our Israelite ancestors in the desert despite the spiritual benefits they received from their exodus experiences. These things happened as "prefigurations" (τύποι) for us—Paul and his Corinthian audience—"that we might not be cravers (ἐπιθυμητὰς) of evil things, just as they indeed craved (ἐπεθύμησαν)" (10:6).[12] The emphatic

---

wise *pneumatics*." See also B. J. Oropeza, "Echoes of Isaiah in the Rhetoric of Paul: New Exodus, Wisdom, and the Humility of the Cross in Utopian-Apocalyptic Expectations," in *The Intertexture of Apocalyptic Discourse in the New Testament* (ed. Duane F. Watson; SBLSymS 14; Atlanta: Society of Biblical Literature, 2002), 87–112. For a denial of Corinthian overconfidence in sacraments here, see Karl-Gustav Sandelin, "Does Paul Argue against Sacramentalism and Over-Confidence in 1 Cor 10.1–14?" in *The New Testament and Hellenistic Judaism* (ed. Peder Borgen and Søren Giversen; Peabody, Mass.: Hendrickson, 1995), 165–82. Cf. Wolfgang Schrage, "Einige Hauptprobleme der Diskussion des Herrenmahls im 1. Korintherbrief," in *The Corinthian Correspondence* (ed. Reimund Bieringer; BETL 125; Louvain: Louvain University Press, 1996), 191–92; Cheung, *Idol Food*, 144–45 n. 187.

11. Gary D. Collier, " 'That We Might Not Crave Evil': The Structure and Argument of 1 Corinthians 10.1–13," *JSNT* 55 (1994): 61; Koet, "1 Cor 10,7–8," 610; Oropeza, *Paul and Apostasy*, 129. On the criteria for determining a chiasm, see n. 8 in ch. 8 above.

12. Hays, *First Corinthians*, 162: "Paul is claiming that the biblical events happened as prefigurations of the situation in which his Christian readers now find themselves." On the issue of a "typological" sense of τύπος here, Gerd Schunack ("τύπος," *EDNT* 3.374–75) states that "in 1 Cor 10:6, 11 one should proceed from the exegetically proven use *formative model, prefiguration*. . . . Only eschatologically qualified and interpreted human existence can be τύπος . . . and past existence is so perceived critically and antithetically because it is already written down. Hence if 1 Corinthians 10 employs 'typology' at all, then it is in the critical-antithetical use of Scripture." See also Thiselton, *Corinthians*, 731–32; Oropeza, *Paul and Apostasy*, 130–32. Fee, *Corinthians*, 452: "As typology the passage breaks down precisely at the point

double occurrence of the word "crave" reminds the audience of similar emphatic expressions of the people's craving or lusting in the scriptural traditions of Israel's wandering in the wilderness after the exodus.

According to LXX Ps 105:14, "But they craved with craving (ἐπεθύμησαν ἐπιθυμίαν) in the desert, and tested God in the waterless land." That this excessive "craving" is oriented toward the meat that the people remembered from Egypt and desired instead of the manna that God provided is indicated in LXX Num 11:4: "And the mixed multitude among them craved with craving (ἐπεθύμησαν ἐπιθυμίαν) and sitting down, they and the sons of Israel wept and said, 'Who will give us meat to eat?'" (cf. Num 11:5–6).[13] Thus, "we," especially those of "strong" conscience with knowledge that idols are nothing (1 Cor 8:1–6), must not follow the bad example of our Israelite ancestors by excessively "craving" the meat sacrificed to idols (10:6), lest we, like they, be "struck down" (10:5).[14]

---

of warning. Paul does not want what happened to Israel to be repeated." Sandnes, *Belly*, 204: "[T]he desire of some of the Corinthians to join the tables in the temples is a passion for forbidden food, just as the Jews were longing for meat, not finding God's providence sufficient."

13. For other scriptural expressions of the intense "craving" for meat by Israel in the wilderness, see LXX Num 11:34–35; 33:16–17; Ps 78:29–31. First Corinthians 10:6 begins a pre-Pauline midrash based on the quotation of Exod 32:6b in 1 Cor 10:7b according to Wayne A. Meeks, "'And Rose Up to Play': Midrash and Paraenesis in 1 Corinthians 10:1–22," *JSNT* 16 (1982): 64–78. But Numbers 11 is the basis for the midrash according to Collier, "1 Corinthians 10.1–13," 55–75. That Paul used a Jewish text into which he inserted Exod 32:6b is argued by Karl-Gustav Sandelin, "'Do Not Be Idolaters!' (1 Cor 10:7)," in *Texts and Contexts: Biblical Texts in Their Textual and Situational Contexts. Essays in Honor of Lars Hartman* (ed. Tord Fornberg and David Hellholm; Oslo: Scandinavian University Press, 1995), 257–73. But Paul himself "weaves together a plethora of scriptural texts on Israel's wilderness experience to warn the Corinthians of the danger of idolatry" with LXX Ps 106 as the prominent text Paul has in mind according to Cheung, *Idol Food*, 144. As Oropeza (*Paul and Apostasy*, 134) notes, "The Exodus and Numbers traditions definitely appear in 1 Corinthians 10:5–10, but when they are placed under the entire rubric of 10:1–13, Paul is borrowing from several detectable sources including Deuteronomic and Isaianic traditions which permeate not only this text but the entire context of 1 Corinthians 8:1–11:1. This observation casts doubt on pre-Pauline 'midrashic' theories concerning this passage. Paul is more likely weaving together the selected wilderness tradition accounts." See also Fee, *Corinthians*, 442 n. 5; Mitchell, *Paul*, 252 n. 364; Smit, *About the Idol Offerings*, 121–34; Thiselton, *Corinthians*, 722–23.

14. Oropeza, *Paul and Apostasy*, 138: "Egypt represented Israel's former state of bondage, and for the people to crave the food of Egypt in general—and meat (κρέα, Num. 11:4) in particular—coincided with the Corinthian situation of eating meat in the context of idols. As the foods of Egypt signified for the Israelites a turning back to the former things of their pre-redemption, so idolatry would be a thing associated with the Corinthians' pre-Christian status (cf. 1 Cor. 6:9–11; 12:2) and eating idol meat with idolaters could draw the Corinthians back to their former status." Collins, *First Corinthians*, 370: "The biblical narrative describes the Israelites' inordinate desire for meat and for the food of Egypt (Num 11:4–6) rather than for the manna provided by YHWH. This inordinate craving led to their death (Num 11:33–34). The Israelites craved for

In the B unit (10:7) of the chiasm the audience begins to hear specific examples of the "craving of evil things" stated in the A unit (10:6).[15] After the first-person plural, "that we might not be cravers of evil things, just as they indeed craved" (10:6b), in the A unit, Paul addresses the audience more directly with the second-person plural negative command in the B unit: "Do not become idolaters as some of them" (10:7a).[16] How the idolatry of some of them exemplified the craving of evil things, particularly food and drink other than what God had provided for them in the desert, is then indicated by the quotation of Exod 32:6b in 10:7b of the B unit: "The people sat down to eat and drink and stood up to play."

In startling contrast and contradiction to "all" (πάντες 5x in 10:1–4) of the Israelite ancestors, that is, all of the people of God, who "ate" (ἔφαγον) the same spiritual food (10:3) and "drank" (ἔπιον) the same spiritual drink, for they "drank" (ἔπινον) from the spiritual rock which was the Christ (10:3–4), some of them, nevertheless, as "the people" (ὁ λαὸς) of God, sat down to "eat" (φαγεῖν) and "drink" (πεῖν) from the peace offerings that had been sacrificed to the idolatrous golden calf and then, as disparate and rebellious individuals, stood up to the further idolatrous behavior of "playing" before the golden calf (10:7b).[17] The craving for and partaking of

---

'meat' (κρέα, 11:4 13[2x], 18[3x], 21, 33 [LXX]). In his discussion on food offered to idols Paul emphatically referred to 'meat,' κρέα, which he would gladly forego for the sake of his brothers and sisters (8:13). 'Crave' (ἐπιθυμέω) suggests a strong desire to satisfy a felt need, often in excessive fashion. Paul's use of the same verb in reference to both the Israelites and the Corinthians suggests that their experiences are comparable."

15. Fee, *Corinthians*, 453: "The verses that follow (7–10), then, give four 'examples' of how 'privileged' Israel 'lusted after evil things,' causing the demise of most of them." Newton, *Deity and Diet*, 327: "Paul introduces this section with a statement that the experiences of ancient Israel constitute warnings for Corinthian Christians not to desire evil in the ways that Israel of old desired evil. Paul then traces four of those acts of the people of Israel which brought down the judgment of God and he sets them out in 10.7–10." Oropeza, *Paul and Apostasy*, 138–39: "In both the Numbers and Corinthian contexts, lusting after evil things is associated with the pre-redemptive status, and the vices which follow in Paul's account may be specific examples of lusting after evil things." Fotopoulos, *Food*, 230: "The *conclusio* (v 6) from the events in Israel's history are clear *exempla* (τύποι) for the Corinthians to follow so that they do not desire evil, expounded in a series of Pauline exhortations (vv 7–13) supported by proofs which demonstrate the consequences of Israel's negative example."

16. Newton, *Deity and Diet*, 327 n. 128: "In 1 Cor. 6.9 Paul informs the Corinthians that in addition to certain other groups, 'idolaters' will not inherit the kingdom of God."

17. Fotopoulos, *Food*, 231: "[T]he Israelites committed idolatry by eating and drinking and rising up to play (Exod. 32:6 and 1 Cor. 10:7), a connection with the consumption of sacrificial food before a cult statue in 8:1–13 (cf. 1 Cor. 8:10, ἐν εἰδωλείῳ). For Paul, eating sacrificial food before a cult statue while reclining in a pagan temple equals idolatry." Oropeza, *Paul and Apostasy*, 139: "The quotation may have been intended to stress idolatry over the other vices since this was the focus of his paraenesis in chapters 8–10. The golden-calf incident would appeal to

idolatrous sacrificial food and drink on the part of "some" of them contradicted the unity of "all" who shared the same spiritual food and drink in the desert.[18] With the scriptural quote in the B unit, then, Paul warns that those among his audience who eat the meat sacrificed to idols not only may lead others into idolatry but also will become idolaters themselves and thus contradict the community's unity and status as the body of Christ (cf. 6:15; 8:12).[19]

Relation to the Subsequent Context in 1 Corinthians 10:8–11

Whereas Paul addressed his audience with a second-person plural negative command in the B unit (10:7), he reverts in the C unit to the first-person plural, as in the A unit (10:6), with the negative exhortation: "Let us not commit sexual immorality, as some of them committed sexual immorality and twenty-three thousand fell on one day" (10:8). This exhortation against sexual immorality follows closely from the standing up "to play" (παίζειν) with its sexual connotations after the people sat down to eat and drink according to the scriptural quote of Exod 32:6b in the B unit (10:7).[20] And it fits the Corinthian situation in which the sitting down to eat and drink the sacrificial food offered to idols was often followed by sexual immorality.[21]

Paul's argument because it was the epitome of God's chosen people committing apostasy through idolatry." See also Fee, *Corinthians*, 454; Garland, *1 Corinthians*, 460–61.

18. Mitchell, *Paul*, 252: "[I]n 10:1-13 Paul continues to treat, not merely the divisive issue of idol meat in itself, but retains his own chosen focus on the unity of the church in the face of controversies surrounding such practices. The emphasis in the verses which set up the analogy, 10:1-4, is most pronounced: *all* Israel was unified at the beginning in *common* baptism, *common* experiences and *common* spiritual food and drink. But despite this auspicious beginning, tragedy befell the community when factions appeared and sought their own advantage over that of all Israel. Their rebellions through sinful acts brought harm to almost all the people Israel." Fotopoulos, *Food*, 229: "Paul's choice of Israel's wilderness *exemplum* serves a twofold purpose in his argumentation: (1) it mirrors the problems of factious behavior and community divisions in the Corinthian church; and (2) it confronts the socio-theological problems that are causing the divisions within the community, i.e. sacrificial food, idolatry, and sexual immorality."

19. Cheung, *Idol Food*, 145: "However much they want to say that an idol is nothing, or that idol food is nothing, there is the danger of losing. No one can get involved in idolatry with immunity. There will be serious spiritual consequences."

20. Gardner, *Gifts*, 151: "[T]he text of Exodus 32:6 used in 10:7b may imply Corinthian involvement in πορνεία. The word παίζειν referred to the cultic use of dance and games, translating the Hebrew צחק which also may have had an erotic sense of cultic licentiousness. The Corinthian idolatrous rites may have involved sexual sin. On the other hand, the traditions regularly linked idolatry with immorality as is the case in both Exodus 32 and Numbers 25 which Paul cited in vv 7–8."

21. Fotopoulos, *Food*, 231: "The citation of Exod. 32:6 leads Paul to interpret παίζειν (1 Cor. 10:7) as sexual immorality in 10:8, rather than as cultic dancing.... [I]t seems likely that

That "twenty-three thousand (εἴκοσι τρεῖς χιλιάδες) fell (ἔπεσαν) on one day (ἡμέρᾳ)" in the C unit (10:8) continues to remind the audience of the golden-calf incident referred to in the scriptural quote from Exod 32:6b in the B unit (10:7) in which "the people" (ὁ λαός) sat down to eat and drink and stood up to play, as it alludes to the Levites slaying a great number of the people who engaged in this idolatrous eating, drinking, and sexual immorality in Exod 32:28b: "and there fell (ἔπεσαν) from the people (τοῦ λαοῦ) on that day (ἡμέρᾳ) about three thousand (τρισχιλίους) men." It also alludes to another incident in which the eating of idol sacrifices and sexual immorality likewise resulted in the deaths of a great number of the people in Num 25:9: "and those that died in the plague were four and twenty thousand (εἴκοσι χιλιάδες)."[22]

Paul has thus conflated the "three thousand" from Exod 32:28b with the "twenty thousand" from Num 25:9 to arrive at "twenty-three thousand" to express the large number who died in 1 Cor 10:8. That "twenty-three thousand fell on one day" further delineates God's punishment on those Israelite ancestors with whom he was not pleased in 10:5, "for they were struck down in the desert." And it supplies the punishment for those in the scriptural quote of Exod 32:6b who sat down to eat and drink idolatrous food and stood up to engage in sexual immorality.[23] The Corinthian audience is thus warned that if they eat the meat sacrificed to idols and

---

Paul is explicitly exhorting against sexual immorality in the context of dining rather than offering a general exhortation against sexual immorality. The συμπόσιον portion of the meal, which frequently involved intoxication and sexual play with flute girls, prostitutes, or boyish wine-servers, stands as a logical context for Corinthian πορνεία in association with the consumption of sacrificial food." Sandnes, *Belly*, 211: "[T]emple banquets included a sexual 'after dinner' as well.... [E]ating, drinking and sex are allied with apostasy in 1 Cor. 10; and it all derives from their craving for food, i.e. to participate in temple-meals." See also Oropeza, *Paul and Apostasy*, 145–49.

22. John William Wevers, *Notes on the Greek Text of Numbers* (SBLSCS 46; Atlanta: Scholars Press, 1998), 425: "The reference to 'the plague' is to the order by Moses to the tribes to kill relatives who worshipped Beel-phogor."

23. Koet, "1 Cor 10,7–8," 612–13: "[I]t is highly probable that in 10,8c Paul does not make a mistake, but refers deliberately to the punishment for the idolatry of the Golden Calf as described in Ex 32,28. This is much more probable because of the fact that Paul already quoted Ex 32,6. In 10,8 Paul places in a skillful way Ex 32,28 in the context of Num 25. Paul does not need to mention the punishment as described in 32,28 in 10,7, because he will use reminiscences to do it in 10,8c. In this way Paul kills two birds with one stone: 10,8c reminds the hearers of the punishment for idolatrous relations with the Moabite women as well as for the idolatry of the Golden Calf. This explains the absence of a punishment in 10,7. When Paul quotes Ex 32,6 and alludes to Ex 32,28, it is clear that he expects his hearers to be familiar with the material."

commit the sexual immorality that often accompanies it, they may likewise incur God's punishment.[24]

As in the C unit (10:8) of the chiasm so also in the C´ unit (10:9), Paul addresses his audience with a negative exhortation in the first-person plural: "Let us not put Christ to the test, as some of them tested and were being destroyed by the serpents."[25] That some of the Israelite ancestors "tested" (ἐπείρασαν, 10:9b) God and/or Christ continues to remind the audience of the scriptural tradition of the wandering in the wilderness of which the quotation of Exod 32:6b in 10:7b is a part and in which the people of Israel "tested" God with regard to their craving for food and drink.[26] As noted above, in LXX Ps 105:14, "But they craved with craving [cf. 1 Cor 10:6] in the desert, and tested (ἐπείρασαν) God in the waterless land" (cf. LXX Ps 77:41, 56).

In "testing" God the people were also "testing" Christ inasmuch as the rock that followed them and by which God gave them water in the desert was Christ (10:4). But despite the fact that God brought water out of the rock (LXX Ps 77:16) that was Christ, they "put to the test" (ἐξεπείρασαν) God in asking for food (LXX Ps 77:18; cf. Exod 17:2–7). For thus "testing" God in their intense craving for food and drink that eventually led to their idolatry, as expressed in the scriptural quote of Exod 32:6b in 10:7b that "the people sat down to eat and drink and stood up to play," they were being destroyed by "the serpents" (τῶν ὄφεων, 10:9c), an allusion to LXX Num 21:6, where the Lord sent "the serpents" (τοὺς ὄφεις) that bit and

---

24. Oropeza, *Paul and Apostasy*, 145: "[T]he gist of Paul's argument is not effected so much by the exact number of those who died as in the affirmation that a very large number of Isaelites did in fact die, emphasising the corporate influence of the vice and the notion of mass slaughter in the wilderness (cf. 10:5). Paul wishes to stress that God did not spare the Israelites who sinned, and by implication, neither will he spare the Corinthians."

25. We translate the compound verb ἐκπειράζωμεν in 10:9a as "put to the test" to distinguish it from the simple form ἐπείρασαν, "they tested," in 10:9b in light of its intensive connotation. According to Robertson and Plummer (*Corinthians*, 205), the compound form "implies prolonged and severe testing." According to Lockwood (*1 Corinthians*, 329), "It signifies 'willfully put to the test,' 'boldly challenge.' " See also Thiselton, *Corinthians*, 740–41. For the text-critical preference for the reading "Christ" rather than "Lord" or "God" in 10:9, see Carroll D. Osburn, "The Text of 1 Corinthians 10:9," in *New Testament Textual Criticism: Its Significance for Exegesis. Essays in Honour of Bruce M. Metzger* (ed. Eldon Jay Epp and Gordon D. Fee; Oxford: Clarendon, 1981), 201–12; Thiselton, *Corinthians*, 740; Oropeza, *Paul and Apostasy*, 153–55.

26. Although "Christ" is the explicit object of the testing in the exhortation "let us not put Christ to the test" in 10:9a, there is no explicit object to the testing in the comparative clause, "as some of them tested," in 10:9b, leaving the object open-ended and thus allowing for the object of Israel's testing to be God and/or Christ.

killed many of the people because they "spoke against" and thus tested God with regard to food and drink (Num 21:5, 7).[27]

Paul's exhortation to his audience, "let us not put Christ to the test" (10:9a), reminds them of what he said about misleading a fellow believer to eat the meat sacrificed to idols in 8:10-12. If someone sees a Christian reclining at table in the temple of an idol—thus actualizing the scriptural quote of Exod 32:6b in 10:7b that "the people sat down to eat and drink and stood up to play"—he may be provoked to eat the meat sacrificed to idols (8:10). Then a brother for whom Christ died is destroyed (8:11). When they sin against their brothers in this way, they are sinning against and thus "putting to the test" Christ (8:12).[28]

If Paul's Corinthian audience puts Christ to the test by eating the meat sacrificed to idols and thus actualizing the scriptural quote of Exod 32:6b in 10:7b, not only may they be the cause of a brother "being destroyed" (ἀπόλλυται, 8:11), but, like some of the Israelite ancestors who tested God and/or Christ in their craving for the food and drink that led to idolatry and were thus "being destroyed" (ἀπώλλυντο, 10:9), they may likewise be destroyed. They would thus be in the realm of those "being destroyed" (ἀπολλυμένοις, 1:18) in an eschatological, eternal sense, outside the realm of those being saved.[29]

As in the B unit (10:7) of the chiasm so also in the B′ unit (10:10), Paul addresses his audience with a negative command in the second-person plural: "Do not grumble, just as some of them grumbled and were destroyed by the destroyer." The Israelites of the wilderness generation "grumbled" against Moses and God in their intense craving for food and drink (Exod 15:24; 16:2-9; 17:2-3; Num 11:1, 4).[30] Although God heard their grum-

---

27. Oropeza, *Paul and Apostasy*, 150: "Although the Numbers tradition does not actually speak of 'testing God' in the bronze serpent incident, Paul may have been prompted by the poetic parallelism of Psalm 77[78]:18-19 to equate 'they tested God' (Psa. 77[78]:18) with 'they spoke against God' (Psa. 77[78]:19). For the psalmist, speaking against God *is conceptually* the same thing as putting God to the test. Paul may have had a similar or the same conception in his assessment of Israel's vice and punishment in Numbers 21."

28. In Num 21:7, the people "sinned" because they "spoke against" the Lord and Moses, and in LXX Ps 77:18-19 "speaking against" God is parallel to "putting God to the test." Mitchell, *Paul*, 128 n. 386: "To 'sin against Christ' implies the metaphor of the σῶμα Χριστοῦ. The brother is a member of one's own body, the body of Christ."

29. Oropeza, *Paul and Apostasy*, 151: "Paul's language is sharp when he describes that Israel's calamity was a result of their testing Christ: they were being destroyed by serpents.... He uses the imperfect tense of ἀπόλλυμι, indicating that this judgement may have had some sense of prolongation about it.... In essence, ἀπόλλυμι refers to moral ruin or eternal damnation."

30. With regard to the terminology of "grumbling" (γογγύζειν) in 1 Cor 10:10, Sandnes (*Belly*, 105) notes: "In particular the demand for food and meat is echoed in Paul's use of

bling and gave them spiritual food and drink (1 Cor 10:3–4), they nevertheless craved for idolatrous food and drink in accord with the scriptural quote of Exod 32:6b in 10:7b that "the people sat down to eat and drink and stood up to play."

For their "grumbling" for food and drink that led to idolatry they eventually "were destroyed by the destroyer" (ἀπώλοντο ὑπὸ τοῦ ὀλοθρευτοῦ, 10:10b)—a climactic intensification of the punishments listed within the chiasm for the idolatrous eating and drinking expressed by the quote of Exod 32:6b in 10:7b.[31] If those in Paul's audience "grumble" to eat the meat sacrificed to idols, they may, like their Israelite ancestors, not only "fall" (10:8), and "be destroyed by serpents" (10:9), but "be destroyed by the destroyer" (10:10).[32]

As in the A unit (10:6) of the chiasm so in the A′ unit (10:11), Paul speaks of the "things" that happened to the people of Israel in the wilderness traditions as "prefigurations."[33] These prefigurations "were written for our warning, upon whom the end of the ages has come" (10:11b). That they "were written" (ἐγράφη) for our warning refers the audience not only to the explicit quotation of Exod 32:6b in 10:7b, introduced by "as it is written (γέγραπται)," but to all of the many allusions to the scriptural wilderness

---

γογγύζειν in 1 Cor. 10:10. . . . The density of this terminology is especially high in texts about demands for food, meat and drink in the desert."

31. For suggestions of specific passages within the scriptural wilderness traditions as the background for 10:10, see Collier, "1 Corinthians 10.1–13," 63–67; Cheung, *Idol Food*, 144; Oropeza, *Paul and Apostasy*, 157–60; Garland, *1 Corinthians*, 464; Matthias Konradt, *Gericht und Gemeinde: Eine Studie zur Bedeutung und Funktion von Gerichtsaussagen im Rahmen der paulinischen Ekklesiologie und Ethik im 1 Thess und 1 Kor* (BZNW 117; Berlin: De Gruyter, 2003), 378–79. But the scriptural patterns rather than specific verses are more pertinent in this case as stated by Thiselton, *Corinthians*, 743: "Paul elsewhere refers to OT patterns rather than necessarily to specific verses, which often provide *more* powerful, *not less* powerful, *formative models* than a single passage may do." On the "destroyer" (ὀλοθρευτοῦ), Fee, *Corinthians*, 457 n. 38: "The LXX speaks of ὁ ὀλοθρεύων, 'the destroying one,' in Exod. 12:23 (cf. Heb. 11:28) and Wis. 18:25. Although the word 'angel' is not in the text, Paul is almost certainly thinking of the destroying angel as responsible for whichever judgment he has in mind"; Garland, *1 Corinthians*, 464 n. 23: "The noun ὄλεθρον appears in 1 Cor. 5:5, where Paul instructs them to deliver the incestuous man to Satan for the 'destruction' of his flesh."

32. Collier, "1 Corinthians 10.1–13," 62 n. 27: "It is not the verbs ἔπεσαν, ἀπώλλυντο and ἀπώλοντο in vv. 8–10 which alone indicate a crescendo in punishment, but the full language of Israel's fate: it is bad enough to fall (v. 8), but the language of 'being destroyed by the angel of destruction' (v. 10) is certainly more ominous and is held till the end." See also Oropeza, *Paul and Apostasy*, 161 n. 172.

33. Oropeza, *Paul and Apostasy*, 168: "[T]he 'things' hypothetically prefigure God's judgements on Israel in the wilderness (10:7–10). Paul intended the Corinthians to take warning from Israel's mistakes."

traditions throughout the chiasm in 10:6–11.[34] These scriptural prefigurations regarding the Israelite ancestors warn Paul's audience not to eat the meat sacrificed to idols as they did in order not to be severely punished as they were. That the "end of the ages has come" upon us underscores the eschatological urgency of the warning provided by these scriptural prefigurations.[35]

In sum, within the chiastic structure of 1 Cor 10:6–11 the scriptural quotation of Exod 32:6b, with its expression of the idolatrous "playing" that followed the eating and drinking of the people of Israel before an idol in the B unit of the chiasm (10:7), represents a scriptural "prefiguration" warning Paul's audience not to reenact this quote by eating the meat sacrificed to idols. If they do, they risk the eschatological destruction prefigured by the severe destructions suffered by the Israelite ancestors of the scriptural wilderness traditions alluded to in the chiasm. The rhetorical power of the explicit quotation of Exod 32:6b as an urgent warning is thus enhanced by the audience's recall of the entire scriptural complex of traditions regarding Israel's idolatrous, disastrous downfall while wandering in the wilderness.

Summary on 1 Corinthians 10:7b

1. Introduced by the formula "as it is written," the statement that "the people sat down to eat and drink and stood up to play" in 1 Cor 10:7b is a direct quotation of Exod 32:6b. It refers to the people of Israel's communal eating and drinking of the "peace offering" that was sacrificed together with holocausts for the feast of the idolatrous golden calf that Aaron fashioned for them (32:1–6a), which was followed by idolatrous "playing."

2. The people complemented their sitting down "to eat and drink" a banquet of idolatrous food with their standing up "to play," that is, to fur-

---

34. Oropeza, *Paul and Apostasy*, 168: "Paul's use of ἐγράφη implies that he considered these as authoritative examples; he uses γράφω when referring to statements found in the Hebrew/LXX scripture traditions. . . . [T]he chiasm begins and ends with a sense of warning, stressing Paul's anxiety over the reality of divine judgement that could occur in the Corinthian situation. The Israelite events were written to place a stern sense of caution in the mind of the readers."

35. Collins, *First Corinthians*, 373: "This eschatological identification of those for whose sake the Scriptures were written suggests that in Paul's vision the Scriptures themselves have eschatological significance." Fee, *Corinthians*, 458–59: "In this sentence one captures a sense of Paul's view that both the historical events and the inscripturated narrative are not simply history or isolated texts in Scripture; rather, behind all these things lies the eternal puposes of the living God, who knows the end from the beginning, and who therefore has himself woven the prefigurement into these earlier texts for the sake of his final eschatological people."

ther riotous, idolatrous behavior with orgiastic connotations. The audience is to realize that although the people "sat down" as a single entity to eat and drink, they "stood up" as a disparate group of individuals to rebellious, idolatrous playing, contradicting their status as "the people" of God.

3. The quotation of Exod 32:6b in 1 Cor 10:7b reinforces Paul's warning to his audience that those who have the knowledge that idols are nothing (8:1–6) not lead those who do not have this knowledge into idolatry.

4. With the scriptural quote of Exod 32:6b in the B unit (10:7) of the chiasm in 10:6–11, Paul warns that those among his audience who eat the meat sacrificed to idols not only may lead others into idolatry but also will become idolaters themselves and thus contradict the community's unity and status as the body of Christ (cf. 6:15; 8:12).

5. The scriptural quotation of Exod 32:6b in the B unit of the chiasm (10:7) represents a scriptural "prefiguration" warning Paul's audience not to reenact this quote by eating the meat sacrificed to idols. If they do, they risk the eschatological destruction prefigured by the severe destructions suffered by the Israelite ancestors of the scriptural wilderness traditions. The rhetorical power of the explicit quotation of Exod 32:6b as an urgent warning is enhanced by the audience's recall of the entire scriptural complex of traditions regarding Israel's idolatrous, disastrous downfall while wandering in the wilderness.

CHAPTER 11

1 Corinthians 10:26

To the Lord are the earth and its fullness.

Old Testament Background

Although not explicitly introduced as a scriptural quotation, the statement that "to the Lord are the earth and its fullness" in 1 Cor 10:26, a quotation of LXX Ps 23:1a, is distinguished from its context by its self-contained formulation lacking an explicit verb.[1] The only difference from the LXX is the insertion of the conjunction "for" (γάρ).

MT Ps 24:1a: לַיהוָה הָאָרֶץ וּמְלוֹאָהּ
LXX Ps 23:1a: τοῦ κυρίου ἡ γῆ καὶ τὸ πλήρωμα αὐτῆς
1 Cor 10:26: τοῦ κυρίου γὰρ ἡ γῆ καὶ τὸ πλήρωμα αὐτῆς

While 1 Cor 10:26 directly quotes LXX Ps 23:1a, it also resonates with similar expressions in several other OT texts. First of all, it is paralleled by the rest of the verse in Ps 23:1b: "To the Lord are the earth and its fullness, the world and all who dwell in it (ἡ οἰκουμένη καὶ πάντες οἱ κατοικοῦντες ἐν αὐτῇ)." In Exod 19:5, God announces, "for to me is all the earth (ἐμὴ γάρ ἐστιν πᾶσα ἡ γῆ)."[2] In Deut 10:14, Moses declares, "behold, to the Lord your God . . . is the earth and all things that are in it" (ἡ γῆ καὶ πάντα ὅσα ἐστὶν ἐν αὐτῇ; cf. LXX Ps 23:1b). In LXX Job 41:3, God asserts that "all that is under heaven is mine (πᾶσα ἡ ὑπ' οὐρανὸν ἐμή ἐστιν)." In LXX Ps 49:12, God insists, "for mine is the world and its fullness (ἐμὴ γάρ ἐστιν ἡ

---

1. Koch, *Schrift*, 14: "Durch seine sentenzenartige, in sich abgeschlossene Formulierung, die durch das Fehlen der Kopula noch verstärkt wird, unterscheidet sich auch die Anführung von Ψ23,1a in 1 Kor 10,26 von jetzigen Kontext."

2. Wevers, *Exodus*, 295: "A final γάρ clause gives the basis for the Lord's taking on Israel as a personal possession; the entire earth belongs to him (cf Ps 23:1), so that he has every right to choose whatever and whomever he wills."

οἰκουμένη καὶ τὸ πλήρωμα αὐτῆς)." And in LXX Ps 88:12, the psalmist praises God: "yours is the earth, the world and its fullness (σή ἐστιν ἡ γῆ τὴν οἰκουμένην καὶ τὸ πλήρωμα αὐτῆς) you have founded" (cf. LXX Ps 101:26).

Paul does not necessarily expect his audience to recall the quotation in 1 Cor 10:26 as a direct citation of LXX Ps 23:1a. Indeed, he does not even introduce it as a scriptural quotation, much less as a quotation of the Psalm. Rather, his audience is simply to recognize it as an authoritative statement, stylistically distinguished from its context in the letter, expressing that the whole earth and everything in it belongs to the Lord God—an expression found in several places in the OT, with which Paul expects his audience to be generally familiar. This enhances the rhetorical power of the quotation, endowing it with the authority not only of a single scriptural verse but of the scriptures in general and as a whole.[3]

Literary-Rhetorical Analysis

The scriptural quotation in 1 Cor 10:26 begins with an emphasis upon the Lord God—"To the *Lord* [and not to anyone or anything else, e.g. demons or idols] are the earth and its fullness."[4] That to the Lord God belongs not only the earth in general but also its "fullness" (πλήρωμα), that is, everything that fills the earth or everything that the earth contains, impresses upon the audience, with the authority of the scriptural word of God, that there is nothing whatsoever in the created order outside of the dominion and sovereignty of God, the Creator.[5] The scriptural quote, then, eliminates from the audience concern with any other lordship over creation other than that of the sovereign Lord God, instills in them a respect for everything on earth as a creature of the Lord God, and calls for their allegiance and gratitude to the Lord God in their use of all that the Lord God has created.[6]

---

3. Collins, *First Corinthians*, 387: "In 1 Corinthians Paul typically identifies scriptural citations by means of a formal introductory lemma, but that is not always the case. The use of the explanatory, postpositive γάρ, 'for,' in 10:26 (cf. 2:16; 15:25) suggests that Paul is citing Scripture as if it were a well-known adage."

4. Robertson and Plummer, *Corinthians*, 220: "The emphasis is on τοῦ Κυρίου, 'To the *Lord* belongs the earth.'"

5. Lockwood, *1 Corinthians*, 348: But like מְלֹא, the Hebrew word used in Ps 24:1 (which is quoted here) and in the similiar phrases in Pss 50:12 and 89:12 (ET 89:11), πλήρωμα means 'that which fills it,' 'its contents.' See . . . LXX Ps 95:11 [MT/ET 96:11]: ἡ θάλασσα καὶ τὸ πλήρωμα αὐτῆς, 'the sea and that which fills her.'" Thiselton, *Corinthians*, 786: "Nothing exists that is not lent or given by *the Lord*."

6. On the relation of the Psalm verse to the Jewish blessing at meals, see Wolff, *Erste Brief*, 238; Lindemann, *Erste Korintherbrief*, 231–32; Fee, *Corinthians*, 482; Tomson, *Paul*, 205;

Relation to the Antecedent Context in 1 Corinthians 10:23-25

The scriptural quotation of LXX Ps 23:1a in 10:26 functions within the following chiastic arrangement in 10:23-11:1:

A   ²³ "*All things* are permitted" but not *all things* are *beneficial!* "*All things* are permitted" but not *all things* build up! ²⁴ Let no one *seek* what is for oneself but what is for the other.

    B   ²⁵ All that is sold in the market eat, not raising questions because of *conscience,* ²⁶ for "to the Lord are the earth and its fullness" (LXX Ps 23:1a). ²⁷ If one of the unbelievers invites you and you want to go, all that is placed before you eat, not raising questions because of *conscience.*

    B′   ²⁸ But if someone says to you, "This was sacrificed in a temple," do not eat it because of the one reporting it, that is, because of *conscience.*[7] ²⁹ The *conscience,* I mean, not of oneself but that of the other. For why is my freedom to be condemned by another's *conscience?* ³⁰ If I partake with gratitude, why am I blasphemed for what I give thanks?

A′   ³¹ So whether you eat or drink, or whatever you do, do *all things* for the glory of God. ³² Be inoffensive, whether to Jews or Greeks or the church of God, ³³ just as I try to please everyone in *all things,* not *seeking* my own *benefit* but that of the many, that they may be saved. ^{11:1} Be imitators of me, just as I am of Christ.[8]

This chiastic structure is constituted by the following parallels (itali-

---

Cheung, *Idol Food,* 155; Garland, *1 Corinthians,* 492; Thiselton, *Corinthians,* 786: "[A]lthough there is no evidence that Ps 24:1 was used as a grace in Judaism, nevertheless the implications of the verse were pressed as an argument that grace at meals ought to be said."

7. We take the καὶ here to be explicative; see BDAG, 495; Smit, *About the Idol Offerings,* 143 n. 28.

8. This chiastic structure for 10:23-11:1 differs from that offered by Fee (*Corinthians,* 478) and Hays (*First Corinthians,* 174). They separate 10:28-30 (my B′ unit) into two units—10:28-29a and 10:29b-30. But the coordinating conjunction "for" (γάρ), as well as the repetition of the word "conscience" (συνειδήσεως) in 10:29b, indicates that 10:29b-30 is closely connected to 10:28-29a, so that 10:28-30 forms a single unit. On the criteria for determining a chiasm, see n. 8 in ch. 8 above.

cized above): "All things" (πάντα, 4x in 10:23), "beneficial" (συμφέρει, 10:23a), and "seek" (ζητείτω, 10:24) in the A unit (10:23-24) are paralleled by "all things" (πάντα, 2x in 10:31, 33), "benefit" (σύμφορον, 10:33), and "seeking" (ζητῶν, 10:33) in the A´ unit (10:31-11:1). These terms occur only in the A and A´ units of the chiasm. "Conscience" (συνείδησιν, 2x in 10:25, 27) in the B unit is paralleled by "conscience" (συνείδησιν, 2x in 10:28b, 29a; συνειδήσεως, 10:29b) in the B´ unit, and occurs only in these units within the chiasm.

In the A unit (10:23-24) of the chiasm, the twice-proclaimed maxim "all things are permissible" (10:23; cf. 6:12) characterizes the position of those in the Corinthian audience who think that they are permitted, that they have the "right" (8:9), to eat meat sacrificed to idols because of their knowledge that idols are nothing (8:1-6).[9] Paul counters with a double refutation that "not all things are beneficial" and "not all things build up" (10:23). That not all things "build up (οἰκοδομεῖ)" recalls how it is love, not "knowledge," that "builds up (οἰκοδομεῖ)" (8:1). Therefore, no one in the audience is to seek only what is good for himself but what is good for the other (10:24). Those in the audience who think they are permitted to eat idol food must give up this "right" for the benefit and building up of others and thus of the community in general.[10]

In the B unit (10:25-27) of the chiasm, Paul raises the issue of eating meat bought in the marketplace that may or may not have been sacrificed

---

9. For a rhetorical analysis of the maxims in 10:23, see Watson, "1 Corinthians 10:23-11:1," 303-4; Ramsaran, *Liberating Words*, 57-59; Smit, *About the Idol Offerings*, 140-42; Fotopoulos, *Food*, 237-38. Winter, *After Paul*, 95: "[T]he nexus between the term ἐξουσία, which Paul used extensively in 1 Corinthians 8-9, and ἔξεστιν (10:23) is not always recognised. What is a 'right' (ἐξουσία) can be expressed in the verbal form 'it is permitted' (ἔξεστιν)."

10. Newton, *Deity and Diet*, 375: "In a real sense, 10.23-24 thus constitute the climax and consolidation of all that the apostle has argued thus far in 1 Cor. 8.1-10.22." Smit, *About the Idol Offerings*, 141: "In cases in which the general permission (πάντα ἔξεστιν) gives conflicts with the obligation to strive for the other's benefit (ζητείτω) the obligation prevails over the permission which, consequently, should not be used." Collins, *First Corinthians*, 386: "For Paul such radical individualism is not advantageous. What is advantageous is what builds up the community. In Paul the verb οἰκοδομέω, 'to build up,' 'to edify,' usually has a specifically ecclesial reference. It is a matter of building up the church (cf. 8:1)." Mitchell, *Paul*, 37: "By the parallel structure of verses 10:23a and 23b, one is led to deduce that the advantageous act is that which builds up the community. Building language, especially the term (ἐπ)οικοδομεῖν and cognates, is very important in 1 Corinthians, and is found throughout the letter."

to idols in temples.¹¹ With strong emphasis on "all" (πᾶν),¹² Paul commands not just part of his audience—either the so-called strong or weak—but everyone in his audience: "*All* that is sold in the market eat, not raising questions because of conscience" (10:25).¹³ In other words, his Corinthian audience can eat anything bought in the market without worrying their moral consciousness.¹⁴ They need not investigate whether the meat they buy and eat has previously been part of a sacrifice to idols.

Paul's command for his audience to eat anything that is sold in the market is bolstered by the authoritative scriptural maxim in 10:26: "For to the Lord are the earth and its fullness" (LXX Ps 23:1a). Because everything sold in the market has been created by God, it is part of the earth's "fullness" that belongs to God and thus is ultimately under the sovereignty of God's lordship. Even if it has previously been sacrificed to idols, anyone in Paul's audience may freely and unquestioningly eat it.¹⁵

---

11. Fee, *Corinthians*, 481: "The reason for addressing this issue is that what was sold in the *macellum* often contained meat butchered by the priests, much of it having been part of the pagan sacrifices." For the argument that not all food sold in the market place came from temple sacrifices, see Dietrich-Alex Koch, "'Alles, was ἐν μακέλλῳ verkauft wird, eβt . . .': Die *macella* von Pompeji, Gerasa und Korinth und ihre Bedeutung für die Auslegung von 1Kor 10,25," *ZNW* 90 (1999): 194–219. Cheung, *Idol Food*, 154–55: "[T]here are indications that non-sacrificed meat was readily available. Therefore one must not exaggerate the plight of the Corinthians as having *nothing* to eat unless it were sacrificial meat. In any case, 1 Cor. 10.25 makes clear that not all food was previously sacrificed. Otherwise, what is the point of 'not asking'?" Garland, *1 Corinthians*, 491–92: "Paul's permission to eat whatever is sold in the market presumes that not everything offered for sale had been contaminated by idolatrous rituals." On the location of the *macellum* in Corinth, see David W. J. Gill, "The Meat-Market at Corinth (1 Corinthians 10:25)," *TynBul* 43 (1992): 389–93; Fotopoulos, *Food*, 139–42.

12. Fee, *Corinthians*, 480 n. 19: "Paul's word order is emphatic: *Anything* sold in the meat market, eat, etc."

13. Garland, *1 Corinthians*, 490: "Paul gives general advice to all Christians about buying and eating food sold in the provision market and does not distinguish between the so-called strong and weak."

14. For the view that "conscience" (συνείδησις) here refers not to moral consciousness but to self-consciousness or self-awareness, see Gardner, *Gifts*, 175–76; Thiselton, *Corinthians*, 784–85. Fee, *Corinthians*, 482: "[H]e [Paul] is contending that 'conscience' is not involved at all, so an investigation is irrelevant. Thus, do not raise any questions 'for conscience' sake' because this matter lies outside the concerns of conscience altogether." Cheung, *Idol Food*, 153: "There is no need to inquire 'for the sake of consciousness,' that is, for the sake of knowing the nature of the food with the entailed moral obligations. . . . συνείδησις need not be involved at all in the case of food of unspecified origin."

15. Fee, *Corinthians*, 482: "God is the ultimate source of the food—even that sold in the *macellum*. For that reason it can be taken with thanksgiving." Smit, *About the Idol Offerings*, 142–43: "[T]his statement is further supported by an argument from authority, namely a very appropriate quotation from Ps. 24:1, which forms the heart of this part: for 'the earth is the Lord's and everything it contains.' Because the earth and everything it contains is the Lord's be-

But to whom does "the Lord" in the scriptural quote refer—God or Jesus Christ? Certainly, in its original context within the OT scriptures "to the Lord" (τοῦ κυρίου) refers to the God of creation, and Paul's audience may understand it in this way. But in its new context within 1 Corinthians the audience may well take "to the Lord" to refer to the Lord Jesus Christ. Indeed, every occurrence of "Lord" (κύριος) in the singular in 8:1–10:22 refers to "the Lord" Jesus Christ (8:6; 9:1 [2x], 2, 5, 14; 10:21 [2x], 22).[16]

An especially noteworthy occurrence of the "Lord" Jesus Christ appears in 8:6: "But for us there is one God, the Father, from whom all things are and for whom we exist, and one Lord (κύριος), Jesus Christ, through whom all things are and through whom we exist." This indicates that there is a sense in which Jesus Christ has a role of "Lord," paralleled with that of God as Father, over all of creation, which accords with the quote in 10:26. For Paul's rhetorical strategy, then, it does not matter whether his audience understands "to the Lord" in the scriptural quote to refer to Jesus Christ or to God. Because of their roles in creation, both God the Father and the Lord Jesus Christ (and not the idols or demons) have absolute dominion over "the earth and its fullness" (10:26), so that the audience may eat anything they buy in the marketplace (10:25).[17]

---

lievers do not need to question anything and are permitted to eat everything offered." Cheung, *Idol Food*, 155: "Idols have no magical power over the food per se because 'the earth is the Lord's, and all it contains.'" Fotopoulos, *Food*, 239: "[I]f it is uncertain whether the food is sacrificial or not, Paul advises that there is no need to raise questions on the grounds of moral consciousness. However, Paul does not give explicit permission to eat sacrificial food in 10:25–26 but states that Christians can eat whatever is sold without raising questions, behavior which is supported by an inartificial proof from the outside authority of Scripture, 'the earth and its fullness are the Lord's.'" Thiselton, *Corinthians*, 785–86: "[T]he quotation from Ps 24:1 performs three functions. (1) It lifts the attention from self and from overscrupulous anxiety to the reminder that the sovereign to whom everything belongs (including the care of the believer) is *the Lord*; (2) It reminds the anxious that even what may or may not have passed through pagan temples still belongs to *the totality of God's creation* over which he (not the so-called gods of 1 Cor 8:1–6) reigns as sovereign.... (3) Most especially it implies that every good gift of God is to be accepted *with gratitude* as *the Lord's* gift." Garland, "Dispute," 195: "The premise behind this instruction comes from Ps 24:1 (cf. 50:12; 89:11), which, in Judaism, shaped the prayer to be voiced before a meal (*b. Šabb.* 119a). It affirms that God is sovereign over all things (8:6) and that everything created by God is good (cf. 1 Tim 4:4). The whole creation belongs to God, not part to God and part to idols. Idol food therefore loses its character as idol food as soon as it leaves the idol's arena and the idolater's purposes."

16. There is a plural reference to "gods" and "lords" (κύριοι) in 8:5.

17. For Lindemann (*Erste Korintherbrief*, 231), "Lord" in 10:26 seems to refer to God as in the quoted text from LXX Ps 23:1a. For Koch (*Schrift*, 287 n. 11) and Wolff (*Erste Brief*, 238 n. 421), "Lord" here can only refer to Christ in the thought of Paul and within the context of 1 Corinthians. But for Schrage (*Erste Brief*, 467 n. 516), the evidence is inconclusive: "Gleichwohl ist keine eindeutige Entscheidung möglich." We maintain that for Paul the audience may

Relation to the Subsequent Context in
1 Corinthians 10:27–11:1

In the conclusion of the B unit (10:25-27) of the chiasm, Paul brings up the possibility of members of his audience being invited to the home of an unbeliever for a meal: "If one of the unbelievers invites you and you want to go, all that is placed before you eat, not raising questions because of conscience" (10:27).[18] Paul's command for his audience to eat without questioning repeats and parallels that in 10:25: "All that is sold in the market eat, not raising questions because of conscience." The authoritative basis for both commands, then, is the scriptural quotation in 10:26. They may eat the food set before them by an unbeliever, even if it has possibly been part of a sacrifice to idols, because the Lord God/Lord Jesus Christ (cf. 8:6) has ultimate dominion over it and not the idols or demons—"To the *Lord* are the earth and its fullness."[19]

The theme of concern for "conscience" or "consciousness" (συνείδησις) in the B unit (10:25-27) of the chiasm continues in the B′ unit (10:28-30), but with a transition from concern for one's own conscience to concern for that of the other. If, when you are dining in the home of an unbeliever (10:27a), someone informs you that what is placed before you to eat (10:27b) has been "sacrificed to a god" (ἱερόθυτόν), then you are not to eat it because of the conscience of the one reporting it (10:28).[20] That you are

---

understand "Lord" in 10:26 as either God or Jesus Christ, as is the case for "Lord" in the scriptural quotation in 1:31 (see ch. 3 above).

18. A meal in the home of an unbeliever is the most likely context for the situation referred to in 10:27. For the discussion and elimination of other possibilities, see Newton, *Deity and Diet*, 376; Fotopoulos, *Food*, 242-43. On "if you want to go" in 10:27, Garland (*1 Corinthians*, 493) notes: "[E]verything depends on the Christian 'wanting to go.' Paul does not encourage Christian dinner guests to go but leaves it for them to decide."

19. Cheung, *Idol Food*, 157: "Therefore at meals in private homes, as in the case of marketplace food, there is no necessary or presumptive connection between food and idolatry. Further, it is possible that some of the foods being served are not εἰδωλόθυτα even though the rest have been hallowed (defiled) by sacrificial rites. This kind of meal is unlike both temple meals (in which εἰδωλόθυτα are most probably served) and meals hosted by Christians (in which εἰδωλόθυτα are not supposed to be served). Paul's advice in this case is the same as his instruction about marketplace food: simply eat; it is not necessary to know the nature of the food."

20. Garland, *1 Corinthians*, 494: "The term ἱερόθυτον appears only here in the Bible and is the more dignified term that a devotee of other gods and goddesses would use rather than the pejorative εἰδωλόθυτον used by Christians. It means 'sacrificed in a temple,' 'slain as sacred,' or 'sacrificial food.'" Lockwood, *1 Corinthians*, 348: "Literally this term means 'sacrificed in a temple.' It was the normal term used by pagans themselves for their sacrifices. Earlier Paul had used the regular Jewish-Christian designation for pagan sacrifices, εἰδωλόθυτον, 'meat sacrificed to idols' (8:1, 4, 7, 10; 10:19; see also Acts 15:29; 21:25; Rev 2:14, 20), which pagans themselves would not have used because of its thrust against idolatry." Although this leads many to suppose a

not to eat such sacrificial food out of respect for the conscience "not of oneself but that of the other" (οὐχὶ τὴν ἑαυτοῦ ἀλλὰ τὴν τοῦ ἑτέρου, 10:29a) further delineates for his audience what Paul commanded in the A unit: "Let no one seek what is for oneself but what is for the other" (μηδεὶς τὸ ἑαυτοῦ ζητείτω ἀλλὰ τὸ τοῦ ἑτέρου, 10:24).

With the paradigmatic first-person singular, representing not only Paul himself but anyone claiming that "all things are permissible" (10:23 in the A unit of the chiasm), Paul explains (γάρ, 10:29b) why one should not eat such sacrificial food for the sake of the conscience of "the other."[21] For why should I risk my freedom, in accord with the dictum of the scriptural quote that "to the Lord are the earth and its fullness" (10:26), to eat what has been sacrificed to a god if it may mean being "condemned" (κρίνεται) by the conscience of anyone (either a fellow Christian or an unbeliever) who thinks such food still to be under the dominion of a pagan god (10:29b)? If eating such food leads another to condemn you, then you have not benefited or built up the other (10:23–24).

Furthermore, if I partake of food sacrificed to a pagan idol with gratitude and thanks to God, as intimated by the scriptural quote that "to the Lord are the earth and its fullness" (10:26), why should I risk being "blasphemed" (βλασφημοῦμαι) by anyone who thinks such food still belongs to the pagan idol (10:30)? I would then ironically be "blasphemed," which often has the connotation of speaking against God, for what I gave thanks

---

pagan informant, the informant could also be a fellow Christian—the "someone" (τις, 10:28) is indefinite. See Newton, *Deity and Diet*, 376–77; Fotopoulos, *Food*, 244–46; Cheung, *Idol Food*, 160: "It is possible that the informant is (purposely or otherwise) left indefinite because it does not matter who broaches the issue.... [I]f its idolatrous prehistory is pointed out (by whatever means), one must abstain." Garland, *1 Corinthians*, 496: "The case is hypothetical, and there is no need to identify or to untangle the motives of the informer." On 10:28, Collins (*First Corinthians*, 388) notes: "Some manuscripts, including the majority of medieval texts, again (cf. v. 26) cite Ps 24:1 at the end of this verse.... The weight of the manuscript tradition and the possibility of scribal error coalesce in leading to the judgment that a citation of Ps 24:1 was originally not to be found in v. 28." See also Garland, *1 Corinthians*, 503–4.

21. In the rhetorical questions of 10:29b–30, then, Paul is not (as some maintain) characterizing the objections of one who holds that "all things are permissible" or the objections of a so-called strong Christian (a term not used by Paul in this context). Rather, he is providing for such persons, among whom he includes himself with the first-person singular, further considerations for his instruction not to eat food that is known to have been sacrificed to a pagan god. For the discussion, see Watson, "1 Corinthians 10:23–11:1," 308–18; Smit, *About the Idol Offerings*, 143–44; Newton, *Deity and Diet*, 377–79; Fotopoulos, *Food*, 246–47; Garland, *1 Corinthians*, 497–500; Cheung, *Idol Food*, 161: "It seems best to see vv. 29b–30 as Paul's reasons for the restrictions in vv. 28–29a. In effect, Paul says, 'Why eat, if eating causes so much trouble and misunderstanding?' Paul is not asking hypothetical questions but rhetorical questions for which no answer need to be provided, because the answer is clear: do not eat!"

to God for!²² The "condemnation" and "blaspheming" that may result from such eating, then, would neither benefit nor build up the other (10:23–24) by leading the other, in accord with the scriptural quote in 10:26, to acknowledge, praise, and thank God as *the Lord*, to whom belongs "the earth and its fullness."²³

Countering the slogan in the A unit (10:23–24) of the chiasm that "all things" (πάντα) are permissible (10:23), Paul in the A´ unit (10:31–11:1) exhorts his audience to do "all things" (πάντα) for the glory of God (10:31b).²⁴ This resonates with and follows from the scriptural quote in 10:26 that "to the Lord are the earth and its fullness." And further countering the repeated slogan that "all things" (πάντα) are permissible, Paul exhorts his audience to imitate him as he imitates Christ (11:1) in trying to please everyone in "all things" (πάντα, 10:33a).²⁵

The audience is to imitate the Paul who personally takes up and extends his exhortation in the A unit that "no one seek what is for oneself

---

22. BDAG, 178; Otfried Hofius, "βλασφημία," *EDNT* 1.219–21.

23. A paraphrase of the rhetorical questions in 10:29b–30 is offered by Willis, *Idol Meat*, 249: "Why should I as a Christian conscious of my freedom to eat or not eat exercise freedom by eating if I know another person's awareness will lead him to condemn me?" and "How can I offer grace over food, knowing that I will be blasphemed for eating that over which I have said a blessing?" Watson ("1 Corinthians 10:23–11:1," 310) objects to the position that the rhetorical questions in 10:29b–30 provide further explanation for 10:28–29a, because it "makes Paul's response trifling, for he in essence is made to counsel the strong to refrain from eating meat offered to idols *merely* to avoid being verbally abused by those of weaker conscience" (my emphasis). But Watson greatly undervalues the strong language of condemning and blaspheming. It is not mere verbal abuse but contradicts the benefiting and building up of the other that Paul calls for in 10:23–24. Garland (*1 Corinthians*, 499) also criticizes this position and Willis's paraphrases: "This argument, again, mistakenly assumes that a weak Christian will be offended by these actions and will condemn the so-called strong for eating and imposes that view on the text. When Paul specifically mentions those with a weak conscience, however, he is more concerned that they will fall into idolatry and be destroyed than that they would be offended by idolatry (8:7–13)." But either a weak Christian or a non-Christian (cf. 9:21–22; 10:32) may be offended by the eating of sacrificial food. Furthermore, the weak Christian may not necessarily be led into idolatry, but be led to condemning and/or blaspheming his fellow Christian, rather than being benefited and built up (10:23–24).

24. Fotopoulos, *Food*, 247: "The slogan that Paul proposes, πάντα εἰς δόξαν θεοῦ ποιεῖτε, is an appropriate alternative to πάντα ἔξεστιν (10:23; 6:12)." Fee, *Corinthians*, 488: "All such things must finally be 'for the glory of God.' This seems in particular to pick up on the theme of 'thanksgiving' in v. 30, that God is to be blessed because everything is his and thus to his glory." Garland, *1 Corinthians*, 500: "The πάντα excludes the possibility of compartmentalizing one's life so that one might reserve a segment of it to do as one pleases. It also sounds a striking counterpoint to the maxim quoted at the beginning of this unit, 'All things are permissable' (10:23). Only those things that bring glory to God are permitted."

25. Garland, *1 Corinthians*, 502: "Seeking to please everyone in all things while not seeking one's own advantage counters the catchphrase cited in 10:23, 'All things are permissible.'"

but what is for the other (τὸ τοῦ ἑτέρου)" (10:24) by "not seeking my own benefit but that of the many (τὸ τῶν πολλῶν), that they may be saved" (10:33b) in the A′ unit.[26] Paul's audience is to be "inoffensive," particularly by abstaining from sacrificial food (10:28–30), "whether to Jews or Greeks or the church of God" (10:32), so that they may be saved (cf. 9:19–22).[27] Paul's inclusive concern for the salvation of all God's people has its scriptural foundation in the quote in 10:26: "To the Lord are the earth and its fullness." The scriptural quotation in 10:26, then, not only justifies the eating of all that is bought in the market (10:25) and all that is offered by an unbeliever (10:27), but also serves as the basis for a concern for the salvation of all people as creatures of God—as part of "the earth and its fullness," a concern which includes not eating sacrificial food for the sake of the salvation of others (10:28–30) for the glory of God (10:31b).[28]

Summary on 1 Corinthians 10:26

1. Although a direct citation of LXX Ps 23:1a, "To the Lord are the earth and its fullness," the scriptural quotation in 1 Cor 10:26 is not introduced as a scriptural quotation. Paul's audience is simply to recognize it as an authoritative statement, stylistically distinguished from its context in the letter, expressing that the whole earth and everything in it belongs to the Lord God—an expression found in several places in the OT, with which

---

26. Garland, *1 Corinthians*, 502: "'The many' does not refer to the church community but to the majority of people inside and outside the church. It is a Semitism for 'all.' . . . Following his example in this instance entails two things: (1) submitting to his authority and his injunctions to dissociate themselves from anything overtly connected to idolatry; and (2) imitating his personal example by forgoing the exercise of perceived rights so that one achieves a greater benefit for others."

27. Margaret M. Mitchell, "Pauline Accommodation and 'Condescension' (συγκατάβασις): 1 Cor 9:19–23 and the History of Influence," in *Paul beyond the Judaism/Hellenism Divide* (ed. Troels Engberg-Pedersen; Louisville: Westminster John Knox, 2001), 197–214.

28. Cheung, *Idol Food*, 161–62: "It is possible to see the 'glorifying God' in v. 31 as being defined in terms of seeking the good of others in vv. 32–33. But, more probably, here as in various places in Scripture, the injunction to give God the glory has something more specific in view, namely, to avoid sinning that affronts God's glory. Just as glorifying God in one's body means abstaining from πορνεία, eating and drinking to God's glory means avoiding εἰδωλόθυτα. In this way v. 31 summarizes the argument of ch. 10." Newton, *Deity and Diet*, 380: "In 10.31 Paul calls the believers to do all things to the glory of God and he makes specific mention of eating and drinking. Such an injunction is at the same time a very broad general principle, yet spans every facet of the idol food issue. Clearly, in Paul's mind, God would not be honoured if believers fell from faith, if there was division in the church, if honour was given to false gods or if unbelievers were prevented in any way from coming to Christian faith. 10.31 thus summarizes the entirety of Paul's intent thoughout 1 Corinthians 8–10."

Paul expects his audience to be generally familiar. This enhances the rhetorical power of the quotation, endowing it with the authority not only of a single scriptural verse but of the scriptures in general and as a whole.

2. The scriptural quote in 10:26 eliminates from the audience concern with any other lordship over creation other than that of the sovereign Lord God, instills in them a respect for everything on earth as a creature of the Lord God, and calls for their allegiance and gratitude to the Lord God in their use of all that the Lord God has created.

3. It does not matter whether Paul's audience understands "to the Lord" in the scriptural quote in 10:26 to refer to Jesus Christ or to God. Because of their roles in creation both God the Father and the Lord Jesus Christ (and not the idols or demons) have absolute dominion over "the earth and its fullness," so that the audience may eat anything they buy in the marketplace (10:25).

4. The scriptural quotation in 10:26 not only justifies the eating of all that is bought in the market (10:25) and all that is offered by an unbeliever (10:27), but also serves as the basis for a concern for the salvation of all people as creatures of God—as part of "the earth and its fullness," a concern which includes not eating sacrificial food for the sake of the salvation of others (10:28–30) for the glory of God (10:31b).

Chapter 12

1 Corinthians 11:7–12

> For man, on the one hand, should not have his head covered, being the image and glory of God, the woman, on the other hand, is the glory of man. For man is not from woman but woman from man. For indeed man was not created on account of the woman but woman on account of the man. For this reason the woman should have authority over her head, on account of the angels. But neither is woman apart from man nor man apart from woman in the Lord. For just as the woman is from the man, so also the man is through the woman; but all things are from God.

Old Testament Background

Although not explicitly introduced as a scriptural citation, 1 Cor 11:7–12 contains such obvious and prominent references to the scriptures that their treatment is not only justified but demanded in this investigation of the rhetorical role of scripture in Paul's argumentation in 1 Corinthians. Indeed, the references to the scriptural traditions regarding the order of creation appear to be crucial and fundamental to Paul's rhetorical strategy within 1 Cor 11:2–16. While the accounts of the creation of man and woman from Genesis are primary, they are not the only scriptural references at play in 1 Cor 11:7–12.[1]

That man is the "image and glory (εἰκὼν καὶ δόξα) of God" in 1 Cor

---

1. Joël Delobel, "1 Cor 11,2–16: Towards a Coherent Interpretation," in *L'Apôtre Paul: Personnalité, style et conception du ministère* (ed. Albert Vanhoye; BETL 73; Louvain: Louvain University Press, 1986), 380: "[O]ne cannot imagine Paul referring to the order in the cosmos without the biblical creation belief in his mind and vv. 7–12 prove that the creation stories themselves played a role in the argumentation of this pericope."

11:7a reminds the audience of several OT texts. In LXX Gen 1:26–27, God said, "Let us make man according to our image and likeness (κατ' εἰκόνα ἡμετέραν καὶ καθ' ὁμοίωσιν) . . . and God made man, according to the image (κατ' εἰκόνα) of God he made him."[2] In LXX Gen 5:1b, "according to the image (κατ' εἰκόνα) of God he made him." In LXX Gen 9:6b, "for in the image (ἐν εἰκόνι) of God I made the man." In Sir 17:3, "He [the Lord; cf. 17:1] endowed them [human beings; cf. ἄνθρωπον in 17:1] with strength like his own, and made them according to his image (κατ' εἰκόνα αὐτοῦ)." And in Wis 2:23, "for God created the man for immortality, and he made him an image (εἰκόνα) of his own eternity."

But 1 Cor 11:7a states that man is not only the image but also the "glory" (δόξα) of God. This reminds the audience of yet other OT texts. In LXX Ps 8:6, the "glory" of a human being includes his lofty status just below the angels in the order of creation: "You [the Lord; cf. 8:1] have made him [man; cf. ἄνθρωπος in 8:5] a little lower than the angels, with glory (δόξῃ) and honor you have crowned him." In LXX Ps 7:6, a human being's God-given "glory" is paralleled with both his "soul" and his "life": "Let the enemy pursue my soul and take it, and let him trample my life to the ground and cause my glory (δόξαν) to dwell in the dust." In LXX Isa 40:6b, the "glory" of a human being is compared with the transitory nature of grass in contrast with the abiding character of God's word (cf. 40:7–8): "All flesh is grass and all glory (δόξα) of man as the flower of grass."

That "the woman is the glory (δόξα) of man" in 1 Cor 11:7b also reminds the audience of several scriptural texts. In LXX Prov 11:16a, "A gracious woman raises up glory (δόξαν) to a man" (cf. 31:30–31). In 1 Esd 4:17b, "they [women; cf. 4:15] bring glory (δόξαν) to men."[3] And, employing the word "honor" (τιμή), which is often synonymously paralleled with "glory" (δόξα) (cf. LXX Ps 8:6; Prov 11:16; 1 Cor 11:14–15), LXX Esth 1:20b states: "all the women will surround their husbands with honor (τιμήν), from the poor to the rich."

That "man is not from woman, but woman from man (ἐξ ἀνδρός)" in 1 Cor 11:8 reminds the audience of LXX Gen 2:23b: "This one will be called

---

2. John William Wevers, *Notes on the Greek Text of Genesis* (SBLSCS 35; Atlanta: Scholars Press, 1993), 14: "That ἄνθρωπος is something quite apart from that which God made in vv. 20–25 is emphasized not only by the first plural verb but also by the coordinate prepositional phrases κατ' εἰκόνα ἡμετέραν καὶ καθ' ὁμοίωσιν. The fact that both phrases are κατά phrases shows that they probably mean the same thing. It is actually difficult to distnguish between εἴκων and ὁμοίωσις. Both mean 'likeness, resemblance,' though only εἴκων can be used of 'image.' . . . In some way then God intends to make man in his own image, in some way reflecting himself."

3. Zipora Talshir, *I Esdras: From Origin to Translation* (SBLSCS 47; Atlanta: Society of Biblical Literature, 1999), 69–70; idem, *I Esdras: A Text Critical Commentary* (SBLSCS 50; Atlanta: Society of Biblical Literature, 2001), 191–92.

'woman,' for out of her man (ἐκ τοῦ ἀνδρὸς αὐτῆς) this one was taken." And that "man was not created on account of the woman but woman on account of the man" in 1 Cor 11:9 recalls for the audience from the same context in Gen 2:20–23 that the woman was formed from the side of the man in order to create from the man a "helper like him" (2:20b; cf. 2:18), which could not be found among all of the animals that the man had named.

That "neither is woman apart from (χωρὶς) man nor is man apart from woman (χωρὶς γυναικὸς)" in 1 Cor 11:11 reminds the audience of 1 Esd 4:17c: "and the men are not able to exist apart from the women (χωρὶς τῶν γυναικῶν)." And that "man is through the woman" in 1 Cor 11:12b continues to remind the audience of the creation account in Genesis, where God tells the woman, "You will give birth to children" (Gen 3:16; cf 1 Esd 4:15–17).

Finally, "but all things (πάντα) are from God (θεοῦ)" in 1 Cor 11:12c recalls for the audience several OT texts. In LXX Gen 1:31, "God (θεὸς) saw all things (πάντα) that he had made, and, behold, they were very good." In LXX Eccl 3:11a, "He [God; cf. θεὸς in 3:10] has made all things (πάντα) good." In Sir 36:1a, "Have mercy on us, God (θεὸς), master of all things (πάντων)." In LXX Amos 5:8a, "He [the Lord; cf. 5:6] is the one who makes all things (πάντα)." And in LXX Isa 45:7b, "I am the Lord God (θεὸς) who makes all (πάντα) these things."

In sum, although 1 Cor 11:7–12 reminds the audience primarily of the accounts about the creation of the first human beings in Genesis (1:26–27, 31; 2:18, 20–23; 3:16; 5:1; 9:6), a number of other scriptural texts concerning creation are also recalled or alluded to. Paul is thus relying upon his implied audience's familiarity with the whole complex of scriptural traditions regarding the divine order of creation.

The Role of 1 Corinthians 11:7–12 in the Argument of 1 Corinthians 11:2–16

We now examine the literary-rhetorical role that the scriptural references in 1 Cor 11:7–12 play within their epistolary context, the argument of 1 Cor 11:2–16. We begin with our translation and literary structure of 1 Cor 11:2–16, as illustrated by the following schema:[4]

---

4. This schema represents a new proposal for the structure of 1 Cor 11:2–16 in contrast to the chiastic structure proposed by Sheila E. McGinn, "ἐξουσίαν ἔχειν ἐπὶ τῆς κεφαλῆς: 1 Cor 11:10 and the Ecclesial Authority of Women," *Listening* 31 (1996): 91–104, and taken over

The Structure of 1 Corinthians 11:2–16

Introduction: Traditions (11:2)

² I praise you because you remember me in everything and, just as I handed them down to you, you hold fast to the traditions.

I. 11:3–7: Man, Woman, and Their Respective "Heads"

A¹: Man–Woman (11:3–4)

³ But I want you to know that the head of every *man* is Christ, and the head of *woman* is *man*, and the head of Christ is God. ⁴ Every *man* praying or prophesying while having something [long hair] hanging down the head shames his head.

B¹: Woman (11:5–6)

⁵ But every *woman* praying or prophesying with head uncovered [by long hair] shames her head, for it is one and the same as if she were shaved. ⁶ For if a *woman* is not covered [by long hair], then let her have her hair cut off. But if it is shameful to have her hair cut off or shaved, let her be covered [by long hair].

A²: Man–Woman (11:7)

⁷ For *man*, on the one hand, should not have his head covered [by long hair], being the image and glory of God, the *woman*, on the other hand, is the glory of *man*.

II. 11:8–12: Man, Woman, and the Woman's Head

A³: Man–Woman–Woman–Man (11:8–9)

⁸ For *man* is not from *woman*, but *woman* from *man*. ⁹ For indeed *man* was not created on account of the *woman* but *woman* on account of the *man*.

B²: Woman (11:10)

¹⁰ For this reason a *woman* should have authority over her head, on account of the angels.

A⁴: Woman–Man–Man–Woman (11:11–12)

¹¹ But neither is *woman* apart from *man* nor *man* apart from *woman* in the Lord. ¹² For just as the *woman* is from the *man*, so also the *man* is through the *woman*; but all things are from God.

(without attribution) by Garland, *1 Corinthians*, 511. It also differs from the structures proposed by Fee, *Corinthians*, 493–94; Kenneth T. Wilson, "Should Women Wear Headcoverings?" *BSac* 148 (1991): 442.

III. 11:13–15: Man, Woman, and Their Respective Long Hair
B³: Woman (11:13)
¹³ Judge for yourselves: Is it proper for a *woman* uncovered [by long hair] to pray to God?
A⁵: Man (11:14)
¹⁴ Does not nature itself teach you that if a *man*, on the one hand, has long hair it is a dishonor for him,
B⁴: Woman (11:15)
¹⁵ but if a *woman*, on the other hand, has long hair it is glory for her, because long hair has been given to her for a covering?

Conclusion: Custom (11:16)
¹⁶ But if anyone is inclined to be contentious, we do not have such a custom, nor do the churches of God.⁵

First Corinthians 11:2–16 is framed by an introduction concerning the "traditions" Paul has handed down to the Corinthians (11:2) and a conclu-

---

5. For some of the vast bibliography on 1 Cor 11:2–16, in addition to the works already cited, see John P. Meier, "On the Veiling of Hermeneutics (1 Cor 11:2–16)," *CBQ* 40 (1978): 212–26; Jerome Murphy-O'Connor, "Sex and Logic in 1 Corinthians 11:2–16," *CBQ* 42 (1980): 482–500; idem, "1 Corinthians 11:2–16 Once Again," *CBQ* 50 (1988): 265–74; Alan G. Padgett, "Paul on Women in the Church: The Contradictions of Coiffure in 1 Corinthians 11.2–16," *JSNT* 20 (1984): 69–86; Cynthia L. Thompson, "Hairstyles, Head-Coverings, and St. Paul: Portraits from Roman Corinth," *BA* 51 (1988): 99–115; David W. J. Gill, "The Importance of Roman Portraiture for Head-Coverings in 1 Corinthians 11:2–16," *TynBul* 41 (1990): 245–60; Gail Paterson Corrington, "The 'Headless Woman': Paul and the Language of the Body in 1 Cor 11:1–16," *PRSt* 18 (1991): 223–31; L. Ann Jervis, "'But I Want You to Know . . .': Paul's Midrashic Intertextual Response to the Corinthian Worshipers (1 Cor 11:2–16)," *JBL* 112 (1993): 231–46; Lone Fatum, "Image of God and Glory of Man: Women in the Pauline Congregations," in *The Image of God: Gender Models in Judeo-Christian Tradition* (ed. Kari Elisabeth Børresen; Minneapolis: Fortress, 1995), 50–133; Ben Witherington, *Women in the Earliest Churches* (Cambridge: Cambridge University Press, 1988), 78–90; idem, *Conflict*, 231–40; Martin, *Corinthian Body*, 242–49; David E. Blattenberger, *Rethinking 1 Corinthians 11:2–16 through Archaeological and Moral-Rhetorical Analysis* (Studies in the Bible and Early Christianity 36; Lewiston, N.Y.: Mellen, 1997); Judith M. Gundry-Volf, "Gender and Creation in 1 Corinthians 11:2–16: A Study in Paul's Theological Method," in *Evangelium, Schriftauslegung, Kirche: Festschrift für Peter Stuhlmacher zum 65. Geburtstag* (ed. Jostein Ådna et al.; Göttingen: Vandenhoeck & Ruprecht, 1997), 151–71; Harold R. Holmyard, "Does 1 Corinthians 11:2–16 Refer to Women Praying and Prophesying in Church?" *BSac* 154 (1997): 461–72; Ritva Williams, "Lifting the Veil: A Social-Science Interpretation of 1 Corinthians 11:2–16," *Consensus* 23 (1997): 53–60; Khiok-Khng Yeo, "Differentiation and Mutuality of Male-Female Relations in 1 Corinthians 11:2–16," *BR* 43 (1998): 7–21; Marlis Gielen, "Beten und Prophezeien mit unverhülltem Kopf? Die Kontroverse zwischen Paulus und der korinthischen Gemeinde um

sion concerning the "custom" of the churches of God (11:16). In between this introduction and conclusion are three units, each dealing with the interrelation between men and women in a Corinthian liturgical setting of praying or prophesying (11:4–5, 13).

In the first unit, 11:3–7 (I), dealing with man, woman, and their respective "heads," subunits concerning the interrelation between man and woman, 11:3–4 (A^1) and 11:7 (A^2), frame a subunit concerned solely with woman and her respective "heads," 11:5–6 (B^1). In the second unit, 11:8–12 (II), dealing with man, woman, and the woman's head, subunits concerning the interdependence of man and woman, 11:8–9 (A^3) and 11:11–12 (A^4), frame a subunit concerned solely with woman and her authority over her head, 11:10 (B^2). And in the third unit, 11:13–15 (III), dealing with man, woman, and their respective long hair, subunits concerning a woman's uncovered and covered head, 11:13 (B^3) and 11:15 (B^4), frame a subunit concerned solely with a man's long hair, 11:14 (A^5).

That the subunits concerning woman or man individually are framed by subunits concerning both man and woman underscores how the main theme of 1 Cor 11:2–16 is the interrelationship and interdependence between man and woman in a liturgical setting of praying or prophesying. In other words, the problem addressed is not a primarily "man" or primarily "woman" problem, but a problem involving their mutual relationship in a worship setting.[6] Indeed, 1 Cor 11:2–16 illustrates how man and woman, when they pray or prophesy together and interdependently, can give glory to God. The theme of giving glory (δόξα) while prophesying or praying to God appears explicitly in both the first (11:7) and third unit (11:15), and in the second unit that "all things (πάντα) are from God"

---

die Wahrung der Geschlechtsrollensymbolik in 1Kor 11,2–16," *ZNW* 90 (1999): 220–49; Gwen Ince, "Judge for Yourselves: Teasing Out Some Knots in 1 Corinthians 11:2–16," *ABR* 48 (2000): 59–71; Francis Watson, *Agape, Eros, Gender: Towards a Pauline Sexual Ethic* (Cambridge: Cambridge University Press, 2000), 40–89; idem, "The Authority of the Voice: A Theological Reading of 1 Cor 11.1–16," *NTS* 46 (2000): 520–36; Birgitte Graakjaer Hjort, "Gender Hierarchy or Religious Androgyny? Male-Female Interaction in the Corinthian Community—A Reading of 1 Cor. 11,2–16," *ST* 55 (2001): 58–80; Linda L. Belleville, "Κεφαλή and the Thorny Issue of Headcovering in 1 Corinthians 11:2–16," in *Paul and the Corinthians: Studies on a Community in Conflict. Essays in Honour of Margaret Thrall* (ed. Trevor J. Burke and J. Keith Elliott; NovTSup 109; Leiden: Brill, 2003), 215–31; James W. Thompson, "Creation, Shame, and Nature in 1 Cor 11:2–16: The Background and Coherence of Paul's Argument," in *Early Christianity and Classical Culture: Comparative Studies in Honor of Abraham J. Malherbe* (ed. John T. Fitzgerald et al.; NovTSup 110; Leiden: Brill, 2003), 237–57; Bruce W. Winter, *Roman Wives, Roman Widows: The Appearance of New Women and the Pauline Communities* (Grand Rapids: Eerdmans, 2003), 77–96.

6. In 1 Cor 11:2–16 "man" occurs 14 times and "woman" 15 times.

(11:12) recalls Paul's injunction in 10:31b that "whatever you do, do all things (πάντα) for the glory (δόξαν) of God."

The First Unit: 1 Corinthians 11:3–7

A¹: *Man–Woman (11:3–4)*. After congratulating his Corinthian audience for remembering him in everything and holding fast to the traditions as he handed them down to them (11:2), Paul begins to discuss yet another tradition he wants them to know when he states that "the head of every man is Christ, and the head of woman is man, and the head of Christ is God" (11:3). That the audience is to understand the metaphorical use of "head" (κεφαλή) here to refer to that which is preeminent or prior in the created order began to be indicated in 3:23:[7] The Corinthians belong to Christ as preeminent to them, who in turn belongs to God as preeminent to him. And in 8:6, we exist through the one Lord Jesus Christ as preeminent to us, who in turn comes from the one God, the Father, as preeminent to him in the hierarchy of the created order. Since we exist for God (8:6a), we are to do all things for the glory of God (10:31b) in accord with our respective positions within the created order in which the "head" of woman is man as her preeminent partner or representative.[8]

That "every man praying or prophesying while having something [long hair] hanging down the head shames his head" (11:4) means that he shames

---

7. For the debate over the metaphorical meaning of "head" here, see Wayne A. Grudem, "Does *Kephale* ('Head') Mean 'Source' or 'Authority Over' in Greek Literature? A Survey of 2,336 Examples," *TJ* 6 (1985): 38–59; idem, "The Meaning of Κεφαλή ('Head'): A Response to Recent Studies," *TJ* 11 (1990): 3–72; Joseph A. Fitzmyer, "*Kephale* in I Corinthians 11:3," *Int* 47 (1993): 52–59; idem, "Another Look at ΚΕΦΑΛΗ in 1 Corinthians 11.3," *NTS* 35 (1989): 503–11. For arguments in favor of the meaning of "preeminence," "priority," or "representative," rather than "authority over" or "source," see Richard S. Cervin, "Does Κεφαλή Mean 'Source' or 'Authority Over' in Greek Literature? A Rebuttal," *TJ* 10 (1989): 85–112; Andrew C. Perriman, "The Head of a Woman: The Meaning of κεφαλή in I Cor. 11:3," *JTS* 45 (1994): 602–22; Delobel, "1 Cor 11,2–16," 378–79; Gundry-Volf, "Gender," 158–59; Lindemann, *Erste Korintherbrief*, 239–40; Thiselton, *Corinthians*, 816–22; Garland, *1 Corinthians*, 516. For OT evidence, see LXX Isa 7:8–9; 9:13; Lam 1:5; Deut 28:44; Jer 38:7.

8. Gundry-Volf, "Gender," 159: "For the head signifies that which is preeminent, just as the physical head is preeminent in relation to the body.... As that which is preeminent, the head is in a position to receive honor or glory." Delobel, "1 Cor 11,2–16," 378–79: "In each of these relationships, there is one who has the priority as κεφαλή, and one who comes in the second place: so is the order in the cosmos. At the same time, it is made clear from 3a and 3c that it is not a shame to have a κεφαλή: that Christ is every man's κεφαλή and that God is Christ's κεφαλή cannot possibly have a negative meaning whatsoever. On the contrary, there is nothing negative then in woman's having man as her κεφαλή. For Paul, it is her proper place to come after man." Perriman, "Head," 621–22: "At issue between the man and the woman in this passage is neither authority nor origin, but the question of whether the woman's behaviour in worship brings glory

not only his literal head, that is, himself as a male, but also his metaphorical head, that is, Christ as the one preeminent to him in the created order (11:3a). Thus, the praying or prophesying male among Paul's Corinthian audience is not to have anything "hanging down" his literal head, that is, he is not to have the long hair that is characteristic of women in the natural order hanging down from his head but the short hair that is natural for men (cf. 11:14–15), in order to honor and thus give glory to his metaphorical head, Christ, and thereby give glory to God (10:31b), the head of Christ (11:3c).[9]

B^1: *Woman (11:5–6)*. That "every woman praying or prophesying with head uncovered [by long hair] shames her head" (11:5a) means that she shames not only her literal head, that is, herself as a female, but also her metaphorical head, that is, the man as the one preeminent to her in the created order. For a woman to pray or prophesy with her head uncovered by long hair is the same as if she were to have her head shaved bald (11:5b). Indeed, if such a woman is not covered by long hair, she might as well have her hair cut off completely (11:6a). But since it is shameful for her to have her hair completely cut off or shaved bald, she should be covered by long hair (11:6b).[10] Thus, the praying or prophesying female among Paul's Corinthian audience is not to have her literal head "uncovered" but rather covered with the long hair characteristic of women in order to honor and

---

or dishonour on the man. The point seems to be, therefore, that the behaviour of the woman reflects upon the man who as her head is representative of her, the prominent partner in the relationship, or that the woman's status and value is summed up in the man. We might almost say that 'man is the head of woman' and 'woman is the glory of man' are reciprocal statements."

9. For recent arguments that "having down the head" (κατὰ κεφαλῆς ἔχων) in 11:4 refers to long hair rather than to a veil and that "uncovered" (ἀκατακαλύπτῳ) in 11:5 refers to a woman not having long hair rather than not having a veil, see Schrage, *Erste Brief*, 2.504–6; Blattenberger, *Rethinking*; Horsley, *1 Corinthians*, 153–54; Gielen, "Beten," 220–49; Lindemann, *Erste Korintherbrief*, 240–41. Note with Gielen that the issue is not between bound or unbound long hair but between long and short hair. Whatever may have been the connection between long hair for males and homosexuality (cf. Schrage, *Erste Brief*, 2.506), it should be noted that Paul does not use this as motivation in his argument. He argues that men should have short hair to distinguish them from women, not from homosexuals. According to Belleville, "Κεφαλή," 219: "If a covering of long, human hair were in view, Paul surely would have used the standard Greek term κομᾷ, rather than the oblique κατὰ κεφαλῆς ἔχων." But Paul uses this oblique phrase because it contains the word "head," which is so important for his argument in 11:3–4. The term κομᾷ, however, is used in 11:14–15.

10. The use of "have oneself shaved" (ξυρᾶσθαι) together with "have one's hair cut" (κείρασθαι) radicalizes the shame. The two occurrences of "shave" (11:5b and 11:6b) serve as the encompassing idea as they frame the two occurrences of "cut off" (11:6a and 11:6b); see Gielen, "Beten," 224; Thiselton, *Corinthians*, 832–33.

thus give glory to her metaphorical head, the man, which will give glory to the man's head, Christ, and to Christ's head, God (10:31b; 11:3).

A^2: *Man–Woman (11:7)*. A praying or prophesying man should not have his head covered (by long hair), because he is not only the living "image" or "likeness" (εἰκών) but also, and most especially for Paul's argument, the "glory" (δόξα) of God (11:7a).[11] That man is the "glory of God" (δόξα θεοῦ) expresses a double meaning based on the nuances of this genitival phrase. On the one hand, it can be taken as a subjective genitive, so that man is the "glory of God" in the sense that he radiates and manifests the glory that God bestowed on him within the created order (cf. LXX Ps 8:6). On the other hand, it can also be taken as an objective genitive, so that man is the "glory of God" in the sense that as the man he was created to be he renders honor or gives glory to the Creator (cf. 1 Cor 10:31b).[12]

Similarly, that the woman, on the other hand, is the "glory of man" (δόξα ἀνδρός, 11:7b) means both that the woman radiates and manifests the glory she received by being created from the side of man (Gen 2:21–23) and that the woman as the woman she was created to be, that is, as the suitable "helper" of man (Gen 2:18, 20), renders honor or gives glory to the man. As the "glory of man," then, the woman completes the creation of mankind in the image of God in accord with Gen 1:27: "And God made the man, according to the image of God he made him, male and female he made them."[13]

---

11. Fee, *Corinthians*, 515: "Paul's own interest, however, is finally not in man as being God's image, but in his being God's glory." Garland, *1 Corinthians*, 522–23: "Paul's purpose is not to establish that man, not woman, is made in the image of God. The term 'image' leads him to the term 'glory,' which then becomes the key term in 1 Cor. 11:7–9 and counterbalances the notion of 'shame' in 11:4–6."

12. Schrage (*Erste Brief*, 2.511) takes it primarily as a subjective gentive, while Fee (*Corinthians*, 516) takes it as an objective genitive. But both are operative within Paul's argumentation here. On the rich complexity of the term "glory" in Paul, see *TLNT* 1.368: "Paul is the writer who uses the word *glory* most often. As part of his largely Septuagint-based vocabulary, δόξα has a depth of meaning that cannot be expressed by a simple translation."

13. On LXX Gen 1:27, Wevers (*Genesis*, 15–16) notes: "The final clause adds the statement that he created them male and female. The change from αὐτόν in the middle clause to αὐτούς in the last raises the question (also for the Hebrew) whether the writer intended this equation of 'him' and 'them' to reflect on the εἰκόνα θεοῦ." Gundry-Volf, "Gender," 156: "Paul's oft-noted failure to state that woman too is the image of God, as the first creation account implies, need not be taken as a denial. It is best understood as an intentional omission for the sake of stressing that woman is the glory of man. Paul wants to relate woman *to man* as his *glory*, since in the social order she owed honor to man. To affirm that woman is created in the image of God would

The Second Unit: 1 Corinthians 11:8–12

A³: Man–Woman–Woman–Man (11:8-9). The double meaning of woman being the "glory of man" (11:7b) is confirmed by the argument of 11:8–9, which is based on the scriptural account of the creation of woman both from and for the man. After God formed the rib that he took from the man into a woman and brought the woman to the man (Gen 2:21–22), the man declared: "This now is bone of my bones and flesh of my flesh, this one will be called 'woman' because out of her man (ἐκ τοῦ ἀνδρὸς αὐτῆς) this one was taken" (LXX Gen 2:23). That man is not from woman but woman is "from man" (ἐξ ἀνδρός, 1 Cor 11:8), then, illustrates the subjective genitive sense that the woman is the "glory of man." The woman radiates and manifests the glory she received by being created from the man.

According to the scriptural account of creation, woman was created not only from but also for the sake of or on account of man. In LXX Gen 2:18, the Lord God said, "It is not good for the man to be alone, let us make for him a helper suitable to him (βοηθὸν κατ' αὐτόν)."[14] After all of the animals were created and named by the man (Gen 2:19–20a), "there was not found a helper like him (βοηθὸς ὅμοιος αὐτῷ)" (LXX Gen 2:20b), and so woman was created in Gen 2:21–23 for the sake of or on account of man.[15] That man was not created on account of the woman but woman on account of the man (1 Cor 11:9), then, illustrates the objective genitive sense that the woman is the "glory of man" (11:7b). The woman renders honor or gives glory to the man by being the woman she was created to be on account of the man.[16]

---

simply obstruct Paul's parenetic goal.... He is saying that woman ought to bring glory to man rather than shaming her 'head' by an unfeminine hairstyle, for she *is* the glory of man by creation" (Gundry-Volf's emphasis).

14. Whereas MT Gen 1:26 uses the plural for God, "Let us make man," MT Gen 2:18 uses the singular, "I will make." As noted by Wevers (*Genesis*, 31), the LXX uses the plural in both places: "[W]ith fine literary feeling [the LXX] has the plural cohortative ποιήσωμεν" in Gen 1:26 and 2:18. "To (LXX) Gen if this plural of self-determination was fitting for the creation of τὸν ἄνθρωπον it was equally fitting for γυναῖκα (v.22), here defined as βοηθόν 'helper.'"

15. On "helper suitable to him" (βοηθὸν κατ' αὐτόν) in LXX Gen 2:18, Wevers (*Genesis*, 31) notes: "Difficult is the prepositional phrase κατ' αὐτόν which modifies βοηθόν.... The phrase occurs only here and v.20 where, however, it is translated by ὅμοιος αὐτῷ 'similar to him.' Presumably what κατ' αὐτόν means here is 'according to him,' i.e. 'like him,' more or less the same as the interpretation of v.20."

16. Gundry-Volf, "Gender," 156–57: "The second ground for this claim (that woman is the glory of man) is woman's creation 'for the man,' which alludes to Gen 2:18. God created Eve to be a 'helper suitable for him,' for 'it is not good for the man to be alone.' Paul makes out of this a general statement about the woman's creation 'for the man' in order to support the specific obligation of bringing glory to man. She fulfills this obligation simply by being woman. But if she re-

B²: Woman (11:10). "For this reason" or "on account (διά) of this" in 11:10a not only refers back to the scripturally based argument that woman is the glory of man in 11:7b-9, but also anticipates the added and parallel reason to be given in 11:10b—"on account (διά) of the angels."[17] Because she is the glory of man in the order of creation, the woman should have "authority" or "control" (ἐξουσίαν) over her literal head, meaning that she should wear her hair long while praying or prophesying in communal worship with men.[18] By doing so, she will maintain and respect the differentiation between males and females established by the scriptural order of creation and thus be acting in accord with her creational status as the glory of man.[19]

But there is a closely related additional reason why a woman should have long hair covering her head while praying or prophesying—"on account of the angels (ἀγγέλους)" (11:10b). This means that the woman should take account not only of her creational status as the glory of man, but also of the creational status of both men and women as having a glory and honor that approaches that of the angels. According to LXX Ps 8:5-6: "What are human beings that you are mindful of them, or mortals that you attend to them? You assigned them a status a little lower than that of angels (ἀγγέλους); you crowned them with glory (δόξῃ) and honor."[20] A praying or prophesying woman, then, should exercise authority over her head by having it covered with long hair not only to maintain her status as the glory (δόξα) of man (11:7b), but also to do her part in order that both men and

---

jects the culturally-encoded symbol of her female identity, a covered head, she calls this purpose into question and falls short of it by shaming herself and her 'head,' the man (11:3, 5–6)."

17. Fee, *Corinthians*, 518: "Most likely 'for this reason' functions here, as it often does in Paul, in both directions at once. It first of all indicates that what is about to be said is the proper inference from what has immediately preceded: the woman ought to have authority over her head because she is man's glory. At the same time it anticipates yet another closely allied reason to be given in the conclusion that is being advanced. The NIV has caught the sense—and the difficulties—by translating, 'for this reason, and because of the angels.'" See also Lockwood, *1 Corinthians*, 369–70.

18. Collins, *First Corinthians*, 411: "The natural meaning of Paul's phrase is that a woman has authority or power over her head. She presumably exercises [proper] control over her head when she wears her hair appropriately, that is, as is fitting in the context of worship." See also Delobel, "1 Cor 11,2–16," 387; Schrage, *Erste Brief*, 2.514; Gielen, "Beten," 244; Thiselton, *Corinthians*, 839; Garland, *1 Corinthians*, 525.

19. In addition to the scriptural accounts of creation, see LXX Deut 22:5: "The apparel of a man shall not be on a woman, neither shall a man be clothed in a woman's dress; for every one that does these things is an abomination to the Lord your God." See also Wevers, *Deuteronomy*, 350–51; P. J. Harland, "Menswear and Womenswear: A Study of Deut 22:5," *ExpTim* 110 (1998): 73–76.

20. Translation from Pietersma, *Psalms*, 6.

women can maintain their lofty creational status of a glory and honor that is just short of that of the angels (11:10b).[21]

A[4]: *Woman–Man–Man–Woman (11:11-12).* With a strongly adversative "but" (πλὴν), Paul emphasizes what is important here—"woman is not apart from man nor man apart from woman" while praying or prophesying "in the Lord" (11:11).[22] While emphasizing the interdependence of man and woman, this statement adds a new dimension to the argument. Until this point the burden was on the woman not to dishonor but to give glory to the man as her "head" by not having her literal head uncovered with long hair (11:5-10). The man, on the other hand, was not to dishonor his "head," Christ, by having long hair down his literal head (11:3-4). Now, however, not only must the woman have respect for the man by not having her head uncovered, since "woman is not apart from man," but the man also must have respect for the woman by not having his head covered with long hair, since "man is not apart from woman." Neither should act independently of the other with regard to their hair styles while praying or prophesying in the Lord.[23]

Paul confirms this assertion by further reminding the audience of the

---

21. This interpretation of "on account of the angels" in 11:10b accords much better with Paul's rhetorical argumentation, which is based on status within the created order, than does the other proposed interpretations of this notoriously difficult text. For other interpretations, see Joseph A. Fitzmyer, "A Feature of Qumran Angelology and the Angels of 1 Cor 11:10," *NTS* 4 (1957-58): 48-58; Jacques Winandy, "Un curieux *casus pendens*: 1 Corinthiens 11.10 et son interprétation," *NTS* 38 (1992): 621-29; Jason David BeDuhn, "'Because of the Angels': Unveiling Paul's Anthropology in 1 Corinthians 11," *JBL* 118 (1999): 295-320; Loren T. Stuckenbruck, "Why Should Women Cover Their Heads Because of the Angels? (1 Corinthians 11:10)," *Stone-Campbell Journal* 4 (2001): 205-34. For an overview and critique of many past interpretations, see Garland, *1 Corinthians*, 526-29. As Delobel ("1 Cor 11,2-16," 386) explains: "[T]he behaviour of women in worship has to respect the order of creation symbolised by the angels who are indeed present in worship and watching the observance of this order." But whether the angels were thought to be present and what their role may have been while men and women were praying or prophesying at Corinth are open questions. In our interpretation of 11:10 the woman is to take account of the angels in general, who are right above human beings in the created order, whether or not they are thought to be present during worship.

22. According to BDAG, 826, πλὴν here means "only, in any case, on the other hand, but, breaking off a discussion and emphasizing what is important." See also Gundry-Volf, "Gender," 160-61.

23. Fee, *Corinthians*, 523: "While it is true that woman is man's glory, having been created for his sake (v. 9), Paul now affirms that that does not mean that woman exists for man's purposes, as though in some kind of subordinate position to his aims and will. To the contrary, God has so arranged things that 'in the Lord' the one cannot exist without the other, not meaning of course that every Christian man and woman must be married, but that as believers man and woman are mutually dependent on each other.... The preposition 'without' ('apart from'; cf.

scriptural account of creation in 11:12ab. "For just as the woman is from the man (ἐκ τοῦ ἀνδρός)" (11:12a) repeats 11:8b, "woman is from man (ἐξ ἀνδρός)," and again recalls LXX Gen 2:23b: "This one will be called 'woman,' for out of her man (ἐκ τοῦ ἀνδρὸς αὐτῆς) this one was taken." And "so also the man is through the woman (διὰ τῆς γυναικός)" (11:12b) recalls the establishment of this as the natural order of creation in Gen 3:16 where God tells the woman that she will give birth to children.[24]

Thus, the mutuality and interdependence of woman and man in 11:11–12 complements that of man and woman in 11:8–9. Whereas the chiasm of man-woman-woman-man in both 11:8 and 11:9, in which "man" frames "woman," expresses primarily the dependence of woman upon man from the scriptural order of creation, the chiasm of woman-man-man-woman in both 11:11 and 11:12, in which "woman" frames "man," asserts the dependence not only of the woman upon the man but especially of the man upon the woman "in the Lord," as confirmed by the fact that man is now given birth into the world through woman in accord with God's scriptural plan of creation.[25]

That "all things (πάντα) are from God" in 11:12c reminds the audience not only that both the man and the woman have their ultimate origin in God, but that in their mutual interdependence upon one another while praying or prophesying, they are finally dependent upon God. Since everything they are and have comes from God, then, they should, recalling 10:31b, "do all things (πάντα) for the glory of God," which in this context means praying or prophesying with the hair style proper to their respective gender.

The Third Unit: 1 Corinthians 11:13–15

B^3: *Woman (11:13)*. With a pointed question Paul further persuades his audience to agree with his argument as he directs them to judge for themselves (11:13a; cf. 10:15) whether what he has been saying about the scrip-

---

4:8) then means not simply that they cannot exist without each other, but that they are not intended to exist independent of one another" (n. 42).

24. Gundry-Volf, "Gender," 162–63: "This comparison cancels out the exclusive privilege of man: just as in the beginning Eve was made from Adam's rib, in all subsequent history man is born through woman. Thus both man and woman are 'from/through' each other, though in different ways.... Paul's frame of reference for the idea of the woman's priority is thus the created order, while for the man's priority it is creation in primal history. By switching from ἐκ to διά, then, Paul maintains the difference between man and woman and avoids a flat contradiction with 11:8, 'man is *not* from (ἐκ) woman,' while asserting that both can be seen to have a position of priority over the other in 'creation.' "

25. On the double chiasms in 11:8–9 as well as in 11:11–12, see Fee, *Corinthians*, 523.

tural order of God's creation is correct. "Is it proper for a woman uncovered (by long hair) to pray to God?" (11:13b). In other words, is it proper or appropriate not just in the eyes of society but most especially in the eyes of the God (τοῦ θεοῦ) who, as the ultimate origin of both man and woman (11:12c), created woman to be the glory of man (11:7b), the God (θεοῦ) for whose glory we are to do all things (10:31), to pray to this God (τῷ θεῷ) with her rather than the man's head uncovered by long hair? The audience must answer, "No."[26]

A^5: *Man (11:14)*. Paul then puts another question to his audience. Does not "nature" (φύσις) itself, that is, the natural order of things that is based upon and accords with the scriptural order of God's creation, teach them that if a man has long hair it is a "dishonor" (ἀτιμία) for him? (11:14).[27] The audience must agree and answer, "Yes." That a man with long hair dishonors himself, his literal head, recalls and reinforces for the audience what Paul asserted in 11:4: Every man praying or prophesying with long hair hanging down his head "shames" (καταισχύνει) not only his literal head, himself, but also his metaphorical "head," Christ, as well as Christ's metaphorical

---

26. Wolff, *Erste Brief*, 255: "Betont wird vom Beten 'zu Gott' gesprochen, um die Ehrfurchtslosigkeit bloßzustellen, die sich in einem Beten der Frauen mit unbedecktem Kopf äußert." Lockwood, *1 Corinthians*, 376: "Normally the verb 'to pray' (προσεύχομαι) does not have an object. The addition of the words 'to God' in 11:13 reminds the Corinthians of the solemn nature of worship. Here they approach the almighty and holy God. . . . In his presence the women should show due decorum."

27. According to BDAG, 1070, φύσις in 1 Cor 11:14 means "the regular or established order of things, nature." For Paul this natural order of things is based upon the scriptural order of God's creation. C. E. B. Cranfield, *A Critical and Exegetical Commentary on the Epistle to the Romans* (2 vols.; ICC; Edinburgh: Clark, 1975, 1979), 1.125-26: ἡ φύσις αὐτὴ in 1 Cor 11:14 "might almost be translated 'the very way God has made us.' . . . The decisive factor in Paul's use of it [φύσις] is his biblical doctrine of creation. It denotes that order which is manifest in God's creation." See also Joseph A. Fitzmyer, *Romans: A New Translation with Introduction and Commentary* (AB 33; New York: Doubleday, 1993), 286. Marion L. Soards, *1 Corinthians* (NIBC 7; Peabody, Mass.: Hendrickson, 1999), 227: "Paul and the Corinthians would have understood that 'nature' indicates God's will, and so persons should style themselves according to the lines of nature as a copy of nature itself. . . . Paul thinks somehow that culture derives from nature and, in turn, that fashion ultimately goes back to God." See also Barrett, *Corinthians*, 256. Lockwood, *1 Corinthians*, 377: "Paul's appeal to nature's teaching with respect to hair lengths probably means that (despite variations across the centuries and cultures) human beings generally have an instinctive sense that long hair makes a more glorious and fitting adornment on a woman than it does on a man, and that, conversely, short or closely cropped hair (not to mention baldness!) is more acceptable and 'natural' for a man than for a woman. Normally—though with numerous exceptions—this instinctive sense of what accords with the created order has been reflected in hairstyles through the ages."

"head," God (11:3). He thereby fails to give glory to the God (11:7a; 10:31b) to whom he is praying (11:13) or for whom he is prophesying.

B⁴: *Woman (11:15)*. Paul then completes his questioning of his audience with regard to the hair styles of both men and women. Does not nature itself (11:14), that is, what accords with the scriptural order of God's creation, teach them that if a woman has long hair it is "glory" for her, because long hair has been given to her for a covering? (11:15).[28] The audience must again agree and answer, "Yes." The long hair "has been given" (δέδοται, with the perfect passive indicating that it was given definitively in the past when the woman was created and still holds in the present) to the woman by God (divine passive) "for use as" (ἀντὶ) a covering for her head.[29] That God has given the woman long hair as a covering intended to be her "glory" (δόξα) means that by praying or prophesying with her head covered by long hair she gives "glory" (δόξα) not only to her literal head but also to her metaphorical "head," the man (11:7b), and thereby plays her part in doing all things for the "glory" (δόξαν) of God (11:7a; 10:31b).[30]

The Conclusion in 1 Corinthians 11:16

In 11:2 Paul introduced his argument in 11:3–15 by praising his Corinthian audience for remembering him in everything and for holding fast to the traditions just as Paul has handed them down to his audience. This motivates his audience again to remember what Paul is going to say in 11:3–15 and to hold fast to it as another tradition handed down to them.

The conclusion in 11:16 adds to this motivation for Paul's audience to practice what he is advocating in 11:3–15. If anyone in his audience is inclined (cf. 3:18; 8:2; 10:12) to be contentious about the matter of male and female hair styles for those praying or prophesying in their communal worship, "we," not just Paul alone (as in 11:2) but also those associated

---

28. Collins, *First Corinthians*, 413: " 'To her' (αὐτῇ) is absent from some manuscripts, but the weight of the manuscript evidence is sufficient to suggest that the reading 'to her' was part of the original text."

29. On ἀντί in 11:15 as meaning "for use as" in the sense of equivalence, so that Paul is asserting that women already have the equivalent of a covering, namely long hair, see Alan G. Padgett, "The Significance of ἀντί in 1 Corinthians 11:15," *TynBul* 45 (1994): 181–87; BDAG, 88; Hubert, Frankemölle, "ἀντί," *EDNT* 1.108.

30. For a provocative but, in our opinion, unconvincing view that 11:13–15 accords with ancient physiology in which a woman's long hair was considered part of her genitalia that she has been given instead of a testicle (περιβόλαιον, 11:15), and therefore should be veiled in worship, see Troy W. Martin, "Paul's Argument from Nature for the Veil in 1 Corinthians 11:13–15: A Testicle Instead of a Head Covering," *JBL* 123 (2004): 75–84. If a woman's long hair was part of her genitalia, shouldn't it be covered at all times in public and not just in worship?

with him, do not have such a custom of allowing either men to pray or prophesy with long (feminine) hair or women to pray or prophesy with short (masculine) hair.[31]

Continuing his concern that the Corinthians conform with all of the other churches (4:17; 7:17) and that they avoid giving offense to the church of God (10:32), Paul adds that neither do the churches of God have such a custom (11:16b). In order for the Corinthians, then, truly to be a church of God that does everything for the glory of God (10:31b) they too must behave, while praying or prophesying in communal worship, in accord with the scriptural order of God's creation (11:3–15), as do all of the other churches.[32] Men and women are to wear the hair styles proper to their gender out of respect for themselves as individuals (11:4, 5–6, 13, 14, 15), for one another as men and women (11:8–9, 11–12), for the other churches (11:16), and for the angels (11:10), Christ (11:3), and God (11:3, 7, 12), to whom they are to do everything for "glory" (10:31b).

Summary on 1 Corinthians 11:7–12

1. Although 1 Cor 11:7–12 reminds the audience primarily of the scriptural accounts about the creation of the first human beings in Genesis (1:26–27, 31; 2:18, 20–23; 3:16; 5:1; 9:6), a number of other scriptural texts concerning creation are also recalled or alluded to. Paul is thus rely-

---

31. Thiselton (*Corinthians*, 847) states that "contentious" (φιλόνεικος) in 11:16 means "striving to contend, or trying to force an argument for the sake of becoming 'a winner' rather than primarily to discover truth." That "custom" here refers to being contentious, with the meaning that Paul and fellow Christians do not have such a custom of being contentious, so that Paul in the end leaves the decision up to the Corinthians and will not insist on his on view, see Troels Engberg-Pedersen, "1 Corinthians 11:16 and the Character of Pauline Exhortation," *JBL* 110 (1991): 679–89. But against this interpretation, see Thiselton, *Corinthians*, 847: "It seems self-evident that *the custom* (συνήθειαν) to which Paul alludes concerns gender distinction in public worship ... addressed both to men and to women equally. The *custom* is the acceptance of an equality of status in accordance with which woman may lead in public prayer or preaching side by side with a recognition that gender differences must not be blurred but appreciated, valued, and expressed in appropriate ways in response to God's unrevoked decree." See also Garland, *1 Corinthians*, 532.

32. Garland, *1 Corinthians*, 532: "His conclusion to his argument does not signal that he has misgivings about the strength of his arguments and consequently makes a preemptive strike by attacking any who might disagree as being 'contentious.'... Paul's concluding statement basically means that when all is said and done, they must be mindful of the universal practice in other churches." Thiselton, *Corinthians*, 848: "[W]e should not allow the rhetoric of a closing act of pronouncement to obscure the patience and tenacity of Paul's argument.... Paul *declares* them marginalized only if or because they have chosen to marginalize themselves."

ing upon his implied audience's familiarity with the whole complex of scriptural traditions regarding the divine order of creation.

2. That the subunits concerning woman (11:5–6, 10, 13, 15) or man (11:14) individually are framed by subunits concerning both man and woman (11:3–4, 7, 8–9, 11–12) underscores how the main theme of 1 Cor 11:2–16 is the interrelationship and interdependence between man and woman in a liturgical setting of praying or prophesying. First Corinthians 11:2–16 illustrates how man and woman, when they pray or prophesy together and interdependently, can give glory to God.

3. Man is the "glory of God" (11:7a) in the sense that he radiates and manifests the glory that God bestowed on him within the scriptural created order (cf. LXX Ps 8:6). On the other hand, man is the "glory of God" in the sense that as the man he was created to be he renders honor or gives glory to the Creator (cf. 1 Cor 10:31b). Similarly, that the woman is the "glory of man" (11:7b) means both that the woman radiates and manifests the glory she received by being created from the side of man (Gen 2:21–23) and that the woman, as the suitable "helper" of man (Gen 2:18, 20), renders honor or gives glory to the man. As the "glory of man," then, the woman completes the creation of mankind in the image of God in accord with Gen 1:27: "And God made the man, according to the image of God he made him, male and female he made them."

4. Because she is the glory of man in the order of creation, the woman should have "authority" or "control" over her literal head (11:10a), meaning that she should wear her hair long while praying or prophesying in communal worship with men. By doing so, she will maintain and respect the differentiation between males and females established by the scriptural order of creation and thus be acting in accord with her creational status as the glory of man.

5. A praying or prophesying woman should exercise authority over her head by having it covered with long hair to do her part in order that both men and women can maintain their lofty creational status of a glory and honor that is just short of that of the angels (11:10b; cf. LXX Ps 8:5–6).

6. The mutuality and interdependence of woman and man in 11:11–12 complements that of man and woman in 11:8–9. Whereas the chiasm of man-woman-woman-man in both 11:8 and 11:9, in which "man" frames "woman," expresses primarily the dependence of woman upon man from

the scriptural order of creation, the chiasm of woman-man-man-woman in both 11:11 and 11:12, in which "woman" frames "man," asserts the dependence not only of the woman upon the man but especially of the man upon the woman "in the Lord," as confirmed by the fact that man is now given birth into the world through woman in accord with God's scriptural plan of creation (Gen 3:16).

7. In order for the Corinthians truly to be a church of God they must behave, while praying or prophesying in communal worship, in accord with the scriptural order of God's creation (11:3–15), as do all of the other churches (11:16). Men and women are to wear the hair styles proper to their gender out of respect for themselves as individuals (11:4, 5–6, 13, 14, 15), for one another as men and women (11:8–9, 11–12), for the other churches (11:16), and for the angels (11:10), Christ (11:3), and God (11:3, 7, 12), to whom they are to do everything for "glory" (10:31b).

CHAPTER 13

1 Corinthians 14:21, 25

> *In foreign tongues and in lips of foreigners*
> *I will speak to this people, and not even thus will they*
> *listen to me, says the Lord.*
>
> God is really among you!

Old Testament Background

Because they occur so closely together in the same contextual unit of 1 Cor 14:20–25, we will treat the scriptural quotations in 14:21 and 14:25 together in this chapter.

1 Corinthians 14:21

Introduced by "in the law it is written" (cf. 1 Cor 9:9), the divinely authoritative promise that "in foreign tongues and in lips of foreigners I will speak to this people, and not even thus will they listen to me, says the Lord" in 1 Cor 14:21 appears to be primarily inspired by Isa 28:11–12. But the Pauline quote differs significantly from both the MT and LXX versions:

> MT Isa 28:11: כִּי בְּלַעֲגֵי שָׂפָה וּבְלָשׁוֹן אַחֶרֶת יְדַבֵּר אֶל־הָעָם הַזֶּה
> For in mocking speech and in a strange tongue he will speak to this people.

> MT Isa 28:12: אֲשֶׁר אָמַר אֲלֵיהֶם זֹאת הַמְּנוּחָה הָנִיחוּ לֶעָיֵף
> וְזֹאת הַמַּרְגֵּעָה וְלֹא אָבוּא שְׁמוֹעַ
> He said to them: "This is the rest; give rest to the weary; and this is the repose," but they would not listen.

> LXX Isa 28:11: διὰ φαυλισμὸν χειλέων διὰ γλώσσης ἑτέρας ὅτι λαλήσουσιν τῷ λαῷ τούτῳ

Through contempt of lips, through another tongue; for they will speak to this people,

LXX Isa 28:12: λέγοντες αὐτῷ τοῦτο τὸ ἀνάπαυμα τῷ πεινῶντι καὶ τοῦτο τὸ σύντριμμα καὶ οὐκ ἠθέλησαν ἀκούειν
saying to it, "This is the rest for the hungry; and this is the destruction," but they would not listen.

1 Cor 14:21:   ἐν ἑτερογλώσσοις καὶ ἐν χείλεσιν ἑτέρων λαλήσω τῷ λαῷ τούτῳ καὶ οὐδ οὕτως εἰσακούσονταί μου, λέγει κύριος
In foreign tongues and in lips of foreigners I will speak to this people, and not even thus will they listen to me, says the Lord.[1]

That Paul introduces the quote in 1 Cor 14:21 not with "in Isaiah it is written" but rather "in the law it is written," with "the law" here standing for the scriptures in general, and that the quote differs so significantly from Isa 28:11–12 indicate that Paul did not expect his scriptural quote to remind his audience only of the text from Isaiah.[2] There are numerous instances, for example, of scriptural statements of the failure of people to listen to God speaking to them through others: LXX Num 14:22; Jer 7:13, 24, 26; 13:11; 25:7; 33:5; 41:14, 17; 42:16; 51:4–5; Ps 80:12. But there are two texts in particular that are quite similar to Isa 28:11–12. They offer additional OT background for 1 Cor 14:21 by stating the failure to listen to God speaking through foreigners: LXX Deut 28:49 and Jer 5:15.

In its OT context, Isa 28:11–12 pronounces God's judgment on the people for failing to listen to and obey God. Since they did not listen to the

---

1. For discussions of the differences between the Pauline scriptural quote in 1 Cor 14:21 and the MT and LXX versions of Isa 28:11–12, see Malan, "Use," 154–56; Koch, *Schrift*, 63–66; Stanley, *Paul*, 197–205; Bruce C. Johanson, "Tongues, a Sign for Unbelievers? A Structural and Exegetical Study of I Corinthians xiv. 20–25," *NTS* 25 (1979): 181–86; Wayne A. Grudem, "1 Corinthians 14.20–25: Prophecy and Tongues as Signs of God's Attitude," *WTJ* 41 (1979): 382–86; idem, *The Gift of Prophecy in 1 Corinthians* (Washington, D.C.: University Press of America, 1982), 185–201; Lanier, "With Stammering Lips," 259–85; Karl Olav Sandnes, "Prophecy—A Sign for Believers (1 Cor 14,20–25)," *Bib* 77 (1996): 6–9; Wilk, *Bedeutung*, 27–30, 49–50; Garland, *1 Corinthians*, 646–47. With reference to 1 Cor 14:21, Origen (*Philocalia* 9.2) claims: "I found the equivalent of this saying in the translation of Aquila." But since we do not have Aquila's translation at this point, we do not know what Origen meant by "equivalent" (τὰ ἰσοδυναμοῦντα). Stanley (*Paul*, 199 n. 58) suggests that it means no more than "similar to" or "agreed in part." Nor can we be sure that the Aquila translation was not influenced by the Pauline quote. Instead, Garland (*1 Corinthians*, 647) proposes that the "differences from the LXX and the MT fit Paul's purposes so well, however, that it seems more likely that 14:21 represents an interpretive paraphrase of the text that he adapts to this context."

2. Thiselton, *Corinthians*, 1120: "*The Law* may be used to denote the whole of Jewish and Christian scripture in the OT, not just the Pentateuch (Rom 3:19; cf. also John 10:34)."

intelligible words God spoke to them through the prophet, he sent foreigners to them to speak his word in a language they cannot understand, so that they continue in failing to listen to and obey God.[3] LXX Deut 28:49 and its context says something similar and perhaps even more clearly than Isa 28:11–12.

LXX Deut 28:45 speaks of all the curses that will come upon Israel by which God will destroy and kill them because "you did not obey the voice of the Lord your God." Because Israel "did not serve the Lord your God (28:47), ... you will serve your enemies which the Lord will send upon you in hunger and in thirst and in nakedness and in want of all things; and he will place on your neck a yoke of iron until he destroys you" (28:48). Indeed, "the Lord will bring upon you a nation from the end of the earth, like a violent rush of a vulture, a nation whose voice you will not understand" (28:49).[4] In ironic correspondence to the fact that "you did not obey (εἰσήκουσας) the voice (φωνῆς) of the Lord your God" (28:45), God will bring upon Israel a foreign nation whose "voice" (φωνῆς) they will not even "understand" (ἀκούσῃ) (28:49).[5] Similarly, in 1 Cor 14:21, God will speak to this people in foreign tongues and in lips of foreigners and not even thus "will they obey (εἰσακούσονταί) me."

In LXX Jer 5:13, the people of Israel stated that "our prophets became wind, and the word of the Lord was not in them." In reply God declared that because they have said this, he has given his words into "your mouth," that is, the mouth of the prophet, "as fire, and this people as wood, and it will devour them" (5:14). Indeed, as God further promises, "I will bring

---

3. Garland, 1 Corinthians, 645–46: "In Isaiah's context, the prophet pronounces a judgment against Israel. Since Israel refused to heed what God spoke to them in understandable language through the prophet, God will now approach them by means of the foreign language of the conquering Assyrians. ... Since they will not be able to understand this message, it assures their unbelief and becomes a sign of God's judgment."

4. On LXX Deut 28:49, Wevers (Deuteronomy, 448) states: "The translator took the image of the swooping of the eagle to refer to the silence of the attack, and so translates the continuation as 'a nation whose voice (or better "the sound of which") they did not hear'; it would be a surprise attack." But this is questionable. In a context that emphasizes the oppressive destruction (28:45–48) that the foreign nation will inflict it seems preferable to translate ὅρμημα not as a silent "swooping" but as a "violent rush." Furthermore, ἀετοῦ might well be translated in this context of violent destruction not as "eagle" but as "vulture" (cf. BDAG, 22). Rather than silence, the suddenness and violence of the attack seems to be connoted. Finally, in accord with the literal sense of the grammar it is not the "sound" of the "swooping" but the "voice" (φωνῆς) of the "nation" (ἔθνος) that they will not "understand" (ἀκούσῃ; cf. BDAG, 38), as also in the MT.

5. Wevers, Deuteronomy, 446: "The reason for the threatened annihilation of Israel is expressed in the ὅτι clause—it was Israel's disobedience: 'you did not obey the voice of the Lord your God.' ... [T]he translator preferred to use the compound (εἰσήκουσας) so as to stress the notion of obedience."

upon you a nation from afar, O house of Israel, says the Lord, a nation the sound of whose tongue you will not understand" (5:15).

Like Isa 28:11–12, LXX Jer 5:15 provides references to both "this people" (τῷ λαῷ τούτῳ in Isa 28:11, also in MT; τὸν λαὸν τοῦτον in Jer 5:14; cf. τῷ λαῷ τούτῳ in 1 Cor 14:21) and the "tongue" of foreigners (γλώσσης in Isa 28:11 [also in MT] and Jer 5:15; cf. ἑτερογλώσσοις in 1 Cor 14:21) as points of contact with 1 Cor 14:21. But LXX Jer 5:15 provides additional key points of contact with 1 Cor 14:21 not found in either LXX or MT Isa 28:11–12.

Whereas both MT and LXX Isa 28:11–12 are narrated in the third person, LXX Jer 5:15, like 1 Cor 14:21, is narrated in the first-person future tense (cf. the emphatic "I will bring upon" [ἐγὼ ἐπάγω] in Jer 5:15 and "I will speak" [λαλήσω] in 1 Cor 14:21). Furthermore, whereas LXX (and MT) Isa 28:12 employs the past-tense "they were not willing to listen (ἠθέλησαν ἀκούειν)," LXX Jer 5:15 (as well as Deut 28:49) uses the future-tense "you will not understand (ἀκούσῃ)," as does 1 Cor 14:21: "they will not listen (εἰσακούσονταί)." And finally, unlike Isa 28:11–12, both LXX Jer 5:15 and 1 Cor 14:21 underline the prophetic promise of God with "says the Lord" (λέγει κύριος).

In sum, introduced by "in the law [scriptures] it is written," Paul's scriptural quotation in 1 Cor 14:21 reminds his audience not only of Isa 28:11–12 but also of Deut 28:45–49 and Jer 5:13–15. Indeed, both of these texts from Deuteronomy and Jeremiah provide points of contact with 1 Cor 14:21 that are not found in Isa 28:11–12.

1 Corinthians 14:25

Introduced by the words "he [an unbeliever or uninstructed person; cf. 1 Cor 14:24] will worship God announcing" (14:25b), the exclamation in 14:25c that "God is really among you!" reminds the audience of several OT passages. Although not explicitly introduced as a scriptural quotation, this exclamation is preceded by the expression "falling on his face (πεσὼν ἐπὶ πρόσωπον)" in 14:25b, which is reminiscent of scriptural language regarding worship (for a few of the many examples, see LXX Gen 17:3, 17; Lev 9:24; Num 16:22; Ezek 11:13), and thus prepares the audience for the scriptural reference in the exclamation in 14:25c.[6]

---

6. On 1 Cor 14:24–25, Fee (*Corinthians*, 687) states: "The language is thoroughly steeped in the OT. First, 'he will thus fall on his face and worship God.' This is biblical language for obeisance and worship.... The thoroughly biblical language used throughout vv. 24–25 to describe the effect of prophecy on the unbeliever is further evdidence that this phenomenon in Paul is to be understood in light of his Jewish heritage and not similar phenomena in Hellenism" (n. 65).

The exclamation that "God is really among you!" (ὄντως ὁ θεὸς ἐν ὑμῖν ἐστιν) in 14:25 reminds the audience of those OT passages in which people acknowledge that the one and only true God is present among the people of Israel. In 1 Kgs (3 Kgdms in LXX) 18:39, after the prophet Elijah dramatically discredited the prophets of Baal on Mount Carmel, all the people of Israel who had been attracted to the worship of Baal "fell on their face" (ἔπεσεν . . . ἐπὶ πρόσωπον αὐτῶν; cf. 1 Cor 14:25b) and said: "Truly the Lord is God, he is God" (ἀληθῶς κύριός ἐστιν ὁ θεός αὐτὸς ὁ θεός).

Several of the elements of the statement in 1 Cor 14:25 that "the secrets (κρυπτὰ) of his heart will become manifest (φανερὰ) and so, falling on his face (πεσὼν ἐπὶ πρόσωπον), he will worship (προσκυνήσει) God, announcing, 'God is really among you (ὄντως ὁ θεὸς ἐν ὑμῖν ἐστιν)!'" remind the audience of LXX Dan 2:46–47: King Nebuchadnezzar, "falling on his face (πεσὼν ἐπὶ πρόσωπον) to the ground, worshiped (προσεκύνησε) Daniel . . . the king said to Daniel, 'In truth your God is the God of Gods (ἐπ᾽ ἀληθείας ἐστὶν ὁ θεὸς ὑμῶν θεὸς τῶν θεῶν) and Lord of kings, who manifests (ἐκφαίνων) secret (κρυπτὰ) mysteries.'"[7]

The exclamation by an unbeliever or uninstructed person that "God is really among you (ὄντως ὁ θεὸς ἐν ὑμῖν ἐστιν)!'" in 1 Cor 14:25c also reminds the audience of the prophecy in LXX Zech 8:23, according to which foreigners of different languages will acknowledge that God is with the Jewish people: "Thus says the Lord almighty: 'In those days if ten men of all the languages of the nations take hold, indeed take hold of the hem of a Jewish man, saying, "Let us go with you, for we have heard that God is with you (ὁ θεὸς μεθ᾽ ὑμῶν ἐστιν)."'"[8]

And that an unbeliever or uninstructed person "will worship (προσκυνήσει) God, announcing, 'God is really among you (ὄντως ὁ θεὸς ἐν ὑμῖν ἐστιν)!'" in 1 Cor 14:25c reminds the audience of the prophecy in LXX Isa 45:14, according to which non-Israelites will confess that the true God is among the people of Israel: "Thus says the Lord of hosts: 'Egypt labored and the merchandise of the Ethiopians and of the Sabeans, men of stature, will cross over to you, and they will be your slaves, and they will follow behind you bound in handcuffs, and they will worship (προσκυνήσουσίν)

---

7. For the comparison of 1 Cor 14:24 with LXX Dan 2:46–47, see Wilk, *Bedeutung*, 331-32; Lindemann, *Erste Korintherbrief*, 310.

8. Collins, *First Corinthians*, 510: "Zechariah 8:23 explicitly mentions language. It has the prophetic formula 'says the Lord' (λέγει κύριος, cf. 14:21). These expressions in Zechariah may be the verbal links that allow Paul to express his reflections on the impact of the exercise of the gift of tongues on outsiders with a brace of biblical allusions that speak of the relationship between the God of Israel and non-Israelites."

you and pray among you, because God is among you (ἐν σοὶ ὁ θεός ἐστιν), and they will say, 'There is (ἔστιν) no God (θεὸς) but yours.' "[9]

To sum up, although not explicitly introduced as a scriptural quotation, the biblical language used in the context of the exclamation that "God is really among you!" in 1 Cor 14:25 helps to remind Paul's audience of those OT passages where previously nonbelieving people come to faith as they acknowledge and confess that the one and only true God is indeed really with the people of Israel.

Literary-Rhetorical Analysis

1 Corinthians 14:21

That it is introduced by the formula, "in the law it is written," with "law" as a reference to the scriptures in general, endows the quotation in 1 Cor 14:21 with the divine authority expressed throughout the scriptures. The quotation begins with a parallel pair of prepositional phrases with synonymous expressions for means of communication—"tongues" and "lips," but with emphasis upon the *foreignness* of this communication—"in foreign tongues (ἑτερογλώσσοις) and in lips of foreigners (ἑτέρων)." This foreign communication is emphatically and prophetically promised by the first-person future verb, "I will speak," to recipients designated as "this people." Even with this alternative, different, and foreign means of communication, however, this people still will not "listen" (εἰσακούσονταί) in the sense of "heed" or "obey" the speaker—"not even thus will they listen to me."[10] A final formula, "says the Lord," explicitly and emphatically identifies the speaker of the prophetic promise as God himself.[11]

---

9. On the recall of Isa 45:14 in 1 Cor 14:25, Fee (*Corinthians*, 687) states: "God, speaking through the prophet, says that the Egyptians will come over to you, and 'will worship' before you, and say, 'Surely God is with you.' Paul simply changes the singular 'with you,' referring to Israel, into a plural, 'among you,' referring to the gathered community." Wilk, *Bedeutung*, 333: "Im Sinne des Paulus verheißt Jes 45:14 demnach die Hinwendung der Ungläubigen zur Gemeinde Christi als Folge der eschatologischen Präsenz Gottes in der Gemeinde—einer Präsenz, die sich zumal in geistgewirkter 'Prophetie' realisiert." Garland, *1 Corinthians*, 653: "It is the confession of the vanquished in Isa. 45:14 (see also 1 Kings 18:39; Dan. 2:47; Zech. 8:23), but in this case they are vanquished by the word."

10. On the meaning of the compound verb εἰσακούω in 14:21 as not just "hearing" but "listening" in the sense of "heeding" or "obeying," see Lockwood, *1 Corinthians*, 488; Garland, *1 Corinthians*, 646; BDAG, 293: "to obey on the basis of having listened carefully."

11. Collins, *First Corinthians*, 508: "Paul further emphasizes the force of his citation by adding an oracular 'thus says the Lord' (cf. Rom 12:19; compare Isa 28:12a)." Garland, *1 Corinthians*, 647: "Paul adds the phrase 'says the Lord' to add punch to the quotation (cf. Rom

In sum, the scriptural quotation of 1 Cor 14:21 emphatically expresses an authoritative prophetic promise to its audience that even when God himself speaks in and through an alternative, different, and foreign means of communication, the people will not heed or obey him.[12] The implication is that if they did not listen and obey when God spoke to them in their own intelligible language, then they certainly will not listen and obey when God speaks to them in a language they cannot understand.

1 Corinthians 14:25

The exuberant exclamation that "God is really among you!" in 14:25 is introduced by "and thus, falling upon his face, he [the unbeliever or uninstructed person; cf. 14:24] will worship God, announcing." The exclamation thus functions as a confession indicating a conversion to faith in and worship of the one and only true God based on an authentic manifestation that God is "really," "in all reality," or "indeed" (ὄντως) "among you," the community of believers which the unbeliever or uninstructed person has encountered.[13]

Relation to the Antecedent Context in 1 Corinthians 14:1-20

In 1 Cor 14:1, after Paul exhorts his audience that in their pursuit of love they should strive eagerly for the spiritual gifts, he wishes above all that "you may prophesy (προφητεύητε)," that is, speak publicly the word of God in a way that can be readily understood and appreciated.[14] Paul prefers that

---

12:19)." Thiselton, *Corinthians*, 1122: "The use of the first person λαλήσω is intensified by perceiving the prophet or apostle in a context of divine agency by the addition of λέγει κύριος."

12. Garland, *1 Corinthians*, 646: "Not even when God's communication takes this unusual form of expression will they listen."

13. Thiselton, *Corinthians*, 1130: "The adverb ὄντως, formed from the adjectival participle ὤν, *being*, is generally translated *really* or *certainly*, but in modern English these words have become thinned down by overuse ('I am really pleased to say . . .'). Here the portentous nature of this profound revaluation and new grasp of truth invites a more weighty, even sonorous rendering. In this context the words convey some such confession as *in all reality*, or, to maintian *really*, the insertion of *indeed* captures the note of revised conviction. In all *reality* they encounter not simply human religion which constructs or projects a god; they encounter *God*, who draws forth authentic worship as he is authentically active and present among the believers."

14. Thiselton (*Corinthians*, 1094) states that "prophesying" here "is the performing of intelligible, articulate, communicative speech-acts, the operative currency of which depends on the active agency of the Holy Spirit mediated through human minds and lives to build up, to encourage, to judge, to exhort, and to comfort others in the context of interpersonal relations. . . . [T]he nearest modern parallel is probably that of an informed pastoral sermon which proclaims grace and judgment, or requires change of life, but which also remains open to question and correction by others."

his audience prophesy in the liturgical assembly because one who speaks (λαλῶν) in a tongue (γλώσσῃ) does not speak (λαλεῖ) to human beings but to God, for no one (οὐδεὶς) listens (ἀκούει); indeed he speaks (λαλεῖ) mysteries in spirit (14:2).[15] The unintelligibility of the spiritual gift of speaking in tongues is reinforced by the example of God himself speaking through foreign "tongues" (languages) to his people in the scriptural quote in 1 Cor 14:21: "In foreign tongues (ἑτερογλώσσοις) and in lips of foreigners I will speak (λαλήσω) to this people, and not even (οὐδ') thus will they listen (εἰσακούσονταί) to me, says the Lord."[16]

Paul's preference for prophesying rather than speaking in tongues centers around the issue of "edification" (οἰκοδομή; cf. 14:3, 5, 12, 26), "building up" or "edifying" (οἰκοδομέω; cf. 14:4, 17) the assembly (ἐκκλησία; cf.14:4, 5, 12) or a member in the assembly (14:17).[17] In contrast to speaking to God in tongues (14:2), prophesying speaks to human beings for edification (οἰκοδομὴν) and encouragement and consolation (14:3). Whoever speaks in a tongue edifies (οἰκοδομεῖ) himself, but whoever prophesies edifies (οἰκοδομεῖ) the entire assembly (14:4). Unless one speaking in

---

15. On the meaning of "tongue" (γλῶσσα) here, BDAG (201) states that it is "an utterance outside the normal patterns of intelligible speech and therefore requiring special interpretation." Gerhard Dautzenberg, "γλῶσσα," *EDNT* 1.253: "In 1 Corinthians 12–14 Paul uses the term γλῶσσα in a variety of phrases to describe a charisma.... On the basis of the phrase λαλεῖν γλώσσῃ, this spiritual gift is called 'glossolalia' ... speech that is unintelligible (14:2, 16, 23) and highly ecstatic." On "speaking in tongues" in 1 Cor 14, Fee (*Corinthians*, 598) states: "(*a*) It is Spirit-inspired utterance; that is made explicit in both vv. 7 and 11 and in 14:2. (*b*) The regulations for its use in 14:27–28 make it clear that the speaker is not in 'ecstasy' or 'out of control.' Quite the opposite; the speakers must speak in turn, and they must remain silent if there is no one to interpret. (*c*) It is speech essentially unintelligible both to the speaker (14:14) and to other hearers (14:16). (*d*) It is speech directed basically toward God (14:2, 14–15, 28); one may assume, therefore, that what is 'interpreted' is not speech directed toward others, but the 'mysteries' spoken to God." Speaking in tongues is "ecstatic only in the technical sense of being automatic speech in which the conscious mind played no part, but not ecstatic in the more common sense of 'produced or accompanied by exalted states of feeling, rapture, frenzy,' " according to James D. G. Dunn, *Jesus and the Spirit: A Study of the Religious and Charismatic Experience of Jesus and the First Christians as Reflected in the New Testament* (London: SCM, 1975), 243.

16. For an unconvincing proposal that the problem treated in 1 Cor 14 was the use of non-Greek languages spoken without translation, see Robert Zerhusen, "The Problem of Tongues in 1 Cor 14: A Reexamination," *BTB* 27 (1997): 139–52. For a refutation, see Garland, *1 Corinthians*, 584.

17. Josef Pfammatter, "οἰκοδομή," *EDNT* 2.496–97: "When the Pauline Epistles use οἰκοδομή as a *nomen actionis* (the action or process of building or edification: Rom 14:19; 15:2 1 Cor 14:3, 5, 12, 26; 2 Cor 12:19), what is built is never a building but always the ἐκκλησία.... Statistically and in terms of content the main focus of the theologically relevant occurrences of οἰκοδομέω is the meaning *build up, edify*. The objects of this vb., explicit and implicit, are always the ἐκκλησία (Matt 16:18; 1 Cor 14:4b) or an individual member of the ἐκκλησία (Acts 20:32; 1 Cor 8:1; 10:23; 14:4a, 17; 1 Thess 5:11; cf. 1 Pet 2:5)."

tongues interprets what he says, the assembly does not receive edification (οἰκοδομὴν) (14:5). And so, Paul's point that no one will know what is being spoken if one speaking in tongues does not produce an intelligible word for edification, but merely speaks to the air (14:9), is bolstered by the scriptural quote in 14:21 in which God himself will speak in unintelligible foreign tongues and not even thus will the people listen and be edified.

Paul goes on to say that although there are so many different languages in the world and none is meaningless (14:10), anyone who does not know the meaning of the language will be a foreigner (βάρβαρος) to the one who speaks it, and the one who speaks it a foreigner (βάρβαρος) to that person (14:11). This is what happens when one speaks in tongues in the assembly. Moreover, this receives an authoritative illustration in the scriptural citation in 14:21: When God himself speaks in foreign tongues (ἑτερογλώσσοις) and in the lips of foreigners (ἑτέρων) to his people, God becomes a foreigner to them and they a foreigner to God, so that they are not able to understand even God himself speaking in tongues, and thus they are not edified.

As Paul further explains, speaking in tongues involves the spirit but not the mind (14:14). In the liturgical assembly it is necessary not only to pray and sing with the spirit by speaking in tongues, but also to pray and sing with the mind in intelligible words (14:15). Otherwise, an uninstructed member within the assembly will not be able to participate in the prayer of thanksgiving in order to be edified (14:17), since he does not even know what one who is speaking in tongues is saying (14:16). This also is reaffirmed by the scriptural quote in 14:21, in which people will not even know what God is saying to them, and thus not be edified, if God himself were to speak to them in "tongues."

Although Paul is grateful to God that he speaks in tongues more than any of the Corinthians (14:18), in the liturgical assembly he would rather speak five (intelligible) words with his mind, in order to instruct and thus edify others and not just himself, than ten thousand (unintelligible) words in a tongue (14:19).[18] Paul thus exhorts his audience not to become children in their thinking (cf. 3:1–12; 13:11); with regard to evil they are to be as children but in their thinking they are to become as mature adults (14:20). They will not be children but adults in their thinking if they prophesy to edify rather than speak in tongues to confuse the assembly. For speaking in tongues does not result in listening, understanding, and obeying the word of God that edifies the assembly, as authoritatively confirmed by the scrip-

---

18. On the contrast between speaking in the spirit and speaking with the mind in 1 Cor 14:14–19, see Hans-Josef Klauck, "Mit Engelszungen? Vom Charisma der verständlichen Rede in 1 Kor 14," *ZTK* 97 (2000): 276–99.

tural quote in 14:21: When God himself speaks in foreign tongues/languages, "they will not listen to me."

In sum, the scriptural quotation in 1 Cor 14:21 reinforces with the divine authority of what is written in the Law Paul's previous points about the unintelligibility of speaking in tongues so that they do not edify the worshiping assembly (14:2, 9, 11, 16–17, 20). Not even if God himself were to speak in foreign tongues/languages would people listen, understand, and obey the word of God for their edification. Through the authoritative scriptural quote in 14:21, then, Paul is strengthening his rhetorical strategy of convincing his Corinthian implied audience to prophesy rather than speak in tongues when they worship together as an assembly.

Relation to the Subsequent Context in 1 Corinthians 14:22–25

The scriptural quotation in 1 Cor 14:21 about God's speaking in foreign tongues not leading people to listen to and thus to believe in God leads to a pair of interpretive assertions about the respective values of speaking in tongues and prophesying in 14:22 based on this scriptural quotation: "Therefore tongues are a sign not resulting in believers but resulting in unbelievers; whereas prophecy [is a sign] not resulting in unbelievers but resulting in believers."[19]

That speaking in tongues is a "sign not resulting in believers but resulting in unbelievers" (14:22a) is illustrated in 14:23: "If then the whole assembly comes together in one place and all are speaking in tongues, and uninstructed people or unbelievers should come in, will they not say that you are insane?" This illustration further develops the scriptural quote's expression of the negative effects of speaking in tongues as a sign for acknowledging God's presence. Speaking in unintelligible tongues, even if done by God himself, results not only in people not listening or heeding (14:21) in order to be edified to believe, but even in people concluding that

---

19. For the rationale justifying this translation of 14:22 in its context, see Robert J. Gladstone, "Sign Language in the Assembly: How Are Tongues a Sign to the Unbeliever in 1 Cor 14:20–25?" *Asian Journal of Pentecostal Studies* 2 (1999): 185–92. See Gladstone ("Sign Language," 182–83) and Garland (*1 Corinthians*, 650) for negative critiques of Joop F. M. Smit, "Tongues and Prophecy: Deciphering 1 Cor 14,22," *Bib* 75 (1994): 175–90. On the meaning of "sign" (σημεῖον) in 14:22, Gladstone ("Sign Language," 180) notes: "It is most natural and consistent with Paul's parallel rhetoric to understand both tongues and prophecy as 'signs.' I take the second half of v. 22 to be an ellipsis assuming the predicate of the first half. As tongues 'are a sign,' so is prophecy. By definition, in the present context a 'sign' is a supernatural, perceptible manifestation of God's power that signifies His presence among His people, proving the truth of their message and implicitly demanding a response from outside observers."

those speaking in tongues are actually out of their minds, so that they turn away without being edified by coming to believe in God.

That prophesying, however, is a sign "not resulting in unbelievers but resulting in believers" (14:22b) is illustrated in 14:24–25: "But if all are prophesying, and any unbeliever or uninstructed person should come in, he is convinced by all, judged by all. The secrets of his heart become manifest, and thus, falling upon his face, he will worship God, announcing, 'God is really among you!' "[20] This illustration concludes with a scriptural allusion in 14:25, the exclamation "God is really among you!" which complements the more explicit scriptural quotation in 14:21.

The scriptural quotation in 14:21 authoritatively establishes that speaking in unintelligible tongues, even when done by God himself, is a sign that does not edify its audience to believe in God, as indicated by a clause introduced by "thus"—"and not even thus (οὕτως) will they listen to me, says the Lord." The scriptural allusion in 14:25 complements this by establishing that prophesying, on the other hand, is a sign that does edify its audience to believe in God, as indicated by a clause introduced by "thus"—"and thus (οὕτως), falling upon his face, he [the unbeliever or uninstructed person] will worship God, announcing, 'God is really among you!' "[21]

How the references to scripture in 14:21 and 14:25 work together in a complementary way within Paul's rhetorical strategy of persuading his audience to prophesy rather than speak in unintelligible tongues for the edification of the worshiping assembly in 14:20–25 can be outlined as follows:

Introductory Exhortation (14:20)
Argument (14:21–25)
    Exemplary Text from Scripture (14:21)
    Two Interpretive Assertions (14:22)

---

20. On the importance of prophecy in the worshiping assembly for the missionary activity of the Christian community in 1 Cor 14:24–25, see Walter Rebell, "Gemeinde als Missionsfaktor im Urchristentum: I Kor 14,24f. als Schlüsselsituation," *TZ* 44 (1988): 117–34. See also Petr Pokorný, "Christliche Verkündigung als Modell des hermeneutishcen Prozesses nach 1 Kor 14,23–25," in *Philosophical Hermeneutics and Biblical Exegesis* (ed. Petr Pokorný and Jan Roskovec; WUNT 153; Tübingen: Mohr Siebeck, 2002), 245–51.

21. As Gladstone ("Sign Language," 191) notes, in 14:21 "glossolalia's result of dissuading obedience from 'this people' follows (the inserted) οὕτως directly. Likewise, prophecy's result of evoking a response of faith from the visitor follows οὕτως directly in 14:25. Both applications of οὕτως seem to be in apposition to one another, paralleling the two results in the two different signs."

Two Illustrations (14:23–25a)
Exemplary Text from Scripture (14:25b)[22]

To sum up, whereas with the scriptural quotation in 14:21, Paul persuades his Corinthian audience against speaking in unintelligible tongues in the worshiping assembly, because it is a sign that results in unbelief in God, with the scriptural allusion in 14:25 he complements his rhetorical strategy by persuading his audience to prophesy, because it is a sign that results in belief in God.

Summary on 1 Corinthians 14:21, 25

1. Introduced by "in the law [scriptures] it is written," Paul's scriptural quotation in 1 Cor 14:21 reminds his audience not only of Isa 28:11–12 but also of Deut 28:45–49 and Jer 5:13–15. Indeed, the texts from Deuteronomy and Jeremiah provide points of contact with 1 Cor 14:21 that are not found in Isa 28:11–12.

2. Although not explicitly introduced as a scriptural quotation, the biblical language used in the context of the exclamation that "God is really among you!" in 1 Cor 14:25 helps to remind Paul's audience of those scriptural passages where previously nonbelieving people come to faith as they acknowledge and confess that the one and only true God is indeed really with the people of Israel.

3. The scriptural quotation of 1 Cor 14:21 emphatically expresses an authoritative prophetic promise to its audience that even when God himself speaks in and through an alternative, different, and foreign means of communication, the people will not heed or obey him. The implication is that if they did not listen and obey when God spoke to them in their own intelligible language, then they certainly will not listen and obey when God speaks to them in a language they cannot understand.

4. The exclamation that "God is really among you!" in 14:25 functions as a confession indicating a conversion to faith in and worship of the one and only true God based on an authentic manifestation that God is "really," "in all reality," or "indeed" (ὄντως) "among you," the community of believers that the unbeliever or uninstructed person has encountered.

---

22. Gladstone, "Sign Language," 191.

5. The scriptural quotation in 1 Cor 14:21 reinforces with the divine authority of what is written in the Law Paul's previous points about the unintelligibility of speaking in tongues so that they do not edify the worshiping assembly (14:2, 9, 11, 16–17, 20). Not even if God himself were to speak in foreign tongues/languages would people listen, understand, and obey the word of God for their edification. Through the authoritative scriptural quote in 14:21, then, Paul is strengthening his rhetorical strategy of convincing his Corinthian implied audience to prophesy rather than speak in tongues when they worship together as an assembly.

6. Whereas with the scriptural quotation in 14:21 Paul persuades his Corinthian audience against speaking in unintelligible tongues in the worshiping assembly, because it is a sign that results in unbelief in God, with the scriptural allusion in 14:25 he complements his rhetorical strategy by persuading his audience to prophesy, because it is a sign that results in belief in God.

CHAPTER 14

1 Corinthians 15:25, 27

*He reign until He places
all the enemies under his feet.*

All things He subjected under his feet.

Old Testament Background

Because they are linked for mutual interpretation by the words "all" and "under his feet," which they have in common, we consider the next two scripture quotations in 1 Cor 15:25, 27 together as yet another example of the Jewish exegetical device that came to be known as *gezera shava*.[1] The first quotation in 1 Cor 15:25 is introduced by "for it is necessary that" (δεῖ γάρ), indicating to Paul's implied Corinthian audience that the words to follow accord with the divine necessity of God's scriptural plan.[2] The quotation itself is an adaptation of an oft-quoted and very familiar Psalm verse in early Christian literature, Ps 110:1 (LXX 109:1): "He reign until He

---

1. For previous uses of *gezera shava* in 1 Corinthians, see chs. 6 and 9 above. With reference to its use in 1 Cor 15:25, 27, see Scott M. Lewis, *"So That God May Be All in All": The Apocalyptic Message of 1 Corinthians 15,12–34* (Tesi Gregoriana 42; Rome: Gregorian University Press, 1998), 60: "In this type of exegesis, one OT passage is explained by comparison with another in which identical terminology and analogous traits are found." See also Scott M. Lewis, "So That God May Be All in All: 1 Corinthians 15:12–34," *SBFLA* 49 (1999): 195–210.

2. Lambrecht, "Paul's Christological Use," 506: "The verb δεῖ is either an apocalyptic term referring to God's fixed and detailed timetable or points to God's plan as it is manifested in scripture. δεῖ, it is often said, confirms that Paul here consciously refers to scripture." Lewis, *So That God*, 62: "The verb δεῖ which is found in verse 25 can be either an apocalyptic term meaning the necessity of God's fixed plan and detailed timetable, or of God's plan expressed in the scriptures, especially the prophetic books. There are probably elements of both." See also Wolff, *Erste Brief*, 387.

places all the enemies under his feet."[3] Because this adapted quotation would be so readily recognizable as scriptural to Paul's audience, he does not need to formally introduce it as a scriptural quotation any more explicitly than he has.[4]

The second quotation in 1 Cor 15:27a quotes from Ps 8:7b: "He subjected all things under his feet." Although introduced simply by the word "for" (γάρ), 1 Cor 15:27a is confirmed as a scriptural quotation by the words that follow it in 15:27b: "But when it says" (ὅταν δὲ εἴπῃ). The implied subject most likely to be supplied by the audience of "it says" is "the scripture" (ἡ γραφή; cf. Gal 4:30; Rom 4:3; 9:17; 10:11; 11:2; 1 Tim 5:18).[5]

---

3. David M. Hay, *Glory at the Right Hand: Psalm 110 in Early Christianity* (SBLMS 18; Nashville: Abingdon, 1973); Terrence Callan, "Psalm 110:1 and the Origin of the Expectation That Jesus Will Come Again," *CBQ* 44 (1982): 622–36; Collins, *First Corinthians*, 553; Lewis, *So That God*, 59: "Of all OT texts, verses 1 and 4 of Psalm 110 are the most often quoted or alluded to in the NT, 33 quotations or allusions in the NT and 7 in other Christian writings before the middle of the 2nd century." Garland, *1 Corinthians*, 711 n. 11: "Psalm 110:1 (109:1 LXX) is the most frequently cited OT passage in the NT (Matt. 22:44/Mark 12:36/Luke 20:42–43; Matt. 26:64/Mark 14:62/Luke 22:69; Acts 2:34–35; Heb. 1:13; see also Eph. 1:20–21; 1 Pet. 3:22)."

4. Despite these indications, neither Koch (*Schrift*, 18–20) nor Stanley (*Paul*, 206 n. 85) considers 1 Cor 15:25 to be a scriptural quotation. For the view that Paul may not be quoting directly from the OT but from christological traditions known to the Corinthians, see Martinus C. de Boer, *The Defeat of Death: Apocalyptic Eschatology in 1 Corinthians 15 and Romans 5* (JSNTSup 22; Sheffield: JSOT, 1988), 118. In a later update, de Boer doubts "that the Corinthians heard the words of v. 25b as an allusion or an appeal to Ps 110,1b. In short, the Corinthians probably heard v. 25b as Paul's own gloss on the christological tradition to which he does allude in v. 25a"; see Martinus C. de Boer, "Paul's Use of a Resurrection Tradition in 1 Cor 15,20–28," in *The Corinthian Correspondence* (ed. Reimund Bieringer; BETL 125; Louvain: Louvain University Press, 1996), 648. But de Boer overstates the differences between 1 Cor 15:25 and Ps 110:1 and underestimates the Corinthian audience's ability to recognize 1 Cor 15:25 as a scriptural quotation. Furthermore, although de Boer and others (see Thiselton, *Corinthians*, 1234) refer to 1 Cor 15:25 as an "allusion" to rather than a "quotation" of Ps 110:1, we prefer the term "quotation" but used in its broadest or loosest sense, keeping in mind that Paul has adapted this quotation, like the others in 1 Corinthians, to fit his rhetorical strategy. Paul expects his audience to recognize the scriptural authority of 1 Cor 15:25, whether considered as a quotation or an allusion to Ps 110:1.

5. Stanley, *Paul*, 206 n. 85; Thiselton, *Corinthians*, 1236; Collins, *First Corinthians*, 554: " 'When it says' (ὅταν δὲ εἴπῃ) is a loose formula that equivalently identifies v. 27a as scriptural." Garland, *1 Corinthians*, 713: " 'When it says' (ὅταν . . . εἴπῃ) refers to what the Scripture says that needs special interpretation, not to Christ's making an announcement or to God's speaking in Scripture." For the questionable view that "Christ" is the implied subject of "says" in 15:27b, see Lambrecht, "Paul's Christological Use," 510; Joseph Plevnik, *Paul and the Parousia: An Exegetical and Theological Investigation* (Peabody, Mass.: Hendrickson, 1997), 132–33. The implied subject of "it says" in 15:27b is, of course, closely related to the issue of whether "Christ" or "God" is the subject of the scriptural quote in 15:27a, which will be discussed below.

1 Corinthians 15:25 and LXX Psalm 109:1

Since MT Ps 110:1 does not significantly differ from LXX Ps 109:1, we may limit our comparison of 1 Cor 15:25 to the LXX version:

> LXX Ps 109:1: τῷ Δαυιδ ψαλμός εἶπεν ὁ κύριος τῷ κυρίῳ μου κάθου ἐκ δεξιῶν μου ἕως ἂν θῶ τοὺς ἐχθρούς σου ὑποπόδιον τῶν ποδῶν σου
> A psalm to David: The Lord said to my Lord, "Sit at my right until I place your enemies as a footstool under your feet."

> 1 Cor 15:25: δεῖ γὰρ αὐτὸν βασιλεύειν ἄχρι οὗ θῇ πάντας τοὺς ἐχθροὺς ὑπὸ τοὺς πόδας αὐτοῦ.
> For it is necessary that he reign until He places all the enemies under his feet.

The direct address in the second person by "the Lord" (God) to "my Lord" (Davidic king) in LXX Ps 109:1b is narrated in the third person in 1 Cor 15:25. The divine decree for the Davidic king to "sit at my right" (κάθου ἐκ δεξιῶν μου) in an authoritative position to rule or reign along with God in the psalm is rendered as the divine scriptural necessity (δεῖ) that "he [Christ] reign" (αὐτὸν βασιλεύειν) in 1 Cor 15:25.[6]

The conjunction "until" (ἕως ἂν) in the psalm, pointing to God's ultimate subjugation of the king's enemies, is changed to the conjunction "until" (ἄχρι οὗ) in 1 Cor 15:25, indicating a temporal limitation to the necessity for Christ to reign.[7] The first-person singular "until I [God] place (θῶ)" in the psalm becomes the third-person singular "until He [God] places (θῇ)" in 1 Cor 15:25.[8]

---

6. Joost Holleman, *Resurrection and Parousia: A Traditio-Historical Study of Paul's Eschatology in 1 Corinthians 15* (NovTSup 84; Leiden: Brill, 1996), 60: "The poet of Psalm 110(109) presents his 'lord' (the king) as remaining passive: he sits on his throne while God is defeating his enemies by making them into a footstool. Yet the idea behind the image is that the king and God are so closely related that, although the king is the actual ruler, it is God who exercises his power through the king."

7. Conzelmann, *1 Corinthians*, 272 n. 92; Lewis, *So That God*, 62; Lambrecht, "Paul's Christological Use," 506–7: "The replacement of ἕως ἂν by ἄχρι οὗ occurred most probably in function of Paul's idea of a temporal limitation of Christ's kingship. In the psalm the expression pointed to a final victory, the ultimate aim of God's action." Andreas Lindemann, "Parusie Christi und Herrschaft Gottes: Zur Exegese von 1 Kor 15,23–28," WD 19 (1987): 95 n. 45: "ἄχρι οὗ markiert stärker den Endpunkt, ἕως ἂν zeigt mehr die Dauer eines Vorgangs an (impliziert freilich auch dessen Endlichkeit)."

8. With regard to the issue of whether "Christ" or "God" is the subject in 1 Cor 15:25b, we follow Holleman, *Resurrection*, 59: "Paul certainly regards God as the subject of the subjection

In the psalm, the object of God's placing is "your enemies" (τοὺς ἐχθρούς σου); in 1 Cor 15:25, it is, more universally and absolutely, "all the enemies" (πάντας τοὺς ἐχθροὺς). In the psalm, God promises to place the king's defeated enemies in total subjugation "as a footstool under your feet" (ὑποπόδιον τῶν ποδῶν σου); in 1 Cor 15:25, God will place all the defeated enemies in the universe in total subjugation "under his feet" (ὑπὸ τοὺς πόδας αὐτοῦ).[9]

Thus, although in a different grammatical form because of its Pauline context, 1 Cor 15:25 contains the same key terms and expresses essentially the same idea as LXX Ps 109:1b: The king reigns according to divine decree until God places defeated enemies in total subjugation under his feet. Because of these strong similarities, the implied Corinthian audience cannot fail to recognize 1 Cor 15:25 as an adapted quotation or allusion to LXX Ps 109:1b, a verse that appears frequently in early Christian literature.[10]

1 Corinthians 15:27a and LXX Psalm 8:7b

MT Ps 8:7b: כֹּל שַׁתָּה תַחַת־רַגְלָיו
All You have placed under his feet.

LXX Ps 8:7b: πάντα ὑπέταξας ὑποκάτω τῶν ποδῶν αὐτοῦ
All things You subjected under his feet.

1 Cor 15:27a: πάντα γὰρ ὑπέταξεν ὑπὸ τοὺς πόδας αὐτοῦ
For all things He subjected under his feet.

---

of the enemies under Jesus' feet (vv. 25b, 27). This can be deduced from verse 28. Thus, there is a change of subjects, from Jesus to God, between verses 25a (δεῖ βασιλεύειν) and 25b (θῇ), where Paul quotes or refers to Ps. 110 (109):1.... In verse 28 it is said that in the end the Son will subject hmself to 'the one who put all things in subjection under him.' The 'one who put all things in subjection' (τῷ ὑποτάξαντι) can only be God. Since God is the subject in verse 28, he must also be the subject of the same action described in verse 27 (ὑπέταξεν, ὑποταξαντος) and 25b (θῇ) (note 4).... One must take into account a change of subjects somewhere between 24b (παραδιδῷ, Jesus) and 25b (θῇ, God). A change at the beginning of the quotation (v. 25b) is the most simple and plausible solution (note 6)." See also Uta Heil, "Theo-logische Interpretation von 1 Kor 15,23–28," ZNW 84 (1993): 29–35.

9. For a list of the differences between 1 Cor 15:25 and LXX Ps 109:1b, see Larry Joseph Kreitzer, *Jesus and God in Paul's Eschatology* (JSNTSup 19; Sheffield: JSOT, 1987), 149.

10. On 1 Cor 15:25 as a quotation of the psalm, Lindemann ("Parusie Christi," 96–97) notes: "Auch in formaler Hinsicht spricht vieles für den Zitatcharacter der Stelle... die Terminologie in V. 25b deutlich von der in V. 24 gebrauchten abweicht; dieser Wechsel in der Terminologie läßt sich leicht von der Annahme her erklären, daß Paulus nun bewußt den biblischen Text aufnimmt." Heil ("Theo-logische Interpretation," 31) adds: "Offensichtlich ist dieser Text sehr bekannt im Urchristentum, was sich aus den häufigen Zitaten ergibt. Aus diesem Grund wurde hier sicher Ps 110,1 wiedererkannt und damit auch Gott als Subjekt gelesen."

The only noteworthy difference between the MT and LXX versions of the psalm verse lies in the verbs—"You have placed" (שַׁתָּה) in the MT but "You subjected" (ὑπέταξας) in the LXX of Ps 8:7b.[11] Hence, 1 Cor 15:27a with "He subjected" (ὑπέταξεν) is closer to the LXX than to the MT.

Just as for the quotation of LXX Ps 109:1b in 1 Cor 15:25, so also the quotation of LXX Ps 8:7b in 1 Cor 15:27a has been transformed from a direct address in the second person (in this case from the psalmist to God) to a third-person narrative to conform it to the Pauline context.[12] Besides the introductory "for" (γάρ) in 1 Cor 15:27a, the only other difference between the Pauline quotation and LXX Ps 8:7b lies in the prepositional phrase "under his feet"—ὑποκάτω τῶν ποδῶν αὐτοῦ in the psalm verse but ὑπὸ τοὺς πόδας αὐτοῦ in 1 Cor 15:27a. Thus, both 1 Cor 15:25 and 15:27a have the identical grammatical form of the prepositional phrase "under his feet," which enhances the *gezera shava* between these two scriptural quotations.[13] Indeed, the identical prepositional phrase "under his feet," as well as the word "all," linking 1 Cor 15:27a to 15:25, further indicates to the audience that not only 1 Cor 15:27a but also 15:25 have the authority of scriptural quotations.[14]

Many who grant that 1 Cor 15:27a is a scriptural quotation deny that same status to 15:25 because of the differences between the psalm verse and the Pauline text. But the Pauline adaptation of LXX Ps 109:1b is not much greater than that of LXX Ps 8:7b. And even after the changes, the essential elements of each psalm verse are still present in their Pauline quotations—reigning until enemies are placed under feet in LXX Ps 109:1b and in 1 Cor 15:25; subjecting all things under his feet in LXX Ps 8:7b and in 1 Cor

---

11. Note that the same Hebrew verb for "place" occurs also in MT Ps 110:1b, quoted in 1 Cor 15:25, which enhances the *gezera shava* between these two psalm verses in the Hebrew version.

12. Stanley, *Paul*, 206: "All in all, there seems little reason to doubt that the third-person form ὑπέταξεν arose out of Paul's desire to conform the wording of his citation to the grammatical constraints of its new context in 1 Cor 15."

13. With regard to Paul's use of the preposition ὑπό in 1 Cor 15:25 rather than ὑποπόδιον as in LXX Ps 109:1b, and in 1 Cor 15:27a rather than ὑποκάτω as in LXX Ps 8:7b, Stanley (*Paul*, 207) notes: "Regardless of the form in which Paul knew either verse, it seems that ὑπό was his word of choice in such situations. The fact that ὑποκάτω appears nowhere in any of Paul's letters while ὑπό is quite common reinforces the impression that Paul has intentionally preferred ὑπό in both 1 Cor 15.25 and 15.27. Though a pre-Pauline origin cannot be ruled out, all the evidence seems to favor the view that Paul has (perhaps unconsciously) adapted the wording of this common quotation to conform to his own linguistic usage."

14. Note that Paul has added "all" (πάντας) to his quotation of LXX Ps 109:1b in 1 Cor 15:25 to further conform it with the "all things" (πάντα) in his quotation of LXX Ps 8:7b in 15:27a, thus enhancing the *gezera shava* that combines the two scriptural quotes in 15:25 and 15:27a.

15:27a. Although both 15:25 and 15:27a have been adapted to Paul's rhetorical strategy, both exhibit enough essential elements of their respective OT sources to warrant the audience's recognition of them as a closely combined pair of scriptural quotations.[15]

Literary-Rhetorical Analysis

That "it is necessary" (δεῖ) makes the audience realize that the Christ who is to hand over the kingdom (βασιλείαν) to the God and Father at the end, when he has destroyed every ruler and every authority and power (15:24), must continue "to reign" (βασιλεύειν) as the Christ who has been raised from the dead (15:20a), in accord with the scriptural plan decreed by God for the king in LXX Ps 109:1b (15:25a). But there is a temporal limitation to and an ultimate goal for this reigning. It is necessary that the risen Christ reign until God places "*all* the enemies," not just every ruler and every authority and power that Christ will destroy, but absolutely *all* the defeated enemies in the universe in total subjugation "under the feet" of Christ (15:25b).[16] This assures the audience that there is an ultimate goal of the necessary reign of the risen Christ for them to look forward to in confident hope—God's absolute and utter defeat of *all* their enemies.

In 15:26, the last of the enemies to be destroyed (καταργεῖται, divine passive) by the God who will place *all* the enemies under the feet of the risen and reigning Christ (15:25) is the personified power of "the death" (ὁ θάνατος) that came into the world through a human being (15:21a). Once God has destroyed death as the last of all enemies, then the audience is assured that LXX Ps 8:7b will be fulfilled: "*All things* He [God] subjected under his [Christ's] feet" (15:27a).

With the quotation of LXX Ps 8:7b in 15:27a, the audience experiences a development of the quotation of LXX Ps 109:1b in 15:25 through the *gezera shava* that combines these two scriptural quotations by the words they have in common. "All (πάντας) the enemies" in 15:25 progresses in 15:27a to absolutely "all things" (πάντα), which embraces not just the negative, the enemies, but also the positive—everything in the universe, including the audience.[17]

---

15. On the Pauline reading of LXX Ps 109:1b in 1 Cor 15:25 and LXX Ps 8:7b in 1 Cor 15:27a, see also J. M. García, "Acontecimientos después de la venida gloriosa (1 Cor 15,23–28)," *EstBib* 58 (2000): 527–59.

16. According to Lewis (*So That God*, 66), this is "reflective of the original intent of the psalm, which places the anointed king at God's right hand while God subdues the king's enemies."

17. Collins, *First Corinthians*, 554: "'All things' (πάντα) are the universe."

"Until He [God] places *all* the enemies under his [Christ's] feet" in 15:25 progresses in 15:27a to "*All things* He [God] subjected under his [Christ's] feet."[18] The quote in 15:25 expresses the negative concept that God "places" (θῇ) *all* defeated enemies in total subjugation "under the feet" of the victorious and triumphantly risen Christ. But the quote in 15:27a asserts the more positive concept that God "subjected" or "subordinated" (ὑπέταξεν), that is, placed in their proper creational order, *all things* in the universe "under the feet" of the risen Christ.[19]

According to 15:21b, Christ is the "human being through whom" (δι ἀνθρώπου) came the resurrection of the dead. But in accord with the quotation of LXX Ps 8:7b in 15:27a, Christ is the "human being" (ἄνθρωπος in LXX Ps 8:5a) under whose feet God "subjected" all things in the universe in their proper order according to God's scriptural plan of creation to subordinate all of creation to humanity. God thus subjected all things under the feet of the risen Christ so that, as "those who belong to Christ" (15:23b) "will be brought to life" (15:22b) "each one in proper order (τάγματι)" (15:23a) after Christ as the "firstfruits" (15:23b), so all things in the universe, including the audience, will be "subordinated" (ὑπέταξεν), that is, placed in their proper creational order under the human being Christ—the first human being to be raised from the dead.[20]

---

18. Lindemann, "Parusie," 100: "V. 27a wiederholt also die Aussage von V. 25b, wobei eine gewisse Änderung natürlich darin liegt, daß ὑποτάσσειν nicht einfach 'unterwerfen' meint, sondern die Errichtung einer neuen Welt 'ordnung' anzudeuten scheint."

19. On the meaning of ὑπέταξεν in 15:27a, Thiselton (*Corinthians*, 1235) points out "its connection with τάσσω and τάγμα or τάξις, *that which is ordered*, with ὑπό, i.e., *sub-ordinate*." BDAG, 1042: "Of submission involving recognition of an ordered structure." Thus, "subjected" or "subordinated" (ὑπέταξεν) in 15:27a recalls "each one in proper order (τάγματι)" in 15:23a. De Boer, *Defeat*, 115: "The verb used here, ὑποτάσσειν, a cognate of the noun τάγμα used in v. 23a, literally means to 'rank or order under,' and thus to 'sub-ord-inate.'" *TLNT* 3.425: "It means first of all accepting the exact place God has assigned, keeping to one's rank in this or that society, accepting a dependent status, especially toward God." Jan Lambrecht, "Structure and Line of Thought in 1 Cor. 15:23-28," *NovT* 32 (1990): 149: "The verb ὑπέταξεν functions as a prophetic aorist."

20. On the biblical metaphor of Christ as "firstfruits" here, see Andy Johnson, "Firstfruits and Death's Defeat: Metaphor in Paul's Rhetorical Strategy in 1 Cor 15:20-28," *WW* 16 (1996): 456-64.

Relation to the Context in 1 Corinthians 15:20–28

1 Corinthians 15:20–23

In further reply to some among his Corinthian audience who say there is no resurrection of the dead (15:12b), Paul asserts that now Christ has been raised from the dead as the "firstfruits" of those "who have fallen asleep" in death (15:20).[21] That Christ is the "firstfruits" guarantees the audience that there will be a further "harvest" of those who will be raised from the dead after Christ.[22] Since death came through a human being (the first human being, Adam), the resurrection of the dead also came through a human being (Christ) (15:21). For just as in Adam all die, so also in Christ all will be brought to life, but each in the proper order—Christ the "firstfruits," then, at his coming, those who belong to Christ (15:22–23).

The Chiasm in 1 Corinthians 15:24–28

At this point the audience begins to hear the following chiasm in 15:24–28, in which the combined pair of scriptural quotations in 15:25 and 27a are embedded as the C and C´ units respectively, which are paralleled around the central and pivotal D unit:

A   [24a] Then [comes] the end,
      [24b] *when* (ὅταν) he hands over the kingdom to the *God* (θεῷ) and Father,

---

21. For the view that 1 Corinthians 15 is addressing the denial of the possibility of further existence after death, see Johan S. Vos, "Argumentation und Situation in 1Kor. 15," *NovT* 41 (1999): 313–33. For the view that Paul is attempting to instill fear in his audience in 1 Corinthians 15, see Anders Eriksson, "Fear of Eternal Damnation: *Pathos* Appeal in 1 Corinthians 15 and 16," in *Paul and Pathos* (ed. Thomas H. Olbricht and Jerry L. Sumney; Atlanta: Society of Biblical Literature, 2001), 117–19.

22. Joost Holleman, "Jesus' Resurrection as the Beginning of the Eschatological Resurrection (1 Cor 15,20)," in *The Corinthian Correspondence* (ed. Reimund Bieringer; BETL 125; Louvain: Louvain University Press, 1996), 653 n. 1: "In 1 Cor 15,20–23 Paul explains the view that 'Jesus has been raised from the dead as the first-fruits (ἀπαρχή) of those who have fallen asleep' in two ways: a) Jesus' resurrection is the beginning of the eschatological resurrection (vv. 20 and 23), thereby emphasizing that Jesus is the *first one* raised; b) Christians will be made alive through participation in Jesus' resurrection (vv. 21–22), thereby emphasizing that Jesus has been raised as the *representative* of those to be raised." See also Holleman, *Resurrection*, 49–51; Thiselton, *Corinthians*, 1223–24; Fee, *Corinthians*, 748–49; Alexander Sand, "ἀπαρχή," *EDNT* 1.116; Collins, *First Corinthians*, 551: "Firstfruits are the harbinger of the harvest to come." Lockwood, *1 Corinthians*, 566: "The NT regularly uses this term of a first installment which betokens a greater fullness to come."

B ²⁴ᶜ *when* (ὅταν) he has destroyed *every* (πᾶσαν) ruler and *every* (πᾶσαν) authority and power.

    C ²⁵ᵃ *For* (γὰρ) it is necessary that he reign
    ²⁵ᵇ "until He has placed *all* (πάντας) the enemies *under his feet* (ὑπὸ τοὺς πόδας αὐτοῦ)" (LXX Ps 109:1b).

        D ²⁶ The *last* (ἔσχατος) enemy to be destroyed is *the death* (ὁ θάνατος).

    C′ ²⁷ᵃ "*For* (γὰρ) *all things* (πάντα) He subjected *under his feet* (ὑπὸ τοὺς πόδας αὐτοῦ)" (LXX Ps 8:7b).

B′ ²⁷ᵇ *But when* (ὅταν δὲ) it says that *all things* (πάντα) have been subjected,
²⁷ᶜ it is clear that excepted is the One who subjected to him *all the things* (τὰ πάντα).

A′ ²⁸ᵃ *But when* (ὅταν δὲ) all the things are subjected to him,
²⁸ᵇ then also the Son himself will be subjected to the One who subjected to him all the things,
²⁸ᶜ so that *God* (θεὸς) may be all things in all things.²³

The A and A′ units in 15:24ab and 15:28. In 15:24ab, the words "end" (τέλος), "hands over" (παραδιδῷ), "kingdom" (βασιλείαν), and "Father"

---

23. For the recognition of this chiasm we are indebted to Charles E. Hill, "Paul's Understanding of Christ's Kingdom in I Corinthians 15:20–28," *NovT* 30 (1988): 300. We will attempt, however, to elucidate and establish it on an even firmer basis. For a rejection of this chiasm in favor of an alternative structure, see Lambrecht, "Structure," 143–51. Lewis (*So That God*, 46 n. 75), however, criticizes Lambrecht's rejection of the chiasm as "an overly subtle analysis" and adds: "Many of the verses he does not find to be 'pure parallels.' It might be pointed out that in a chiastic structure there is seldom a pure parallel. He concentrates on the subtle grammatical differences in the four ὅταν clauses, claiming that these differences affect the meaning of the clauses. Even so, the meanings are not affected enough to alter the *basic* meaning.... Even though vv. 25–28 can be an explanation of a thesis presented in vv. 23–24, there is no reason why that cannot be done in the context of a chiastic structure as established by Hill." We might add that the reason there are seldom pure parallels in a chiasm is that the parallel units are not meant to be mere repetitions, but involve a progression or development from one parallel unit to another. For previous chiasms involving scriptural quotations in 1 Corinthians, see chs. 8, 10, and 11 above. For a proposed structure in accord with the elaboration of the chreia, see Anders Eriksson, "Elaboration of Argument in 1 Cor 15:20–34," *SEÅ* 64 (1999): 101–14.

(πατρί), which occur only here within the chiasm, establish the integrity and distinction of the chiasm's A unit. In 15:28, the word "Son" (υἱός), occurring only here within the chiasm, secures the integrity and distinction of the chiasm's A´ unit. The words "when" (ὅταν) and "God" (θεῷ in 15:24b and θεός in 15:28c), occurring in both the A and A´ units, establish their parallelism. Furthermore, "Son" in the A´ unit complements "Father" in the A unit, and the conclusion of the chiasm in 15:28c, "so that God may be all things in all things," represents a parallel yet fuller expression of "the end," which introduces the chiasm in 15:24a.[24]

The B and B´ units in 15:24c and 15:27bc. In 15:24c, the words "ruler" (ἀρχὴν), "authority" (ἐξουσίαν), and "power" (δύναμιν), occurring only here within the chiasm, establish the integrity and distinction of the chiasm's B unit. In 15:27bc, the words "says" (εἴπῃ), "clear" (δῆλον), and "excepted" (ἐκτὸς), which occur only here within the chiasm, secure the integrity and distinction of the chiasm's B´ unit. The words "when" (ὅταν) and "every/all" (πᾶσαν twice in 15:24c; πάντα in 15:27b and τὰ πάντα in 15:27c), which are found in both the B and B´ units, determine their parallelism.

The C and C´ units in 15:25 and 15:27a. In 15:25, the words "necessary" (δεῖ), "reign" (βασιλεύειν), and "place" (θῇ), found only here within the chiasm, set the integrity and distinction of the chiasm's C unit. In 15:27a, the third-person singular aorist active of the verb "subject" (ὑπέταξεν), occurring only in this form within the chiasm, establishes the integrity and distinction of the chiasm's C´ unit. The words "for" (γὰρ), "all" (πάντας in 15:25b; πάντα in 15:27a), and "under his feet" (ὑπὸ τοὺς πόδας αὐτοῦ), found in both the C and C´ units, establish their parallelism.

The D unit in 15:26. In 15:26, the words "last" (ἔσχατος) and "the death" (ὁ θάνατος), occurring only here within the chiasm, determine the

---

24. Lewis, *So That God*, 46 n. 75: "[T]he τέλος of v. 24 is certainly the parallel of πάντα ἐν πᾶσιν of 28c, the latter being a fuller expression of the former." For a recent unconvincing attempt to interpret τέλος ("end") as the resurrection of non-Christians, see Marlis Gielen, "Universale Totenauferweckung und universales Heil? 1 Kor 15,20–28 im Kontext paulinischer Theologie," *BZ* 47 (2003): 92–95. As Collins (*First Corinthians*, 552) notes: "[N]o known Greek usage allows 'the end' (τὸ τέλος) to be construed as the rest (of those to be raised)." And as Lockwood (*1 Corinthians*, 567) asserts: "τὸ τέλος means 'the end,' particularly in the sense of God's great goal or purpose of redemptive history." See also Lewis, *So That God*, 52–53; Thiselton, *Corinthians*, 1230–31; Garland, *1 Corinthians*, 709.

integrity and distinction of the D unit. It functions as the unparalleled, central, and pivotal unit of the chiasm.

The Role of the Scriptural Quotations in the Chiasm

"For it is necessary that he [Christ] reign" in 15:25a of the C unit of the chiasm is based upon God's command in LXX Ps 109:1b for the Davidic king to "sit at my right," that is, to reign in the authoritative right-hand position along with God. This scriptural necessity for Christ "to reign" (βασιλεύειν) begins to explain to the audience why it is stated in the A unit (15:24ab) that at the end Christ will hand over the "kingdom" (βασιλείαν), in which he has been "reigning" since God raised him from the dead (15:20), to the God and Father who authorized and empowered him "to reign" in this "kingdom" according to LXX Ps 109:1b.

The scriptural necessity for the risen Christ to reign "until He [God] places all the enemies under his [Christ's] feet" in 15:25b of the C unit of the chiasm develops what the audience has heard in the B unit in 15:24c. It is God himself who will place absolutely and emphatically "all" (πάντας) the enemies in the universe in utter defeat and total subjugation "under the feet" of the risen Christ (15:25b), so that, in accord with the scriptural quotation of LXX Ps 109:1b, it is through God's empowerment of the risen Christ to reign (15:25a) that Christ will have destroyed "every" (πᾶσαν) ruler and "every" (πᾶσαν) authority and power (15:24c) at the end when he hands over the kingdom to the God and Father (15:24ab).

The central and pivotal D unit of the chiasm in 15:26 further develops for the audience the scriptural quotation of LXX Ps 109:1b in 15:25b of the C unit. The absolute and emphatic *all* of the defeated "enemies" (ἐχθρούς) that God places under the feet of the risen Christ according to the scriptural quote (15:25b) includes the most important and *last* "enemy" (ἐχθρὸς) to be destroyed (by God, divine passive), namely, the personified power of "the death" (15:26) that came through the first human being, Adam (15:21a), and thus extended its power over all human beings. That God has destroyed "the death" as the last of all enemies brings the negative assertions about the destruction and utter defeat of all inimical powers in the universe in the first half of the chiasm to their climax in the central D unit of the chiasm in 15:26.

But this central D unit also functions as the pivotal unit of the chiasm. With the climax of the negative assertions about the total and utter defeat and destruction of absolutely *all* enemies in the cosmos (15:26), the way is open for a "pivot" in the chiasm to positive assertions about "subjection" or "subordination," the placing of things in their proper creational subordination or order as designed by the Creator (15:27–28).

In the quotation of LXX Ps 8:7b in the C′ unit of the chiasm in 15:27a, the audience hears a progression from "all the enemies" that God places in utter defeat "under the feet" of the risen Christ in the quotation of LXX Ps 109:1b in the C unit in 15:25b to the more comprehensive "all things," including not only negatively all the enemies but positively all things in general, that God "subjected" or "subordinated," that is, placed in their proper creational order in accord with the scriptural quote, "under the feet" of the risen Christ as the first human being to be raised from the dead (15:21). Whereas "under the feet" in the scriptural quote in the C unit (15:25b) indicates negatively the utter defeat and destruction of all the enemies, in the scriptural quote in the C′ unit (15:27a) "under the feet" indicates more positively all things in the universe being subordinated or placed in their proper order under the risen Christ, in order for them to be brought to the goal designed for them by the Creator in accord with Ps 8.[25]

The B′ unit of the chiasm in 15:27bc clarifies for the audience that when the scriptural quotation of LXX Ps 8:7b in the C′ unit in 15:27a says that "all things" have been subjected (15:27b), it is obvious that "all things" do not include God himself, the One who subjected to him, Christ, "all the things" (15:27c). The subtle progression that the audience experiences from "all things" (πάντα) in 15:27b to "all the things" (τὰ πάντα) in 15:27c places added emphasis upon the totality and universality of the subjection

---

25. In accord with Ps 8, the "subordination" expressed in 15:27–28 is positive throughout; there is no need to posit an adaptation from a negative to a positive nuance in 15:28, as stated by Lambrecht, "Paul's Christological Use," 519 n. 24: "It should be noted that in v. 28 with regard to the 'subordination' of Christ, Paul must adapt the rather negative meaning of ὑποτάσσω of v. 27 to a more positive nuance." As Lockwood (1 Corinthians, 571 n. 24) notes: "Psalm 8 can be read as a description of the place of mankind, especially of Adam as the head, in the original creation in Eden. But after the fall into sin, Adam and mankind retained only a corrupted vestige of that original place of honor in creation. Therefore the description in Psalm 8 applies fully, accurately, and literally only to Christ, the head of redeemed humanity, who after his humiliation and death was indeed crowned with glory and honor. Secondarily, then, Psalm 8 also describes the glorification of those in Christ." Malan, "The Use," 159–60: "The Psalmist speaks of God's subjection of all things to man. This subjection the apostle finds realized in Christ. Psalm 8:7 is interpreted in a messianic sense. While Psalm 8 decribes the place God allocated to man in his creation, Paul uses the quotation to describe the place God allocated to Christ in history. He is the man who restores man's rule over God's creation, by conquering the hostile powers which entered creation by means of a man, Adam (v. 20)." Gielen, "Universale Totenauferweckung," 99: "Wie nämlich am Beginn Gott dem Menschen seine Schöpfung unterstellt hat (Ps 8,7), so hat er sie nun Christus, dem Erstling der Entschlafenen und Repräsentanten der eschatologisch auferweckten Menschheit, unterstellt. Er soll alles gottfeindliche in ihr tilgen und so der eschatologischen Neuschöpfung und der vollendeten Gottesherrschaft zum Durchbruch verhelfen."

or subordination to the risen Christ of absolutely everything in the created order outside of the Creator himself.

The B′ unit of the chiasm (15:27bc) develops for the audience the B unit (15:24c) with which it is progressively parallel. The B unit assures the audience that at the end the risen Christ will have destroyed every ruler and every authority and power. But the B′ unit goes beyond this to assure the audience that at the end absolutely all things in the universe except the Creator himself will have been subjected or subordinated to the risen Christ in accord with the quotation of LXX Ps 8:7b in 15:27a. The single occurrence of the negative verb "destroyed" (καταργήσῃ) with Christ as its subject progresses to the double occurrence of the more positive verb "subjected" or "subordinated" (ὑποτέτακται in 15:27b; ὑποτάξαντος in 15:27c) with God as its subject. "Every (πᾶσαν) ruler and every (πᾶσαν) authority and power" expands to absolutely "all things" (πάντα), indeed, "all the things" (τὰ πάντα) in the universe, embracing then even the audience.

The A′ unit of the chiasm in 15:28 continues to draw out for the audience the implications of the quote of LXX Ps 8:7b in the C′ unit (15:27a), as it develops the B′ unit (15:27bc). The A′ unit reiterates the B′ unit's paraphrase of the scriptural quote in the C′ unit with a pointed accent on "to him" in the statement, "But when all the things are subjected *to him*," in 15:28a. The "to him" (αὐτῷ) in the A′ unit emphatically repeats the "to him" (αὐτῷ) in the B′ unit's statement of "the One who subjected *to him* all the things" (15:27c) to impress upon the audience that at the end "all the things" in the universe will be subjected "*to him*" (αὐτῷ), the risen Christ, before the risen Christ as "the Son" will "himself" (αὐτὸς) be subjected to the One who subjected "*to him*" (αὐτῷ) all the things (15:28b). Once the Son, the human being to whom all the things in the universe have been subordinated in accord with Ps 8, has himself been subordinated to God, then all of creation, in the proper order of their subordination, will return to the Creator, "so that God may be all things in all things" (15:28c).[26]

The A′ unit of the chiasm (15:28) develops for the audience the A unit (15:24ab) with which it is progressively parallel. The climactic "so that God

---

26. On the meaning of "all things in all things," Lewis (*So That God*, 69) states: "Although soteriological in purpose, it insists that salvation cannot be understood apart from the redemption of the created order and the defeat of inimical powers, especially death. 'All things' would include the created order, the world, the heavenly powers, and human beings." Garland, *1 Corinthians*, 714: "It applies to the pacification and redemption of the created order and is similar to saying God is over all." Fee, *Corinthians*, 760: "God's will will be supreme in every quarter and in every way. In Paul's view the consummation of redemption includes the whole sphere of creation as well. Nothing lies outside God's redemptive purposes in Christ." See also Adams, *Constructing the World*, 144–45.

may be all things in all things" in the A´ unit (15:28c) is a fuller elaboration of "the end" in the A unit (15:24a). That "the Son" himself will be subjected to God (θεὸς) as the One who subjected all the things to him in the A´ unit (15:28bc) complements the statement in the A unit that the risen Christ will hand over the kingdom to the God (θεῷ) and "Father" (15:24b).[27] And the assurance to the audience in the A unit that at the end Christ will hand over the kingdom in which he reigns in accord with the scriptural quotation of LXX Ps 109:1b in the C unit (15:25) progresses to the assurance to the audience in the A´ unit that at the end the risen Christ, as the Son to whom all the things in creation, including the audience, have been subordinated in accord with the scriptural quotation of LXX Ps 8:7b in the C´ unit (15:27a), will himself be subordinated to the Creator, "so that God may be all things in all things."

In sum, within the chiasm the scriptural quotation of LXX Ps 109:1b, with its promise that God will place all the enemies in defeat and destruction under the feet of the risen Christ (15:25), leads to the central and pivotal point that the last of all of these enemies to be destroyed is the power of death (15:26). God's destruction of death enables the fulfillment of the scriptural quotation of LXX Ps 8:7b, with its assertion that God subordinated or placed in their proper creational order all things in the universe under the feet of the risen Christ (15:27a). The scriptural quotes, then, play a central and pivotal role within the chiasm in 15:24–28 to assure the audience that not only will they, as those who belong to Christ, be brought to life in their proper order after Christ as the "firstfruits" of the resurrection from the dead (15:20–23), but that, once death has been destroyed (15:26), all things in creation will be subordinated to the Creator through their subordination to the risen Christ, "so that God may be all things in all things" (15:28c).

Summary on 1 Corinthians 15:25, 27

1. Although both 15:25 and 15:27a have been adapted and modified to fit Paul's rhetorical strategy, both exhibit enough essential elements of their respective OT sources, LXX Ps 109:1b in 15:25 and LXX Ps 8:7b in 15:27a, to warrant the audience's recognition of them as a closely combined pair of scriptural quotations.

---

27. Garland, *1 Corinthians*, 713: "This is the only place in Paul's letter where the absolute use of the title 'the Son' appears (which corresponds to the absolute use of God the Father in 15:24)." See also Lindemann, *Erste Korintherbrief*, 348.

2. With the quotation of LXX Ps 8:7b in 15:27a, the audience experiences a development of the quotation of LXX Ps 109:1b in 15:25 through the *gezera shava* that combines these two scriptural quotations by the words they have in common. The quote in 15:25 expresses the negative concept that God "places" (θῇ) *all* defeated enemies in total subjugation "under the feet" of the victorious and triumphantly risen Christ. But the quote in 15:27a asserts the more positive concept that God "subjected" or "subordinated" (ὑπέταξεν), that is, placed in their proper creational order, *all things* in the universe, including the audience, "under the feet" of Christ as the "firstfruits" of the resurrection from the dead.

3. The scriptural quotes in 15:25, 27a play a central and pivotal role within the chiasm in 15:24–28 to assure the audience that not only will they, as those who belong to Christ, be brought to life in their proper order after Christ as the "firstfruits" of the resurrection from the dead (15:20–23), but that, once death has been destroyed (15:26) in accord with the quote in 15:25, all things in creation will be subordinated to the Creator through their subordination to the risen Christ in accord with the quote in 15:27a, "so that God may be all things in all things" (15:28c).

CHAPTER 15

1 Corinthians 15:32b

Let us eat and drink, for tomorrow we die.

Old Testament Background

Introduced by a protasis, "if the dead are not raised," the apodosis, "let us eat and drink, for tomorrow we die" in 1 Cor 15:32b, although not explicitly indicated as a quotation from scripture, nevertheless quotes LXX Isa 22:13b verbatim:

MT Isa 22:13b: אָכוֹל וְשָׁתוֹ כִּי מָחָר נָמוּת
Eat and drink, for tomorrow we die.

LXX Isa 22:13b: φάγωμεν καὶ πίωμεν αὔριον γὰρ ἀποθνῄσκομεν
Let us eat and drink, for tomorrow we die.

1 Cor 15:32b: φάγωμεν καὶ πίωμεν, αὔριον γὰρ ἀποθνῄσκομεν
Let us eat and drink, for tomorrow we die.

In its Isaian context the quotation, "let us eat and drink, for tomorrow we die," voices the despondency and despair of the inhabitants of Jerusalem as they face certain death at the hands of their Assyrian conquerors. Although God called for them to weep, lament, shave their heads, and gird themselves with sackcloth (Isa 22:12) in repentance of their sinfulness (22:14), they decided instead to indulge in extravagant feasting while still alive: "But they engaged in joy and gladness, slaying calves, and slaughtering sheep, so as to eat flesh, and drink wine, saying, 'Let us eat and drink, for tomorrow we die'" (22:13).[1]

Although a direct quote from Isa 22:13, "Let us eat (φάγωμεν) and

---

1. Malan, "Use," 160; Hays, *First Corinthians*, 268.

drink (πίωμεν), for tomorrow we die" expresses sentiments found elsewhere in the OT of living well now and feasting by "eating and drinking" since this short life is all there is. According to Wis 2:5-6, "Our time is the passing of a shadow, and there is no escape of our death for it is sealed and no one returns. Come, therefore, let us enjoy the good things that exist." According to Eccl 8:15, "There is no good for a man under the sun, but to eat (φαγεῖν), and drink (πιεῖν), and be merry . . . all the days of his life, which God has given him under the sun." And according to Eccl 9:7-9, "Eat (φάγε) your bread with joy and drink (πίε) your wine with a good heart . . . all the days of your life of futility which are given you under the sun."

Paul, however, does not necessarily expect his implied Corinthian audience to recognize the quotation in 1 Cor 15:32b as a quotation from Isa 22:13b. Indeed, he does not even introduce it as a quotation from scripture, much less from Isaiah.[2] Rather, his audience is to recognize it as a popular slogan, which is incidentally very aptly expressed in Isa 22:13b, that characterizes a lifestyle practiced and promoted by many at the time of Paul— one that has no hope in a resurrection of the dead.[3]

Literary-Rhetorical Analysis

The introduction to the quotation "if the dead are not raised" entertains for the audience the possibility that there is no life after death for

---

2. Wilk (*Bedeutung*, 318–20) draws comparisons between 1 Cor 15:29–34 and Isa 22:11–14, the broader context of the quote from Isa 22:13b in 1 Cor 15:32b. But it is questionable whether Paul expects his audience to recognize these alleged comparisons.

3. Wolfgang Schrage, *Der erste Brief an die Korinther (1 Kor 15,1–16,24)* (EKKNT 7/4; Zürich: Benziger, 2001), 246: "[D]ie Losung, 'Lasset uns essen und trinken, denn morgen sind wir tot' wurde in der damaligen Zeit kräftig praktiziert und propagiert. Eine Aufforderung zum Lebensgenuß angesichts der Kürze des Lebens ist bei Dichtern und in Inschriften immer wieder zu lesen, selbst auf Gräbern" (for examples, see 246 nn. 1195–96). Abraham J. Malherbe, "The Beasts at Ephesus," *JBL* 87 (1968): 76–77: "In hellenistic literature the libertinistic life popularly, if unjustly, associated with the philosophy of Epicurus is frequently summarized as ἐσθίειν καὶ πίνειν. . . . His [Paul's] quotation from Isa 22 13 . . . would be reminiscent of the slogan attributed to the Epicureans and reflects the contemporary anti-Epicurean bias." Thiselton, *Corinthians*, 1252–53: "Is he [Paul] quoting from Isa 22:13, or from an Epicurean slogan, or from an anti-Epicurean slogan which offers an ironic overstatement of Epicurean philosophy? . . . The question which arises is simply whether this quotation *also* coincides with a quotation from hellenistic philosophical or ethical controversy. Epicureanism in its sophisticated form is more than crude materialism, but its opponents readily characterized it as such, especially in popular Stoic-Cynic circles." Garland, *1 Corinthians*, 721–22: "Paul quotes Isa. 22:13 . . . but the sentiment was widespread (Luke 12:19–20)." See also Joseph S. Park, *Conceptions of Afterlife in Jewish Inscriptions: With Special Reference to Pauline Literature* (WUNT 121; Tübingen: Mohr Siebeck, 2000), 181–82.

them. If that is the case, they and Paul might as well live a fully pleasurable life now in accord with the quoted popular slogan, "Let us"—Paul, his audience, and all human beings—"eat and drink"—not just satisfy hunger and thirst, but feast extravagantly and dissolutely—"for tomorrow"—not literally the next day, but in a relatively short time—"we die" without hope for a future life.[4] The quotation, then, shocks the audience with the hopeless consequences not only for their future but present existence, condemned as it is to the pursuit of immediate pleasures only, if there is no resurrection of the dead.

Relation to the Antecedent Context in 1 Corinthians 15:29–32a

When the audience hears "if the dead are not raised, let us eat and drink, for tomorrow we die" in 1 Cor 15:32b, it recalls and reinforces the point of what they heard in 15:29: "Otherwise what will they do who are being baptized on behalf of the dead?[5] If the dead are not raised at all, then why are they being baptized on behalf of them?"[6] And this in turn resonates with what Paul pointedly asked his audience in 15:12: "But if Christ is preached as raised from the dead, how can some among you say that there is no resurrection of the dead?"

---

4. Fee, *Corinthians*, 772: "In Plutarch's anti-Epicurean writings, for example, the language of 'eating and drinking' was a formula for the dissolute life." On the meaning of the adverb "tomorrow" (αὔριον) in 1 Cor 15:32, BDAG, 151: "a brief time lapse without reference to a nocturnal period, *soon, in a short time*," and *EDNT* 1.179: "Αὔριον can also mean *tomorrow* in the sense of *soon thereafter, after a short while*."

5. According to Fee (*Corinthians*, 763 n. 10), the future verb, "will they do" (ποιήσουσιν), "is probably 'logical' (= when they realize what they are doing and that there is no real future for the dead, how will it affect them?)." Thiselton (*Corinthians*, 1241) proposes the translation "What do those people think they are doing who have themselves baptized for the sake of the dead?"

6. For discussions and critiques of the many different ways of understanding the problematical baptism for the dead in 15:29, see Fee, *Corinthians*, 763–67; Lockwood, *1 Corinthians*, 574–78; Thiselton, *Corinthians*, 1242–49; Garland, *1 Corinthians*, 716–19, 723–24. Fee (*Corinthians*, 762–64) aptly points out: "One may consider axiomatic that when there is such a wide divergence of opinion, no one knows what in fact was going on. The best one can do in terms of particulars is point out what appear to be the more viable options, but finally admit to ignorance. What is certain is how the text *functions* in the argument. Whatever it was that some of them were doing, those actions are a contradiction to the position that there is no resurrection of the dead (v. 12). . . . The normal reading of the text is that some Corinthians are being baptized, apparently vicariously, in behalf of some people who have already died. It would be fair to add that this reading is such a plain understanding of the Greek text that no one would ever have imagined the various alternatives were it not for the difficulties involved."

The audience is drawn into a progressive parallelism proceeding from 15:29b to 15:32b:

> 15:29b: If the dead are not raised at all, then why are they being baptized on behalf of them?
> 15:32b: If the dead are not raised, "Let us eat and drink, for tomorrow we die."

This parallelism moves the audience from a realization of the logical and hopeless absurdity of some ("they," third-person plural) among them,[7] but not necessarily themselves, who are being baptized for the dead, if there is no resurrection of the dead (15:29b), to the logical and hopeless absurdity of the audience themselves ("let us," first-person plural inclusive of the audience and indeed all people) engaging in a hedonistic and dissolute lifestyle by festively eating and drinking while still alive, "for tomorrow we die" (15:32b) and there is nothing to follow, if the dead are not raised. The parallelism thus persuades the audience that since some are being baptized with a view to the afterlife and since the audience themselves would not think of living only for the present by engaging in an extremely extravagant way of life, they should have hope for a future life through the resurrection of the dead.

Paul moves his audience from a consideration of the hope for resurrection from the dead implied by those who are baptized for the dead (15:29) to that same hope implied by his apostolic ministry. With an emphatic use of the first-person plural pronoun, "and as for us" (καὶ ἡμεῖς), that is, Paul and his fellow apostles (15:7–11), Paul asks his audience the rhetorical question, "why are *we* in danger every hour?" (15:30).[8] The implication for the audience is that apostles would not undergo the constant dangers

---

7. Fee, *Corinthians*, 766–67: "[T]his unusual use of the third-person plural, when elsewhere Paul always turns such references into a word to the community as a whole (e.g., vv. 12–13, 35–36), suggests that it is not the action of the whole community. On the other hand, there is no reason to deny that it was happening with the full knowledge of the community and probably with their approval. Second, Paul's apparently noncommittal attitude toward it, while not implying approval, would seem to suggest that he did not consider it to be as serious a fault as most interpreters do."

8. Lockwood, *1 Corinthians*, 579: "The pronoun (ἡμεῖς) is emphatic. Paul means 'we apostles and our coworkers.' He speaks of himself and his coworkers similarly with first-person plural forms in, for example, 3:9; 4:1, 6–13." Fee, *Corinthians*, 768 n. 36: "This emphatic 'we' immediately following v. 29 excludes the Corinthians themselves." Thiselton, *Corinthians*, 1249: "καὶ ἡμεῖς should be construed together.... καὶ does not qualify the sentence as a whole but specifically *we*."

threatening their lives throughout their ministry (4:9–13) if they did not have a firm hope in the resurrection from the dead.

Paul then sharpens the focus of the audience to a consideration of his own apostolic ministry, as he moves from speaking in the first-person plural to the first-person singular: "Every day I am dying; I affirm it by the boasting in you that I have in Christ Jesus our Lord" (15:31).[9] Paul wants his audience to realize that his "dying" every day means not only facing the danger of death, but "living out an *identification with the death of Christ* voluntarily assumed, and accepting the *vulnerability and fragility* of life in Christian service in the confident expectation of sharing in Christ's resurrection and *being raised* at the last day."[10] The audience for whom Paul strongly affirms his "dying" is thus motivated to share the hope of being raised implied by this "dying" because of the "boasting" in them that Paul has in Christ Jesus our Lord, that is, because God has brought them to faith in Christ through Paul's apostolic ministry (4:15b; 9:1–2; 15:1–2, 10–11), his "dying" in hope of being raised.[11]

If only "humanly" (κατὰ ἄνθρωπον), that is, on a merely human level or from a merely human viewpoint, without a hope in the resurrection from the dead, Paul metaphorically "fought with wild beasts" in his apostolic ministry at Ephesus, what would be the gain or profit for him? (15:32a).[12]

---

9. On the rhetorical movement from 15:30 to 15:31a, Collins (*First Corinthians*, 559) notes: "The juxtaposition of two temporal elements (hour, day) and the movement from danger to death are an example of Paul's use of the rhetorical device of *klimax* (*gradatio*) and contribute to the strength of his argument. Building up the climax of his appeal, Paul moves from the first-person plural to the first-person singular." For the text-critical reasoning for omitting "brothers" (ἀδελφοί) from 15:31, see Thiselton, *Corinthians*, 1249.

10. Thiselton, *Corinthians*, 1250.

11. Collins, *First Corinthians*, 560: "His [Paul's] use of the strong affirmative particle, νή, is singular in the New Testament. It adds to the *pathos* of his argument." Garland, *1 Corinthians*, 720: "His boast is that the Corinthians are the fruit of his apostolic labor and suffering (1 Cor. 9:1–2). It is not a self-serving boast, but rather confirms that Christ has worked in and through him as his apostle." See also Fee, *Corinthians*, 769–70.

12. On κατὰ ἄνθρωπον in 15:32a, BDAG, 81: "perhaps *like an ordinary man* (opp. as a Christian sure of the resurrection)." Fee, *Corinthians*, 771: "Here he [Paul] means that if there is no hope in the resurrection, then his life or death struggle against the opponents of his gospel is carried on at the merely human level—he is nothing more than a 'mere man' among other 'mere humans.' His point of course is, What sense does it make to live like *this* if we live only at the merely human level as others who have no hope for the future?" Thiselton, *Corinthians*, 1251: "[T]he proper term for denoting the limitations of a merely human view is *only with human horizons*, i.e., with horizons that reach neither beyond the grave nor beyond human capacities to the power of God." On the metaphorical sense of "fought with wild beasts" (ἐθηριομάχησα) in 15:32a, see R. E. Osborne, "Paul and the Wild Beasts," *JBL* 85 (1966): 225–30; Malherbe, "Beasts at Ephesus," 71–80; Fee, *Corinthians*, 770–71: "The fighting 'with wild beasts in Eph-

The audience is to ponder why Paul would risk his life for the gospel at Ephesus, if he did not have a hope in being raised from the dead.

That Paul places a consideration of his own apostolic ministry both in Corinth and Ephesus before his audience in 15:30–32a broadens and intensifies the scope of the first-person plural in the quotation in 15:32b and thus strengthens its impact. If the dead are not raised, "Let us," not only the audience but apostles (15:30) and even the apostle Paul himself (15:31–32a), "eat and drink" festively and extravagantly, "for tomorrow we die." That Paul himself does not live in accord with the dissolute and despondent way proposed by the quotation is further evidence to motivate his audience likewise to reject what the quotation suggests and to share his hope in the resurrection of the dead.

Relation to the Subsequent Context in 1 Corinthians 15:33–34

With a blunt command to his audience, "Stop being led astray," Paul introduces another quotation expressing a popular, proverbial maxim, "Bad company corrupts good morals" (15:33). Much as Paul does not necessarily expect his audience to recognize the scriptural origin of the quotation of Isa 22:13b in 15:32b, so in 15:33 he does not expect his audience to locate the literary origin of the proverbial maxim.[13] The authority and rhetorical force of both of these quotations, then, depend upon the audience's recognition of them as expressions of ideas current and widespread in the culture of their time.

The audience is to "stop being led astray" by those who say there is no

---

esus' must be understood metaphorically, not only because Paul otherwise lived to tell about it if it was literal(!), but because (*a*) such a metaphor was a common phenomenon in the moralistic literature of Hellenism, and (*b*) his Roman citizenship should have excluded him from what would have meant certain death if it were a literal 'fight' in the arena." See also Thiselton, *Corinthians*, 1251–52.

13. Lockwood, *1 Corinthians*, 579: "[T]he proverb cited in this verse occurs in Menander's comedy *Thais* and perhaps as early as Euripides (fifth century B.C.)." Collins, *First Corinthians*, 561: "Paul cites the slogan not as a literary quotation but as a *bon mot* in popular currency." Thiselton, *Corinthians*, 1254: "Jerome seems first to have attributed the quotation to Menander's comedy, but there is clear evidence that it had also become a popular maxim. Paul may well have heard it cited more than once as a maxim, and we may infer neither knowledge nor ignorance of Greek literature on Paul's part from this quotation." Garland, *1 Corinthians*, 722: "This may be a quotation from Menander's (died 292 B.C.) lost comedy, *Thais* (fragment 187 [218]), but one cannot assume that Paul was familiar with Menander any more than one can assume that a person who cites a famous line from a Shakespeare play has read Shakespeare. It had become a cliché, perhaps even before Menander." See also Koch, *Schrift*, 42–45.

resurrection of the dead (15:12b). If they keep "bad company" with such people and their erroneous ideas regarding resurrection, it may "corrupt" their "good morals" (15:33) by leading them into the corrupt and immoral lifestyle proposed by the quotation in 15:32b: "Let us eat and drink, for tomorrow we die."[14]

Paul's command that his audience "sober up" (ἐκνήψατε)[15] "properly" or "as is right" (δικαίως) in 15:34a stands in contradictory contrast to the drunken revelry implied by the festive and extravagant "eating and drinking" in the quotation of 15:32b, further urging the audience to reject a lifestyle without hope in the resurrection of the dead. That the audience is to "stop sinning" (15:34b) in this context warns them to refrain from associating with the ideas and people (15:33) that deny the resurrection of the dead. Indeed, if the dead are not raised, then Christ has not been raised, and the audience is still in their sins (15:16–17).[16]

Paul then accuses "some" (τινες) people in the audience, especially the "some" (τινες) who say there is no resurrection of the dead (15:12b), of having no knowledge of God (15:34c).[17] He says this to "shame" (15:34d; cf. 6:5b) the audience into acquiring the proper knowledge of the God who raised Christ from the dead as the beginning of the resurrection of the dead (15:13–28), so that their lifestyle is not "corrupted" (15:33) into the hope-

---

14. Fee, *Corinthians*, 773: "Since the word translated 'company' (ὁμιλίαι) can mean either 'companionship' or 'conversation,' one wonders whether the emphasis here is more on the 'company' of 'evil conversation' that denies the resurrection, than on simply associating with people who so deny. In that case, it would mean here something like, 'Evil conversations such as those that deny the resurrection of the dead can only have a corrupting effect on your good character.' Otherwise, he would seem to be pointing to the 'some' in v. 12 who are denying the resurrection. By implication, they should thus dissociate from them."

15. Lockwood, *1 Corinthians*, 580: "The compound ἐκνήφω is an intensive form, and in the aorist here means 'sober up.'" Fee, *Corinthians*, 774: "The verb 'sober up' may be a metaphor either for to awake from sleep or to be aroused from a drunken stupor.... [B]oth the context ('let us eat and drink') and the compounded form of the verb suggest that it is the latter. In any case, it is a telling metaphor for their present state of delusion, in which they both deny the resurrection and behave as if there were no future to the kingdom of God."

16. Thiselton, *Corinthians*, 1256: "Most English VSS retain Paul's theological word *sin* (rightly) since here an attitude toward *God*, other people, credal issues of faith, and conduct of life are all at issue. Paul regularly regards *sin* less in terms (if at all) of *acts* (plural) of commission or omission than as an *attitude, stance, and state* in which the human will is granted 'autonomy' to turn away from God and to seek self-gratification as the chief end of human life."

17. Thiselton, *Corinthians*, 1256: "*Some people* simply represents τινες, but picks up the resonance to the Greek ear of the *some* of 15:12 who have, in effect, been the 'opponents' for the whole of the treatise from 15:1 up to this point." See also Collins, *First Corinthians*, 561.

lessness expressed by the quotation of the popular slogan in 15:32b: "Let us eat and drink, for tomorrow we die."[18]

Summary on 1 Corinthians 15:32b

1. Paul's audience is to recognize the quotation in 1 Cor 15:32b as a popular slogan, which is incidentally very aptly expressed in Isa 22:13b, that characterizes a lifestyle practiced and promoted by many at the time of Paul—one that has no hope in a resurrection of the dead.

2. The quotation in 1 Cor 15:32b shocks the audience with the hopeless consequences not only for their future but present existence, condemned as it is to the pursuit of immediate pleasures only, if there is no resurrection of the dead.

3. The parallelism between 15:29b and 15:32b persuades the audience that since some are being baptized with a view to the afterlife (15:29b) and since the audience themselves would not think of living only for the present by engaging in an extremely extravagant way of life as proposed by the quotation in 15:32b, they should have hope for a future life through the resurrection of the dead.

4. That Paul places a consideration of his own apostolic ministry both in Corinth (15:30–31) and Ephesus (15:32a) before his audience broadens and intensifies the scope of the first-person plural in the quotation in 15:32b and thus strengthens its impact. If the dead are not raised, "Let us," not only the audience but apostles (15:30) and even the apostle Paul himself (15:31–32a), "eat and drink" festively and extravagantly, "for tomorrow we die." That Paul himself does not so live as proposed by the quotation is further evidence to motivate his audience likewise to reject what the quotation suggests and to share his hope in the resurrection of the dead.

---

18. Collins, *First Corinthians*, 561: "The God who is known and experienced by his people is one who has raised Christ from the dead and promises resurrection to those who believe the kerygma. Those who deny the resurrection can be equated with people who have not experienced God (1 Thess 4:5), the living God who has raised Jesus from the dead." Fee, *Corinthians*, 774: "[T]hose who deny the resurrection ultimately live in ignorance of God, who through Christ's resurrection has set in motion that chain of events which leads to his finally being all in all.... [H]e says this 'to their shame,' probably in much the same way as in the first occurrence of this clause in 6:5, where his argument itself is an attempt to 'shame' them into a change of thinking and behavior." Garland, *1 Corinthians*, 722–23: "Shaming is one way . . . to prevent persons from behaving and believing inappropriately."

5. Paul "shames" the audience, which is to "sober up" rather than live in the drunken revelry suggested by the quotation, into acquiring the proper knowledge of the God (15:34) who raised Christ from the dead as the beginning of the resurrection of the dead (15:13–28). The "good morals" of their lifestyle are not to be "corrupted" by the "bad company" of those who deny the resurrection of the dead (15:33). They would then be reduced to the utter hopelessness expressed by the quotation of the popular slogan in 15:32b: "Let us eat and drink, for tomorrow we die."

Chapter 16

1 Corinthians 15:45a

The first human, Adam, became a living being.

Old Testament Background

Introduced by the formula "so also it is written" (οὕτως καὶ γέγραπται), the statement that "the first human, Adam, became a living being" in 1 Cor 15:45a quotes from Gen 2:7b:

MT Gen 2:7b: וַיְהִי הָאָדָם לְנֶפֶשׁ חַיָּה
LXX Gen 2:7b: καὶ ἐγένετο ὁ ἄνθρωπος εἰς ψυχὴν ζῶσαν
1 Cor 15:45a: ἐγένετο ὁ πρῶτος ἄνθρωπος Ἀδὰμ εἰς ψυχὴν ζῶσαν[1]

The Pauline quotation omits the initial καί found in the LXX version and adds the adjective "first" (πρῶτος) before the noun "human" (ἄνθρωπος) as well as the proper name "Adam" (Ἀδάμ) after it. Paul added the adjective "first" for the purpose of his argument, as we will see below.[2]

But his addition of the proper name "Adam" may be dependent on a non-LXX version, as it is found in both Theodotion and Symmachus:

---

1. Some have argued that 1 Cor 15:45b, "the last Adam [became] a life-giving Spirit," should be considered as part of the Pauline quotation. But, as Stanley (*Paul*, 209 n. 99) points out, "there seems to be little reason to think that either Paul or his readers would have regarded the citation as extending to the end of v. 45. The very explicitness of the Christological reference in the latter half of the verse (ὁ ἔσχατος Ἀδάμ) would have made it clear to Paul's readers that an interpretive element had been added to the end of what was most likely a well-known verse of Scripture."
2. Stanley, *Paul*, 208: "Nothing in either the Greek or Hebrew textual traditions offers any reason to think that Paul might have found the word πρῶτος in his *Vorlage* of Gen 2.7. . . . Though the insertion would not be out of place in the original text, all the evidence would trace the addition of πρῶτος here to the argumentative interests of the apostle Paul."

Gen 2:7b in Theo. and Sym.: ἐγένετο ὁ Ἀδάμ ἄνθρωπος εἰς ψυχὴν ζῶσαν
Gen 2:7b in 1 Cor 15:45a: ἐγένετο ὁ πρῶτος ἄνθρωπος Ἀδάμ εἰς ψυχὴν ζῶσαν

In place of the adjective "first" (πρῶτος) before "human" (ἄνθρωπος), Theodotion and Symmachus have the proper name "Adam" (Ἀδάμ), which Paul places after "human."[3]

Paul's use of the proper name "Adam" in his quotation of Gen 2:7b, which anticipates its first use as a proper name in LXX Gen 2:16, indicates that Paul's argument is dependent upon his implied audience's familiarity not just with this particular verse of Genesis but with the broader scriptural account of the Adam story (see the reference to "Adam" already in 1 Cor 15:22). Indeed, there are several allusions to the Genesis account of creation both previous and subsequent to Paul's quotation of Gen 2:7b within the rhetorical unit of 1 Cor 15:35–49.

That God gives to each of the seeds (σπερμάτων) its own body (ἴδιον σῶμα) in 1 Cor 15:38 recalls how God creates seed (σπέρμα) according to kind (κατὰ γένος) in LXX Gen 1:11–12.[4] That "not all flesh is the same, but there is one flesh for humans (ἀνθρώπων), another flesh for animals (κτηνῶν), another flesh for birds (πτηνῶν), and another for fish (ἰχθύων)" in 1 Cor 15:39 recalls that God created the human (ἄνθρωπον) to have dominion over the different creatures—the fish (ἰχθύων) of the sea and the birds

---

3. Stanley, *Paul*, 208: "[T]hough none of the LXX manuscripts shows any of the Pauline wording in Gen 2.7, both Theodotion and Symmachus have ὁ Ἀδάμ ἄνθρωπος at this point in their texts. Though the word order is the reverse of Paul's, it seems clear that the ambiguous sense of the Hebrew אָדָם (either a generic term or a proper name) lies behind the dual rendering in both texts." Thus, the versions of Gen 2:7b in Paul, Theodotion, and Symmachus anticipate the LXX's use of "Adam" as a proper name, which does not begin until 2:16. On LXX Gen 2:16, Wevers (*Genesis*, 29–30) notes: "At this stage Gen changes from translating האדם by ὁ ἄνθρωπος to treating the lexeme as a proper noun τῷ Ἀδάμ....With 4:25 אדם becomes a proper noun in the MT as well." Stanley (*Paul*, 209 n. 98) concludes: "There is simply no reason why Paul could not have found the words ὁ Ἀδάμ ἄνθρωπος (or its converse) in his *Vorlage* or tradition and then shaped the ἔσχατος Ἀδάμ figure around it."

4. Bernardin Schneider, "The Corporate Meaning and Background of 1 Cor 15,45b—'O Eschatos Adam Eis Pneuma Zoiopoioun," *CBQ* 29 (1967): 147 n. 11: "It is interesting to note that the ἴδιον σῶμα of v. 38 reflects the לְמִינוֹ (LXX κατὰ γένος) of Gn 1,11." Jean-M. Vincent, "'Avec quel Corps les Morts reviennent-ils?' L'Usage des Écritures dans 1 Corinthiens 15,36–45," *FoiVie* 100 (2001): 64: "Avec la suite 'et à chaque semence de façon particulière' (v. 38) nous sommes clairement renvoyés à la louange du Dieu créateur en Gn 1." See also Garland, *1 Corinthians*, 729.

(πετεινῶν) of the sky and the animals (κτηνῶν) in LXX Gen 1:26 (cf. 1:20–25).[5]

In 1 Cor 15:40, that "there are both heavenly (ἐπουράνια) bodies and earthly (ἐπίγεια) bodies, but the glory of the heavenly (ἐπουρανίων) is one kind and that of the earthly (ἐπιγείων) another" recalls how God commanded that there be lights in the firmament of heaven (οὐρανοῦ) to give light upon the earth (γῆς) in LXX Gen 1:14–15. And in 1 Cor 15:41, that "the glory of the sun is one kind, the glory of the moon another, and the glory of the stars (ἀστέρων) another, for star (ἀστήρ) differs from star (ἀστέρος) in glory" recalls how "God made the two great lights, the greater light [the sun] for regulating the day and the lesser light [the moon] for regulating the night, and the stars (ἀστέρας)" in LXX Gen 1:16 (cf. Sir 43:1–10).[6]

Whereas 1 Cor 15:45a quotes from Gen 2:7b, 1 Cor 15:45b, "the last Adam [became] a life-giving Spirit (πνεῦμα ζῳοποιοῦν)," resonates with LXX Gen 2:7a, "God formed the human of dust from the earth, and breathed (ἐνεφύσησεν) into his face the breath of life (πνοὴν ζωῆς)."[7] And 1 Cor

---

5. Kôshi Usami, " 'How Are the Dead Raised?' (1 Cor 15,35–58)," *Bib* 57 (1976): 481–82: " 'All flesh' signifies the variety of beings on the earth which God created. It is a theological expression which designates the creator's greatness diversified in so many creatures. This variety is further emphasized with the help of a 'list' of creatures in allusion to Gn 1,20–25." Collins, *First Corinthians*, 566: "The division recalls the Priestly author's story of the fifth and sixth days of creation (Gen 1:20–25). Fish, birds, and animals are distinguished from one another. These three are further distinguished from the human being who was also created on the sixth day (Gen 1:26–28)." See also Lindemann, *Erster Korintherbrief*, 357–58; Alan G. Padgett, "The Body in Resurrection: Science and Scripture on the 'Spiritual Body' (1 Cor 15:35–58)," *WW* 22 (2002): 159.

6. Collins, *First Corinthians*, 566–67: "As he speaks of the distinction between heavenly bodies and earthly bodies Paul continues to hark back to the Priestly author's creation narrative.... The story of the fourth day of creation (Gen 1:14–19, v. 16) distinguishes among kinds of heavenly bodies, the sun, the moon, and the stars, just as Paul does in v. 41."

7. On LXX Gen 2:7a, Wevers (*Genesis*, 24–25) notes: "God's creation of man is in two stages: first, man is molded out of dust from the earth, and then he is animated by an infusion of a πνοὴν ζωῆς into his face. This infusion is active; God infused a blast or breath of life." Fee, *Corinthians*, 788–89: "Even though the second line [1 Cor 15:45b] is neither present nor inferred in the Genesis text [Gen 2:7], it nonetheless reflects the language of the prior clause in the LXX, 'and he breathed into his face the breath of life (πνοὴ ζωῆς).' " Jeffrey R. Asher, *Polarity and Change in 1 Corinthians 15: A Study of Metaphysics, Rhetoric, and Resurrection* (HUT 42; Tübingen: Mohr Siebeck, 2000), 114: "Paul has obviously freely adapted language present in Genesis [2:7]; the term πνεῦμα ζῳοποιοῦν [in 1 Cor 15:45b] recalls ἐνεφύσησεν and πνοὴν ζωῆς [in Gen 2:7a], and he has also repeated the title "Αδάμ." Maurizio Teani, *Corporeita e risurrezione: L'interpretazione di I Corinti 15,35–49 nel Novecento* (Aloisiana 24; Rome: Gregorian University, 1994), 250: "πνεῦμα ζῳοποιοῦν è una represa dell'espressione πνοὴ ζωῆς.... In tal mode, l'Apostolo 'legge' nel testo scritturistico l'annuncio della venuta del Cristo, Spirito vivificante."

15:47a, "the first human (ἄνθρωπος) was from earth (γῆς), of dust (χοϊκός)," recalls how "God formed the human (ἄνθρωπον) of dust (χοῦν) from the earth (γῆς)" in LXX Gen 2:7a and that he will return to the earth (γῆν) from which he was taken, "for you are earth (γῆ) and to earth (γῆν) you will return" in LXX Gen 3:19b.[8] Finally, 1 Cor 15:49, "even as we have borne the image (εἰκόνα) of the one of dust, let us also bear the image (εἰκόνα) of the heavenly one,"[9] recalls both how a descendant of Adam is begotten according to his image (εἰκόνα) in LXX Gen 5:3 and how the human was created according to the image (εἰκόνα) of God in LXX Gen 1:26–27.[10]

To sum up, Paul is relying upon his implied audience's recognition that not only the adapted quotation of LXX Gen 2:7b in 1 Cor 15:45a, "the first human, Adam, became a living being," but also the immediate context both before (15:38–44) and after (15:45b–49) the quotation recalls the scriptural account of creation as recorded in Genesis.

Literary-Rhetorical Analysis

The implied audience's recall that it is written in scripture that "the first human," who later was named "Adam," "became a living being" in 1 Cor 15:45a leads them to accept not only Paul's adaptation of the quote itself but his continuation of it in 15:45b, "the second Adam [became] a life-

---

8. Collins, *First Corinthians*, 571: "Paul's own description of the first human is a paraphrase of the biblical text. In doing so he seems to have coined an adjective, 'dusty' (χοϊκός), not found in Hellenistic literature prior to 1 Corinthians. The new adjective occurs four times in 1 Cor 15:47–49. It creates and highlights a contrast between 'dusty' and 'heavenly,' that is, of dust and from the heavens." See also Scott Brodeur, *The Holy Spirit's Agency in the Resurrection of the Dead: An Exegetico-Theological Study of 1 Corinthians 15,44b–49 and Romans 8,9–13* (Tesi Gregoriana: Serie Teologia 14; Rome: Gregorian University Press, 1996), 126. On LXX Gen 3:19b, Wevers (*Genesis*, 47) notes: "The ὅτι clause gives the reason for man's death and burial; 'you are γῆ and to γῆν you will go back,' i.e. you will again become the substance from which you were made."

9. For the reasons to choose the hortatory aorist subjunctive φορέσωμεν, "let us bear," which is the better attested and more difficult reading, rather than the future indicative φορέσομεν, "we will bear," in 1 Cor 15:49, see Andrew T. Lincoln, *Paradise Now and Not Yet: Studies in the Role of the Heavenly Dimension in Paul's Thought with Special Reference to His Eschatology* (SNTSMS 43; Cambridge: Cambridge University Press, 1981), 50–51; S. P. Botha, "1 Korintiërs 15:49b: 'n Hortatief-of futurumlesing? (1 Corinthians 15:49b: A Hortative or Future Reading?)," *HvTSt* 49 (1993): 760–74; Fee, *Corinthians*, 794–95; Brodeur, *Holy Spirit's Agency*, 140–41; Hays, *First Corinthians*, 273–74; Collins, *First Corinthians*, 572.

10. Collins, *First Corinthians*, 572: "The exhortation harks back to the biblical tradition according to which the descendants of Adam bear his image (Gen 5:3). This is combined with the notion that humans are created in the image of God (Gen 1:27)."

giving Spirit," as a legitimate interpretive elaboration of Gen 2:7 that has a scriptural authority equivalent to it.¹¹ But the effect on the audience of the scriptural quotation and its elaboration is based not only on the authority of scripture but on the rhetorical power of the striking syntactical correspondence, with verbal contrasts, between the quote and its elaboration:

1 Cor 15:45a: ἐγένετο ὁ πρῶτος ἄνθρωπος Ἀδὰμ εἰς ψυχὴν ζῶσαν
1 Cor 15:45b: ὁ ἔσχατος   Ἀδὰμ εἰς πνεῦμα ζῳοποιοῦν

Although the noun "human" (ἄνθρωπος) and the verb "became" (ἐγένετο) occur only in the scriptural quote in v. 45a, they are implied in the syntactical correspondence with the quote in v. 45b. Leaving them out of the elaboration in v. 45b eliminates needless repetition and enhances the rhetorical impact upon the audience. The name "Adam" followed by the preposition εἰς establishes a verbal correspondence between the quote and its elaboration.

But the remaining words within the syntactical correspondence present the audience with noteworthy contrasts. The adjective "the first" (ὁ πρῶτος) in v. 45a is contrasted by the adjective "the last" (ὁ ἔσχατος) in v. 45b, the noun "being" (ψυχὴν) in v. 45a is contrasted by the noun "Spirit" (πνεῦμα) in v. 45b, and the participle "living" (ζῶσαν) at the rhetorically emphatic end of the line in v. 45a is contrasted by the participle "life-giving" (ζῳοποιοῦν) at the rhetorically emphatic end of the line in v. 45b.¹²

The rhetorical progression from the scriptural quote in v. 45a to its elaboration in v. 45b brings the audience to the realization that whereas the first Adam, the origin and representative of all humanity, became a "living being" at creation when God breathed into his face the breath of life (LXX Gen 2:7), the last Adam, Christ, became a "life-giving Spirit" when God

---

11. According to Brodeur (*Holy Spirit's Agency*, 112), Paul's use of the proper noun "Adam" here "reveals that he did not merely want to speculate on the nature of the human being. By referring to an historical person in this way, he personalizes his argument, thus making it more compelling thanks to the introduction of a famous and well known character onto the scene."

12. Brodeur, *Holy Spirit's Agency*, 106: "The choice of these adjectives, nouns and participles is not accidental; Paul selected them with great care in order to make his point. Moreover, the syntax of the sentence is quite important. By placing them at the end of each line, Paul puts added emphasis on the nouns and the participles: The first Adam became a being that is *living*, while the second Adam became a Spirit that is *life-giving*. The final position of these verbal forms shows that they represent the important action words of the verse."

raised him from the dead.[13] This imparts to the audience the hope that as they became living, physical beings like the first Adam, so they will become living, spiritual beings by receiving eschatological life from the last Adam, who became not only a "living" but a "life-giving" Spirit capable of giving spiritual life to humanity.[14]

Relation to the Antecedent Context in 1 Corinthians 15:21–22, 35–44

1 Corinthians 15:21–22

The correspondence between the scriptural quote about the first Adam and Christ as the last Adam in 1 Cor 15:45 develops for the audience the previous correspondence between Adam and Christ in 15:21–22. That "the first human (ἄνθρωπος), Adam (Ἀδάμ), became a living being" as quoted from Gen 2:7b in 15:45a complements Paul's earlier statements that "death

---

13. On the origin of the two Adams in Palestinian exegetical traditions (rather than in Philo or Gnosticism) known to Paul, see Stephen J. Hultgren, "The Origin of Paul's Doctrine of the Two Adams in 1 Corinthians 15.45–49," *JSNT* 25, no. 3 (2003): 343–70. Brodeur, *Holy Spirit's Agency*, 112: "[S]ince he was the first man created by God, Adam also represents humanity's progenitor. It is precisely in this sense that Paul uses Ἀδάμ in the typological argument in v. 45. The first Adam designates the reality of the old humanity while the last Adam designates the reality of the new. The first Adam possesses a natural body, the one created for human existence on earth. In this way the Apostle emphasizes the fact that Adam is one with the other creatures in this world." See also Schneider, "Corporate Meaning," 151–52.

14. James D. G. Dunn, "I Corinthians 15:45—Last Adam, Life-Giving Spirit," in *Christ and Spirit in the New Testament: In Honour of Charles Francis Digby Moule* (ed. Barnabas Lindars and Stephen S. Smalley; Cambridge: Cambridge University Press, 1973), 130–31: "The understanding of 'the man' in Gen. 2:7 as πρῶτος Ἀδάμ is determined by Paul's understanding of Jesus as ἔσχατος Ἀδάμ. In other words, the point and force of the citation of Gen. 2:7 lies not in the actual Genesis passage itself, but in the contrast between that Adam and the last Adam—a contrast drawn from Paul's own understanding of Christ." Lincoln, *Paradise*, 43–44: "In this typological relationship between the two Adams verse 45 makes it clear that the first Adam became a living soul (ψυχὴν ζῶσαν) and as such had a body appropriate to this quality of life. The last Adam however has a new quality of life, for as πνεῦμα ζῳοποιοῦν he is no longer merely alive and susceptible to death but rather has now become creatively life-giving. Paul emphasizes that Christ *became* life-giving Spirit, for the verb ἐγένετο belongs to both clauses, and it is clear from his whole discussion that this occurred at the resurrection." David Hodgens, "Our Resurrection Body: An Exegesis of 1 Corinthians 15:42–49," *Melanesian Journal of Theology* 17 (2001): 79: "While Christians will be recreated in the likeness of the second Adam, there will be one decisive difference; Christ is life giving." See also Fatehi, *Spirit's Relation*, 275–89; Richard B. Gaffin, "'Life-Giving Spirit': Probing the Center of Paul's Pneumatology," *JETS* 41 (1998): 573–89; Andy Johnson, "Turning the World Upside Down in 1 Corinthians 15: Apocalyptic Epistemology, the Resurrected Body, and the New Creation," *EvQ* 75 (2003): 291–309.

came through a human (ἀνθρώπου)" in 15:21a and that "in Adam (Ἀδάμ) all die" in 15:22a. The audience realizes, then, that with the first Adam came not only the death of humans but also their life. That the first Adam became a "living being" before death gives the audience hope for life after death through the last Adam.

That "the last Adam [became] a life-giving Spirit" according to the scriptural elaboration in 15:45b reinforces and develops the hope engendered for the audience by Paul's previous statement that "in Christ all will be given life" in 15:22b. Not only will all be "given life" (ζῳοποιηθήσονται) in Christ (15:22b), but they will be given the eschatological, resurrected, spiritual life given by the "life-giving (ζῳοποιοῦν) Spirit" who is the last Adam (15:45b), Christ, the human through whom came the resurrection of the dead (15:21b).

1 Corinthians 15:35–44

With the contrast between the first Adam as a living being and the last Adam as a life-giving Spirit in 15:45, Paul provides his audience with a scriptural confirmation and development of the contrast between physical and spiritual bodies as illustrated by the sowing metaphor for God's creative power in 15:36–38.[15] Something that is sown in the ground is "given life" (ζῳοποιεῖται), that is, physical life (15:36), by the creative power of God who gives it a physical body (15:38), just as the first Adam was made a "living" (ζῶσαν) being with a physical body by the creative power of God (15:45a). But God, by raising him from the dead, made the last Adam a "life-giving (ζῳοποιοῦν) Spirit" (15:45b) with a spiritual body to give eschatological, spiritual life.[16]

With the two related but distinct examples of God's creative power in

---

15. On the structure of Paul's argument in 1 Cor 15:35–49, see Rodolphe Morissette, "La condition de ressuscité: 1 Corinthiens 15,35–49. Structure littéraire de la pericope," *Bib* 53 (1972): 208–28; Normand Bonneau, "The Logic of Paul's Argument on the Resurrection Body in 1 Cor 15:35–44a," *ScEs* 45 (1993): 79–92; Duane F. Watson, "Paul's Rhetorical Strategy in 1 Corinthians 15," in *Rhetoric and the New Testament: Essays from the 1992 Heidelberg Conference* (ed. Stanley E. Porter and Thomas H. Olbricht; JSNTSup 90; Sheffield: Sheffield Academic Press, 1993), 244–47; Brodeur, *Holy Spirit's Agency*, 17–31.

16. Jeffrey R. Asher, "Σπείρεται: Paul's Anthropogenic Metaphor in 1 Corinthains 15:42–44," *JBL* 120 (2001): 108: "Paul's point in vv. 36–38 is to illustrate the creative power of God, not the resurrection of the dead. In other words, the agricultural example is provided not as a parallel to the resurrection but as a way of illustrating the effectual power of God in the generation of life.... Consequently, rather than referring to the burial of human beings in an analogy, the account of the seed and the plant in vv. 36–38 is only used to illustrate the creative power of God in the generation of life. Paul thus sets the stage for his subsequent discussion of the role of God's creative power in the resurrection of the dead."

15:36–41, each of which alludes to the scriptural account of creation (see above), Paul is leading his audience to the realization that, since God gives to something that is sown and dies a body as God wishes (first example in 15:36–38), the God who created both earthly and heavenly bodies that differ in glory (second example in 15:39–41) can transform an earthly body that has died into a heavenly body.[17] With the introduction "So also is the resurrection of the dead" in 15:42a, Paul applies these scriptural examples of God's creative power to the resurrection body in a fourfold series of elegantly balanced antitheses that contrast the body of creation with the body of resurrection in 15:42b–44a:

> v. 42b: it is sown in corruption, it is raised in incorruptibility
> v. 43a: it is sown in dishonor, it is raised in glory
> v. 43b: it is sown in weakness, it is raised in power
> v. 44a: it is sown a physical body, it is raised a spiritual body

Each antithesis presents the audience with a contrast between the same verbs—"it is sown" (σπείρεται) and "it is raised" (ἐγείρεται) with "body" (cf. 15:38, 40) as the implicit subject that becomes explicit in the final antithesis. The sequence first brings the audience through an opening triplet of antitheses with the same grammatical construction in which each verb is modified by contrasting prepositional phrases—"in corruption" (ἐν φθορᾷ)/"in incorruptibility" (ἐν ἀφθαρσίᾳ) in v. 42b, "in dishonor" (ἐν ἀτιμίᾳ)/"in glory" (ἐν δόξῃ) in v. 43a, and "in weakness" (ἐν ἀσθενείᾳ)/"in power" (ἐν δυνάμει) in v. 43b. Then the audience experiences the fourth antithesis in v. 44a as the emphatic climax of the series in which the contrasting prepositional phrases of the first three antitheses progress to the contrast between the adjectives—"physical"/"spiritual"—modifying the now explicitly expressed subject—the "body": "it is sown a physical body (σῶμα ψυχικόν), it is raised a spiritual body (σῶμα πνευματικόν)."[18]

---

17. Bonneau, "The Resurrection Body," 86: "The full import of vv. 36–41 lies in the merging of the main points of the two examples ... to form a new implied question: Can God transform an earthly body into a heavenly body?"

18. Collins, *First Corinthians*, 567: "Paul's emphasis lies on the fourth contrast, between the natural body (σῶμα ψυχικόν; cf. 2:14) and the inspirited body (σῶμα πνευματικόν). The grammatical structure of the fourth contrast is different from that of the first three. Instead of a verb modified by a prepositional phrase, Paul uses the same verbs, 'is sown,' 'is raised,' but supplies the subject that could only have been supposed up to this point. All along Paul has been talking about a physical body and a spiritual body; what has hitherto been implicit becomes explicit in the fourth antithesis." See also John Gillman, "Transformation in 1 Cor 15,50–53," *ETL* 58 (1982): 327; N. D. O'Donoghue, "The Awakening of the Dead," *ITQ* 56 (1990): 49–59. Bonneau, "The Resurrection Body," 87: "The adjectives ψυχικός and πνευματικός of the last con-

With the verb "it is raised" (ἐγείρεται), the second half of each of the four antitheses begins to answer for the audience the opening question of this rhetorical unit in 15:35a, "How are the dead raised (ἐγείρονται)?" with God as the implicit agent of this divine passive verb (cf. 15:15). And the second half of the climactic fourth antithesis, "it is raised a spiritual body (σῶμα)" (15:44a), begins to answer for the audience the second question in the introduction of this rhetorical unit in 15:35b, "With what kind of body (σώματι) do they come?"

But with the verb, "it is sown" (σπείρεται), in the first half of each of the four antitheses the audience experiences a development in the agent of the sowing from the first scriptural example in 15:36–38. A hypothetical "you," the "fool" (ἄφρων), was the agent of the three occurrences of the verb "sow" (σπείρεις) in 15:36–37. But with the assertion in 15:38 that it is God who gives what is sown a "body" (σῶμα), God becomes the implicit agent of all of the creative activity alluded to in the two scriptural examples in 15:36–41. Accordingly, in the first half of each of the four antitheses God is the agent of the verb "it is sown," since the subject is the "body" (σῶμα, 15:44a) that God gives to what is sown (15:38), and in correspondence to the second half of each antithesis in which God is the implicit agent of the verb, "it is raised."

The audience understands, then, that the "sowing" in the first half of each antithesis refers not to the burial of the human body but to God's original creation of mankind (Adam) in accord with all of the scriptural allusions to God's creative activity in the surrounding context.[19] In these antitheses the verb "it is sown" is synonymous with "it is created," but Paul prefers the metaphorical "it is sown" because of the connotation that what is sown must die (15:36) before God gives it a body (15:38). Thus, the body is "sown" (created) by God as a "physical body" (v. 44a) "in corruption" (v. 42b), "in dishonor" (v. 43a), and "in weakness" (v. 43b) since it will die (cf 15:21–22). But the body is raised by God as a "spiritual body" (v. 44a)

---

trasting pair, unlike the ἐν + dative construction of the first three antitheses, qualify the noun 'body.' More than merely describing states of being as do the six preceding substantives, these adjectives recapitulate the preceding states of being and apply them to the body itself as attributes. This move toward the more concrete prepares the way for the two Adams in the argument from Scripture."

19. Asher, "Paul's Anthropogenic Metaphor," 110: "The prepositional phrases that form the predicate of σπείρεται in vv. 42–43 do not describe precisely a dead and buried body, and the noun phrase that serves as the object of σπείρεται in v. 44 indicates that the verb is an anthropogenic metaphor, not one of burial or human existence.... Paul uses the clause σπείρεται σῶμα ψυχικόν to describe the creation of Adam when God animated his body. Moreover, all the predicates of σπείρεται in vv. 42–44 are appropriate designations of the state of humanity upon its creation in the person of Adam." See also Garland, *1 Corinthians*, 733.

"in incorruptibility" (v. 42b), "in glory" (ἐν δόξῃ, v. 43a), and "in power" (v. 43b) in analogous accord with the second scriptural example in 15:39–41, which alludes to God's creation of heavenly or spiritual (cf. 15:46–47) bodies that differ "in glory" (ἐν δόξῃ, v. 41).[20]

After the emphatic and climactic antithesis in 15:44a between the physical body that is sown and the spiritual body that is raised, Paul aims to convince his audience that "if there is a physical body, there is also a spiritual," as he begins a new turn in his argument in 15:44b. Echoing "so also (οὕτως καὶ) is the resurrection of the dead" in 15:42a, "so also (οὕτως καὶ) it is written" in 15:45a introduces the scriptural confirmation and development of the conviction for a spiritual body, as the kind of body for those raised from the dead (15:35).[21] The scriptural quotation of Gen 2:7b, "The first human, Adam, became a living being (ψυχὴν)" (15:45a), confirms for the audience that there is a "physical (ψυχικόν) body" (15:44b), indeed one that is "living" but, as it was "sown" (created) by God in corruption, in dishonor, and in weakness (15:42b–43), destined to die (15:21–22, 36).

The elaboration of the scriptural quotation "the last Adam [became] a life-giving Spirit (πνεῦμα)" (15:45b) confirms for the audience that there is a "spiritual" (πνευματικόν) body (15:44b), indeed one that is "life-giving," as it was raised by God in incorruptibility, in glory, and in power (15:42b–43), a spiritual body with glory analogous to the glory of a heavenly rather than earthly body (15:40–41).[22] That the last Adam was raised by God into a not merely living but life-giving Spirit aims to engender hope in the audience. In the first Adam they were "sown" (created) by God as living beings with physical bodies destined for death (15:36–38, 42–44) in accord with

---

20. Asher, "Paul's Anthropogenic Metaphor," 105: "In four successive antitheses, Paul implies, by means of the two verbs σπείρεται and ἐγείρεται, that, like the original creation of humankind, the resurrection is a creative act of God and, by means of the predicates of each verb, that the resurrection body, like Adam's, qualitatively conforms to the polar distinction between the celestial and terrestrial realms as places of somatic habitation. Paul demonstrates that the resurrection, like the original creation of Adam, is a creative act of God and that it does not violate the metaphysical strictures of the contrariety that exists between heaven and earth."

21. Bonneau, "The Resurrection Body," 90: "In effect, the conclusion reached in the argument from analogy becomes the premise for the next argument. In v. 44a, the phrases 'psychical body' and 'pneumatic body,' structured with the verbs 'is sown' and 'is raised,' encapsulate the essence of all that was gleaned from vv. 35–43. By repeating these same substantival phrases in v. 44b, but here with the 'if . . . also' construction, Paul recapitulates the argument from analogy and uses the conclusions from this first argument as the foundation of the argument from scripture."

22. Brodeur, Holy Spirit's Agency, 124: "The πνευματικός is that which is characteristic of the Spirit. Thus when Paul teaches that the risen body is spiritual, he means that it has been created by God through the agency of the Spirit and formed for heaven, the ideal and appropriate environment for the new creation."

the scriptural quote of Gen 2:7b in 15:45a. They now may have the hope of being raised from the dead and given spiritual bodies (15:35), with glory analogous to the glory of the heavenly bodies (15:39–41), by the life-giving Spirit, the last Adam, Christ, in accord with the elaboration of the scriptural quote in 15:45b.

Relation to the Subsequent Context in 1 Corinthians 15:46–49

Rhetorically, that "the spiritual was not first but the physical, then the spiritual" (15:46) reinforces the emphasis on the spiritual that follows upon the physical (15:44), as it takes the audience through a sequential movement from a focus on the spiritual to the physical and back to the spiritual. That "the spiritual" (τὸ πνευματικόν), referring to both the spiritual body (σῶμα πνευματικόν, 15:44b) and the life-giving Spirit (πνεῦμα ζῳοποιοῦν, 15:45b), was not first but rather "the physical" (τὸ ψυχικόν) clarifies for the audience that the scripture quote's "living being" (ψυχὴν ζῶσαν, 15:45a), the first Adam, though living, is not spiritual. Nevertheless, the audience is assured that "the physical" is followed in temporal sequence by "the spiritual" with the spiritual body that came into existence with the last Adam, the not merely living but life-giving Spirit, in accord with the elaboration of the scripture quote in 15:45b.[23]

That "the first human (πρῶτος ἄνθρωπος) was from the earth, of dust" (15:47a) develops the scripture quote's statement that "the first human (πρῶτος ἄνθρωπος), Adam, became a living being" (15:45a). Paul's intensified assertion that the first human was not only "from the earth (γῆς)" but also "of dust (χοϊκός)" reminds the audience that in accord with the scriptural account of creation not only was the first human formed by God from the dust (χοῦν) of the earth (γῆς) (LXX Gen 2:7a), but is also destined to die and return to the earth from which he was taken: "for you are earth (γῆ) and to earth (γῆν) you will return" (LXX Gen 3:19b). This emphasis on the earthly origin and destiny of the first human heightens the audience's real-

---

23. On "the spiritual" and "the physical" in 15:46 referring to both the body (15:44) and the two Adams of the scripture quote and its elaboration (15:45), see Rodolphe Morissette, "L'Antithèse entre le 'psychique' et le 'pneumatique' en 1 Corinthiens, XV, 44 à 46," *RevScRel* 46 (1972): 118; Teani, *Corporeità*, 258. Lincoln, *Paradise*, 44: "What started out as a comparison between two forms of bodily existence moved to a comparison between the two representatives of those forms and now proceeds to include the two world-orders which the first and last Adam exemplify. In other words, in verse 46 τὸ ψυχικόν and τὸ πνευματικόν should not be restricted simply to a reference to the body but have become descriptive of two contrasting orders of existence which have bodily expression."

ization that although the first human became a living being (15:45a), as recorded in scripture, he was mortal and earthbound, as also recorded in scripture.[24]

That "the second human is from heaven" (15:47b) develops the scripture quote's elaboration that "the last Adam [became] a life-giving Spirit" (15:45b). The progression from "last" (ἔσχατος) Adam to "second" (δεύτερος) human awakens the audience's hope in a newness that transcends the first human, Adam.[25] Whereas the first human was "from the earth, of dust" (15:47a), the second is "from heaven" (15:47b), and thus possesses a glory surpassing that of the merely earthly (15:40). But that the second human, as the last Adam of the scripture quote's elaboration, is a life-giving Spirit awakens the audience's hope that the second human not only possesses the glorious life of a heavenly body but can give that life to fellow human beings, who are otherwise mortal and bound to the earth as descendants of the first human.

"As the one of dust, so also those of dust" (15:48a) makes the audience, as those of dust—made from and destined to return to the earth—realize that although they are living beings like the scripture quote's first human (15:45a), "the one of dust," they are, nevertheless, also "from the earth, of dust" (15:47a) and thus mortal and earthbound. "But as the one of heaven, so also those of heaven" (15:48b) gives the audience hope that the life-giving Spirit of the scripture quote's elaboration (15:45b), who is "the one of heaven," will give earthbound humans the life of those of heaven.

With a transition from a third-person to an inclusive first-person plural discourse that draws the audience more explicitly and directly to Paul and his scriptural argumentation, Paul concludes the argument with a climactic exhortation in 15:49: "Even as we have borne the image of the one of dust,

---

24. On the adjective "of dust" (χοϊκός) in 15:45a, Fee (*Corinthians*, 792 n. 24) notes: "The use of the adjective indicates that Paul's interest is not in the 'stuff' or dust of the earth per se, but in describing Adam's body as being 'earthy,' that is, subject to decay and death." Brodeur, *Holy Spirit's Agency*, 130: "Paul coined χοϊκός to fit his understanding of the passing nature of the first human being. Adam is χοϊκός in as much as he is weak and perishable. A frail mortal in this passing world, he is a creature made of earth and formed for life on earth. Given his earthly nature then, it is impossible for him to leave this world and pass to heaven."

25. Lorenz Oberlinner, "δεύτερος," *EDNT* 1.292: "δεύτερος can be used to emphasize the specifically *new*, which surpasses and excels the 'first.'" Brodeur, *Holy Spirit's Agency*, 131: "In v. 47, however, δεύτερος adopts a different nuance by stressing something that is brand new. This human being is not merely the last in the line of earthly people, which is the assumption of v. 45. Rather, by calling him 'the second human being,' Paul is suggesting that he exceeds the first due to his glorious resurrection from the dead. Hence he represents a new prototype for humanity, a new possibility for human beings to live in the eschatological age.... In him, humanity at last discovers a reason to hope in heaven."

let us also bear the image of the heavenly one."²⁶ In accord with the scriptural account of creation, that we have borne the image (εἰκόνα) of "the one of dust" (15:49a), the first human, means that although, like Adam, we are "living beings" (LXX Gen 2:7b in 15:45a) created according to the image (εἰκόνα) and likeness of God (LXX Gen 1:26–27), as descendants of Adam we are born according to the image (εἰκόνα) of Adam (LXX Gen 5:3) as "the one of dust," so that we are destined to die and return to the earth.²⁷

The exhortation "let us also bear the image of the heavenly one" (15:49b) presents the audience with a rhetorical surprise analogous to that of the elaboration of the scriptural quote (15:45b). After the audience hears the scriptural quote of Gen 2:7b that "the first human, Adam, became a living being" (15:45a), they expect to hear in the elaboration of it that "the last Adam [became] a living Spirit." Instead, what they hear includes yet transcends what they expected to hear: "the last Adam [became]," not merely a *living*, but "a *life-giving* Spirit" (15:45b), not only possessing but capable of giving the spiritual, glorious life of the heavenly one to humanity.

Similarly, after the audience hears "Even as we have borne the image of the one of dust" (15:49a), they expect to hear, "we will also bear the image of the heavenly one." Instead, the exhortation that they hear includes, yet surpasses, what they expected to hear: "let us also bear the image of the heavenly one" (15:49b), that is, with the assistance of the life-giving Spirit that is "the heavenly one," let us already begin to live the spiritual, heavenly life for which we are destined in the future.²⁸ For the audience already to bear the image of the heavenly one means for them to live as those who are "spiritual" (πνευματικός, 2:13–15; 3:1; 14:37) with the assured hope that

---

26. Brodeur, *Holy Spirit's Agency*, 138: " 'To bear the image of someone' means to put him on (as one would a garment) and so resemble him." BDAG, 1064: "*bear the image of the earthly person*, i.e. represent in one's own appearance."

27. Brodeur, *Holy Spirit's Agency*, 140: " 'The image of the one like dust' of v. 49a obviously refers to the first Adam, ὁ χοϊκός. All those connected to Adam, their representative and forefather, bear his εἰκών. In other words, those who bear the image of the first Adam share in his natural condition, one which is subject to decay and death."

28. On the text-critical preference of the hortatory subjunctive, "let us bear," over the future indicative, "we will bear," Fee (*Corinthians*, 795) points out that "it is nearly impossible to account for anyone's having changed a clearly understandable future to the hortatory subjunctive so early and so often that it made its way into every textual history as the predominant reading. For that reason it must be the original, and if original it must be intentional on Paul's part as a way of calling them to prepare now for the future that is to be." Brodeur, *Holy Spirit's Agency*, 143: "Christian living ought to start now and thereby become the hallmark of all who hope to resemble 'the one like heaven,' the last Adam. If all people already bear the image of the one like earth, the first Adam, the Apostle now exhorts the Corinthians to be true to their vocation and bear the image of the one like heaven."

after death they will receive a "spiritual body" (σῶμα πνευματικόν, 15:44, 46) appropriate for life in heaven from the life-giving Spirit, the last Adam, who is the heavenly one.[29]

To sum up, the climactic exhortation, "let us bear the image of the heavenly one" (15:49b), urges the audience to conform their lives even now to the confident hope of exceeding their earthbound condition and resembling "the heavenly one" after their deaths. This is a hope they may have based on Paul's scriptural argumentation that the first human, Adam, who became a living being (LXX Gen 2:7b in 15:45a) created in the image of God (LXX Gen 1:26–27 in 15:49a) but destined to die as earthly and of dust (LXX Gen 3:19 in 15:47), and in whose image all humans have been created (LXX Gen 5:3 in 15:49a), is followed by a new, second human from heaven (15:47), the last Adam, the life-giving Spirit (15:45b), capable of transforming our physical, earthbound bodies that will die into spiritual, heavenly bodies (15:46) like that of "the heavenly one."

Summary on 1 Corinthians 15:45a

1. Paul is relying upon his implied audience's recognition that not only the adapted quotation of LXX Gen 2:7b in 1 Cor 15:45a, "the first human, Adam, became a living being," but also the immediate context both before (15:38–44) and after (15:45b–49) the quotation recall the scriptural account of creation as recorded in Genesis.

2. The rhetorical progression from the scriptural quote in v. 45a to its elaboration in v. 45b imparts to the audience the hope that as they became living, physical beings like the first Adam, so they will become living, spiritual beings by receiving eschatological life from the last Adam, who became at his resurrection from the dead not only a "living" but a "life-giving" Spirit capable of giving spiritual life to humanity.

3. That "the last Adam [became] a life-giving Spirit" according to the scriptural elaboration in 15:45b reinforces and develops the hope engendered for the audience by Paul's previous statement that "in Christ all will be given life" in 15:22b.

---

29. Brodeur, *Holy Spirit's Agency*, 141: "[T]he Apostle is exhorting them to adopt the Spirit-filled life of the last Adam even now during their earthly existence.... Those who bear the image of the last Adam already partly share in his supernatural condition thanks to the Spirit whom believers received at baptism. They are already called through their life in the Spirit to resemble him now in their natural bodies. At the eschaton they will come to resemble him completely when they at last put on their spiritual bodies."

4. That the last Adam was raised by God into a not merely living but life-giving Spirit aims to engender hope in the audience. In the first Adam they were "sown" (created) by God as living beings with physical bodies destined for death (15:36–38, 42–44) in accord with the scriptural quote of Gen 2:7b in 15:45a. They now may have the hope of being raised from the dead and given spiritual bodies (15:35), with glory analogous to the glory of the heavenly bodies (15:39–41), by the life-giving Spirit, the last Adam, Christ, in accord with the elaboration of the scriptural quote in 15:45b.

5. The audience's hope of exceeding their earthbound condition and resembling "the heavenly one" (15:49b) both now and after their deaths is based on Paul's scriptural argumentation that the first human, Adam, who became a living being (LXX Gen 2:7b in 15:45a) created in the image of God (LXX Gen 1:26–27 in 15:49a) but destined to die as earthly and of dust (LXX Gen 3:19 in 15:47), and in whose image all humans have been created (LXX Gen 5:3 in 15:49a), is followed by a new, second human from heaven (15:47), the last Adam, the life-giving Spirit (15:45b), capable of transforming our physical, earthbound bodies that will die into spiritual, heavenly bodies (15:46) like that of "the heavenly one."

Chapter 17

1 Corinthians 15:54b–55

> *Death is swallowed up in victory.*
> *Where, O death, is your victory?*
> *Where, O death, is your sting?*

Old Testament Background

Joined together in an interpretive interrelationship by the words "death" and "victory," which they have in common, the final two scripture quotations in 1 Corinthians (15:54b–55) offer yet another example of the Jewish exegetical device that came to be known as *gezera shava*.[1] Unlike previous uses of this device in 1 Corinthians (3:19b–20; 9:9–10; 15:25, 27), where the combination more-or-less preserved a distinction between two different quotations, the *gezera shava* in 1 Cor 15:54b–55 combines and presents two quotations as if they were a single citation of scripture. This is confirmed by the way their combination is introduced as a single "word" or "saying" of scripture: "then will come to be the word (λόγος) that is written" (15:54b).[2] The audience, then, need not recall the original source or context of either quotation, but merely accept the combination as a single

---

1. For previous uses of *gezera shava* in 1 Corinthians, see chs. 6, 9, and 14 above. With regard to its use in 1 Cor 15:54b–55, see Rodolphe Morissette, "Un midrash sur la mort (I Cor. xv, 54c à 57)," *RB* 79 (1972): 165 n. 1.
2. Morissette, "Midrash," 167: "Les deux passages de l'Écriture sont cités selon le procédé de l'amalgame, c'est-à-dire sans transition ou sans que le deuxième texte soit introduit par une nouvelle formule." Stanley, *Paul*, 209–10: "Paul gives his reader no indication that vv. 54b–55 might represent anything other than a continuous quotation from a single biblical passage. Equally typical of Paul is the way the two verses have been knit together through a series of thoughtful adaptations to form a coherent, well-rounded rhetorical unit with a single, transparent theme. Here again the evidence supports the view that the various combined citations that appear in Paul's epistles are the carefully cultivated fruit of a sophisticated literary artistry and not the unfortunate by-product of a rather careless citation technique."

prophecy from scripture yet to be fulfilled. Once again Paul is relying upon his audience's recognition of scriptural authority in general.³

Noteworthy is the formula that introduces the scriptural combination in 15:54b-55. It is the only time in 1 Corinthians that Paul quotes a scriptural prophecy yet to be fulfilled.⁴ The main verb of the formula, "will come to be" or "will become operative" (γενήσεται), expresses a future fulfillment.⁵ The combination of quotations into a single "word" (λόγος) that "has been and still is written" (γεγραμμένος, perfect passive) has the scriptural authority of a prophecy written in the past that has a present impact upon the audience, who awaits its future fulfillment.⁶

1 Corinthians 15:54b and Isaiah 25:8a

The combined scriptural quotation's first line in 1 Cor 15:54b is dependent upon a version of Isa 25:8a:

MT Isa 25:8a: בִּלַּע הַמָּוֶת לָנֶצַח
    He [God] will swallow up death forever.
LXX Isa 25:8a: κατέπιεν ὁ θάνατος ἰσχύσας
    Being strong death has swallowed up [all the nations; cf. v. 7].
Aquila Isa 25:8a: καταποντίσει τὸν θάνατον εἰς νῖκος
    He [God] will drown death in victory.
Symmachus Isa 25:8a: καταποθῆναι ποιήσει τὸν θάνατον εἰς τέλος
    He [God] will cause death to be swallowed up to the uttermost.
Theodotion (Uncial Q) Isa 25:8a: κατεπόθη ὁ θάνατος εἰς νῖκος
    Death is swallowed up in victory.
Theodotion (Syrohexapla) Isa 25:8a: κατέπιεν ὁ θάνατος εἰς νῖκος

---

3. Lindemann, "Schrift," 224: "Denn der Hinweis auf den endgültigen Sieg über den Tod ist im Rahmen von 1 Kor 15 unverzichtbar; und ebenso ist klar, daß es nach dem hier von Paulus verwendeten Schema von Verheißung und Erfüllung ein Wort der Schrift sein muß, das 'erfüllt' werden wird. Den ursprünglichen Sinn und den Kontext der zitierten Texte braucht man dabei selbstverständlich nicht zu kennen."

4. Fee, *Corinthians*, 803: "Paul ... [is] citing two OT texts that he understands as yet to be fulfilled: 'Then the saying that is written will come true.' This is the only instance of his citing yet unfulfilled prophecy; but as always he cites the OT in light of the death and resurrection of Jesus. So these two passages are in fact fulfilled in Christ; they simply have yet to be realized." See also Thiselton, *Corinthians*, 1298.

5. Thiselton, *Corinthians*, 1298: "Hence γενήσεται bears some such sense as 'shall become operative,' or 'shall come into force.'"

6. Morissette, "Midrash," 167: "C'est le plus souvent à l'aide du verbe γράφειν au parfait passif que Paul amène une citation de l'Écriture. Au parfait, afin de souligner la valeur et l'importance de 'ce qui a été écrit' pour le temps présent et pour l'avenir."

> Death has swallowed up [the
> nations] in victory.
1 Cor 15:54b: κατεπόθη ὁ θάνατος εἰς νῖκος
> Death is swallowed up in victory.

Paul does not appear to be quoting from either the Hebrew, which has "forever" instead of "in victory," or the LXX, in which "death" is the subject of an active rather than passive form of the verb, and which also lacks "in victory."[7] Although the Theodotion version in uncial Q is identical to the Pauline version, it may be a later assimilation to 1 Cor 15:54b, especially since it occurs as a marginal gloss, and the Syrohexapla reading of Theodotion has the active rather than passive form of the verb. But the fact that Aquila and both Theodotion readings have "in victory" for the Hebrew "forever," and Symmachus as well as the Theodotion uncial Q reading have the passive form of the verb, indicates a common tradition behind these translations. The agreements between them and Paul point to Paul's dependence upon a preexisting, non-LXX Greek text of Isa 25:8a.[8]

1 Corinthians 15:55 and Hosea 13:14b

The combined scriptural quotation's second line in 1 Cor 15:55 represents a Pauline adaptation of Hos 13:14b:

MT Hos 13:14b: אֱהִי דְבָרֶיךָ מָוֶת אֱהִי קָטָבְךָ שְׁאוֹל
> Where are your plagues, O death? Where is your destruction, O sheol?

LXX Hos 13:14b: ποῦ ἡ δίκη σου θάνατε ποῦ τὸ κέντρον σου ᾅδη
> Where is your punishment, O death? Where is your sting, O hades?

1 Cor 15:55: ποῦ σου, θάνατε, τὸ νῖκος; ποῦ σου, θάνατε, το κέντρον;

---

7. Harm W. Hollander and Joost Holleman, "The Relationship of Death, Sin, and Law in 1 Cor 15:56," *NovT* 35 (1993): 273–74: "Paul introduces, or takes over, the formula εἰς νῖκος, not used in Isa 25:8 LXX, but a more or less common LXX idiom for the translation of the Hebrew לנצח, 'for ever', which is found in Isa 25:8 MT. By taking εἰς νῖκος literally, meaning 'to victory', he can interpret 'the victory over death through Jesus Christ' (v. 57) as the fulfillment of Isaiah's proclamation in Isa 25:8."

8. Koch, *Schrift*, 63: "Paulus hier weder frei variiert noch eigenständig ad hoc übersetzt. Vielmehr folgt er einer vorgegebenen, die LXX korrigierenden Vorlage, die auch auf die späteren Übersetzungen eingewirk hat." Stanley, *Paul*, 211: "Paul has most likely followed a pre-existing Greek text at this point, one that may have exercised at least a measure of influence over the subsequent translations of Aquila, Symmachus, and (possibly) Theodotion." For fuller discussions of all the details involved in comparing the various versions of Isa 25:8a, see Morissette, "Midrash," 168–70; Koch, *Schrift*, 61–63; Stanley, *Paul*, 210–11; Thiselton, *Corinthians*, 1299.

Where, O death, is *your* victory? Where, O death, is *your* sting?

In MT Hos 13:14a, God, who has already decided to destroy the people of Israel (13:9), asks, "Shall I ransom them from the power of sheol? Shall I redeem them from death?" Consequently, the questions in 13:14b, "Where are your plagues, O death? Where is your destruction, O sheol?" are calling upon a personified death and Sheol to work their destruction upon the people. Similarly, in LXX Hos 13:14a, God asks, "Shall I rescue them [the people] out of the hand of hades and shall I redeem them from death?" so that the questions in 13:14b, "Where is your punishment, O death? Where is your sting, O hades?" are invoking a personified death and Hades to destroy Israel. But in 1 Cor 15:55 the questions "Where, O death, is *your* victory? Where, O death, is *your* sting?" following upon the first part of the combined quotation in 15:54b, "Death is swallowed up in victory," function rather as an emphatic taunting of an utterly defeated personified death to work its destructive power.[9]

Instead of the MT's "plagues" (דְּבָרֶיךָ) and the LXX's "punishment" (δίκη), Paul's quotation of Hos 13:14b has "victory" (νῖκος), which strengthens the *gezera shava* combination with the quotation of Isa 25:8a in 1 Cor 15:54b. Both quotes thus have not only the word "death" but also the word "victory" in common for their mutual interpretation.[10]

Paul has advanced both occurrences of the pronoun "your" (σου) to a position in front of the vocative "death" and thus separated them from the nouns they modify, "victory" and "sting" respectively, to create a powerful rhetorical emphasis that heightens the taunting effect of both questions of the quotation of Hos 13:14b. Since death is swallowed up, and thus overwhelmed and annihilated, in a victory that is God's (1 Cor 15:54b), "Where, O death, is *your* victory? Where, O death, is *your* sting?" (15:55).[11]

Whereas both the MT and the LXX of Hos 13:14b address personified

---

9. Garland, *1 Corinthians*, 745: "Paul's citation... interprets the passage from the perspective of Christ's resurrection by turning it into a taunt. The rhetorical questions now sneer defiantly at death's impotence before the power and mercy of God."

10. Stanley, *Paul*, 214: "[I]t seems clear that Paul has introduced the words τὸ νῖκος into the text to create a closer verbal and rhetorical link with the excerpt from Isa 25.8 in v. 54, where the notion of 'victory' plays an equally prominent role." Collins, *First Corinthians*, 578: "Paul has adapted the texts so that they might be read together and be mutually interpretive." Hollander and Holleman, "1 Cor 15:56," 274: "Both OT texts are now supplementary and strengthen each other in their function of showing the end of the power of death." See also Koch, *Schrift*, 169.

11. Koch, *Schrift*, 107: "Die außergewöhnlich weite Voranstellung des Possessivpronomens, das jeweils durch den Vokativ θάνατε vom Bezugswort getrennt ist, verleiht dem Zitat eine

"death" in the first question and its synonym, the personified place of death, "sheol" and "hades" respectively, in the second question, the Pauline quote addresses personified "death" in both questions. The result is a triplet of references to personified "death" in the combined quotation of Isa 25:8a and Hos 13:14b in 1 Cor 15:54b–55 to create a potent rhetorical unit that emphatically underscores for the audience the utter devastation of the power of death.[12]

To sum up, using the exegetical device of *gezera shava*, Paul in 1 Cor 15:54b–55 adapted and combined two distinct scriptural texts, Isa 25:8a and Hos 13:14b, by the words "death" and "victory" that they have in common into a single scriptural quotation of prophecy that functions as a powerful rhetorical unit whose authority is based not on any one particular scriptural text but on the authority of scripture in general.

Literary-Rhetorical Analysis

The introduction to the combined scriptural quotation in 1 Cor 15:54b–55, "Then will come to be the word that is written," prepares the audience to hear a "word" or "saying" (λόγος) written in the past with a scriptural authority that remains valid for the present time of the audience, as expressed by the perfect tense of the Greek participle "written" (γεγραμμένος). That it "will come to be" (γενήσεται) assures the audience of its certain fulfillment in the future, based on its authority as God's scriptural "word" of prophecy.[13]

The first part of the scriptural "word" that the audience hears is the assertion that when this prophetic "word" is fulfilled, "Death is swallowed up in victory" (15:54b). In accord with Jewish apocalyptic eschatology, "the death" (ὁ θάνατος) here is regarded as a personified cosmic power that is

---

starke rhetorische Wirkung." Stanley, *Paul*, 212: "The reason for the altered order is purely rhetorical: separating two elements that would otherwise belong together (here the noun and its attributive) is a common way of indicating emphasis in both classical and Hellenistic Greek."

12. Stanley, *Paul*, 215: "The effect of this and other modifications to vv. 54–5 . . . is to produce a tightly knit, three-membered 'word of Scripture' structured around a threefold repetition of the word θάνατος, in which the first two lines are further united by the repetition of the keyword νῖκος and the last two by a thoroughgoing verbal parallelism. In this form, the verse serves as a rhetorical flourish to notify the hearers that the discussion is fast coming to an end. The fundamentally Pauline origin of this carefully structured rhetorical unit can hardly be doubted." See also Koch, *Schrift*, 168–70.

13. Collins, *First Corinthians*, 582: "The unusual introductory lemma—Paul typically uses a perfect passive form of the verb to write, γέγραπται, in a formulaic, 'it is written,' sometimes incorporating a postpositive γάρ; cf. 1:19, 31; 2:9; 3:19; 9:9; 10:7; 14:21; 15:45—underscores the dynamic reality of God's word: Then the word will come to pass (γενήσεται ὁ λόγος)."

God's last enemy (cf. 15:26) or opponent in the great eschatological battle for ultimate control over all of creation.[14] That death "is swallowed up" (κατεπόθη) by God (divine passive)[15] in the manner that a wild animal completely consumes its prey or the waves of the sea drown something so that it disappears assures the audience of death's utter destruction and disappearance, rendering it powerless.[16] Ironically, the death that swallows and devours the living is itself swallowed up. And that death is swallowed up by God "in victory" (εἰς νῖκος) assures the audience that God will be the victor in the great eschatological battle and ultimately triumph over the cosmic power of death.[17]

The second part of the scriptural "word" draws the audience into a taunting interrogation of the personified power of death by means of a parallel pair of penetrating rhetorical questions: "Where, O death, is *your* victory? Where, O death, is *your* sting?" (15:55). Since the inimical power of death will ultimately be swallowed up and completely defeated in God's victory (15:54b), the first question, with its emphasis upon the pronoun "your" (σου) and taunting direct address of a personified "death" (θάνατε), mocks any claim death may think it has to "the victory" (τὸ νῖκος).[18] In contrast to *God's* complete victory over death, "Where, O death, is *your* victory?" (15:55a).[19] The audience realizes that the implied answer is

---

14. According to de Boer (*Defeat*), "death itself is here regarded as a cosmic reality, a mark of the perverted and corrupted creation" (47), "the annihilation of the human person by an alien, inimical power" (184). John Gillman, "A Thematic Comparison: 1 Cor 15:50–57 and 2 Cor 5:1–5," *JBL* 107 (1988): 444–45: "Death, ὁ θάνατος, here considered as a power in its own right, has a double sense: (1) For those who have died it is understood as the experience marking a radical end to earthly life. (2) For those who are still living, death is understood as a power continually threatening and constraining earthly life."

15. Lindemann, *Erste Korintherbrief*, 370: "Logisches Subj. des pass. κατεπόθη ist offenbar Gott."

16. According to BDAG (524), καταπίνω means "to destroy completely, in the figure of one devouring or swallowing something . . . to cause the end of something."

17. Schrage, *Erste Brief*, 4.379: "Der Sinn des Bildes vom καταπίνεσθαι des Todes ist nicht ganz sicher (vgl. auch 2Kor 5,4). Die einen denken an das Verschlungenwerden von Raubtieren, andere dagegen an das Hineingezogenwerden in einen Meeresstrudel. Obwohl man auch erwogen hat, daß hier keine Alternative vorliegt, spricht εἰς νῖκος eher für das Bild eines Strudels, in dem der Tod untergeht. Der Tod ist am Ende in den Sieg hineinverschlungen, ist völlig besiegt und restlos abgetan."

18. Thiselton, *Corinthians*, 1301: "To press home the powerlessness of death to damage, to intimidate, or to dismay, Paul uses the vocative of address as a *taunt*, like a taunt to a hostile but disarmed, bound, and powerless attacker."

19. For similar rhetorical uses of the interrogative "where" (ποῦ) previously in 1 Corinthians, see 1:20 (3x); 12:17 (2x); 12:19.

"nowhere" and is thus assured of the ultimate defeat of the cosmic power of death over them.

The second taunting question, "Where, O death, is *your* sting?" (15:55b), reinforces and develops the rhetorical impact of the first (15:55a). In contrast to *God's* overwhelming and complete "swallowing up" of the inimical power of death, the question mocks a personified death by asking where is "the sting" (τὸ κέντρον) that is *yours?* Not only can death no longer swallow up the living because it has itself been swallowed up, but it no longer has any "sting" to harm the living, in the manner of the poisonous sting of a wild animal or the piercing sting of a goad.[20] Thus, the audience is assured that not only will death have no claim to final victory over them (15:55a), but it will ultimately have no power ("sting") to harm them (15:55b).[21]

In sum, the combined scriptural quotation in 1 Cor 15:54b–55, as God's authoritative "word" of prophecy destined to be fulfilled, assures the audience of God's final victory over the inimical power of death in the great cosmic battle for ultimate control of all of creation (15:54b), so that death has absolutely no claim to that final victory (15:55a) nor any poisonous or piercing power ultimately to harm the living (15:55b).

Relation to the Antecedent Context in 1 Corinthians 15:21–26, 50–54a

1 Corinthians 15:21–26

After reminding the audience that "death" (θάνατος) came through a human being (15:21a), so that in that human being, Adam, all die (15:22a), Paul explains that at the end when all the rulers, authorities, and powers in creation are destroyed (15:24c), the last enemy to be destroyed is "the death" (ὁ θάνατος) (15:26). In 15:54b–55, the apocalyptic-eschatological

---

20. Hollander and Holleman, "1 Cor 15:56," 277: "In the context, and applied to the connection between death and man, it means that death 'stings' men, making them perishable, mortal."

21. Garland, *1 Corinthians*, 745–46: "The noun τὸ κέντρον can refer to a goad that drives on or wounds (Acts 26:14; Prov. 26:3; Sir. 38:25; Ps. Sol. 16:4), or to a stinger (Rev. 9:10 [of scorpions]; 4 Macc. 14:19 [of insects]. Does Paul picture death wielding a goad in its hand to rule over humans and torture them? Or does it puncture the flesh with its poison-filled stinger? Here it must refer to something that harms far more seriously than either a goad or a stinger, and it must be synonymous with 'power' in 1 Cor. 15:56. It enables death to exercise its dominion over the entire world, but its venom has been absorbed by Christ and drained of its potency so that the victory over death now belongs to God and to God's people, who benefit from it." See also Schrage, *Erste Brief*, 4.380–81.

imagery of death as an enemy to be defeated in the great battle for control of creation reaches a climax in the scriptural prophecy assuring the audience that "the death" (ὁ θάνατος) will ultimately be swallowed up by God in victory, so that it can be taunted as having absolutely no claim to that final victory, having been rendered totally powerless with no "sting" to harm the living.

1 Corinthians 15:50–54a

The theme of the possible victory of "death" as a personified, militaristic enemy (15:26) in the apocalyptic-eschatological battle for control of creation emerges in Paul's declaration to his audience in 15:50 that "flesh and blood cannot inherit the kingdom of God [cf. 15:24], nor does corruption inherit incorruptibility."[22] Within the synonymous parallelism of this verse, "flesh and blood," that is, earthly human beings with physical bodies (cf. 15:39–41), cannot inherit the final kingdom of God because "flesh and blood" is synonymous with "corruption" (φθορά).[23] Human beings cannot inherit the final kingdom of God, which is synonymous with "incorruptibility" (ἀφθαρσίαν), because their bodies are susceptible to the corruption caused by the menacing enemy that is "death."[24]

By rendering human beings corruptible, "death" could claim "victory" in the final battle by making it impossible for them to inherit the incorrupt-

---

22. Johannes H. Friedrich, "κληρονομέω," *EDNT* 2.299: "In 1 Cor 15:50 'inherit the kingdom' is intended in an explicitly eschatological way, as in this passage it is a synonym for 'rise from the dead.'" Collins, *First Corinthians*, 579: "'Kingdom of God' is an expression that occurs only seven times in Paul's letters, but five of the occurrences are in 1 Corinthians (4:20; 6:9, 10; 15:24; cf. Rom 14:17; Gal 5:21; compare 1 Thess 2:12). The phrase is a cipher for God's ultimate reign. In the NT 'to inherit' (κληρονομέω) is frequently used with eschatological connotations."

23. For the arguments for a synonymous rather than synthetical parallelism in 15:50, in which "flesh and blood" would refer to the living and "corruption" to the dead according to Joachim Jeremias, "Flesh and Blood Cannot Inherit the Kingdom of God (1 Cor 15.50)," *NTS* 2 (1955–56): 151–59, see Rodolphe Morissette, "'La chair et le sang ne peuvent hériter du Règne de Dieu' (I Cor., XV, 50)," *ScEs* 26 (1974): 46–48; Andrew C. Perriman, "Paul and the Parousia: 1 Corinthians 15.50-7 and 2 Corinthians 5.1–5," *NTS* 35 (1989): 513–15; Plevnik, *Paul and the Parousia*, 149–52; Fee, *Corinthians*, 798; Collins, *First Corinthians*, 579; Asher, *Polarity*, 152–54; Garland, *1 Corinthians*, 741.

24. De Boer, *Defeat*, 132: "Neither mortality nor corruption denotes for Paul a necessary and natural process of decay, nor can either of them be equated with death as such. Rather, human mortality refers to the susceptibility of living human beings with their 'natural' bodies to the onslaught of death (conceived as a cosmological power), an onslaught that culminates in corruption, the decay of these bodies upon physical demise. Death thereby attains its victory (v. 55). It is thus because of death's great power that flesh and blood *cannot* inherit the kingdom of God and that corruption *does not* inherit incorruption."

ible kingdom of God. But the scriptural quotation in 15:54b–55 proclaims that at the end, when the dead are raised "incorruptible" (ἄφθαρτοι) (15:52) and when all of us—those who have died and those still living—are clothed with "incorruptibility" (ἀφθαρσίαν) and "immortality" (ἀθανασίαν) (15:53–54a), "death is swallowed up in victory!" (15:54b). Thus, the apparent victory that death might have claimed can be taunted—"Where, O death, is *your* victory?" (15:55a). The audience is assured that death cannot claim its victory in preventing us, by its power to corrupt our bodies of "flesh and blood," from inheriting the incorruptible kingdom of God (15:50).

In accord with the "mystery" (μυστήριον) that Paul divulges to his audience, we will all—those who have and those who have not yet "fallen asleep" in death—be changed (15:51).[25] This final transformation will be instantaneous at the end—"in an instant, in the blink of an eye, at the last trumpet" (15:52a). The intensified expression that at the "last" trumpet (σάλπιγγι) it will trumpet (σαλπίσει) signals that the end has arrived, the time for the dead to be raised and for those who have not yet died to be changed (15:52) by being clothed with incorruptibility and immortality (15:53–54a).[26] But, in accord with the imagery of God's eschatological battle with the enemy "death" (15:26), it also signals the triumph of God's victory, as confirmed for the audience by the scriptural quotation that "death is swallowed up in victory!" (15:54a).[27]

In the divine salvific plan "it is necessary" (δεῖ), in accord with the "mystery" that must take place (15:51), for the body that is corruptible to

---

25. On the meaning of "mystery" in the NT, Krämer ("μυστήριον," 447) states: "Out of the Jewish tradition comes a less stringently esoteric and the transcendent, humanly inaccessible *mystery* of God, which is historically set in action by God himself in his acts of salvation and judgment in the past, present, and future, which already now has been made evident to the one who is called and will be made evident to all on the last day. In terms of content, μυστήριον refers primarily to the saving acts of God in Christ." Gillman, "Thematic Comparison," 444: "The mystery is an end-time reality which, according to divine counsel, must take place." For an unconvincing argument for accepting the variant reading, "we will not all be changed," in 15:51, see Sebastian Schneider, "1 Kor 15,51-52: Ein neuer Lösungsvorschlag zu einer alten Schwierigkeit," in *The Corinthian Correspondence* (ed. Reimund Bieringer; BETL 125; Louvain: Louvain University Press, 1996), 661–69.

26. Gillman, "Thematic Comparison," 443: "The instancy imagery 'in a moment, in the twinkling of an eye' (1) emphasizes the equality of the living and the dead, (2) excludes rival views wherein a gradual transformation is represented (cf. the later text, *2 Bar.* 50:1–51:10), and (3) highlights the miraculous, supraterrestrial and ineffable nature of the transformation event. The trumpet imagery marks the transformation as an event occurring on the last day."

27. Thiselton, *Corinthians*, 1296: "*The last trumpet* intensifies the metaphor of suddenness, adding the dimension of divine decree and ordered signal. In both Testaments (Exod 19:16; Zech 9:14; 1 Thess 4:16) manifestations of God are associated with the sound of *the trumpet*. Additionally, however, *the trumpet* awakens a sleeping army to be urgently roused to activity, in-

be clothed with incorruptibility and the body that is mortal to be clothed with immortality (15:53).[28] Not only is it a divine necessity for this to happen, but, as Paul immediately assures the audience with the words "and when" (ὅταν δέ), it will definitely happen as a future certainty (15:54a).[29]

The synonymous parallel between the corruptible being clothed with incorruptibility and the mortal being clothed with immortality in both 15:53 and 15:54a not only emphatically reinforces the expression but with the semantic progression to "mortal" or "subject to death" (θνητὸν) and "immortality" (ἀθανασίαν) prepares the audience for the assertion about "the death" (ὁ θάνατος) itself. The scriptural "word" of prophecy that is divinely "written" and thus must be fulfilled, "death is swallowed up in victory!" (15:54b), further convinces the audience that the divine "mystery" (15:51) of their transformation from what is corruptible and mortal to what is incorruptible and immortal not only "must" (15:53) but certainly will take place (15:54a).

The divine necessity for the corruptible and mortal body "to be clothed" (ἐνδύσασθαι, aorist middle functioning as divine passive) by God (15:53; cf. also 15:54a) presents the audience with imagery depicting how what is corruptible and mortal or subject to the power of death, the last enemy (15:26), is covered over or enveloped by incorruptibility and immortality, so that it can inherit the kingdom of God (15:50).[30] This clothing imagery is further developed by the swallowing imagery of the scriptural quotation in 15:54b. The audience is assured that at the end not only will "what is subject to death" (τὸ θνητὸν) be clothed, covered over, or enveloped by God (15:53–54a), but "the death" (ὁ θάνατος) itself will be

---

cluding possible battle when *the alert* is sounded. . . . Ambrosiaster understands the trumpet sound as a sound of triumph when the battle is over."

28. Gillman, "Thematic Comparison," 444: "The primary force implied by the δεῖ is the compulsion of divine authority. . . . The mysteries are those things which must happen. In the commentaries on 1 Corinthians the correspondence between δεῖ and μυστήριον is usually overlooked" (n. 15).

29. Gillman, "Thematic Comparison," 444: "The repetition of the mortal/immortal, corruptible/incorruptible and clothing terminology in v 54ab is not merely to connect ideas; it also signals a subtle, though significant, advance in the thought (cf. δέ). In v 53 the principle is laid down in paradigmatic fashion that the clothing event *must* take place. Behind v 54 lies the important assumption that, at some point in the future, it *will* take place. The use of ὅταν with the aorist subjunctive . . . points to future eventuality."

30. As noted by BDAG (334), the passive sense is preferable to the middle sense of ἐνδύω in 1 Cor 15:53–54a. Lockwood, *1 Corinthians*, 598: "Thus ἐνδύσασθαι with the passive meaning 'to be clothed' parallels the passive ἀλλαγησόμεθα ('we will be changed') in 15:51–52." On the clothing imagery here, Garland (*1 Corinthians*, 744 n. 5) notes: "Putting on garments of glory as a metaphor for eternal life is familiar in Jewish apocalyptic tradition (see 1 Enoch 62:15–16; 1QS 4:7–8)." See also Schrage, *Erste Brief*, 4.377.

"swallowed up" (κατεπόθη) by God in victory, so that death itself will totally disappear (15:54b), so that its "victory" and "sting" can be taunted (15:55).[31]

In sum, the scriptural quotation in 1 Cor 15:54b–55, "death is swallowed up in victory! Where, O death, is *your* victory? Where, O death, is *your* sting?" reinforces the audience's hope that (1) death as the last enemy will be destroyed (15:26); (2) death cannot claim its victory in preventing them, by its power to corrupt their bodies of "flesh and blood," from inheriting the incorruptible kingdom of God (15:50); (3) the divine "mystery" (15:51) of their transformation from what is corruptible and mortal to what is incorruptible and immortal not only "must" (15:53) but certainly will take place (15:54a); (4) at the end not only will "what is subject to death" be clothed, covered over, or enveloped by God (15:53–54a), but "the death" itself will be "swallowed up" by God in victory, so that death itself will totally disappear (15:54b) without "victory" or "sting" (15:55).

Relation to the Subsequent Context in 1 Corinthians 15:56–58

Employing a catchword connection with the scriptural quote's final taunt, "Where, O death, is *your* sting (κέντρον)?" (15:55b), Paul in 15:56 asserts that "the sting (κέντρον) of death is sin and the power of sin is the law."[32] Paul thus shifts his audience's attention from the scriptural quote's future taunting of death at the end when death is swallowed up in victory to the still-present menace of the enemy death through sin. Death as an apocalyptic power uses another apocalyptic power, sin, as its instrument to

---

31. Henning Paulsen, "ἐνδύω," *EDNT* 1.452: "Ἐνδύω's explicit eschatological character can be seen in 1 Cor 15:53f. The image of the garment is still resonant: the new garment is put on over the old garment, and death is 'swallowed up' by life." For a similar Pauline progression in imagery from "being clothed" to "being swallowed up," see 2 Cor 5:4; Gillman, "Thematic Comparison," 449.

32. For a discussion of the view that 15:56 is a later gloss, see F. W. Horn, "1 Korinther 15,56—Ein exegetischer Stachel," *ZNW* 82 (1991): 88–105. But, as Hollander and Holleman ("1 Cor 15:56," 271) point out, "nowadays there is an almost general agreement about the authenticity of verse 56." Collins, *First Corinthians*, 582: "[T]he verse is part of Paul's text. The remark is not incidental to his argument. It is his commentary on the pair of scriptural passages that he has woven into a single scripture." See also Thomas Söding, " 'Die Kraft der Sünde ist das Gesetz' (1 Kor 15,56): Anmerkungen zum Hintergrund und zur Pointe einer gesetzeskritischen Sentenz des Apostels Paulus," *ZNW* 83 (1992): 74–84. For an unconvincing attempt to translate 15:56 as "The sting of death is our error and the force against error is our Law," see J. M. García Pérez, "1 Co 15,56: ¿Una polémica contra la ley judía?" *EstBib* 60 (2002): 405–14.

inject the poisonous "sting" that brings about death.[33] This reminds the audience that the death that came from the first human, Adam (15:21-22), was a result of his sin (Gen 2:17; 3:6, 19).[34] Though they may look forward in confident hope to the scripture quote's future taunting of death's "sting," they presently still experience the death-bringing "sting" of the power of sin in their lives (6:18; 7:28, 36; 8:12; 15:3, 17, 34) through the law (9:8-9, 20; 14:21, 34) that makes sin a reality.[35]

Although we still experience the "sting" of death through our sins (15:56), in 15:57 Paul exclaims, "But thanks be to God who gives us the victory (τὸ νῖκος) through our Lord Jesus Christ!" The scriptural quote's future "victory" when "death is swallowed up in victory (νῖκος)!" (15:54b) is given by God to us—Paul, his audience, and all believers—through our Lord Jesus Christ, the one who died for our sins (15:3) and was raised from the dead so that we are no longer in our sins (15:17), the sins that inject us with the poisonous "sting" of death (15:56). That we have been given by God "the victory" (τὸ νῖκος), that *the* victory over death as the last enemy (15:26) is *ours*, intensifies the scriptural quote's taunt—"Where, O death, is *your* victory (τὸ νῖκος)?" (15:55a).[36]

In 15:58, Paul exhorts his Corinthian audience to "become firm,

---

33. Hollander and Holleman, "1 Cor 15:56," 277: "Death injects mortality in man, and the means by which it does so is sin.... According to Paul, there is a clear connection between death and sin, between the power of death and the power of sin, both being active in the life of mankind."

34. According to Collins (*First Corinthians*, 582), Paul is "convinced that death itself is the result of sin. This thought, which will be explicitly elaborated in his later letters (Romans, Galatians, Philippians), is a key element in his anthropology, derived from Judaism. Philo (*Creation* 134-169; *Questions on Genesis* 1.51) and Jewish apocalyptic (4 Ezra 3:7; 2 *Apoc. Bar.* 17:2-3) were at one in considering that the death of Adam was the result of his transgression." See also Hollander and Holleman, "1 Cor 15:56," 275-79.

35. Hollander and Holleman, "1 Cor 15:56," 276, 279: "In 1 Cor 15:54-55, Paul, too, derides death, but underlines that the triumph over death will be achieved not until the *parousia*. For the time being, death is still a power to be taken quite seriously.... The parallelism between verse 56a and 56b invites us to interpret δύναμις as the 'power' through which sin is brought about. The law is the stimulus of sin; it empowers men to sin. That is the meaning of verse 56b. In Paul's opinion, sin, being the sting of death, is incited by the law."

36. On 15:57, Thiselton (*Corinthians*, 1303-4) states: "Here is a classic illocutionary speech-act (an act performed *in* the saying of an utterance): Paul gives thanks for the gracious gift of victory over death and over death's empowerment by sin and by the law in alliance. It is an *act* of thanksgiving; a verbal equivalent to throwing one's arm around someone in gratitude; or like throwing one's hat in the air *in sheer exultation*.... [E]ven if the last resurrection is still future, the basis of the victory is a present gift, providing grounds for present exultation and thanksgiving. It is not a mere present of future certainty about resurrection; it also expresses the present gift of grace to believers for whom the destructive potential of sin, the law, and death as a terrifying prospect has been broken. The present reality is that the sting of death has been

unmovable, abounding in the work of the Lord always, knowing that your labor is not in vain in the Lord." They can be assured that their labor is not in vain in the Lord (κυρίῳ), so that they may abound in the work of the Lord (κυρίου), because it is through the resurrection of the Lord (κυρίου) Jesus Christ that they and all believers are given "*the* victory" by God (15:57)—the victory in which the power of death is completely swallowed up by God, as proclaimed in the scriptural quote in 15:54b–55. That the victory over death belongs to the audience ensures that their work (cf. 3:13–15; 9:1) and labor (cf. 3:8) in bringing others to faith and living it themselves is not "in vain" or "empty" (κενός) in the Lord (15:58).[37] Indeed, the preaching of the apostles is not in vain (κενόν), and the faith of the Corinthians is not in vain (κενή) (15:14), because they include an assured hope in the victory over death announced by the scriptural quote in 15:54b–55.

To sum up, although Paul's Corinthian audience may look forward in confident hope to the scripture quote's future taunting of death's "sting" (15:55b), they presently still experience the death-bringing "sting" of the power of sin in their lives through the law that makes sin a reality (15:56). But that we believers have been given by God "the victory" over death as the last enemy (15:26) so that *the* victory is *ours* (15:57) intensifies the scriptural quote's taunt—"Where, O death, is *your* victory?" (15:55a). And the audience can be assured that their evangelizing labor is not in vain in the Lord, so that they may abound in the work of the Lord (15:58), because it is through the resurrection of the Lord Jesus Christ that they and all believers are given "*the* victory" by God (15:57)—the victory in which the power of death that can render their work and lives meaningless is completely swallowed up by God, as proclaimed in the scriptural quote in 15:54b–55.

Summary on 1 Corinthians 15:54b–55

1. Using the exegetical device of *gezera shava*, Paul in 1 Cor 15:54b–55 adapted and combined two distinct scriptural texts, Isa 25:8a and Hos 13:14b, by the words "death" and "victory" that they have in common into a single scriptural quotation of prophecy that functions as a powerful

---

drawn out by Christ's victory. Believers already in some measure share in this victory, even though the final appropriation of all that this entails has yet to be appropriated and experienced fully at the last day."

37. Collins, *First Corinthians*, 583: "In Paul's rhetorical lexis 'work' and 'toil' are almost technical terms used to describe the work of evangelization. On the 'work' of the Corinthians see 3:10–17. It is a work of building up the community."

rhetorical unit whose authority is based not on any one particular scriptural text but on the authority of scripture in general.

2. The combined scriptural quotation in 1 Cor 15:54b–55, as God's authoritative "word" of prophecy destined to be fulfilled, assures the audience of God's final victory over the inimical power of death in the great cosmic battle for ultimate control of all of creation (15:54b), so that death has absolutely no claim to that final victory (15:55a) nor any poisonous or piercing power ultimately to harm the living (15:55b).

3. The scriptural quotation in 1 Cor 15:54b–55 reinforces the audience's hope that (1) death as the last enemy will be destroyed (15:26); (2) death cannot claim its victory in preventing them, by its power to corrupt their bodies of "flesh and blood," from inheriting the incorruptible kingdom of God (15:50); (3) the divine "mystery" (15:51) of their transformation from what is corruptible and mortal to what is incorruptible and immortal not only "must" (15:53) but certainly will take place (15:54a); (4) at the end not only will "what is subject to death" be clothed, covered over, or enveloped by God (15:53–54a) but "the death" itself will be "swallowed up" by God in victory, so that death itself will totally disappear (15:54b) without "victory" or "sting" (15:55).

4. Although Paul's Corinthian audience may look forward in confident hope to the scripture quote's future taunting of death's "sting" (15:55b), they presently still experience the death-bringing "sting" of the power of sin in their lives through the law that makes sin a reality (15:56). But that we believers have been given by God "the victory" over death so that *the* victory is *ours* (15:57) intensifies the scriptural quote's taunt—"Where, O death, is *your* victory?" (15:55a). And the audience can be assured that their evangelizing labor is not in vain in the Lord, so that they may abound in the work of the Lord (15:58), because it is through the resurrection of the Lord Jesus Christ that they and all believers are given "*the* victory" by God (15:57)—the victory in which the power of death that can render their work and lives meaningless is completely swallowed up by God, as proclaimed in the scriptural quote in 15:54b–55.

Chapter 18

Conclusion

In this concluding chapter we limit ourselves to the key generalizations regarding the rhetorical use of scripture in 1 Corinthians. For the details on each of the scriptural quotes or references see the summary at the end of each of the preceding chapters.

In his scriptural references in 1 Corinthians, Paul presupposes his audience's acceptance not only of the divine authority of the Jewish scriptures but of the interrelation of all scriptural texts. The significance of each scriptural quote or reference derives not only from a particular context within the scriptures but from the global context of all the scriptures. Just as important as the original context of each scriptural quote or reference is its interrelation with other similar scriptural texts within the whole of the scriptures. Each scriptural quote or reference thereby speaks with the divine authority of the scriptures in general.

Each scriptural quote or reference in 1 Corinthians impacts the audience not only with its divine authority but with its rhetorical power. In some cases Paul has skillfully adapted or reshaped his scriptural quotes and references to enhance their rhetorical effectiveness for the particular purposes of his argumentative strategy. Paul thus relies not only upon the divine authority but upon the rhetorical effectiveness of each of his scriptural quotes or references to engage and powerfully persuade his Corinthian audience.

Each scriptural quote or reference in 1 Corinthians plays a key rhetorical role in relation to both its antecedent and subsequent epistolary contexts. There is at least one scriptural quote or reference in each of the main rhetorical units of the letter. In some cases the scriptural quote or reference is part of a carefully constructed chiastic structure. But in all cases the scriptural quotes and references are intricately and elegantly embedded as effective rhetorical elements within Paul's various rhetorical strategies that powerfully persuade his audience in his first letter to the Corinthians.

Bibliography

Aageson, James W. *Written Also for Our Sake: Paul and the Art of Biblical Interpretation*. Louisville: Westminster John Knox, 1993.
Adams, Edward. *Constructing the World: A Study in Paul's Cosmological Language*. Edinburgh: Clark, 2000.
Adeyemi, M. E. "The Rulers of This Age in First Corinthians 2:6–8: An Exegetical Exposition." *Deltion Biblikon Meleton* 28 (1999): 38–45.
Alexander, Loveday. "IPSE DIXIT: Citation of Authority in Paul and in the Jewish and Hellenistic Schools." Pp. 103–27 in *Paul beyond the Judaism/Hellenism Divide*. Edited by Troels Engberg-Pedersen. Louisville: Westminster John Knox, 2001.
Alter, Robert. *The Art of Biblical Poetry*. New York: Basic, 1985.
Amador, J. David Hester. *Academic Constraints in Rhetorical Criticism of the New Testament: An Introduction to a Rhetoric of Power*. JSNTSup 174. Sheffield: Sheffield Academic Press, 1999.
Anderson, R. Dean. *Ancient Rhetorical Theory and Paul: Revised Edition*. CBET 18. Louvain: Peeters, 1998.
Asher, Jeffrey R. *Polarity and Change in 1 Corinthians 15: A Study of Metaphysics, Rhetoric, and Resurrection*. HUT 42. Tübingen: Mohr Siebeck, 2000.
———. "Σπείρεται: Paul's Anthropogenic Metaphor in 1 Corinthains 15:42–44." *JBL* 120 (2001): 101–22.
Aune, David E. "Chiasmus." Pp. 93–96 in *The Westminster Dictionary of New Testament and Early Christian Literature and Rhetoric*. Louisville: Westminster John Knox, 2003.
Austin, John Langshaw. *How to Do Things with Words*. Cambridge: Harvard University Press, 1962.
Bailey, Kenneth E. "Paul's Theological Foundation for Human Sexuality: I Cor. 6:9–20 in the Light of Rhetorical Criticism." *Near East School of Theology Theological Review* 3 (1980): 27–41.
Baldanza, Giuseppe. "L'uso della metafora sponsale in 1 Cor 6,12–20: Riflessi sull'ecclesiologia." *Rivista biblica italiana* 46 (1998): 317–40.
Balz, Horst. "ἅγιος." *EDNT* 1:16–20.
———. "μάταιος." *EDNT* 2:396.
Barclay, John M. G. "Matching Theory and Practice: Josephus's Constitutional Ideal and Paul's Strategy in Corinth." Pp. 139–63 in *Paul beyond the Judaism/Hellenism Divide*. Edited by Troels Engberg-Pedersen. Louisville: Westminster John Knox, 2001.

Barnett, Paul. "Paul, Apologist to the Corinthians." Pp. 313–26 in *Paul and the Corinthians: Studies on a Community in Conflict: Essays in Honour of Margaret Thrall*. Edited by Trevor J. Burke and J. Keith Elliott. NovTSup 109. Leiden: Brill, 2003.

Barrett, Charles K. "Boasting (καυχᾶσθαι, κτλ.) in the Pauline Epistles." Pp. 363–68 in *L'Apôtre Paul: Personnalité, style et conception du ministère*. Edited by Albert Vanhoye. BETL 73. Louvain: Louvain University Press, 1986.

———. *A Commentary on the First Epistle to the Corinthians*. HNTC. New York: Harper & Row, 1968.

———. "Sectarian Diversity at Corinth." Pp. 287–302 in *Paul and the Corinthians: Studies on a Community in Conflict. Essays in Honour of Margaret Thrall*. Edited by Trevor J. Burke and J. Keith Elliott. NovTSup 109. Leiden: Brill, 2003.

BeDuhn, Jason David. "'Because of the Angels': Unveiling Paul's Anthropology in 1 Corinthians 11." *JBL* 118 (1999): 295–320.

Belleville, Linda L. "Κεφαλή and the Thorny Issue of Headcovering in 1 Corinthians 11:2–16." Pp. 215–31 in *Paul and the Corinthians: Studies on a Community in Conflict. Essays in Honour of Margaret Thrall*. Edited by Trevor J. Burke and J. Keith Elliott. NovTSup 109. Leiden: Brill, 2003.

Bender, Wilhelm. "Bemerkungen zur Übersetzung von 1 Korinther 1:30." *ZNW* 71 (1980): 263–68.

Berger, Klaus. "Zur Diskussion über die Herkunft von I Kor. ii. 9." *NTS* 24 (1978): 270–83.

Berkley, Timothy W. *From a Broken Covenant to Circumcision of the Heart: Pauline Intertextual Exegesis in Romans 2:17–29*. SBLDS 175. Atlanta: Society of Biblical Literature, 2000.

Betz, Otto. "Der gekreuzigte Christus, unsere Weisheit und Gerechtigkeit (Der alttestamentliche Hintergrund von 1.Korinther 1–2)." Pp. 195–215 in *Tradition and Interpretation in the New Testament: Essays in Honor of E. Earle Ellis for His Sixtieth Birthday*. Edited by Gerald F. Hawthorne and Otto Betz. Grand Rapids: Eerdmans, 1987.

Binder, Donald D. *Into the Temple Courts: The Place of the Synagogues in the Second Temple Period*. SBLDS 169. Atlanta: Society of Biblical Literature, 1999.

Black, David Alan. *Paul, Apostle of Weakness: Astheneia and Its Cognates in the Pauline Literature*. New York: Lang, 1984.

Blattenberger, David E. *Rethinking 1 Corinthians 11:2–16 through Archaeological and Moral-Rhetorical Analysis*. Studies in the Bible and Early Christianity 36. Lewiston, N.Y.: Mellen, 1997.

Blomberg, Craig L. "The Structure of 2 Corinthians 1–7." *CTR* 4 (1989): 3–20.

Bonneau, Normand. "The Logic of Paul's Argument on the Resurrection Body in 1 Cor 15:35–44a." *Science et esprit* 45 (1993): 79–92.

Borghi, Ernesto. "La notion de conscience dans le Nouveau Testament: Une proposition de lecture." *Filologia Neotestamentaria* 10 (1997): 85–98.

Botha, S. P. "1 Korintiërs 15:49b: 'n Hortatief–of futurumlesing? (1 Corinthians

15:49b: A Hortative or Future Reading?)." *Hervormde teologiese studies* 49 (1993): 760–74.
Braxton, Brad Ronnell. *The Tyranny of Resolution: 1 Corinthians 7:17–24*. SBLDS 181. Atlanta: Society of Biblical Literature, 2000.
Brewer, David Instone. "1 Corinthians 9.9–11: A Literal Interpretation of 'Do Not Muzzle the Ox.'" *NTS* 38 (1992): 554–65.
———. *Techniques and Assumptions in Jewish Exegesis Before 70 CE*. TSAJ 30. Tübingen: Mohr Siebeck, 1992.
Brodeur, Scott. *The Holy Spirit's Agency in the Resurrection of the Dead: An Exegetico-Theological Study of 1 Corinthians 15,44b–49 and Romans 8,9–13*. Tesi Gregoriana: Serie Teologia 14. Rome: Gregorian University Press, 1996.
Brodie, Thomas L. "The Systematic Use of the Pentateuch in 1 Corinthians." Pp. 441–57 in *The Corinthian Correspondence*. Edited by Reimund Bieringer. BETL 125. Louvain: Louvain University Press, 1996.
Brown, Alexandra R. *The Cross and Human Transformation: Paul's Apocalyptic Word in 1 Corinthians*. Minneapolis: Fortress, 1995.
Bryant, Robert A. *The Risen Crucified Christ in Galatians*. SBLDS 185. Atlanta: Society of Biblical Literature, 2001.
Bullmore, Michael A. *St. Paul's Theology of Rhetorical Style: An Examination of I Corinthians 2.1–5 in the Light of First Century Graeco-Roman Rhetorical Culture*. San Francisco: International Scholars, 1995.
Button, M. Bruce, and Fika J. van Rensburg. "The 'House Churches' in Corinth." *Neot* 37 (2003): 1–28.
Bünker, Michael. *Briefformular und rhetorische Disposition im 1 Korintherbrief*. GTA 28. Göttingen: Vandenhoeck & Ruprecht, 1984.
Byrne, Brendan. "Sinning against One's Own Body: Paul's Understanding of the Sexual Relationship in 1 Corinthians 6:18." *CBQ* 45 (1983): 608–16.
Byron, John. "Slave of Christ or Willing Servant? Paul's Self-Description in 1 Corinthians 4:1–2 and 9:16–18." *Neot* 37 (2003): 179–98.
Callan, Terrence. "Psalm 110:1 and the Origin of the Expectation That Jesus Will Come Again." *CBQ* 44 (1982): 622–36.
Callow, Kathleen. "The Disappearing Δέ in 1 Corinthians." Pp. 183–93 in *Linguistics and New Testament Interpretation: Essays on Discourse Analysis*. Edited by David Alan Black, Katherine Barnwell, and Stephen Levinsohn. Nashville: Broadman, 1992.
———. "Patterns of Thematic Development in 1 Corinthians 5:1–13." Pp. 194–206 in *Linguistics and New Testament Interpretation: Essays on Discourse Analysis*. Edited by David Alan Black, Katherine Barnwell, and Stephen Levinsohn. Nashville: Broadman, 1992.
Campbell, Barth. "Flesh and Spirit in 1 Cor 5:5: An Exercise in Rhetorical Criticism of the NT." *JETS* 36 (1993): 331–42.
Caragounis, Chrys C. "ΟΨΩΝΙΟΝ: A Reconsideration of Its Meaning." *NovT* 16 (1974): 35–57.
Carr, Wesley A. "The Rulers of This Age—I Corinthians II.6–8." *NTS* 23 (1976): 20–35.

Carter, Warren. *Matthew and Empire: Initial Explorations*. Harrisburg, Pa.: Trinity Press International, 2001.

Carter, Warren, and John Paul Heil. *Matthew's Parables: Audience-Oriented Perspectives*. CBQMS 30. Washington, D.C.: Catholic Biblical Association, 1998.

Cervin, Richard S. "Does Κεφαλή Mean 'Source' or 'Authority Over' in Greek Literature? A Rebuttal." *TJ* 10 (1989): 85–112.

Chester, Stephen J. *Conversion at Corinth: Perspectives on Conversion in Paul's Theology and the Corinthian Church*. London: Clark, 2003.

Cheung, Alex T. *Idol Food in Corinth: Jewish Background and Pauline Legacy*. JSNTSup 176. Sheffield: Sheffield Academic Press, 1999.

Chow, John K. *Patronage and Power: A Study of Social Networks in Corinth*. JSNTSup 75. Sheffield: JSOT, 1992.

Ciampa, Roy E. *The Presence and Function of Scripture in Galatians 1 and 2*. WUNT 102. Tübingen: Mohr Siebeck, 1998.

Clarke, Andrew D. *Secular and Christian Leadership in Corinth: A Socio-historical and Exegetical Study of 1 Corinthians 1–6*. AGJU 18. Leiden: Brill, 1993.

———. *Serve the Community of the Church: Christians as Leaders and Ministers*. Grand Rapids: Eerdmans, 2000.

Classen, Carl Joachim. *Rhetorical Criticism of the New Testament*. WUNT 128. Tübingen: Mohr Siebeck, 2000.

Collier, Gary D. "'That We Might Not Crave Evil': The Structure and Argument of 1 Corinthians 10.1–13." *JSNT* 55 (1994): 55–75.

Collins, Raymond F. *First Corinthians*. SP 7. Collegeville, Minn.: Liturgical Press, 1999.

———. "'It Was Indeed Written for Our Sake' (1 Cor 9,10): Paul's Use of Scripture in the First Letter to the Corinthians." *SNTSU* 20 (1995): 151–70.

Conzelmann, Hans. *1 Corinthians*. Hermeneia. Philadelphia: Fortress, 1975.

Corrington, Gail Paterson. "The 'Headless Woman': Paul and the Language of the Body in 1 Cor 11:1–16." *PRSt* 18 (1991): 223–31.

Cranfield, C. E. B. *A Critical and Exegetical Commentary on the Epistle to the Romans*. 2 vols. ICC. Edinburgh: Clark, 1975, 1979.

Dautzenberg, Gerhard. "γλῶσσα." *EDNT* 1.251–55.

———. "διακρίνω." *EDNT* 1:305–7.

Davis, James A. *Wisdom and Spirit: An Investigation of 1 Corinthians 1.18–3.20 against the Background of Jewish Sapiential Traditions in the Greco-Roman Period*. Lanham, Md.: University Press of America, 1984.

Dawes, Gregory W. "The Danger of Idolatry: First Corinthians 8:7–13." *CBQ* 58 (1996): 82–98.

de Boer, Martinus C. *The Defeat of Death: Apocalyptic Eschatology in 1 Corinthians 15 and Romans 5*. JSNTSup 22. Sheffield: JSOT, 1988.

———. "Paul's Use of a Resurrection Tradition in 1 Cor 15,20–28." Pp. 639–51 in *The Corinthian Correspondence*. Edited by Reimund Bieringer. BETL 125. Louvain: Louvain University Press, 1996.

de Vos, Craig Steven. *Church and Community Conflicts: The Relationships of the*

Thessalonian, Corinthian, and Philippian Churches with Their Wider Civic Communities. SBLDS 168. Atlanta: Scholars Press, 1999.
———. "Stepmothers, Concubines, and the Case of Πορνεία in 1 Corinthians 5." *NTS* 44 (1998): 104–14.
Delobel, Joël. "Coherence and Relevance of 1 Cor 8–10." Pp. 177–90 in *The Corinthian Correspondence.* Edited by Reimund Beiringer. BETL 125. Louvain: Louvain University Press, 1996.
———. "1 Cor 11,2–16: Towards a Coherent Interpretation." Pp. 369–89 in *L'Apôtre Paul: Personnalité, style et conception du ministère.* Edited by Albert Vanhoye. BETL 73. Louvain: Louvain University Press, 1986.
Deming, Will. "The Unity of 1 Corinthians 5–6." *JBL* 115 (1996): 289–312.
Derrett, J. Duncan M. "Right and Wrong Sticking (1 Cor 6,18)?" *EstBib* 55 (1997): 89–106.
Dewey, Joanna. "Textuality in an Oral Culture: A Survey of the Pauline Traditions." *Semeia* 65 (1995): 37–65. The theme of the issue is "Orality and Textuality in Early Christian Literature."
Dodd, Brian J. "Paul's Paradigmatic 'I' and 1 Corinthians 6.12." *JSNT* 59 (1995): 39–58.
Donaldson, Terence L. *Paul and the Gentiles: Remapping the Apostle's Convictional World.* Minneapolis: Fortress, 1997.
Dunn, James D. G. "I Corinthians 15:45—Last Adam, Life-Giving Spirit." Pp. 127–41 in *Christ and Spirit in the New Testament: In Honour of Charles Francis Digby Moule.* Edited by Barnabas Lindars and Stephen S. Smalley. Cambridge: Cambridge University Press, 1973.
———. *Jesus and the Spirit: A Study of the Religious and Charismatic Experience of Jesus and the First Christians as Reflected in the New Testament.* London: SCM, 1975.
Eastman, Brad. *The Significance of Grace in the Letters of Paul.* Studies in Biblical Literature 11. New York: Lang, 1999.
Elliott, John H. "The Jesus Movement Was Not Egalitarian but Family-Oriented." *BibInt* 11 (2003): 173–210.
Ellis, E. Earle. *Paul's Use of the Old Testament.* Edinburgh: Oliver and Boyd, 1957.
———. "*Soma* in First Corinthians." *Int* 44 (1990): 132–44.
Engberg-Pedersen, Troels. "1 Corinthians 11:16 and the Character of Pauline Exhortation." *JBL* 110 (1991): 679–89.
Engels, Donald. *Roman Corinth: An Alternative Model for the Classical City.* Chicago: University of Chicago Press, 1990.
Enns, P. E. "The 'Movable Well' in 1 Corinthians 10:4: An Extra-biblical Tradition in an Apostolic Text." *BBR* 6 (1996): 23–38.
Eriksson, Anders. "Elaboration of Argument in 1 Cor 15:20–34." *SEÅ* 64 (1999): 101–14.
———. "Fear of Eternal Damnation: *Pathos* Appeal in 1 Corinthians 15 and 16." Pp. 115–26 in *Paul and Pathos.* Edited by Thomas H. Olbricht and Jerry L. Sumney. Atlanta: Society of Biblical Literature, 2001.

———. *Traditions as Rhetorical Proof: Pauline Argumentation in 1 Corinthians.* ConBNT 29. Stockholm: Almqvist & Wiksell, 1998.
Fatehi, Mehrdad. *The Spirit's Relation to the Risen Lord in Paul: An Examination of Its Christological Implications.* WUNT 128. Tübingen: Mohr Siebeck, 2000.
Fatum, Lone. "Image of God and Glory of Man: Women in the Pauline Congregations." Pp. 50–133 in *The Image of God: Gender Models in Judeo-Christian Tradition.* Edited by Kari Elisabeth Børresen. Minneapolis: Fortress, 1995.
Fee, Gordon D. *The First Epistle to the Corinthians.* NICNT. Grand Rapids: Eerdmans, 1987.
Fernández Marcos, Natalio. *The Septuagint in Context: Introduction to the Greek Versions of the Bible.* Leiden: Brill, 2000.
Fiore, Benjamin. "'Covert Allusion' in 1 Corinthians 1–4." *CBQ* 47 (1985): 85–102.
———. *The Function of Personal Example in the Socratic and Pastoral Epistles.* AnBib 105. Rome: Biblical Institute, 1986.
———. "Passion in Paul and Plutarch: 1 Corinthians 5–6 and the Polemic against Epicureans." Pp. 135–43 in *Greeks, Romans, and Christians: Essays in Honor of Abraham J. Malherbe.* Edited by David L. Balch, Everett Ferguson, and Wayne A. Meeks. Minneapolis: Fortress, 1990.
Fisk, Bruce N. "Eating Meat Offered to Idols: Corinthian Behavior and Pauline Response in 1 Corinthians 8–10." *TJ* 10 (1989): 49–70.
———. "ΠΟΡΝΕΥΕΙΝ as Body Violation: The Unique Nature of Sexual Sin in 1 Corinthians 6.18." *NTS* 42 (1996): 540–58.
Fitzmyer, Joseph A. "Another Look at ΚΕΦΑΛΗ in 1 Corinthians 11.3." *NTS* 35 (1989): 503–11.
———. "A Feature of Qumran Angelology and the Angels of 1 Cor 11:10." *NTS* 4 (1957–58): 48–58.
———. "*Kephale* in I Corinthians 11:3." *Int* 47 (1993): 52–59.
———. *Romans: A New Translation with Introduction and Commentary.* AB 33. New York: Doubleday, 1993.
Foley, John Miles. *Immanent Art: From Structure to Meaning in Traditional Oral Epic.* Bloomington: Indiana University Press, 1991.
Fotopoulos, John. *Food Offered to Idols in Roman Corinth: A Social-Rhetorical Reconsideration of 1 Corinthians 8:1–11:1.* WUNT 151. Tübingen: Mohr Siebeck, 2003.
Frankemölle, Hubert. "ἀντί." *EDNT* 1.108–9.
———. "λαός." *EDNT* 2.339–44.
Frid, Bo. "The Enigmatic ΑΛΛΑ in 1 Corinthians 2.9." *NTS* 31 (1985): 603–11.
Friedrich, Gerhard. "δύναμις." *EDNT* 1.355–58.
Friedrich, Johannes H. "κληρονομέω." *EDNT* 2.298–99.
Gaffin, Richard B. "'Life-Giving Spirit': Probing the Center of Paul's Pneumatology." *JETS* 41 (1998): 573–89.
García, J. M. "Acontecimientos después de la venida gloriosa (1 Cor 15,23–28)." *EstBib* 58 (2000): 527–59.
García Pérez, J. M. "1 Co 15,56: ¿Una polémica contra la ley judía?" *EstBib* 60 (2002): 405–14.
Gardner, Paul Douglas. *The Gifts of God and the Authentication of a Christian: An*

Exegetical Study of 1 Corinthians 8–11:1. Lanham, Md.: University Press of America, 1994.
Garland, David E. *1 Corinthians*. BECNT. Grand Rapids: Baker, 2003.
———. "The Dispute Over Food Sacrificed to Idols (1 Cor 8:1–11:1)." *PRSt* 30 (2003): 173–97.
Gathercole, Simon J. *Where Is Boasting? Early Jewish Soteriology and Paul's Response in Romans 1–5*. Grand Rapids: Eerdmans, 2002.
Gielen, Marlis. "Beten und Prophezeien mit unverhülltem Kopf? Die Kontroverse zwischen Paulus und der korinthischen Gemeinde um die Wahrung der Geschlechtsrollensymbolik in 1Kor 11,2–16." *ZNW* 90 (1999): 220–49.
———. "Universale Totenauferweckung und universales Heil? 1 Kor 15,20–28 im Kontext paulinischer Theologie." *BZ* 47 (2003): 86–104.
Gill, David W. J. "The Importance of Roman Portraiture for Head-Coverings in 1 Corinthians 11:2–16." *TynBul* 41 (1990): 245–60.
———. "In Search of the Social Elite in the Corinthian Church." *TynBul* 44 (1993): 323–37.
———. "The Meat-Market at Corinth (1 Corinthians 10:25)." *TynBul* 43 (1992): 389–93.
Gillman, John. "A Thematic Comparison: 1 Cor 15:50–57 and 2 Cor 5:1–5." *JBL* 107 (1988): 439–54.
———. "Transformation in 1 Cor 15,50–53." *ETL* 58 (1982): 309–33.
Given, Mark D. *Paul's True Rhetoric: Ambiguity, Cunning, and Deception in Greece and Rome*. Emory Studies in Early Christianity 7. Harrisburg, Pa.: Trinity Press International, 2001.
Gladstone, Robert J. "Sign Language in the Assembly: How Are Tongues a Sign to the Unbeliever in 1 Cor 14:20–25?" *Asian Journal of Pentecostal Studies* 2 (1999): 177–94.
Gooch, Peter David. *Dangerous Food: 1 Corinthians 8–10 in Its Context*. Studies in Christianity and Judaism 5. Waterloo, Ontario: Wilfrid Laurier University Press, 1993.
Goodwin, Mark J. *Paul, Apostle of the Living God: Kerygma and Conversion in 2 Corinthians*. Harrisburg, Pa.: Trinity Press International, 2001.
Gorman, Michael J. *Apostle of the Crucified Lord: A Theological Introduction to Paul and His Letters*. Grand Rapids: Eerdmans, 2004.
———. *Cruciformity: Paul's Narrative Spirituality of the Cross*. Grand Rapids: Eerdmans, 2001.
Goulder, Michael D. "Libertines? (1 Cor. 5–6)." *NovT* 41 (1999): 334–48.
———. *Paul and the Competing Mission in Corinth*. Peabody, Mass.: Hendrickson, 2001.
Gräbe, Petrus J. *The Power of God in Paul's Letters*. WUNT 123. Tübingen: Mohr Siebeck, 2000.
Grant, Robert M. *Paul in the Roman World: The Conflict at Corinth*. Louisville: Westminster John Knox, 2001.
Grindheim, Sigurd. "Wisdom for the Perfect: Paul's Challenge to the Corinthian Church (1 Corinthians 2:6–16)." *JBL* 121 (2002): 689–709.

Grudem, Wayne A. "1 Corinthians 14.20–25: Prophecy and Tongues as Signs of God's Attitude." *WTJ* 41 (1979): 381–96.
———. "Does *Kephale* ('Head') Mean 'Source' or 'Authority Over' in Greek Literature? A Survey of 2,336 Examples." *TJ* 6 (1985): 38–59.
———. *The Gift of Prophecy in 1 Corinthians*. Washington, D.C.: University Press of America, 1982.
———. "The Meaning of Κεφαλή ('Head'): A Response to Recent Studies." *TJ* 11 (1990): 3–72.
Gundry-Volf, Judith M. "Gender and Creation in 1 Corinthians 11:2–16: A Study in Paul's Theological Method." Pp. 151–71 in *Evangelium, Schriftauslegung, Kirche: Festschrift für Peter Stuhlmacher zum 65. Geburtstag*. Edited by Jostein Ådna, Scott J. Hafemann, and Otfried Hofius. Göttingen: Vandenhoeck & Ruprecht, 1997.
Hall, David R. "A Disguise for the Wise: μετασχηματισμός in 1 Corinthians 4.6." *NTS* 40 (1994): 143–49.
Hanges, James C. "1 Corinthians 4:6 and the Possibility of Written Bylaws in the Corinthian Church." *JBL* 117 (1998): 275–98.
Harland, P. J. "Menswear and Womenswear: A Study of Deut 22:5." *ExpTim* 110 (1998): 73–76.
Harris, Gerald. "The Beginnings of Church Discipline: 1 Corinthians 5." *NTS* 37 (1991): 1–21.
Harrisville, Roy A. *I Corinthians*. ACNT. Minneapolis: Augsburg, 1987.
Harvey, John D. *Listening to the Text: Oral Patterning in Paul's Letters*. Grand Rapids: Baker, 1998.
Hay, David M. *Glory at the Right Hand: Psalm 110 in Early Christianity*. SBLMS 18. Nashville: Abingdon, 1973.
Hays, Richard B. "The Conversion of the Imagination: Scripture and Eschatology in 1 Corinthians." *NTS* 45 (1999): 391–412.
———. *Echoes of Scripture in the Letters of Paul*. New Haven: Yale University Press, 1989.
———. *First Corinthians*. Interpretation. Louisville: Knox, 1997.
Hegermann, Harald. "σοφία." *EDNT* 3:258–61.
———. "σοφός." *EDNT* 3:261–62.
Heil, John Paul. "The Chiastic Structure and Meaning of Paul's Letter to Philemon." *Bib* 82 (2001): 178–206.
Heil, Uta. "Theo-logische Interpretation von 1 Kor 15,23–28." *ZNW* 84 (1993): 27–35.
Hengel, Martin. *The Four Gospels and the One Gospel of Jesus Christ: An Investigation of the Collection and Origin of the Canonical Gospels*. Harrisburg, Pa.: Trinity Press International, 2000.
Hester, James D. "Speaker, Audience, and Situations: A Modified Interactional Model." *Neot* 32 (1998): 75–94.
Hickling, C. J. A. "Paul's Use of Exodus in the Corinthian Correspondence." Pp. 367–76 in *The Corinthian Correspondence*. Edited by Reimund Bieringer. BETL 125. Louvain: Louvain University Press, 1996.

Hill, Charles E. "Paul's Understanding of Christ's Kingdom in I Corinthians 15:20–28." *NovT* 30 (1988): 297–320.
Hjort, Birgitte Graakjaer. "Gender Hierarchy or Religious Androgyny? Male-Female Interaction in the Corinthian Community—A Reading of 1 Cor. 11,2–16." *ST* 55 (2001): 58–80.
Hodgens, David. "Our Resurrection Body: An Exegesis of 1 Corinthians 15:42–49." *Melanesian Journal of Theology* 17 (2001): 65–90.
Hofius, Otfried. "βλασφημία." *EDNT* 1.219–21.
———. "Das Zitat 1 Kor 2,9 und das koptische Testament des Jakob." *ZNW* 66 (1975): 140–42.
Holland, Glenn. "Paul's Use of Irony as a Rhetorical Technique." Pp. 234–48 in *The Rhetorical Analysis of Scripture: Essays from the 1995 London Conference*. Edited by Stanley E. Porter and Thomas H. Olbricht. JSNTSup 146. Sheffield: Sheffield Academic Press, 1997.
Hollander, Harm W. "The Meaning of the Term 'Law' (ΝΟΜΟΣ) in 1 Corinthians." *NovT* 40 (1998): 117–35.
Hollander, Harm W., and Joost Holleman. "The Relationship of Death, Sin, and Law in 1 Cor 15:56." *NovT* 35 (1993): 270–91.
Holleman, Joost. "Jesus' Resurrection as the Beginning of the Eschatological Resurrection (1 Cor 15,20)." Pp. 653–60 in *The Corinthian Correspondence*. Edited by Reimund Bieringer. BETL 125. Louvain: Louvain University Press, 1996.
———. *Resurrection and Parousia: A Traditio-Historical Study of Paul's Eschatology in 1 Corinthians 15*. NovTSup 84. Leiden: Brill, 1996.
Holmyard, Harold R. "Does 1 Corinthians 11:2–16 Refer to Women Praying and Prophesying in Church?" *BSac* 154 (1997): 461–72.
Horn, F. W. "1 Korinther 15,56—Ein exegetischer Stachel." *ZNW* 82 (1991): 88–105.
Horrell, David G. "Domestic Space and Christian Meetings at Corinth: Imagining New Contexts and the Buildings East of the Theatre." *NTS* 50 (2004): 349–69.
———. "'The Lord Commanded . . . but I Have Not Used . . .': Exegetical and Hermeneutical Reflections on 1 Cor 9.14–15." *NTS* 43 (1997): 587–603.
Horsley, Richard A. *1 Corinthians*. Nashville: Abingdon, 1998.
———. "Rhetoric and Empire—and 1 Corinthians." Pp. 72–102 in *Paul and Politics: Ekklesia, Israel, Imperium, Interpretation. Essays in Honor of Krister Stendahl*. Edited by Richard A. Horsley. Harrisburg, Pa.: Trinity Press International, 2000.
Hughes, Frank Witt. "Rhetorical Criticism and the Corinthian Correspondence." Pp. 336–50 in *The Rhetorical Analysis of Scripture: Essays from the 1995 London Conference*. Edited by Stanley E. Porter and Thomas H. Olbricht. JSNTSup 146. Sheffield: Sheffield Academic Press, 1997.
———. "The Rhetoric of Letters." Pp. 194–240 in *The Thessalonians Debate: Methodological Discord or Methodological Synthesis?* Edited by Karl P. Donfried and Johannes Beutler. Grand Rapids: Eerdmans, 2000.
Hultgren, Stephen J. "The Origin of Paul's Doctrine of the Two Adams in 1 Corinthians 15.45–49." *JSNT* 25, no. 3 (2003): 343–70.

Hyldahl, Niels. "Paul and Hellenistic Judaism in Corinth." Pp. 204–16 in *The New Testament and Hellenistic Judaism*. Edited by Peder Borgen and Søren Giverson. Peabody, Mass.: Hendrickson, 1995.
Ince, Gwen. "Judge for Yourselves: Teasing Out Some Knots in 1 Corinthians 11:2–16." *ABR* 48 (2000): 59–71.
Jacobs, Lambert D. "Establishing a New Value System in Corinth: 1 Corinthians 5–6 as Persuasive Argument." Pp. 374–87 in *The Rhetorical Analysis of Scripture: Essays from the 1995 London Conference*. Edited by Stanley E. Porter and Thomas H. Olbricht. JSNTSup 146. Sheffield: Sheffield Academic Press, 1997.
Jeremias, Joachim. "Flesh and Blood Cannot Inherit the Kingdom of God (1 Cor 15.50)." *NTS* 2 (1955–56): 151–59.
Jervis, L. Ann. " 'But I Want You to Know . . .': Paul's Midrashic Intertextual Response to the Corinthian Worshipers (1 Cor 11:2–16)." *JBL* 112 (1993): 231–46.
Jewett, Robert. *Paul's Anthropological Terms: A Study of Their Use in Conflict Sayings*. AGJU 10. Leiden: Brill, 1971.
Jobes, Karen H., and Moisés Silva. *Invitation to the Septuagint*. Grand Rapids: Baker Academic, 2000.
Johanson, Bruce C. "Tongues, a Sign for Unbelievers? A Structural and Exegetical Study of I Corinthians xiv. 20–25." *NTS* 25 (1979): 180–203.
Johnson, Andy. "Firstfruits and Death's Defeat: Metaphor in Paul's Rhetorical Strategy in 1 Cor 15:20–28." *WW* 16 (1996): 456–64.
———. "Turning the World Upside Down in 1 Corinthians 15: Apocalyptic Epistemology, the Resurrected Body, and the New Creation." *EvQ* 75 (2003): 291–309.
Kaiser, W. C. "The Current Crisis in Exegesis and the Apostolic Use of Deuteronomy 25:4 in 1 Corinthians 9:8–10." *JETS* 21 (1978): 3–18.
Kammler, Hans-Christian. *Kreuz und Weisheit: Eine exegetische Untersuchung zu 1 Kor 1,10–3,4*. WUNT 159. Tübingen: Mohr Siebeck, 2003.
Ker, D. P. "Paul and Apollos—Colleagues or Rivals?" *JSNT* 77 (2000): 75–97.
Kertelge, Karl. "ἀπολύτρωσις." *EDNT* 1:138–40.
———. "δικαιοσύνη." *EDNT* 1:325–30.
Kim, Seyoon. "*Imitatio Christ* (1 Corinthians 11:1): How Paul Imitates Jesus Christ in Dealing with Idol Food (1 Corinthians 8–10)." *BBR* 13 (2003): 193–226.
———. *Paul and the New Perspective: Second Thoughts on the Origin of Paul's Gospel*. Grand Rapids: Eerdmans, 2002.
Kirchhoff, Renate. *Die Sünde gegen den eigenen Leib: Studien zu πόρνη und πορνεία in 1 Kor 6,12–20 und dem sozio-kulturellen Kontext der paulinischen Adressaten*. Studien zur Umwelt des Neuen Testaments 18. Göttingen: Vandenhoeck & Ruprecht, 1994.
Kistemaker, Simon J. " 'Deliver This Man to Satan' (1 Cor 5:5): A Case Study in Church Discipline." *Master's Seminary Journal* 3 (1992): 33–46.
Klauck, Hans-Josef. "Mit Engelszungen? Vom Charisma der verständlichen Rede in 1 Kor 14." *ZTK* 97 (2000): 276–99.
Klein, George L. "Hos 3:1–3—Background to 1 Cor 6:19b–20." *CTR* 3 (1989): 373–75.
Koch, Dietrich-Alex. " 'Alles, was ἐν μακέλλῳ verkauft wird, eβt . . .': Die *macella* von

Pompeji, Gerasa und Korinth und ihre Bedeutung für die Auslegung von 1Kor 10,25." *ZNW* 90 (1999): 194–219.

———. *Die Schrift als Zeuge des Evangeliums: Untersuchungen zur Verwendung und zum Verständnis der Schrift bei Paulus.* BHT 69. Tübingen: Mohr Siebeck, 1986.

Koet, Bart J. "As Close to the Synagogue as Can Be: Paul in Corinth (Acts 18,1–18)." Pp. 397–415 in *The Corinthian Correspondence*. Edited by Reimund Bieringer. BETL 125. Louvain: Louvain University Press, 1996.

———. "The Old Testament Background to 1 Cor 10,7–8." Pp. 607–15 in *The Corinthian Correspondence*. Edited by Reimund Bieringer. BETL 125. Louvain: Louvain University Press, 1996.

Konradt, Matthias. *Gericht und Gemeinde: Eine Studie zur Bedeutung und Funktion von Gerichtsaussagen im Rahmen der paulinischen Ekklesiologie und Ethik im 1 Thess und 1 Kor.* BZNT 117. Berlin: De Gruyter, 2003.

———. "Die korinthische Weisheit und das Wort vom Kreuz: Erwägungen zur korinthischen Problemkonstellation und paulinischen Intention in 1 Kor 1–4." *ZNW* 94 (2003): 181–214.

Köstenberger, Andreas J. "Women in the Pauline Mission." Pp. 221–47 in *The Gospel to the Nations: Perspectives on Paul's Mission*. Edited by Peter Bolt and Mark Thompson. Downers Grove, Ill.: InterVarsity, 2000.

Krämer, Helmut. "μυστήριον." *EDNT* 2:446–49.

Kreitzer, Larry Joseph. "1 Corinthians 10:4 and Philo's Flinty Rock." *CV* 35 (1993): 109–26.

———. *Jesus and God in Paul's Eschatology.* JSNTSup 19. Sheffield: JSOT, 1987.

Kuck, David W. *Judgment and Community Conflict: Paul's Use of Apocalyptic Judgment Language in 1 Corinthians 3:5–4:5.* NovTSup 66. Leiden: Brill, 1992.

Lambrecht, Jan. "Paul's Christological Use of Scripture in 1 Cor. 15.20–28." *NTS* 28 (1982): 502–27.

———. "Structure and Line of Thought in 1 Cor. 15:23–28." *NovT* 32 (1990): 143–51.

Lamp, Jeffrey S. *First Corinthians 1–4 in Light of Jewish Wisdom Traditions: Christ, Wisdom and Spirituality.* Studies in Bible and Early Christianity 42. Lewiston, N.Y.: Mellen, 2000.

Lampe, Peter. "Theological Wisdom and the 'Word about the Cross': The Rhetorical Scheme in I Corinthians 1–4." *Int* 44 (1990): 117–31.

Lanier, David E. "With Stammering Lips and Another Tongue: 1 Cor 14:20–22 and Isa 28:11–12." *CTR* 5 (1991): 259–85.

Lautenschlager, Markus. "Abschied vom Disputierer: Zur Bedeutung von συζητητή in 1 Kor 1,20." *ZNW* 83 (1992): 276–85.

Lewis, Scott M. *"So That God May Be All in All": The Apocalyptic Message of 1 Corinthians 15,12–34.* Tesi Gregoriana 42. Rome: Gregorian University Press, 1998.

———. "So That God May Be All in All: 1 Corinthians 15:12–34." *Studii biblici Franciscani liber annus* 49 (1999): 195–210.

Lim, Timothy H. *Holy Scripture in the Qumran Commentaries and Pauline Letters*. Oxford: Clarendon, 1997.

———. " 'Not in Persuasive Words of Wisdom, but in the Demonstration of the Spirit and Power' (I Cor. 2:4)." *NovT* 29 (1987): 137–49.

Limbeck, Meinrad. "ἀθετέω." *EDNT* 1:35.

Lincoln, Andrew T. *Paradise Now and Not Yet: Studies in the Role of the Heavenly Dimension in Paul's Thought with Special Reference to His Eschatology*. SNTSMS 43. Cambridge: Cambridge University Press, 1981.

Lindemann, Andreas. *Der erste Korintherbrief*. HNT 9. Tübingen: Mohr Siebeck, 2000.

———. "Parusie Christi und Herrschaft Gottes: Zur Exegese von 1 Kor 15,23–28." *WD* 19 (1987): 87–107.

———. "Die Schrift als Tradition: Beobachtungen zu den biblischen Zitaten im Ersten Korintherbrief." Pp. 199–225 in *Schrift und Tradition: Festschrift für Josef Ernst zum 70. Geburtstag*. Edited by Knut Backhaus and Franz Georg Untergassmair. Paderborn, Germany: Schöningh, 1996.

Litfin, Duane. *St. Paul's Theology of Proclamation: 1 Corinthians 1–4 and Greco-Roman Rhetoric*. SNTSMS 79. Cambridge: Cambridge University Press, 1994.

Lockwood, Gregory J. *1 Corinthians*. Concordia Commentary. St. Louis: Concordia, 2000.

Lohse, Eduard. " 'Kümmert sich Gott etwa um die Ochsen?' Zu 1 Kor 9,9." *ZNW* 88 (1997): 314–15.

Malan, François S. "The Use of the Old Testament in 1 Corinthians." *Neot* 14 (1981): 134–70.

Malherbe, Abraham J. "The Beasts at Ephesus." *JBL* 87 (1968): 71–80.

———. "ΜΗ ΓΕΝΟΙΤΟ In the Diatribe and Paul." *HTR* 73 (1980): 231–40.

Marsh, Clive. " 'Who Are You For?' 1 Corinthians 1:10–17 as Christian Scripture in the Context of Diverse Methods of Reading." Pp. 157–76 in *Paul and the Corinthians: Studies on a Community in Conflict. Essays in Honour of Margaret Thrall*. Edited by Trevor J. Burke and J. Keith Elliott. NovTSup 109. Leiden: Brill, 2003.

Marshall, Peter. *Enmity in Corinth: Social Conventions in Paul's Relations with the Corinthians*. WUNT 2/23. Tübingen: Mohr, 1987.

Martin, Dale B. *The Corinthian Body*. New Haven: Yale University Press, 1995.

———. *Slavery as Salvation: The Metaphor of Slavery in Pauline Christianity*. New Haven: Yale University Press, 1990.

Martin, Troy W. "Paul's Argument from Nature for the Veil in 1 Corinthians 11:13–15: A Testicle Instead of a Head Covering." *JBL* 123 (2004): 75–84.

McConville, J. Gordon. "Singular Address in the Deuteronomic Law and the Politics of Legal Adminstration." *JSOT* 97 (2002): 19–36.

McGinn, Sheila E. "ἐξουσίαν ἔχειν ἐπὶ τῆ κεφαλῆ: 1 Cor 11:10 and the Ecclesial Authority of Women." *Listening* 31 (1996): 91–104.

McKay, Kenneth L. "Aspect in Imperatival Constructions in New Testament Greek." *NovT* 27 (1985): 201–16.

McLay, R. Timothy. *The Use of the Septuagint in New Testament Research*. Grand Rapdis: Eerdmans, 2003.
Meeks, Wayne A. " 'And Rose Up to Play': Midrash and Paraenesis in 1 Corinthians 10:1–22." *JSNT* 16 (1982): 64–78.
———. "Corinthian Christians as Artificial Aliens." Pp. 129–38 in *Paul beyond the Judaism/Hellenism Divide*. Edited by Troels Engberg-Pedersen. Louisville: Westminster John Knox, 2001.
———. *The First Urban Christians: The Social World of the Apostle Paul*. New Haven: Yale University Press, 1983.
Meggitt, Justin J. "Meat Consumption and Social Conflict in Corinth." *JTS* 45 (1994): 137–41.
———. *Paul, Poverty, and Survival*. Edinburgh: Clark, 1998.
Meier, John P. "On the Veiling of Hermeneutics (1 Cor 11:2–16)." *CBQ* 40 (1978): 212–26.
Merklein, Helmut. *Der erste Brief an die Korinther: Kapitel 1–4*. ÖTK 7. Gütersloh: Gütersloher Verlagshaus, 1992.
Merz, A. "Why Did the Pure Bride of Christ (2 Cor. 11.2) Become a Wedded Wife (Eph. 5.22–33)? Theses about the Intertextual Transformation of an Ecclesiological Metaphor." *JSNT* 79 (2000): 131–47.
Metzger, Bruce M. *A Textual Commentary on the Greek New Testament*. New York: United Bible Societies, 1971.
Miller, J. I. "A Fresh Look at I Corinthians 6.16f." *NTS* 27 (1980): 125–27.
Mitchell, Margaret M. *Paul and the Rhetoric of Reconciliation: An Exegetical Investigation of the Language and Composition of 1 Corinthians*. HUT 28. Tübingen: Mohr, 1991.
———. "Pauline Accommodation and 'Condescension' (συγκατάβασις): 1 Cor 9:19–23 and the History of Influence." Pp. 197–214 in *Paul beyond the Judaism/Hellenism Divide*. Edited by Troels Engberg-Pedersen. Louisville: Westminster John Knox, 2001.
———. "Rhetorical Shorthand in Pauline Argumentation: The Functions of 'the Gospel' in the Corinthian Correspondence." Pp. 63–88 in *Gospel in Paul: Studies on Corinthians, Galatians, and Romans for Richard N. Longenecker*. Edited by L. Ann Jervis and Peter Richardson. JSNTSup 108. Sheffield: Sheffield Academic Press, 1994.
Morissette, Rodolphe. "L'Antithèse entre le 'psychique' et le 'pneumatique' en 1 Corinthiens, XV, 44 à 46." *RevScRel* 46 (1972): 97–143.
———. " 'La chair et le sang ne peuvent hériter du Règne de Dieu' (I Cor., XV, 50)." *Science et esprit* 26 (1974): 39–67.
———. "La condition de ressuscité: 1 Corinthiens 15,35–49. Structure littéraire de la pericope." *Bib* 53 (1972): 208–28.
———. "Un midrash sur la mort (I Cor. xv, 54c à 57)." *RB* 79 (1972): 161–88.
Muraoka, Takamitsu. *A Greek-English Lexicon of the Septuagint: Chiefly of the Pentateuch and the Twelve Prophets*. Louvain: Peeters, 2002.
Murphy-O'Connor, Jerome. "Co-authorship in the Corinthian Correspondence." *RB* 100 (1993): 562–79.

———. "Corinthian Slogans in 1 Cor 6:12–20." *CBQ* 40 (1978): 391–96.
———. "1 Corinthians 11:2–16 Once Again." *CBQ* 50 (1988): 265–74.
———. "Sex and Logic in 1 Corinthians 11:2–16." *CBQ* 42 (1980): 482–500.
Nasuti, Harry P. "The Woes of the Prophets and the Rights of the Apostle: The Internal Dynamics of 1 Corinthians 9." *CBQ* 50 (1988): 246–64.
Newton, Derek. *Deity and Diet: The Dilemma of Sacrificial Food at Corinth.* JSNTSup 169. Sheffield: Sheffield Academic Press, 1998.
Newton, Michael. *The Concept of Purity at Qumran and in the Letters of Paul.* SNTSMS 53. Cambridge: Cambridge University Press, 1985.
Oberlinner, Lorenz. "δεύτερος." *EDNT* 1.291–92.
O'Day, Gail R. "Jeremiah 9:22–23 and 1 Corinthians 1:26–31: A Study in Intertextuality." *JBL* 109 (1990): 259–67.
O'Donoghue, N. D. "The Awakening of the Dead." *Irish Theological Quarterly* 56 (1990): 49–59.
Olbricht, Thomas H., and Jerry L. Sumney, eds. *Paul and Pathos.* SBLSymS 16. Atlanta: Society of Biblical Literature, 2001.
Ollrog, Wolf-Henning. *Paulus und seine Mitarbeiter: Untersuchungen zu Theorie und Praxis der paulinischen Mission.* WMANT 50. Neukirchen-Vluyn: Neukirchener Verlag, 1979.
Omanson, Roger L. "Acknowledging Paul's Quotations." *The Bible Translator* 43 (1992): 202–13.
Oropeza, B. J. "Echoes of Isaiah in the Rhetoric of Paul: New Exodus, Wisdom, and the Humility of the Cross in Utopian-Apocalyptic Expectations." Pp. 87–112 in *The Intertexture of Apocalyptic Discourse in the New Testament.* Edited by Duane F. Watson. SBLSymS 14. Atlanta: Society of Biblical Literature, 2002.
———. "Laying to Rest the Midrash: Paul's Message on Meat Sacrificed to Idols in Light of the Deuteronomistic Tradition." *Bib* 79 (1998): 57–68.
———. *Paul and Apostasy: Eschatology, Perseverance, and Falling Away in the Corinthian Congregation.* WUNT 115. Tübingen: Mohr Siebeck, 2000.
Osborne, R. E. "Paul and the Wild Beasts." *JBL* 85 (1966): 225–30.
Osburn, Carroll D. "The Text of 1 Corinthians 10:9." Pp. 201–12 in *New Testament Textual Criticism: Its Significance for Exegesis. Essays in Honour of Bruce M. Metzger.* Edited by Eldon Jay Epp and Gordon D. Fee. Oxford: Clarendon, 1981.
Ostmeyer, Karl-Heinrich. "Satan und Passa in 1.Korinther 5." *Zeitschrift für Neues Testament* 9 (2002): 38–45.
Padgett, Alan G. "The Body in Resurrection: Science and Scripture on the 'Spiritual Body' (1 Cor 15:35–58)." *WW* 22 (2002): 155–63.
———. "Paul on Women in the Church: The Contradictions of Coiffure in 1 Corinthians 11.2–16." *JSNT* 20 (1984): 69–86.
———. "The Significance of ἀντί in 1 Corinthians 11:15." *TynBul* 45 (1994): 181–87.
Palzkill, Angela. "πίνω." *EDNT* 3.88–90.
Park, Joseph S. *Conceptions of Afterlife in Jewish Inscriptions: With Special Reference to Pauline Literature.* WUNT 121. Tübingen: Mohr Siebeck, 2000.

Pascuzzi, Maria. *Ethics, Ecclesiology, and Church Discipline: A Rhetorical Analysis of 1 Corinthians 5*. Tesi Gregoriana 32. Rome: Gregorian University Press, 1997.
Pate, C. Marvin. *The Reverse of the Curse: Paul, Wisdom, and Law*. WUNT 114. Tübingen: Mohr Siebeck, 2000.
Paulsen, Henning. "ἐνδύω." *EDNT* 1.451–52.
Penna, Romano. "The Gospel as 'Power of God' according to 1 Corinthians 1:18–25." Pages 169–80 in *Paul the Apostle: Jew and Greek Alike*. Theological and Exegetical Study 1. Collegeville, Minn.: Liturgical Press, 1996.
———. "Paul's Attitude toward the Old Testament." Pages 61–91 in *Paul the Apostle: Wisdom and Folly of the Cross*. Theological and Exegetical Study 2. Collegeville, Minn.: Liturgical Press, 1996.
Perriman, Andrew C. "The Head of a Woman: The Meaning of κεφαλή in I Cor. 11:3." *JTS* 45 (1994): 602–22.
———. "Paul and the Parousia: 1 Corinthians 15.50-7 and 2 Corinthians 5.1–5." *NTS* 35 (1989): 512–21.
Peterson, Brian K. *Eloquence and the Proclamation of the Gospel in Corinth*. SBLDS 163. Atlanta: Scholars Press, 1998.
Petzke, Gerd. "διαλογισμός." *EDNT* 1:308.
Pfammater, Josef. "οἰκοδομή." *EDNT* 2:495–98.
Pickett, Raymond. *The Cross in Corinth: The Social Significance of the Death of Jesus*. JSNTSup 143. Sheffield: Sheffield Academic Press, 1997.
Pietersma, Albert. *A New English Translation of the Septuagint: The Psalms*. New York: Oxford University Press, 2000.
Plag, Christoph. "Paulus und die *Gezera schawa*: Zur Übernahme rabbinischer Auslegungskunst." *Jud* 50 (1994): 135–40.
Plank, Karl A. *Paul and the Irony of Affliction*. Atlanta: Scholars Press, 1987.
Plevnik, Joseph. *Paul and the Parousia: An Exegetical and Theological Investigation*. Peabody, Mass.: Hendrickson, 1997.
Pogoloff, Stephen M. *Logos and Sophia: The Rhetorical Situation of 1 Corinthians*. SBLDS 134. Atlanta: Scholars Press, 1992.
Pokorný, Petr. "Christliche Verkündigung als Modell des hermeneutishcen Prozesses nach 1 Kor 14,23–25." Pp. 245–51 in *Philosophical Hermeneutics and Biblical Exegesis*. Edited by Petr Pokorný and Jan Roskovec. WUNT 153. Tübingen: Mohr Siebeck, 2002.
Ponsot, Hervé. "D'Isaïe LXIV, 3 à I Corinthiens II, 9." *RB* 90 (1983): 229–42.
Popkes, Wiard. "1 Kor 2,2 und die Anfänge der Christologie." *ZNW* 95 (2004): 64–83.
Porter, Stanley E. "How Should κολλώμενος in 1 Cor 6,16.17 Be Translated?" *ETL* 67 (1991): 105–6.
———. *Verbal Aspect in the Greek of the New Testament, with Reference to Tense and Mood*. Studies in Biblical Greek 1. New York: Lang, 1993.
Probst, Hermann. *Paulus und der Brief: Die Rhetorik des antiken Briefes als Form der paulinischen Korintherkorrespondenz (1 Kor 8–10)*. WUNT 45. Tübingen: Mohr, 1991.

Radcliffe, Timothy. " 'Glorify God in Your Bodies': 1 Corinthians 6,12–20 as a Sexual Ethic." *New Blackfriars* 67 (1986): 306–14.
Ramsaran, Rollin A. *Liberating Words: Paul's Use of Rhetorical Maxims in 1 Corinthians 1–10*. Valley Forge, Pa.: Trinity Press International, 1996.
Rebell, Walter. "Gemeinde als Missionsfaktor im Urchristentum: I Kor 14,24f. als Schlüsselsituation." *TZ* 44 (1988): 117–34.
Reinmuth, Eckart. "Narratio und argumentatio—Zur Auslegung der Jesus-Christus-Geschichte im Ersten Korintherbrief: Ein Beitrag zur mimetischen Kompetenz des Paulus." *ZTK* 92 (1995): 13–27.
Richardson, Neil. *Paul's Language about God*. JSNTSup 99. Sheffield: Sheffield Academic Press, 1994.
Richardson, Peter. "Temples, Altars, and Living from the Gospel (1 Cor. 9.12b–18)." Pp. 89–110 in *Gospel in Paul: Studies on Corinthians, Galatians, and Romans for Richard N. Longenecker*. Edited by L. Ann Jervis and Peter Richardson. JSNTSup 108. Sheffield: Sheffield Academic Press, 1994.
Rissi, Mathias. "κρίνω." *EDNT* 2:318–21.
Robbins, Vernon. K. "Oral, Rhetorical, and Literary Cultures: A Response." *Semeia* 65 (1995): 75–91. The theme of the issue is "Orality and Textuality in Early Christian Literature."
Robertson, Archibald, and Alfred Plummer. *A Critical and Exegetical Commentary on the First Epistle of St Paul to the Corinthians*. ICC. Edinburgh: Clark, 1914.
Robertson, C. K. *Conflict in Corinth: Redefining the System*. Studies in Biblical Literature 42. New York: Lang, 2001.
Roloff, Jürgen. "ἐκκλησία." *EDNT* 1:410–15.
Rosner, Brian S. "The Function of Scripture in 1 Cor 5,13b and 6,16." Pp. 513–18 in *The Corinthian Correspondence*. Edited by Reimund Bieringer. BETL 125. Louvain: Louvain University Press, 1996.
———. " 'Οὐχὶ μᾶλλον ἐπενθήσατε'—Corporate Responsibility in 1 Corinthians 5." *NTS* 38 (1992): 470–73.
———. *Paul, Scripture, and Ethics: A Study of 1 Corinthians 5–7*. AGJU 22. Leiden: Brill, 1994.
———. "A Possible Quotation of *Test. Reuben* 5:5 in 1 Corinthians 6:18a." *JTS* 43 (1992): 123–27.
———. "Temple and Holiness in 1 Corinthians 5." *TynBul* 42 (1991): 137–45.
———. "Temple Prostitution in 1 Corinthians 6:12–20." *NovT* 40 (1998): 336–51.
Rothaus, Richard M. *Corinth, the First City of Greece: An Urban History of Late Antique Cult and Religion*. Religions in the Greco-Roman World 139. Leiden: Brill, 2000.
Sand, Alexander. "ἀπαρχή." *EDNT* 1.116–17.
———. "καρδία." *EDNT* 2:249–51.
———. "νοῦς." *EDNT* 2:478–79.
Sandelin, Karl-Gustav. "Does Paul Argue against Sacramentalism and Over-Confidence in 1 Cor 10.1–14?" Pp. 165–82 in *The New Testament and Hellenistic Judaism*. Edited by Peder Borgen and Søren Giversen. Peabody, Mass.: Hendrickson, 1995.
———. " 'Do Not Be Idolaters!' (1 Cor 10:7)." Pp. 257–73 in *Texts and Contexts:*

Biblical Texts in Their Textual and Situational Contexts. Essays in Honor of Lars Hartman. Edited by Tord Fornberg and David Hellholm. Oslo: Scandinavian University Press, 1995.

———. "Drawing the Line: Paul on Idol Food and Idolatry in 1 Cor 8:1–11:1." Pp. 108–25 in *Neotestamentica et Philonica: Studies in Honor of Peder Borgen.* Edited by David E. Aune, Torrey Seland, and Jarl Henning Ulrichsen. NovTSup 106. Leiden: Brill, 2003.

Sanders, Jack T. "Paul between Jews and Gentiles in Corinth." *JSNT* 65 (1997): 67–83.

Sandnes, Karl Olav. *Belly and the Body in the Pauline Epistles.* SNTSMS 120. New York: Cambridge University Press, 2002.

———. "Prophecy—A Sign for Believers (1 Cor 14,20–25)." *Bib* 77 (1996): 1–15.

Sänger, Dieter. "Die δυνατοι in I Kor 1:26." *ZNW* 76 (1985): 285–91.

Saw, Insawn. *Paul's Rhetoric in 1 Corinthians 15: An Analysis Utilizing the Theories of Classical Rhetoric.* Lewiston, N.Y.: Mellen, 1995.

Schaller, Berndt. "Zum Textcharakter der Hiobzitate im paulinischen Schrifttum." *ZNW* 71 (1980): 21–26.

Schneider, Bernardin. "The Corporate Meaning and Background of 1 Cor 15,45b—'O Eschatos Adam Eis Pneuma Zoiopoioun.'" *CBQ* 29 (1967): 144–61.

Schneider, Sebastian. "1 Kor 15,51–52: Ein neuer Lösungsvorshlag zu einer alten Schwierigkeit." Pp. 661–69 in *The Corinthian Correspondence.* Edited by Reimund Bieringer. BETL 125. Louvain: Louvain University Press, 1996.

Schrage, Wolfgang. "Einige Hauptprobleme der Diskussion des Herrenmahls im 1. Korintherbrief." Pp. 191–98 in *The Corinthian Correspondence.* Edited by Reimund Bieringer. BETL 125. Louvain: Louvain University Press, 1996.

———. *Der erste Brief an die Korinther (1 Kor 1,1–6,11).* EKKNT 7/1. Zürich: Benziger, 1991.

———. *Der erste Brief an die Korinther (1 Kor 6,12–11,16).* EKKNT 7/2. Düsseldorf: Benziger, 1995.

———. *Der erste Brief an die Korinther (1 Kor 15,1–16,24).* EKKNT 7/4. Zürich: Benziger, 2001.

Schreiner, Josef. "Jeremia 9,22.23 als Hintergrund des paulinischen 'Sich-Rühmens.'" Pp. 530–42 in *Neues Testament und Kirche: Für Rudolf Schnackenburg.* Edited by Joachim Gnilka. Freiburg: Herder, 1974.

Schunack, Gerd. "τύπος." *EDNT* 3.372–76.

Schüssler Fiorenza, Elisabeth. "Rhetorical Situation and Historical Reconstruction in I Corinthians." *NTS* 33 (1987): 386–403.

Selby, Gary S. "Paul, the Seer: The Rhetorical Persona in 1 Corinthians 2.1–16." Pp. 351–73 in *The Rhetorical Analysis of Scripture: Essays from the 1995 London Conference.* Edited by Stanley E. Porter and Thomas H. Olbricht. JSNTSup 146. Sheffield: Sheffield Academic Press, 1997.

Shillington, V. George. "Atonement Texture in 1 Corinthians 5.5." *JSNT* 71 (1998): 29–50.

Sibinga, Joost Smit. "The Composition of 1 Cor. 9 and Its Context." *NovT* 40 (1998): 136–63.

Smit, Joop F. M. *"About the Idol Offerings": Rhetoric, Social Context, and Theology of Paul's Discourse in First Corinthians 8:1–11:1.* CBET 27. Louvain: Peeters, 2000.

———. "Epideictic Rhetoric in Paul's First Letter to the Corinthians 1–4." *Bib* 84 (2003): 184–201.

———. "1 Cor 8,1–6: A Rhetorical *Partitio*. A Contribution to the Coherence of 1 Cor 8,1–11,1." Pp. 577–91 in *The Corinthian Correspondence*. Edited by Reimund Bieringer. BETL 125. Louvain: Louvain University Press, 1996.

———. "Tongues and Prophecy: Deciphering 1 Cor 14,22." *Bib* 75 (1994): 175–90.

———. "'What Is Apollos? What Is Paul?' In Search for the Coherence of First Corinthians 1:10–4:21." *NovT* 44 (2002): 231–51.

———. "'You Shall Not Muzzle a Threshing Ox': Paul's Use of the Law of Moses in 1 Cor 9,8–12." *EstBib* 58 (2000): 239–63.

Smith, Dennis E. *From Symposium to Eucharist: The Banquet in the Early Christian World.* Minneapolis: Fortress, 2002.

Smith, D. Moody. "The Pauline Literature." Pp. 265–91 in *It Is Written: Scripture Citing Scripture. Essays in Honour of Barnabas Lindars.* Edited by D. A. Carson and H. G. M. Williamson. Cambridge: Cambridge University Press, 1988.

Soards, Marion L. *1 Corinthians.* New International Biblical Commentary 7. Peabody, Mass.: Hendrickson, 1999.

Söding, Thomas. "'Die Kraft der Sünde ist das Gesetz' (1 Kor 15,56): Anmerkungen zum Hintergrund und zur Pointe einer gesetzeskritischen Sentenz des Apostels Paulus." *ZNW* 83 (1992): 74–84.

Sollamo, Raija. "The Significance of Septuagint Studies." Pp. 497–512 in *Emanuel: Studies in Hebrew Bible, Septuagint, and Dead Sea Scrolls in Honor of Emanuel Tov.* Edited by Shalom M. Paul et al. VTSup 94. Leiden: Brill, 2003.

Son, Sang-Won (Aaron). *Corporate Elements in Pauline Anthropology: A Study of Selected Terms, Idioms, and Concepts in the Light of Paul's Usage and Background.* AnBib 148. Rome: Biblical Institute, 2001.

South, James T. "A Critique of the 'Curse/Death' Interpretation of 1 Corinthians 5.1–8." *NTS* 39 (1993): 539–61.

Sparks, Hedley Frederick Davis. "1 Kor 2,9: A Quotation from the Coptic Testament of Jacob?" *ZNW* 67 (1976): 269–76.

Stamps, Dennis L. "The Christological Premise in Pauline Theological Rhetoric: 1 Corinthians 1.4–2.5." Pp. 441–57 in *Rhetorical Criticism and the Bible.* Edited by Stanley E. Porter and Dennis L. Stamps. JSNTSup 195. London: Sheffield Academic Press, 2002.

Standhartinger, Angela. "Weisheit in *Joseph und Aseneth* und den paulinischen Briefen." *NTS* 47 (2001) 482–501.

Stanley, Christopher D. "Biblical Quotations as Rhetorical Devices in Paul's Letter to the Galatians." *SBLSP* 37 (1998): 700–730.

———. "'Neither Jew Nor Greek': Ethnic Conflict in Graeco-Roman Society." *JSNT* 64 (1996): 101–24.

———. *Paul and the Language of Scripture: Citation Technique in the Pauline Epis-*

tles and Contemporary Literature. SNTSMS 69. Cambridge: Cambridge University Press, 1992.

———. "'Pearls before Swine': Did Paul's Audiences Understand His Biblical Quotations?" *NovT* 41 (1999): 124–44.

———. "The Rhetoric of Quotations: An Essay on Method." Pp. 44–58 in *Early Christian Interpretation of the Scriptures of Israel: Investigations and Proposals*. Edited by Craig A. Evans and James A. Sanders. JSNTSup 148. Sheffield: Sheffield Academic Press, 1997.

Stenschke, Christoph W. *Luke's Portrait of Gentiles Prior to Their Coming to Faith*. WUNT 108. Tübingen: Mohr Siebeck, 1999.

Sterling, Gregory E. "'Wisdom among the Perfect': Creation Traditions in Alexandrian Judaism and Corinthian Christianity." *NovT* 37 (1995): 355–84.

Still, E. Coye. "The Meaning and Uses of ΕΙΔΩΛΟΘΥΤΟΝ in First-Century Non-Pauline Literature and 1 Cor 8:1–11:1: Toward Resolution of the Debate." *TJ* 23 (2002): 225–34.

———. "Paul's Aims Regarding Εἰδωλόθυτα: A New Proposal for Interpreting 1 Corinthians 8:1–11:1." *NovT* 44 (2002): 333–43.

Stockhausen, Carol Kern. *Moses' Veil and the Glory of the New Covenant: The Exegetical Substructure of II Cor. 3,1–4,6*. AnBib 116. Rome: Biblical Institute, 1989.

———. "2 Corinthians 3 and the Principles of Pauline Exegesis." Pp. 143–64 in *Paul and the Scriptures of Israel*. Edited by Craig A. Evans and James A. Sanders. JSNTSup 83. Sheffield: Sheffield Academic Press, 1993.

Stone, Michael E., and John Strugnell. *The Books of Elijah, Parts 1–2*. SBLTT 18. Missoula, Mont.: Scholars Press, 1979.

Strüder, Christof W. "Preferences Not Parties: The Background of 1 Cor 1,12." *ETL* 79 (2003): 431–55.

Stuckenbruck, Loren T. "Why Should Women Cover Their Heads Because of the Angels? (1 Corinthians 11:10)." *Stone-Campbell Journal* 4 (2001): 205–34.

Sumney, Jerry L. *'Servants of Satan,' 'False Brothers,' and Other Opponents of Paul*. JSNTSup 188. Sheffield: Sheffield Academic Press, 1999.

Talbert, Charles H. *Reading Corinthians: A Literary and Theological Commentary on 1 and 2 Corinthians*. New York: Crossroad, 1987.

Talshir, Zipora. *I Esdras: A Text Critical Commentary*. SBLSCS 50. Atlanta: Society of Biblical Literature, 2001.

———. *I Esdras: From Origin to Translation*. SBLSCS 47. Atlanta: Society of Biblical Literature, 1999.

Teani, Maurizio. *Corporeita e risurrezione: L'interpretazione di I Corinti 15,35–49 nel Novecento*. Aloisiana 24. Rome: Gregorian University, 1994.

Theis, Joachim. *Paulus als Weisheitslehrer: Der Gekreuzigte und die Weisheit Gottes in 1 Kor 1–4*. Biblische Untersuchungen 22. Regensburg: Pustet, 1991.

Theissen, Gerd. "Social Conflicts in the Corinthian Community: Further Remarks on J. J. Meggitt, *Paul, Poverty, and Survival*." *JSNT* 25, no. 3 (2003): 371–91.

———. *The Social Setting of Pauline Christianity: Essays on Corinth*. Philadelphia: Fortress, 1982.

Thiselton, Anthony. C. *The First Epistle to the Corinthians: A Commentary on the Greek Text*. NIGTC. Grand Rapids: Eerdmans, 2000.

Thompson, Cynthia L. "Hairstyles, Head-Coverings, and St. Paul: Portraits from Roman Corinth." *BA* 51 (1988): 99–115.

Thompson, James W. "Creation, Shame, and Nature in 1 Cor 11:2–16: The Background and Coherence of Paul's Argument." Pp. 237–57 in *Early Christianity and Classical Culture: Comparative Studies in Honor of Abraham J. Malherbe*. Edited by John T. Fitzgerald, Thomas H. Olbricht, and Michael L. White. NovTSup 110. Leiden: Brill, 2003.

Thomson, Ian H. *Chiasmus in the Pauline Letters*. JSNTSup 111. Sheffield: Sheffield Academic Press, 1995.

Thrall, Margaret E. "The Initial Attraction of Paul's Mission in Corinth and of the Church He Founded There." Pp. 59–73 in *Paul, Luke, and the Graeco-Roman World: Essays in Honour of Alexander J. M. Wedderburn*. Edited by Alf Christophersen et al. JSNTSup 217. London: Sheffield Academic Press, 2002.

Tomson, Peter J. *Paul and the Jewish Law: Halakha in the Letters of the Apostle to the Gentiles*. CRINT 1. Minneapolis: Fortress, 1990.

Tuckett, Chistopher M. "Paul and Jesus Tradition: The Evidence of 1 Corinthians 2:9 and *Gospel of Thomas* 17." Pp. 55–73 in *Paul and the Corinthians: Studies on a Community in Conflict. Essays on Honour of Margaret Thrall*. Edited by Trevor J. Burke and J. Keith Elliott. NovTSup 109. Leiden: Brill, 2003.

———. "Paul, Scripture, and Ethics: Some Reflections." *NTS* 46 (2000): 403–24.

Tyler, Ronald L. "First Corinthians 4:6 and Hellenistic Pedagogy." *CBQ* 60 (1998): 97–103.

———. "The History of the Interpretation of τὸ μὴ ὑπὲρ ἃ γέγραπται in 1 Corinthians 4:6." *ResQ* 43 (2001): 243–52.

Usami, Kôshi. "'How Are the Dead Raised?' (1 Cor 15,35–58)." *Bib* 57 (1976): 468–93.

Vander Broek, Lyle D. "Discipline and Community: Another Look at 1 Corinthians 5." *Reformed Review* 48 (1994): 5–13.

van der Minde, Hans-Jürgen. "ἐσθίω." *EDNT* 2.58–60.

Verheyden, Joseph. "Origen on the Origin of 1 Cor 2,9." Pp. 491–511 in *The Corinthian Correspondence*. Edited by Reimund Bieringer. BETL 125. Louvain: Louvain University Press, 1996.

Verhoef, Eduard. "The Senders of the Letters to the Corinthians and the Use of 'I' and 'We.'" Pp. 417–25 in *The Corinthian Correspondence*. Edited by Reimund Bieringer. BETL 125. Louvain: Louvain University Press, 1996.

Vincent, Jean-M. "'Avec quel Corps les Morts reviennent-ils?' L'Usage des Écritures dans 1 Corinthiens 15,36–45." *Foi et vie* 100 (2001): 63–70.

von Nordheim, Eckard. "Das Zitat des Paulus in 1 Kor 2,9 und seine Beziehung zum koptischen Testament Jakobs." *ZNW* 65 (1974): 112–20.

Vos, Johan S. "Argumentation und Situation in 1Kor. 15." *NovT* 41 (1999): 313–33.

———. *Die Kunst der Argumentation bei Paulus: Studien zur antiken Rhetorik*. WUNT 149. Tübingen: Mohr Siebeck, 2002.

———. "Der ΜΕΤΑΣΞΗΜΑΤΙΣΜΟΣ in 1 Kor 4,6." *ZNW* 86 (1995): 154–72.
Wagner, J. Ross. " 'Not Beyond the Things Which Are Written': A Call to Boast Only in the Lord (1 Cor 4.6)." *NTS* 44 (1998): 279–87.
Walker, William O. *Interpolations in the Pauline Letters.* JSNTSup 213. Sheffield: Sheffield Academic Press, 2001.
Wanamaker, Charles A. "A Rhetoric of Power: Ideology and 1 Corinthians 1–4." Pp. 115–37 in *Paul and the Corinthians: Studies on a Community in Conflict. Essays in Honour of Margaret Thrall.* Edited by Trevor J. Burke and J. Keith Elliott. NovTSup 109. Leiden: Brill, 2003.
Watson, Duane F. "1 Corinthians 10:23–11:1 in the Light of Greco-Roman Rhetoric: The Role of Rhetorical Questions." *JBL* 108 (1989): 301–18.
———. "Paul and Boasting." Pp. 77–100 in *Paul in the Greco-Roman World: A Handbook.* Edited by J. Paul Sampley. Harrisburg, Pa.: Trinity Press International, 2003.
———. "Paul's Rhetorical Strategy in 1 Corinthians 15." Pp. 231–49 in *Rhetoric and the New Testament: Essays from the 1992 Heidelberg Conference.* Edited by Stanley E. Porter and Thomas H. Olbricht. JSNTSup 90. Sheffield: Sheffield Academic Press, 1993.
Watson, Francis. *Agape, Eros, Gender: Towards a Pauline Sexual Ethic.* Cambridge: Cambridge University Press, 2000.
———. "The Authority of the Voice: A Theological Reading of 1 Cor 11.1–16." *NTS* 46 (2000): 520–36.
Wedderburn, A. J. M. "ἐν τῇ σοφίᾳ τοῦ θεοῦ—1 Kor 1.21." *ZNW* 64 (1973): 132–34.
———. "Some Observations on Paul's Use of the Phrases 'in Christ' and 'with Christ.' " *JSNT* 25 (1985): 83–97.
Weiser, Alfons. "διακονέω." *EDNT* 1:302–4.
Welborn, Laurence L. "A Conciliatory Principle in 1 Cor. 4:6." *NovT* 29 (1987): 320–46.
———. "Μωρὸς γενέσθω: Paul's Appropriation of the Role of the Fool in 1 Corinthians 1–4." *BibInt* 10 (2002): 420–35.
———. *Politics and Rhetoric in the Corinthian Epistles.* Macon, Ga.: Mercer University Press, 1997.
Welch, John W. "Criteria for Identifying and Evaluating the Presence of Chiasmus." Pp. 157–74 in *Chiasmus Bibliography.* Edited by John W. Welch and Daniel B. McKinlay. Provo, Utah: Research, 1999.
Wevers, John William. *Notes on the Greek Text of Deuteronomy.* SBLSCS 39. Atlanta: Scholars Press, 1995.
———. *Notes on the Greek Text of Exodus.* SBLSCS 30. Atlanta: Scholars Press, 1990.
———. *Notes on the Greek Text of Genesis.* SBLSCS 35. Atlanta: Scholars Press, 1993.
———. *Notes on the Greek Text of Numbers.* SBLSCS 46. Atlanta: Scholars Press, 1998.
Wilk, Florian. *Die Bedeutung des Jesajabuches für Paulus.* FRLANT 179. Göttingen: Vandenhoeck & Ruprecht, 1998.

Williams, David J. *Paul's Metaphors: Their Context and Character*. Peabody, Mass.: Hendrickson, 1999.

Williams, H. H. Drake. *The Wisdom of the Wise: The Presence and Function of Scripture within 1 Cor. 1:18–3:23*. AGJU 49. Leiden: Brill, 2001.

Williams, Ritva. "Lifting the Veil: A Social-Science Interpretation of 1 Corinthians 11:2–16." *Consensus* 23 (1997): 53–60.

Willis, Wendell Lee. "An Apostolic Apologia? The Form and Function of 1 Corinthians 9." *JSNT* 24 (1985): 33–48.

———. *Idol Meat in Corinth: The Pauline Argument in 1 Corinthians 8 and 10*. SBLDS 68. Chico, Calif.: Scholars Press, 1985.

———. "The 'Mind of Christ' in 1 Corinthians 2,16." *Bib* 70 (1989): 110–22.

Wilson, Kenneth T. "Should Women Wear Headcoverings?" *BSac* 148 (1991): 442–62.

Winandy, Jacques. "Un curieux *casus pendens*: 1 Corinthiens 11.10 et son interprétation." *NTS* 38 (1992): 621–29.

Winter, Bruce W. *After Paul Left Corinth: The Influence of Secular Ethics and Social Change*. Grand Rapids: Eerdmans, 2001.

———. "Gluttony and Immorality at Elitist Banquets: The Background to 1 Corinthians 6:12–20." *Jian Dao* 7 (1997): 77–90.

———. *Philo and Paul among the Sophists: Alexandrian and Corinthian Responses to a Julio-Claudian Movement*. 2nd ed. Grand Rapids: Eerdmans, 2002.

———. "Philodemus and Paul on Rhetorical Delivery (ὑπόκρισις)." Pp. 323–42 in *Philodemus and the New Testament World*. Edited by John T. Fitzgerald, Dirk Obbink, and Glenn S. Holland. NovTSup 111. Leiden: Brill, 2004.

———. *Roman Wives, Roman Widows: The Appearance of New Women and the Pauline Communities*. Grand Rapids: Eerdmans, 2003.

———. *Seek the Welfare of the City: Christians as Benefactors and Citizens*. Grand Rapids: Eerdmans, 1994.

———. "The 'Underlays' of Conflict and Compromise in 1 Corinthians." Pp. 139–55 in *Paul and the Corinthians: Studies on a Community in Conflict. Essays in Honour of Margaret Thrall*. Edited by Trevor J. Burke and J. Keith Elliott. NovTSup 109. Leiden: Brill, 2003.

Wire, Antoinette C. *The Corinthian Women Prophets: A Reconstruction through Paul's Rhetoric*. Minneapolis: Fortress, 1990.

Wischmeyer, Oda. "ΘΕΟΝ ΑΓΑΠΑΝ bei Paulus: Eine traditionsgeschichtliche Miszelle." *ZNW* 78 (1987): 141–44.

Witherington, Ben. *Conflict and Community in Corinth: A Socio-rhetorical Commentary on 1 and 2 Corinthians*. Grand Rapids: Eerdmans, 1995.

———. *Women in the Earliest Churches*. Cambridge: Cambridge University Press, 1988.

Wolff, Christian. *Der erste Brief des Paulus an die Korinther*. 2nd ed. THKNT 7. Leipzig: Evangelische Verlagsanstalt, 2000.

———. *Jeremia im Frühjudentum und Urchristentum*. TU 118. Berlin: Akademie, 1976.

Wuellner, Wilhelm. "Paul as Pastor: The Function of Rhetorical Questions in First

Corinthians." Pp. 49–77 in *L'Apôtre Paul: Personalité, style et conception du ministère*. Edited by Albert Vanhoye. BETL 73. Louvain: Louvain University Press, 1986.
Yarbro Collins, Adela. "The Function of 'Excommunication' in Paul." *HTR* 73 (1980): 251–63.
Yeo, Khiok-Khng. "Differentiation and Mutuality of Male-Female Relations in 1 Corinthians 11:2–16." *BR* 43 (1998): 7–21.
———. *Rhetorical Interaction in 1 Corinthians 8 and 10: A Formal Analysis with Preliminary Suggestions for a Chinese, Cross-Cultural Hermeneutic*. BIS 9. Leiden: Brill, 1995.
Yinger, Kent L. *Paul, Judaism, and Judgment according to Deeds*. SNTSMS 105. Cambridge: Cambridge University Press, 1999.
Yorke, Gosnell L. O. R. *The Church as the Body of Christ in the Pauline Corpus: A Re-examination*. Lanham, Md.: University Press of America, 1991.
Zaas, Peter S. " 'Cast Out the Evil Man from Your Midst' (1 Cor 5:13b)." *JBL* 103 (1984): 259–61.
———. "Catalogues and Context: 1 Corinthians 5 and 6." *NTS* 34 (1988): 622–29.
Zerhusen, Robert. "The Problem of Tongues in 1 Cor 14: A Reexamination." *BTB* 27 (1997): 139–52.
Zerwick, Maximilian. *Biblical Greek*. Rome: Biblical Institute, 1963.
Zerwick, Maximilian, and Mary Grosvenor. *A Grammatical Analysis of the Greek New Testament*. Rome: Biblical Institute, 1979.
Zmijewski, Josef. "καυχάομαι." *EDNT* 2:276–79.

Author Index

Aageson, James W., 2 n. 3
Adams, Edward., 32 n. 53, 33 n. 55, 34 n. 58, 34 n. 60, 35 n. 63, 47 n. 28, 63 n. 25, 80 n. 8, 82 n. 12, 82 n. 13, 82 n. 14, 85 n. 23, 97 n. 26, 217 n. 26
Adeyemi, M. E., 61 n. 19
Alexander, Loveday., 30 n. 46
Alter, Robert, 22 n. 16, 127 n. 6
Amador, J. David Hester, 4 n. 9
Anderson, R. Dean, 3 n. 6
Asher, Jeffrey R., 233 n. 7, 237 n. 16, 239 n. 19, 240 n. 20, 254 n. 23
Aune, David E., 106 n. 8
Austin, John Langshaw, 5 n. 12

Bailey, Kenneth E., 105 n. 8
Baldanza, Giuseppe, 116 n. 31
Balz, Horst, 24 n. 21, 44 n. 24, 81 n. 10
Barclay, John M. G., 7 n. 17
Barnett, Paul, 26 n. 32
Barrett, Charles K., 28 n. 40, 39 n. 11, 40 n. 14, 80 n. 8, 114 n. 24, 186 n. 27
BeDuhn, Jason David, 184 n. 21
Belleville, Linda L., 178 n. 5, 180 n. 9
Bender, Wilhelm, 42 n. 17
Berger, Klaus, 54 n. 2
Berkley, Timothy W., 5 n. 11
Betz, Otto, 25 n. 27
Binder, Donald D., 9 n. 22
Black, David Alan, 35 n. 62
Blattenberger, David E., 177 n. 5, 180 n. 9
Blomberg, Craig L., 105 n. 8
Bonneau, Normand, 237 n. 15, 238 n. 17, 238 n. 18, 240 n. 21
Borghi, Ernesto, 133 n. 24
Botha, S. P., 234 n. 9
Braxton, Brad Ronnell, 5 n. 10, 7 n. 17
Brewer, David Instone, 11 n. 27, 77 n. 1, 131 n. 16

Brodeur, Scott, 234 n. 8, 234 n. 9, 235 n. 11, 235 n. 12, 236 n. 13, 237 n. 15, 240 n. 22, 242 n. 24, 242 n. 25, 243 n. 26, 243 n. 27, 243 n. 28, 244 n. 29
Brodie, Thomas L., 1 n. 1
Brown, Alexandra R., 5 n. 13, 25 n. 28
Bryant, Robert A., 3 n. 6
Bullmore, Michael A., 3 n. 8, 27 n. 37
Button, M. Bruce, 8 n. 17
Bünker, Michael, 3 n. 7
Byrne, Brendan, 118 n. 36, 119 n. 37
Byron, John, 142 n. 51

Callan, Terrence, 206 n. 3
Callow, Kathleen, 92 n. 11, 93 n. 12, 93 n. 13, 98 n. 30
Campbell, Barth, 94 n. 16
Caragounis, Chrys C., 138 n. 41
Carr, Wesley A., 61 n. 19
Carter, Warren, 6 n. 14, 19 n. 10
Cervin, Richard S., 179 n. 7
Chester, Stephen J., 66 n. 32
Cheung, Alex T., 133 n. 23, 133 n. 24, 136 n. 33, 136 n. 35, 136 n. 36, 137 n. 37, 137 n. 39, 142 n. 52, 150 n. 10, 151 n. 13, 153 n. 19, 157 n. 31, 163 n. 6, 165 n. 11, 165 n. 14, 166 n. 15, 167 n. 19, 168 n. 20, 168 n. 21, 170 n. 28
Chow, John K., 7 n. 17
Ciampa, Roy E., 9 n. 23
Clarke, Andrew D., 7 n. 17, 28 n. 39
Classen, Carl Joachim, 3 n. 6
Collier, Gary D., 150 n. 11, 151 n. 13, 157 n. 31, 157 n. 32
Collins, Raymond F., 1 n. 1, 10 n. 25, 19 n. 11, 23 n. 17, 24 n. 21, 25 n. 28, 26 n. 31, 30 n. 46, 34 n. 59, 37 n. 1, 42 n. 18, 43 n. 21, 45 n. 25, 46 n. 27, 48 n. 31, 54 n. 2, 58 n. 8, 61 n. 21, 64

288   Author Index

(Collins)   n. 28, 65 n. 29, 65 n. 31, 69 n. 3, 70 n. 5, 73 n. 11, 74 n. 14, 80 n. 7, 86 n. 23, 91 n. 6, 98 n. 28, 104 n. 3, 104 n. 4, 112 n. 17, 114 n. 23, 115 n. 26, 116 n. 31, 117 n. 33, 119 n. 37, 121 n. 41, 128 n. 7, 135 n. 29, 135 n. 32, 136 n. 33, 136 n. 35, 138 n. 41, 139 n. 43, 151 n. 14, 158 n. 35, 162 n. 3, 164 n. 10, 168 n. 20, 183 n. 18, 187 n. 28, 195 n. 8, 196 n. 11, 206 n. 3, 206 n. 5, 210 n. 17, 212 n. 22, 214 n. 24, 225 n. 9, 225 n. 11, 226 n. 13, 227 n. 17, 228 n. 18, 233 n. 5, 233 n. 6, 234 n. 8, 234 n. 9, 234 n. 10, 238 n. 18, 250 n. 10, 251 n. 13, 254 n. 22, 254 n. 23, 257 n. 32, 258 n. 34, 259 n. 37
Conzelmann, Hans, 23 n. 18, 31 n. 50, 34 n. 59, 37 n. 1, 80 n. 8, 96 n. 23, 207 n. 7
Corrington, Gail Paterson, 177 n. 5
Cranfield, C. E. B., 186 n. 27

Dautzenberg, Gerhard, 50 n. 36, 198 n. 15
Davis, James A., 22 n. 15, 62 n. 22
Dawes, Gregory W., 133 n. 24, 133 n. 25, 137 n. 36
de Boer, Martinus C., 206 n. 4, 211 n. 19, 252 n. 14, 254 n. 24
de Vos, Craig Steven, 7 n. 17, 93 n. 12
Delobel, Joël, 148 n. 7, 173 n. 1, 179 n. 7, 179 n. 8, 183 n. 18, 184 n. 21
Deming, Will, 99 n. 32
Derrett, J. Duncan M., 115 n. 27
Dewey, Joanna, 7 n. 16, 8 n. 19, 9 n. 22
Dodd, Brian J., 107 n. 10
Donaldson, Terence L., 9 n. 24, 23 n. 19
Dunn, James D. G., 198 n.15, 236 n. 14

Eastman, Brad, 25 n. 25, 33 n. 57, 63 n. 26
Elliott, John H., 8 n. 17
Ellis, E. Earle, 38 n. 5, 114 n. 24
Engberg-Pedersen, Troels, 188 n. 31
Engels, Donald, 7 n. 17
Enns, P. E., 148 n. 9
Eriksson, Anders, 3 n. 7, 4 n. 9, 8 n. 20, 212 n. 21, 213 n. 23

Fatehi, Mehrdad, 71 n. 5, 236 n. 14
Fatum, Lone, 177 n. 5

Fee, Gordon D., 23 n. 17, 23 n. 18, 24 n. 21, 25 n. 24, 27 n. 37, 32 n. 51, 34 n. 58, 34 n. 61, 37n. 1, 39 n. 9, 40 n. 14, 42 n. 18, 43 n. 20, 43 n. 21, 44 n. 22, 44 n. 23, 46 n. 26, 46 n. 27, 47 n. 29, 48 n. 30, 53 n. 1, 54 n. 2, 58 n. 8, 58 n. 9, 58 n. 10, 59 n. 12, 61 n. 19, 61 n. 21, 64 n. 28, 65 n. 31, 66 n. 33, 71 n. 7, 71 n. 8, 72 n. 10, 73 n. 11, 80 n. 8, 86 n. 23, 95 n. 17, 95 n. 18, 96 n. 22, 98 n. 29, 104 n. 3, 114 n. 24, 116 n. 30, 117 n. 33, 121 n. 40, 126 n. 5, 131 n. 18, 132 n. 21, 133 n. 24, 133 n. 25, 135 n. 31, 136 n. 33, 136 n. 34, 137 n. 36, 138 n. 41, 138 n. 42, 140 n. 46, 140 n. 47, 146 n. 2, 150 n. 12, 151 n. 13, 152 n. 15, 153 n. 17, 157 n. 31, 158 n. 35, 162 n. 6, 163 n. 8, 165 n. 11, 165 n. 12, 165 n. 14, 165 n. 15, 169 n. 24, 176 n. 4, 181 n. 11, 181 n. 12, 183 n. 17, 184 n. 23, 185 n. 25, 194 n. 6, 196 n. 9, 198 n. 15, 212 n. 22, 217 n. 26, 223 n. 4, 223 n. 5, 223 n. 6, 224 n. 7, 224 n. 8, 225 n. 11, 225 n. 12, 227 n. 14, 227 n. 15, 228 n. 18, 233 n. 7, 234 n. 9, 242 n. 24, 243 n. 28, 248 n. 4, 254 n. 23
Fernández Marcos, Natalio, 5 n. 10, 129 n. 11
Fiore, Benjamin, 48 n. 33, 112 n. 18
Fisk, Bruce N., 116 n. 29, 118 n. 36, 119 n. 37, 133 n. 23
Fitzmyer, Joseph A., 179 n. 7, 184 n. 21, 186 n. 27
Foley, John Miles, 19 n. 10
Fotopoulos, John, 133 n. 23, 134 n. 26, 134 n. 27, 135 n. 29, 136 n. 33, 137 n. 36, 142 n. 52, 152 n. 15, 152 n. 17, 153 n. 18, 153 n. 21, 164 n. 9, 165 n. 11, 166 n. 15, 167 n. 18, 168 n. 20, 168 n. 21, 169 n. 24
Frankemölle, Hubert, 146 n. 3, 187 n. 29
Frid, Bo, 58 n. 9
Friedrich, Gerhard, 118 n. 34
Friedrich, Johannes H., 254 n. 22

Gaffin, Richard B., 236 n. 14
García, J. M., 210 n. 15
García Pérez, J. M., 257 n. 32

Gardner, Paul Douglas, 135 n. 30, 137 n. 36. 146 n. 2, 153 n. 20, 165 n. 14
Garland, David E., 24 n. 21, 53 n. 1, 78 n. 2, 91 n. 7, 115 n. 27, 125 n. 1, 131 n. 14, 134 n. 29, 136 n. 33, 142 n. 52, 146 n. 2, 153 n. 17, 157 n. 31, 163 n. 6, 165 n. 11, 165 n. 13, 166 n. 15, 167 n. 18, 167 n. 20, 168 n. 21, 169 n. 23, 169 n. 24, 169 n. 25, 170 n. 26, 176 n. 4, 179 n. 7, 181 n. 11, 183 n. 18, 184 n. 21, 188 n. 31, 188 n. 32, 192 n. 1, 193 n. 3, 196 n. 9, 196 n. 10, 196 n. 11, 197 n. 12, 198 n. 16, 200 n. 19, 206 n. 3, 206 n. 5, 214 n. 24, 217 n. 26, 218 n. 27, 222 n. 3, 223 n. 6, 225 n. 11, 226 n. 13, 228 n. 18, 232 n. 4, 239 n. 19, 250 n. 9, 253 n. 21, 254 n. 23, 256 n. 30
Gathercole, Simon J., 40 n. 14
Gielen, Marlis, 177 n. 5, 180 n. 9, 180 n. 10, 183 n. 18, 214 n. 24, 216 n. 25
Gill, David W. J., 7 n. 17, 165 n. 11, 177 n. 5
Gillman, John, 238 n. 18, 252 n. 14, 255 n. 25, 255 n. 26, 256 n. 28, 256 n. 29, 257 n. 31
Given, Mark D., 3 n. 6
Gladstone, Robert J., 200 n. 19, 201 n. 21, 202 n. 22
Gooch, Peter David, 133 n. 23, 137 n. 36
Goodwin, Mark J., 33 n. 57
Gorman, Michael J., 3 n. 6, 30 n. 45
Goulder, Michael D., 27 n. 37, 30 n. 46, 99 n. 32, 108 n. 11
Gräbe, Petrus J., 25 n. 28, 26 n. 31, 42 n. 18
Grant, Robert M., 7 n. 17
Grindheim, Sigurd, 59 n. 12, 60 n. 13, 61 n. 19, 65 n. 31, 73 n. 13
Grosvenor, Mary, 93 n. 13
Grudem, Wayne A., 179 n. 7, 192 n. 1
Gundry-Volf, Judith M., 177 n. 5, 179 n. 7, 179 n. 8, 181 n. 13, 182 n. 16, 184 n. 22, 185 n. 24

Hall, David R., 48 n. 33
Hanges, James C., 49 n. 34
Harland, P. J., 183 n. 19
Harris, Gerald, 94 n. 16

Harrisville, Roy A., 95 n. 18
Harvey, John D., 7 n. 16, 22 n. 16
Hay, David M., 206 n. 3
Hays, Richard B., 1 n. 1, 2 n. 3, 9 n. 24, 26 n. 31, 30 n. 45, 37 n. 2, 49 n. 34, 80 n. 6, 91 n. 8, 150 n. 12, 163 n. 8, 221 n. 1, 234 n. 9
Hegermann, Harald, 27 n. 33, 27 n. 34
Heil, John Paul, 6 n. 14, 106 n. 8
Heil, Uta, 208 n. 8, 208 n. 10
Hengel, Martin, 9 n. 22
Hester, James D., 8 n. 18
Hickling, C. J. A., 1 n. 2
Hill, Charles E., 213 n. 23
Hjort, Birgitte Graakjaer, 178 n. 5
Hodgens, David, 236 n. 14
Hofius, Otfried, 54 n. 2, 169 n. 22
Holland, Glenn, 4 n. 8
Hollander, Harm W., 139 n. 43, 249 n. 7, 250 n. 10, 253 n. 20, 257 n. 32, 258 n. 33, 258 n. 34, 258 n. 35
Holleman, Joost, 207 n. 6, 207 n. 8, 212 n. 22, 249 n. 7, 250 n. 10, 253 n. 20, 257 n. 32, 258 n. 33, 258 n. 34, 258 n. 35
Holmyard, Harold R., 177 n. 5
Horn, F. W., 257 n. 32
Horrell, David G., 8 n. 17, 142 n. 50
Horsley, Richard A., 3 n. 7, 108 n. 12, 180 n. 9
Hughes, Frank Witt, 3 n. 6, 3 n. 7
Hultgren, Stephen J., 236 n. 13
Hyldahl, Niels, 7 n. 17

Ince, Gwen, 178 n. 5

Jacobs, Lambert D., 4 n. 8
Jeremias, Joachim, 254 n. 23
Jervis, L. Ann, 177 n. 5
Jewett, Robert, 70 n. 5
Jobes, Karen H., 37 n. 2, 129 n. 11
Johanson, Bruce C., 192 n. 1
Johnson, Andy, 211 n. 20, 236 n. 14

Kaiser, W. C., 130 n. 14
Kammler, Hans-Christian, 17 n. 1, 17 n. 2, 30 n. 46, 31 n. 48, 31 n. 50, 37 n. 1, 53 n. 1, 61 n. 18, 74 n. 14
Ker, D. P., 26 n. 32

Kertelge, Karl, 44 n. 22, 45 n. 25
Kim, Seyoon, 61 n. 20, 137 n. 36
Kirchhoff, Renate, 103 n. 2, 104 n. 3, 111 n. 16, 113 n. 21, 113 n. 22, 114 n. 23, 114 n. 24, 114 n. 25, 115 n. 26, 115 n. 28, 116 n. 31, 117 n. 33, 122 n. 42
Kistemaker, Simon J., 94 n. 16
Klauck, Hans-Josef, 199 n. 18
Klein, George L., 121 n. 40
Koch, Dietrich-Alex, 2 n. 3, 17 n. 1, 37 n. 2, 38 n. 6, 53 n. 1, 54 n. 2, 69 n. 2, 78 n. 2, 78 n. 3, 91 n. 5, 104 n. 4, 125 n. 1, 127 n. 6, 129 n. 11, 130 n. 12, 161 n. 1, 165 n. 11, 166 n. 17, 192 n. 1, 206 n. 4, 226 n. 13, 249 n. 8, 250 n. 10, 250 n. 11, 251 n. 12
Koet, Bart J., 1 n. 2, 9 n. 22, 150 n. 11, 154 n. 23
Konradt, Matthias, 26 n. 32, 157 n. 31
Köstenberger, Andreas J., 29 n. 42
Krämer, Helmut, 60 n. 14, 255 n. 25
Kreitzer, Larry Joseph, 148 n. 9, 208 n. 9
Kuck, David W., 24 n. 23, 44 n. 23, 48 n. 33, 60 n. 17, 65 n. 30, 65 n. 31, 66 n. 32, 74 n. 15, 80 n. 6, 86 n. 24

Lambrecht, Jan, 1 n. 2, 205 n. 2, 206 n. 5, 207 n. 7, 211 n. 19, 213 n. 23, 216 n. 25
Lamp, Jeffrey S., 26 n. 31, 31 n. 49, 32 n. 54, 33 n. 56, 34 n. 59, 41 n. 16, 42 n. 17, 60 n. 17, 61 n. 19, 62 n. 22, 62 n. 23, 74 n. 15, 74 n. 16
Lampe, Peter, 3 n. 8
Lanier, David E., 1 n. 2, 192 n. 1
Lautenschlager, Markus, 31 n. 48
Lewis, Scott M., 205 n. 1, 205 n. 2, 206 n. 3, 207 n. 7, 210 n. 16, 213 n. 23, 214 n. 24, 217 n. 26
Lim, Timothy H., 2 n. 3, 28 n. 38, 38 n. 4, 69 n. 3
Limbeck, Meinrad, 20 n. 13
Lincoln, Andrew T., 234 n. 9, 236 n. 14, 241 n. 23
Lindemann, Andreas, 1 n. 1, 19 n. 12, 25 n. 28, 33 n. 56, 37 n. 1, 40 n. 12, 41 n. 17, 42 n. 18, 44 n. 24, 46 n. 26, 46 n. 27, 54 n. 2, 55 n. 4, 56 n. 5, 58 n. 9, 65 n. 28, 65 n. 31, 71 n. 8, 73 n. 11, 108 n. 13, 114 n. 24, 128 n, 8, 129 n. 11, 162 n. 6, 166 n. 17, 179 n. 7, 180 n. 9, 195 n. 7, 207 n. 7, 208 n. 10, 211 n. 18, 218 n. 27, 233 n. 5, 248 n. 3, 252 n. 15
Litfin, Duane, 3 n. 8, 28 n. 38, 30 n. 45, 85 n. 21
Lockwood, Gregory J., 17 n. 3, 23 n. 18, 24 n. 22, 25 n. 24, 26 n. 31, 33 n. 57, 37 n. 1, 39 n. 9, 42 n. 17, 42 n. 18, 49 n. 34, 64 n. 28, 69 n. 2, 78 n. 4, 80 n.7, 85 n. 21, 95 n. 18, 104 n. 4, 105 n. 6, 120 n. 39, 136 n. 34, 137 n. 38, 141 n. 48, 146 n. 2, 155 n. 25, 162 n. 5, 167 n. 20, 183 n. 17, 186 n. 26, 186 n. 27, 196 n. 10, 212 n. 22, 214 n. 24, 216 n. 25, 223 n. 6, 224 n. 8, 226 n. 13, 227 n. 15, 256 n. 30
Lohse, Eduard, 131 n. 15

Malan, François S., 1 n. 1, 192 n. 1, 216 n. 25, 221 n. 1
Malherbe, Abraham J., 115 n. 26, 222 n. 3, 225 n. 12
Marsh, Clive, 29 n. 44
Marshall, Peter, 28 n. 38
Martin, Dale B., 94 n. 16, 116 n. 29, 141 n. 48, 177 n. 5
Martin, Troy W., 187 n. 30
McConville, J. Gordon, 89 n. 1
McGinn, Sheila E., 175 n. 4
McKay, Kenneth L., 39 n. 10
McLay, R. Timothy, 73 n. 13, 129 n. 11
Meeks, Wayne A., 7 n. 17, 9 n. 22, 151 n. 13
Meggitt, Justin J., 8 n. 17, 133 n. 23
Meier, John P., 177 n. 5
Merklein, Helmut, 26 n. 30, 42 n. 18
Merz, A., 116 n. 31
Metzger, Bruce M., 58 n. 8, 60 n. 13
Miller, J. I., 115 n. 27
Mitchell, Margaret M., 3 n. 7, 10 n. 25, 28 n. 39, 49 n. 35, 107 n. 10, 108 n. 13, 109 n. 14, 119 n. 38, 122 n. 43, 136 n. 33, 151 n. 13, 153 n. 18, 156 n. 28, 164 n. 10, 170 n. 27
Morissette, Rodolphe, 237 n. 15, 241 n. 23, 247 n. 1, 247 n. 2, 248 n. 6, 249 n. 8, 254 n. 23

Muraoka, Takamitsu, 90 n. 2
Murphy-O'Connor, Jerome, 29 n. 41, 107 n. 10, 177 n. 5

Nasuti, Harry P., 133 n. 22
Newton, Derek, 133 n. 23, 134 n. 28, 136 n. 33, 139 n. 44, 152 n. 15, 152 n. 16, 164 n. 10, 167 n. 18, 168 n. 20, 168 n. 21, 170 n. 28
Newton, Michael, 95 n. 20, 96 n. 21, 96 n. 22

O'Day, Gail R., 1 n. 2, 34 n. 59, 37 n. 1
O'Donoghue, N.D., 238 n. 18
Oberlinner, Lorenz, 242 n. 25
Olbricht, Thomas H., 3 n. 6
Ollrog, Wolf-Henning, 29 n. 41
Omanson, Roger L., 107 n. 10
Oropeza, B. J., 133 n. 23, 135 n. 29, 146 n. 2, 147 n. 5, 148 n. 8, 149 n. 10, 150 n. 11, 150 n. 12, 151 n. 13, 151 n. 14, 152 n. 15, 152 n. 17, 154 n. 21, 155 n. 24, 155 n. 25, 156 n. 27, 156 n. 29, 157 n. 31, 157 n. 32, 157 n. 33, 158 n. 34
Osborne, R. E., 225 n. 12
Osburn, Carroll D., 155 n. 25
Ostmeyer, Karl-Heinrich, 97 n. 25

Padgett, Alan G., 177 n. 5, 187 n. 29, 233 n. 5
Palzkill, Angela, 147 n. 4
Park, Joseph S., 222 n. 3
Pascuzzi, Maria, 4 n. 8, 92 n. 8, 98 n. 27, 99 n. 31
Pate, C. Marvin, 2 n. 4
Paulsen, Henning, 257 n. 31
Penna, Romano, 2 n. 3, 25 n. 29
Perriman, Andrew C., 179 n. 7, 179 n. 8, 254 n. 23
Peterson, Brian K., 4 n. 8
Petzke, Gerd, 81 n. 10
Pfammater, Josef, 198 n.17
Pickett, Raymond, 25 n. 28, 30 n. 45, 96 n. 20, 96 n. 21
Pietersma, Albert, 130 n. 12, 183 n. 20
Plag, Christoph, 11 n. 27, 126 n. 2
Plank, Karl A., 3 n. 8
Plevnik, Joseph, 206 n. 5, 254 n. 23

Plummer, Alfred, 58 n. 10, 78 n. 4, 80 n. 7, 131 n. 18, 136 n. 33, 155 n. 25, 162 n. 4
Pogoloff, Stephen M., 3 n. 7, 6 n. 15, 27 n. 37, 28 n. 38, 30 n. 46, 30 n. 47, 31 n. 48
Pokorný, Petr, 201 n. 20
Ponsot, Hervé, 53 n. 1
Popkes, Wiard, 60 n. 15
Porter, Stanley E., 92 n. 9, 115 n. 27
Probst, Hermann, 3 n. 8

Radcliffe, Timothy, 108 n. 13
Ramsaran, Rollin A., 40 n. 13, 50 n. 37, 86 n. 23, 138 n. 40, 164 n. 9
Rebell, Walter, 201 n. 20
Reinmuth, Eckart, 3 n. 7
Richardson, Neil, 18 n. 4, 48 n. 31, 113 n. 21
Richardson, Peter, 141 n. 49
Rissi, Mathias, 66 n. 33
Robbins, Vernon. K., 7 n. 16
Robertson, Archibald, 58 n. 10, 78 n. 4, 80 n. 7, 131 n. 18, 136 n. 33, 155 n. 25, 162 n. 4
Robertson, C. K., 8 n. 17, 23 n. 17, 108 n. 11
Roloff, Jürgen, 23 n. 17
Rosner, Brian S., 1 n. 2, 2 n. 4, 8 n. 18, 8 n. 20, 91 n. 7, 91 n. 8, 93 n. 12, 94 n. 16, 108 n. 11, 116 n. 31, 118 n. 35
Rothaus, Richard M., 7 n. 17

Sand, Alexander, 59 n. 11, 70 n. 5, 212 n. 22
Sandelin, Karl-Gustav, 134 n. 27, 142 n. 52, 150 n. 10, 151 n. 13
Sanders, Jack T., 93 n. 12
Sandnes, Karl Olav, 111 n. 17, 112 n. 19, 146 n. 2, 151 n. 12, 154 n. 21, 156 n. 30, 192 n. 1
Saw, Insawn, 4 n. 8
Sänger, Dieter, 34 n. 59
Schaller, Berndt, 77 n. 2
Schneider, Bernardin, 232 n. 4, 236 n. 13
Schneider, Sebastian, 255 n. 25
Schrage, Wolfgang, 31 n. 49, 37 n. 2, 37 n. 3, 39 n. 9, 41 n. 17, 42 n. 17, 42 n. 19, 44 n. 22, 44 n. 24, 45 n. 25, 46

(Schrage) n. 26, 46 n. 27, 48 n. 30, 54 n. 2, 58 n. 9, 64 n. 28, 65 n. 31, 71 n. 5, 74 n. 14, 112 n. 20, 114 n. 24, 117 n. 32, 126 n. 4, 126 n. 5, 127 n. 6, 140 n. 45, 146 n. 2, 150 n. 10, 166 n. 17, 180 n. 9, 181 n. 12, 183 n. 18, 222 n. 3, 252 n. 17, 253 n. 21, 256 n. 30
Schreiner, Josef, 39 n. 7
Schunack, Gerd, 150 n. 12
Schüssler Fiorenza, Elizabeth, 3 n. 7
Selby, Gary S., 4 n. 8, 61 n. 18
Shillington, V. George, 94 n. 16
Sibinga, Joost Smit, 142 n. 50
Silva, Moisés, 37 n. 2, 129 n. 11
Smit, Joop F. M., 1 n. 2, 4 n. 8, 26 n. 32, 28 n. 37, 60 n. 16, 126 n. 4, 126 n. 5, 127 n. 6, 131 n. 17, 131 n. 19, 132 n. 20, 132 n. 22, 133 n. 23, 134 n. 28, 137 n. 36, 139 n. 44, 151 n. 13, 163 n. 7, 164 n. 9, 164 n. 10, 165 n. 15, 168 n. 21, 200 n. 19
Smith, D. Moody, 1 n.1
Smith, Dennis E., 98 n. 28
Soards, Marion L., 186 n. 27
Sollamo, Raija, 5 n. 10
Son, Sang-Won (Aaron), 114 n. 24, 117 n. 33
South, James T., 94 n. 16
Söding, Thomas, 257 n. 32
Sparks, Hedley Frederick Davis, 54 n. 2
Stamps, Dennis L., 4 n. 8
Standhartinger, Angela, 27 n. 37
Stanley, Christopher D., 2 n. 3, 2 n. 5, 5 n. 12, 7 n. 17, 8 n. 19, 11 n. 26, 17 n. 1, 17 n. 2, 37 n. 1, 38 n. 6, 40 n. 12, 53 n. 1, 77 n. 2, 78 n. 3, 91 n. 5, 103 n. 1, 125 n. 1, 127 n. 6, 128 n. 7, 129 n. 11, 130 n. 13, 192 n. 1, 206 n. 4, 206 n. 5, 209 n. 12, 209 n. 13, 231 n. 1, 231 n. 2, 232 n. 3, 247 n. 2, 249 n. 8, 250 n. 10, 251 n. 11, 251 n. 12
Stenschke, Christoph W., 9 n. 21
Sterling, Gregory E., 66 n. 34
Still, E. Coye, 134 n. 29, 137 n. 36, 142 n. 52
Stockhausen, Carol Kern, 5 n. 11, 77 n. 1, 126 n. 3
Stone, Michael E., 54 n. 2
Strüder, Christof W., 29 n. 43
Strugnell, John, 54 n. 2
Stuckenbruck, Loren T., 184 n. 21
Sumney, Jerry L., 3 n. 6, 85 n. 22

Talbert, Charles H., 22 n. 16
Talshir, Zipora, 174 n. 3
Teani, Maurizio, 233 n. 7, 241 n. 23
Theis, Joachim, 59 n. 12
Theissen, Gerd, 7 n. 17, 8 n. 17
Thiselton, Anthony. C., 5 n. 13, 7 n. 17, 19 n. 12, 23 n. 18, 24 n. 21, 24 n. 22, 27 n. 37, 31 n. 47, 35 n. 61, 37 n. 1, 41 n. 15, 44 n. 22, 44 n. 23, 44 n. 24, 45 n. 25, 46 n. 26, 46 n. 27, 47 n. 29, 48 n. 33, 49 n. 34, 53 n. 1, 54 n. 2, 55 n. 4, 58 n. 8, 58 n. 9, 59 n. 10, 59 n. 11, 59 n. 12, 60 n. 13, 60 n. 16, 61 n. 19, 61 n. 21, 64 n. 28, 65 n. 30, 65 n. 31, 69 n. 3, 70 n. 5, 71 n. 6, 72 n. 10, 74 n. 14, 78 n. 2, 78 n. 4, 80 n. 7, 82 n. 12, 86 n. 23, 92 n. 10, 93 n. 14, 94 n. 17, 95 n. 18, 95 n. 19, 96 n. 23, 97 n. 24, 99 n. 31, 103 n. 1, 104 n. 4, 105 n. 6, 108 n. 13, 112 n. 17, 112 n. 18, 113 n. 22, 114 n. 24, 115 n. 27, 117 n. 32, 118 n. 35, 121 n. 40, 135 n. 29, 135 n. 31, 136 n. 34, 137 n. 36, 137 n. 37, 138 n. 41, 138 n. 42, 146 n. 2, 150 n. 12, 151 n. 13, 155 n. 25, 157 n. 31, 162 n. 5, 163 n. 6, 165 n. 14, 166 n. 15, 179 n. 7, 180 n. 10, 183 n. 18, 188 n. 31, 188 n. 32, 192 n. 2, 197 n. 11, 197 n. 13, 197 n. 14, 206 n. 4, 206 n. 5, 211 n. 19, 212 n. 22, 214 n. 24, 222 n. 3, 223 n. 5, 223 n. 6, 224 n. 8, 225 n. 9, 225 n. 10, 225 n. 12, 226 n. 12, 226 n. 13, 227 n. 16, 227 n. 17, 248 n. 4, 248 n. 5, 249 n. 8, 252 n. 18, 255 n. 27, 258 n. 36
Thompson, Cynthia L., 177 n. 5
Thompson, James W., 177 n. 5
Thomson, Ian H., 106 n. 8
Thrall, Margaret E., 8 n. 17
Tomson, Peter J., 2 n. 4, 8 n. 18, 8 n. 20, 105 n. 5, 162 n. 6
Tuckett, Chistopher M., 1 n. 1, 8 n. 19, 37 n. 2, 57 n. 7, 91 n. 8

Tyler, Ronald L., 49 n. 34

Usami, Kôshi, 233 n. 5

van der Minde, Hans-Jürgen, 145 n. 1
Vander Broek, Lyle D., 94 n. 16
van Rensburg, Fika J., 8 n. 17
Verheyden, Joseph, 54 n. 2
Verhoef, Eduard, 23 n. 20
Vincent, Jean-M., 232 n. 4
von Nordheim, Eckard, 54 n. 2
Vos, Johan S., 48 n. 33, 60 n. 16, 63 n. 26, 66 n. 33, 70 n. 5, 212 n. 21

Wagner, J. Ross, 37 n. 2, 49 n. 34
Walker, William O., 60 n. 16
Wanamaker, Charles A., 35 n. 64
Watson, Duane F., 3 n. 8, 40 n. 14, 164 n. 9, 168 n. 21, 169 n. 23, 237 n. 15
Watson, Francis, 178 n. 5
Wedderburn, A. J. M., 32 n. 54, 41 n. 16
Weiser, Alfons, 46 n. 27
Welborn, Laurence L., 4 n. 8, 34 n. 60, 49 n. 34
Welch, John W., 196 n. 8
Wevers, John William, 90 n. 3, 145 n. 1, 146 n. 3, 147 n. 6, 154 n. 22, 161 n. 2, 174 n. 2, 181 n. 13, 182 n. 14, 182 n. 15, 183 n. 19, 193 n. 4, 193 n. 5, 232 n. 3, 233 n. 7, 234 n. 8
Wilk, Florian, 2 n. 3, 17 n. 1, 18 n. 6, 18 n. 7, 19 n. 9, 22 n. 15, 66 n. 33, 69 n. 1, 192 n. 1, 195 n. 7, 196 n. 9, 222 n. 2
Williams, David J., 114 n. 24, 131 n. 14

Williams, H. H. Drake, 2 n. 4, 6 n. 14, 8 n. 18, 17 n. 3, 34 n. 59, 37 n. 1, 37 n. 2, 38 n. 6, 53 n. 1, 70 n. 4, 70 n. 5, 73 n. 11, 78 n. 2, 78 n. 3
Williams, Ritva, 177 n. 5
Willis, Wendell Lee, 74 n. 16, 133 n. 23, 136 n. 33, 169 n. 23
Wilson, Kenneth T., 176 n. 4
Winandy, Jacques, 184 n. 21
Winter, Bruce W., 4 n. 8, 28 n. 38, 28 n. 39, 34 n. 59, 39 n. 8, 48 n. 32, 108 n. 11, 112 n. 19, 133 n. 23, 164 n. 9, 178 n. 5
Wire, Antoinette C., 3 n. 7
Wischmeyer, Oda, 57 n. 6
Witherington, Ben, 7 n. 17, 8 n. 19, 10 n. 25, 37 n. 1, 41 n. 15, 177 n. 5
Wolff, Christian, 31 n. 50, 38 n. 6, 42 n. 18, 48 n. 31, 48 n. 33, 53 n. 1, 58 n. 9, 61 n. 19, 64 n. 28, 65 n. 31, 70 n. 5, 85 n. 20, 114 n. 24, 126 n. 5, 162 n. 6, 166 n. 17, 186 n. 26, 205 n. 2
Wuellner, Wilhelm, 3 n. 7, 8 n. 18

Yarbro Collins, Adela, 94 n. 16
Yeo, Khiok-Khng, 4 n. 8, 177 n. 5
Yinger, Kent L., 2 n. 4
Yorke, Gosnell L. O. R., 114 n. 24, 120 n. 39

Zaas, Peter S., 1 n. 2, 94 n. 15, 98 n. 27
Zerhusen, Robert, 198 n. 16
Zerwick, Maximilian, 91 n. 6, 92 n. 9, 93 n. 13
Zmijewski, Josef, 40 n. 14

Scripture Index

Hebrew Bible

Genesis
1   232 n. 4
1:11–12   232
1:11   232 n. 4
1:14–19   233 n. 6
1:14–15   233
1:16   233, 233 n. 6
1:20–25   174 n. 2, 233, 233 n. 5
1:26–28   233 n. 5
1:26–27   174, 175, 188, 234, 243, 244, 245
1:26   182 n. 14, 233
1:27   12, 15, 181, 181 n. 13, 189, 234 n. 10
1:31   175, 188
2:7   13, 15, 231 n. 2, 232 n. 3, 233 n. 7, 235, 236 n. 14
2:7a   233, 233 n. 7, 234, 241
2:7b   231, 232, 232 n. 3, 233, 234, 236, 240, 241, 243, 244, 245
2:16   232, 232 n. 3
2:17   258
2:18   12, 15, 175, 181, 182, 182 n. 14, 182 n. 15, 182 n. 16, 188, 189
2:19–20a   182
2:20–23   175, 188
2:20   181, 182 n. 15, 189
2:20b   175, 182
2:21–24   12, 15
2:21–23   181, 182, 189
2:21–22   182
2:22   182 n. 14
2:23   182
2:23b   174–75, 185
2:24   12, 14, 103 n. 1, 104 n. 3, 104 n. 4, 105 n. 5, 117 n. 33
2:24ab   104
2:24a   105
2:24b   105, 115, 122 n. 42
2:24c   103, 104, 105, 107, 109, 110, 111, 115, 122
3:6   258
3:16   12, 15, 175, 185, 188, 190
3:19   244, 245, 258
3:19b   234, 234 n. 8, 241
4:25   232 n. 3
5:1   175, 188
5:1b   174
5:3   234, 234 n. 10, 243, 244, 245
9:6   175, 188
9:6b   174
17:3   194
17:17   194
26:9   146 n. 2
39   118 n. 35

Exodus
12:23   157 n. 31
15:17   57
15:24   156
16:2–9   156
16:4   148
16:35   148
17:2–7   155
17:2–3   156
17:6   148
19:5   146, 161
19:16   255 n. 27
20:6   57 n. 6
23:20   57
32   153 n. 20
32:1–6a   145, 158
32:4   145
32:6   12, 14, 152 n. 17, 153 n. 20, 153 n. 21, 154 n. 23
32:6a   147

295

(Exodus) 32:6b   145, 146, 147, 149, 151 n. 13, 152–59
32:17   146, 146 n. 2
32:18   146, 146 n. 2
32:19   146, 146 n. 2
32:28   154 n. 23
32:28b   154

Leviticus
9:24   194
11:44   24 n. 21
19:2   24 n. 21
20:26   24 n. 21

Numbers
11   151 n. 13
11:1   156
11:4–6   151 n. 14
11:4   151, 151 n. 14, 156
11:5–6   151
11:13   152 n. 14
11:18   152 n. 14
11:21   152 n. 14
11:33–34   151 n. 14
11:33   149, 152 n. 14
11:34–35   151 n. 13
14:11–12   149
14:16   149
14:22   192
14:28–35   149
16:22   194
20:11   148
21   156 n. 27
21:5   156
21:6   155
21:7   156, 156 n. 28
25   153 n. 20, 154 n. 23
25:9   154
26:64–65   149
33:16–17   151 n. 13

Deuteronomy
4:10   23 n. 17
5:10   57 n. 6
7:9   56
10:14   161
10:21   39 n. 7
13–24   89

13:5   11
13:6   11, 14, 89, 90, 90 n. 3
17:7   11, 14, 89, 90
17:12   11, 14, 89, 90
19:13   11, 14, 89, 90
19:19   11, 14, 89, 90
21:9   11, 14, 89, 90, 90 n. 3
21:21   89, 90
22:5   183 n. 19
22:21   11, 14, 89, 90
22:22   11, 14, 89, 90
22:24   11, 14, 89, 90
23:1–8   22 n. 17
24:7   11, 14, 89, 90
25:4   12, 14, 125, 125 n. 1, 126 n. 4, 126 n. 5, 127, 130, 130 n. 13, 130 n. 14, 131, 131 n. 16, 131 n. 17, 132, 132 n. 20, 139, 142, 143
28:44   179 n. 7
28:45–49   15, 194, 202
28:45–48   193 n. 4
28:45   193
28:47   193
28:48   193
28:49   13, 192, 193, 193 n. 4
29:1–3   55
29:3   55
29:17   135 n. 29

Judges
20:2   22 n. 17
21:21   146 n. 2

1 Kingdoms (1 Samuel)
2:3   57
2:10   11, 14, 37, 37 n. 2, 37 n. 3, 38, 38 n. 6, 39, 50
13:13   57

2 Kingdoms (2 Samuel)
5:12   57
7:12   57
11:11   147 n. 5

3 Kingdoms (1 Kings)
18:26   146 n. 2
18:39   13, 15, 195, 196 n. 9

4 Kingdoms (2 Kings)
12:5   55 n. 4

1 Chronicles
14:2   57
16:35   39 n. 7
17:11   57
29:11   39 n. 7

Nehemiah
5:1   56
8:12   147 n. 5
9:15   148
9:20   148

Esther
1:20b   174

Job
5:12–13   80 n. 6
5:12   78 n. 4
5:13   11, 14, 78 n. 4
5:13a   77, 77 n. 2, 78, 79 n. 5, 80, 86
15:8   70
28:12–28   53 n. 1
41:3   161

Psalms
6:10   35 n. 61
8   216, 216 n. 25, 217
8:7   216 n. 25
8:7b   206
24:1   162 n. 5, 163 n. 6, 165 n. 15, 166 n. 15, 168 n. 20
31:17   35 n. 61
35:4   35 n. 61
35:26–27   35 n. 61
50:12   162 n. 5, 166 n. 15
78:15   148
78:20   148
78:23–25   148
89:11   166 n. 15
89:12   162 n. 5
94:11   80 n. 6
105:40–41   148
110   207 n. 6
110:1   205–6, 206 n. 3, 206 n. 4, 207, 208 n. 8, 208 n. 10, 209 n. 11

110:1b   206 n. 4
110:4   206 n. 3

Psalms (LXX)
4:9   130
5:10a   79
5:12   39 n. 7
7:6   174
8:1   174
8:5–6   183, 189
8:5   174
8:5a   211
8:6   174, 181, 189
8:7b   13, 15, 208, 209, 209 n. 13, 209 n. 14, 210, 210 n. 15, 211, 213, 216, 217, 218, 219
11:3   79
15:9   130
22:5   57
23:1   12, 14, 161 n. 2
23:1a   161, 161 n. 1, 162, 163, 165, 166 n. 17, 170
23:1b   161
31:11   39 n. 7
32:10   18, 18 n. 4, 18 n. 5, 18 n. 6, 18 n. 8, 19
32:11   18
48:7   40 n. 14
49:12   161–62
61:10   79
77:16   155
77:18–19   156 n. 27, 156 n. 28
77:18   155, 156 n. 27
77:19   156 n. 27
77:41   155
77:56   155
78:29–31   151 n. 13
80:12   192
88:12   162
88:18   39 n. 7
88:34   18 n. 5
88:35   17, 17 n. 3, 18
93:11   11, 14, 78, 79, 79 n. 5, 80, 81, 85 n. 19, 86
95:11   162 n. 5
101:26   162
105:14   151, 155
106   151 n. 13

(Psalms [LXX])   109   207 n. 6
109:1   13, 15, 205–6, 206 n. 3, 207, 208 n. 8, 209
109:1b   207, 208, 208 n. 9, 209, 209 n. 13, 209 n. 14, 210, 210 n. 15, 213, 215, 216, 218, 219
131:17   57
138:2b   79
138:20   79
145:4   79
145:20   56
149:5   39 n. 7

Proverbs
8:21   57 n. 6
11:16   174
11:16a   174
26:3   253 n. 21
31:30–31   174

Ecclesiastes (or Qoheleth)
3:10   175
3:11a   175
8:15   222
9:7–9   222

Isaiah
6:9–10   55
7:8–9   179 n. 7
7:25   129 n. 10
9:13   179 n. 7
11:2   118 n. 34
19:11–12   32 n. 52, 79–80
22:11–14   222 n. 2
22:12   221
22:13   221, 222 n. 3
22:13b   13, 15, 221, 222, 222 n. 2, 226, 228
22:14   221
23:18   147 n. 5
25:7   248
25:8   249 n. 7, 250 n. 10
25:8a   14, 15, 248, 249 n. 8, 250, 251, 259
28:11–12   13, 15, 191, 192, 192 n. 1, 193, 194, 202
28:11   191, 194
28:12   191, 192, 194
28:12a   196 n. 11
28:24   12, 14, 128, 129, 130, 130 n. 13, 143
28:24a   128, 129
28:24b–25   128
28:27–28a   128
28:28   12, 14, 128, 129, 130, 130 n. 13, 143
28:28b   129
29:13–14   18
29:14   25 n. 27, 36
29:14b–15   18
29:14b   10, 14, 17, 18 n. 6, 19, 80
29:15   18
32:6a   79
33:18   31
40:6b   174
40:7–8   174
40:13   11, 14, 69, 69 n. 3, 70 n. 4, 74
44:25   32 n. 52
45:7b   175
45:9   12, 14, 128, 128 n. 9, 130, 143
45:9b   128
45:14   13, 15, 195–96, 196 n. 9
48:6   53 n. 1
52:12   53 n. 1
52:13   54
52:14   54
52:15   11, 14, 54
53   25 n. 27
53:1b   54
59:7b   79
64:3   11, 14, 53, 53 n. 1, 54, 57, 66
65:16   11, 14
65:17   53 n. 1, 55 n. 4

Jeremiah
3:16   11, 14, 53 n. 1, 55 n. 4
5:13–15   15, 194, 202
5:13   193
5:14   193, 194
5:15   13, 192, 194
7:13   192
7:24   192
7:26   192
8:8   80
8:9   78
9:22–23   37 n. 2
9:22   34 n. 50, 37, 80
9:23–24   38 n. 4

9:23   11, 14, 37, 37 n. 3, 38, 38 n. 6, 39,
       50
13:11   192
16:8   147 n. 5
17:14   39 n. 7
23:18   70
25:7   192
33:5   192
38:7   179 n. 7
39:35   55 n. 4
41:14   192
41:17   192
42:16   192
51:4–5   192
51:21   55 n. 4

Lamentations
1:5   179 n. 7

Ezekiel
11:13   194
20:6   57
40:4   55
44:5   55

Daniel
2:46–47   13, 15, 195, 195 n. 7
2:47   196 n. 9

Hosea
3:1–3   121 n. 40
13:9   250
13:14a   250
13:14b   14, 15, 249–51, 259

Joel
3:5   24, 24 n. 22, 41 n. 15

Amos
5:6   175
5:8a   175

Zechariah
8:23   13, 15, 195, 195 n. 8, 196 n. 9
9:14   255 n. 27

1 Esdras
4:15–17   175

4:15   174
4:17b   174
4:17c   175
9:54   147 n. 5

Judith
8:14   69–70, 70 n. 4
12:11   147 n. 5

4 Maccabees
14:19   253 n. 21

Sirach
1:1–9   56
1:1a   56
1:1b   56
1:3b   56
1:4   56
1:6a   56
1:6b   56
1:9   56
1:9a   56
1:10   11, 14, 53 n. 1, 56, 56 n. 5, 57, 66
1:10b   56
1:11   39 n. 7
6:19   12, 14, 128, 129, 130, 143
9:16   39 n. 7
10:22   39 n. 7
17:1   174
17:3   174
19:23   78
19:25a   78
21:12   78
25:6   39 n. 7
33:5   79
36:1a   175
38:25   253 n. 21
39:8   39 n. 7
43:1–10   233
47:19   109 n. 15
50:20   39 n. 7

Wisdom
2:5–6   222
2:23   174
9:13   70
9:17   70
18:25   157 n. 31

New Testament

Matthew
10:10   142
16:18   198 n. 17
19:5   103 n. 1
22:44   206 n. 3
26:64   206 n. 3

Mark
10:8   103 n. 1
12:36   206 n. 3
14:62   206 n. 3

Luke
1:17   118 n. 34
10:7   142
12:19–20   222 n. 3
20:42–43   206 n. 3
21:28   45 n. 25
22:69   206 n. 3
24:27   9
24:44–45   9

John
10:34   192 n. 2

Acts
2:21   24 n. 22
2:34–35   206 n. 3
6:5   118 n. 34
6:8   118 n. 34
8:32   9
8:35   9
10:38   118 n. 34
13:16–41   9
13:27   9
13:29   9
13:44   9
13:46   9
13:46–48   9
13:48   9
13:49   9
15:29   167 n. 20
17:2   9
17:11–12   9
18:4   9
18:5–11   9
18:7   9, 29 n. 41
18:11   9
18:24   9
18:28   9
20:32   198 n. 17
21:25   167 n. 20
26:14   253 n. 21

Romans
3:4   115 n. 26
3:6   115 n. 26
3:19   192 n. 2
3:23–26   45 n. 25
3:31   115 n. 26
4:3   206
4:6   38 n. 5
5:11   41 n. 15
6:2   115 n. 26
6:15   115 n. 26
6:23   63 n. 26
7:7   115 n. 26
7:13   115 n. 26
8:11   118 n. 34
8:38   47
9:14   115 n. 26
9:17   206
9:25   38 n. 5
9:27   38 n. 5
9:29   38 n. 5
10:9   41 n. 15
10:11   206
10:13   24 n. 22, 41 n. 15
11:1   115 n. 26
11:2   206
11:9   38 n. 5
11:11   115 n. 26
11:34   69 n. 3
12:9   104 n. 3
12:19   196 n. 11
14:17   254 n. 22
14:19   198 n. 17
15:2   198 n. 17

1 Corinthians
1:1–30   41–45
1:1–18   22–30
1:1–3   22–24, 36
1:1   23, 23 n. 20, 29, 29 n. 41
1:2–9   59
1:2   7, 22, 23, 24, 24 n. 21, 33 n. 57, 42, 44
1:3   42, 63

Scripture Index 301

1:4–9   24–25, 36
1:4   24, 24 n. 24, 50, 63, 63 n. 26
1:5   63
1:6   24, 24 n. 24
1:7–8   24 n. 23
1:7   42, 63
1:8   24, 24 n. 24, 25 n. 25, 25 n. 27, 42, 44, 44 n. 23
1:9   24, 24 n. 24, 42, 44, 45
1:10–4:21   36 n. 64
1:10–18   25–30, 36
1:10–17   29 n. 44, 72, 75
1:10–13   32, 35, 81, 83, 87
1:10   28, 28 n. 39, 42, 48, 74, 74 n. 16, 75
1:11–13   28
1:11–12   85
1:11   29
1:12   26 n. 32, 27 n. 37, 29, 46, 47, 48, 48 n. 31, 50, 51, 85 n. 22, 85 n. 23, 136
1:13   29, 72, 74, 75, 148
1:14–17   148
1:17–3:19a   81–84
1:17–3:4   27 n. 37
1:17–2:13   70
1:17–21   43, 51
1:17–18   83, 87
1:17   26–27, 27 n. 36, 28, 28 n. 37, 29, 30, 31–32, 34, 35, 36, 43, 51, 72, 74, 75, 81, 83, 87
1:18–4:21   10–11, 14
1:18–31   10, 29 n. 41
1:18   22, 24, 25, 26, 26 n. 31, 26 n. 32, 27, 28, 29, 30, 32, 33, 33 n. 56, 34, 34 n. 60, 36, 45, 55, 81, 82, 156
1:18a   33
1:18b   33
1:19–20   32 n. 52
1:19   10, 14, 17–36, 43, 48, 51, 80, 80 n. 6, 81–82, 81 n. 11, 83, 86, 87, 251 n. 13
1:20–4:21   30–35, 36
1:20–21   33 n. 55
1:20   18, 30 n. 46, 32 n. 52, 34 n. 58, 34 n. 60, 35, 36, 43, 47, 51, 82 n. 13, 82 n. 14, 252 n. 19
1:20a   30–31, 32, 32 n. 52
1:20b   32, 34, 82
1:21–2:15   71–72
1:21   32, 33, 43, 45, 47, 51, 55, 71, 84
1:22–24   7

1:22   48 n. 31
1:23–24   43
1:23   33, 72, 74, 75, 82
1:24   33, 33 n. 57, 55
1:25   33, 35 n. 62, 45
1:26–28   33, 42
1:26–27   37
1:26   33, 33 n. 57, 34, 34 n. 59, 35, 37, 82
1:26b   34 n. 59
1:27–29   82 n. 13
1:27–28   41, 50
1:27   35, 35 n. 62, 36, 47, 82
1:27a   34
1:27b   35
1:28   35, 36, 47, 112 n. 17
1:29–30   39, 83
1:29   39 n. 11, 41, 42
1:30   41 n. 16, 42, 42 n. 17, 42 n. 18, 43, 44, 45, 45 n. 25, 48, 51
1:30a   41
1:30b   41
1:31   11, 14, 19 n. 11, 37–51, 80 n. 6, 83, 85, 85 n. 20, 86, 87, 167 n. 17, 251 n. 13
2:1–4:21   45–50, 134 n. 26
2:1–8   60–62
2:1–5   60, 60 n. 16
2:1–2   62, 74, 75, 83, 87
2:1   55, 60, 60 n. 16, 83, 87
2:2   55, 60, 60 n. 15, 60 n. 16, 62, 63, 67, 72, 74, 75
2:3   60 n. 16
2:4–14   70
2:4–5   35
2:4   60 n. 16, 118 n. 34
2:5–10   69 n. 1
2:5–8   67
2:5–6   59
2:5   45, 55, 60, 60 n. 16, 60 n. 17, 61
2:6–3:4   66 n. 34
2:6–16   11, 29 n. 41, 60 n. 16, 65 n. 30
2:6–8   18 n. 8, 82 n. 13
2:6–7   54, 60 n. 17, 65
2:6   18 n. 8, 58, 58 n. 8, 59, 60, 61, 61 n. 19, 65 n. 31, 112 n. 17
2:7–14   75
2:7–8   62, 71, 84
2:7   55, 58, 58 n. 9, 60, 61, 63, 73, 74, 75, 83, 87

(1 Corinthians) 2:7a   56, 58, 72, 75
2:7b–8   58
2:7b–8a   62, 67
2:7b   56, 60 n. 17, 61, 67
2:8–10   61 n. 20
2:8   18 n. 8, 54, 55, 56, 58, 58 n. 8, 58 n. 9, 59, 61, 61 n. 21, 72, 73, 74, 75
2:8b   72 n. 9
2:9–14   75
2:9–12   75
2:9–10a   58 n. 8
2:9   11, 14, 19 n. 11, 45, 48, 53–67, 72, 73, 80 n. 6, 83–84, 84 n. 17, 86, 87, 251 n. 13
2:9b   72 n. 9
2:10–15   62–66
2:10   58 n. 8, 62, 63, 63 n. 26, 64 n. 27, 65, 66, 67, 72 n. 9, 84
2:10a   54, 55, 56, 58, 58 n. 8, 59, 59 n. 12, 61, 62, 63, 67, 73
2:10b   62, 72
2:11   62, 63, 65, 70 n. 5, 71, 72, 72 n. 9, 75, 84
2:11b   72, 73
2:12–3:1   46
2:12–13   45, 65
2:12   47, 50, 62, 63, 63 n. 25, 63 n. 26, 64, 64 n. 27, 66, 67, 72 n. 9, 73, 85, 85 n. 21
2:12a   73
2:12b   64, 72
2:13–15   243
2:13–14   67
2:13   62, 64, 65, 65 n. 28, 73, 85, 148
2:13a   64
2:13b   64, 65 n. 28, 72
2:14–16   73 n. 13
2:14–15   66 n. 33
2:14   45, 62, 65 n. 28, 66, 71, 84, 238 n. 18
2:14a   72, 72 n. 9
2:15   62, 65 n. 28, 66, 73, 149
2:15a   66 n. 33, 72
2:15b   66 n. 33, 72, 75
2:16   11 n. 26, 50, 74 n. 15, 80 n. 6, 85, 85 n. 21, 86, 162 n. 3
2:16a   11, 14, 69–75, 84, 84 n. 18, 87
2:16b   71, 71 n. 8, 72, 73–74, 75, 84, 87
3   122 n. 43

3:1–12   199
3:1   64 n. 28, 149, 243
3:3–4   45, 46, 85, 85 n. 21
3:3   85
3:4–6   136
3:4   50, 85, 85 n. 23
3:5–4:5   48, 86
3:5–9   50
3:5   46, 49
3:6–9   139
3:6–7   46, 49
3:6   138
3:7–8   138
3:8   49, 259
3:9   46, 49, 50, 96 n. 21, 224 n. 8
3:10–17   259 n. 37
3:13–15   259
3:16–17   96 n. 20
3:16   46, 50, 95 n. 18, 113, 120–21
3:18–23   11, 48 n. 32
3:18   82, 187
3:19–20   46
3:19   19 n. 11, 47, 48, 86, 251 n. 13
3:19a   82, 82 n. 14
3:19b–20   77–88, 126 n. 2, 247
3:19b   11, 14
3:20   11, 14
3:21–4:21   84–86
3:21–23   50, 86 n. 23
3:21   45, 46, 47, 48, 50, 51, 85 n. 21, 85 n. 22
3:21a   79 n. 5, 83 n. 16, 84, 85, 86, 88
3:21b–23   85, 88
3:21b   46
3:22   46, 47, 85 n. 22, 136
3:23   48, 179
4:1   49, 224 n. 8
4:3–4   136, 136 n. 33
4:4   48 n. 33, 133 n. 24
4:6–13   224 n. 8
4:6–7   49 n. 35
4:6   48 n. 33, 49, 49 n. 34, 49 n. 35, 86 n. 25, 136
4:6a   48, 48 n. 33
4:6b   48, 86, 88
4:6c   49, 86, 88
4:7   73 n. 12
4:7a   49
4:7b   50, 51

4:8   185 n. 23
4:9–13   225
4:10   37
4:14–15   135
4:14   138
4:15b   225
4:17   188
4:19–20   35
4:20   254 n. 22
5–6   99 n. 32
5   98 n. 28
5:1–13   91, 92
5:1–13a   92–99
5:1–12   92 n. 8
5:1–11   99
5:1–7:40   11–12, 14
5:1–5   23 n. 17
5:1–2   92, 93, 100
5:1   93, 93 n. 12, 94, 94 n. 15, 97–98, 99, 99 n. 32, 100, 101
5:2   91, 93 n. 12
5:2a   93, 93 n. 12, 93 n. 13, 97, 100
5:2b   93, 93 n. 13
5:2c   93, 93 n. 13, 94, 100
5:3–5   92, 94, 100
5:3–4   94
5:3   99
5:5   94, 94 n. 16, 94 n. 17, 97 n. 25, 100, 157 n. 31
5:6–8   92, 95, 97 n. 25, 100
5:6–7   96 n. 20
5:6   97, 113
5:6a   97, 100
5:6b   95, 95 n. 18
5:7   96
5:7a   96, 97 n. 24, 100
5:8   96, 97
5:9–13   12, 92, 97, 99 n. 30, 100, 101
5:9–11   98
5:9   94 n. 15, 97, 98, 101
5:10–11   98 n. 27
5:10   94 n. 15, 97
5:10a   97 n. 26
5:11   94 n. 15, 98, 99, 101
5:12   99 n. 30
5:12a   98, 99
5:12b   98, 99, 101
5:13   11 n. 26
5:13a   98, 98 n. 30, 99

5:13b   11, 14, 89–101
6:1–7:2   99, 101
6:2   95 n. 18, 113
6:3   95 n. 18, 113
6:5   228 n. 18
6:5b   227
6:9–11   8, 151 n. 14
6:9–10   98 n. 27
6:9   95 n. 18, 99, 101, 113, 152 n. 16, 254 n. 22
6:10   254 n. 22
6:11   107, 118, 121
6:12–20   12, 103 n. 2, 105–11, 122 n. 43
6:12–16a   105, 111–16
6:12   106, 107, 108, 108 n. 13, 110, 111, 111 n. 16, 112, 114, 122, 123, 134 n. 26, 164, 169 n. 24
6:12a   109
612b   108 n. 12, 109
6:13–20   106, 107, 108, 108 n. 13, 109, 109 n. 14, 110, 111, 120, 121, 123
6:13–16a   123
6:13–15   113 n. 20
6:13–14   109, 110, 111, 112 n. 19, 113 n. 21, 121, 123
6:13   99, 101, 109, 110, 112 n. 17, 116 n. 31
6:13ab   111
6:13a   109, 110
6:13b   109, 110, 111 n. 17, 113, 121
6:13c–20   105 n. 8
6:13c   112 n. 17, 113, 116, 118, 119
6:14   110, 113, 114 n. 23, 118, 118 n. 34, 121
6:15–17   116 n. 31
6:15   95 n. 18, 109, 110, 111, 113, 115 n. 28, 116 n. 31, 120 n. 38, 121, 123, 153, 159
6:15a   113, 115, 116, 118, 119, 120
6:15b   114, 118
6:15c   114
6:16   95 n. 18, 103 n. 1, 104 n. 3, 115 n. 28
6:16a   103, 109, 110, 111, 115, 116, 117, 118, 119, 119 n. 37, 120, 121, 122, 123
6:16b   12, 14, 103–23
6:17–20   105, 117–22, 123

(1 Corinthians)   6:17   103–4, 104 n. 3, 109, 110, 111, 118, 118 n. 34, 119, 120, 121, 122, 123
6:18–20   120 n. 38
6:18   99, 101, 109, 110, 111, 118, 120 n. 38, 121, 122, 123, 258
6:18a   118
6:18b   118, 118 n. 36
6:18c   119, 119 n. 37, 120
6:19–20   110, 111, 122, 123
6:19   95 n. 18, 120, 121, 122 n. 43
6:20a   121
6:20b   121
7:2   99, 101
7:17   188
7:18   7
7:23   45 n. 25, 121
7:28   258
7:36   258
8:1–11:1   12, 14, 134 n. 27, 151 n. 13
8–10   133 n. 24, 148 n. 7, 152 n. 17, 170 n. 28
8:1–10:22   164 n. 10, 166
8:1–10:7a   147–53
8:1–10–5   147–49
8–9   164 n. 9
8:1–9:8   133–40
8   133 n. 24, 135 n. 29, 148 n. 8
8:1–13   140, 143, 152 n. 17
8:1–12   138
8:1–6   133, 137 n. 36, 148, 151, 159, 164, 166 n. 15
8:1   135, 136, 164, 164 n. 10, 167 n. 20, 198 n. 17
8:2   82 n. 13, 187
8:4   138, 167 n. 20
8:5   166 n. 16
8:6   8, 166, 166 n. 15, 167, 179
8:6a   179
8:7–13   169 n. 23
8:7   8, 133, 136, 137 n. 36, 138, 148, 164 n. 20
8:8   136, 138
8:9   133, 134, 134 n. 26, 136, 137, 137 n. 36, 137 n. 39, 140, 140 n. 47, 141, 141 n. 48, 142, 143, 164
8:10–12   134, 156
8:10   136, 138, 148, 152 n. 17, 156, 164 n. 20

8:11   136, 156
8:11b   8
8:12   153, 156, 159, 258
8:13   134, 135, 135 n. 29, 136, 141, 141 n. 48, 152 n. 14
9   135 n. 29, 137 n. 39
9:1–14   12
9:1–7   140, 143
9:1–2   225, 225 n. 11
9:1   138, 166, 259
9:1a   135
9:1bc   135
9:1d   135
9:2   135, 136, 166
9:3   136
9:4–7   139
9:4–6   139 n. 43
9:4–5   137, 137 n. 38
9:4   136, 136 n. 35, 137
9:5   137, 137 n. 37, 166
9:6   131, 136, 137, 139
9:7   138
9:7a   138
9:7b   138
9:7c   138
9:8–10   130 n. 14
9:8–9   258
9:8   130
9:8a   138 n. 40, 139
9:8b   139
9:9–10   125–43, 247
9:9   12, 14, 19 n. 11, 38 n. 5, 126 n. 5, 127, 191, 251 n. 13
9:9a   139
9:9b   125, 126, 126 n. 4, 127, 130, 139, 142, 142 n. 50
9:9c–10b   131 n. 16
9:9c–10a   125
9:9c   131, 139
9:10   12, 14, 126 n. 5, 127 n. 6, 140, 140 n. 46
9:10a   131, 139
9:10b   125, 126 n. 2, 127 n. 6, 130, 130 n. 13, 131, 139, 142
9:10c   125–26, 127, 127 n. 6, 128, 128 n. 7, 128 n. 8, 129, 130, 130 n. 12, 131, 131 n. 16, 132, 132 n. 21, 139, 142, 143
9:11–18   140–42

Scripture Index   305

9:11   127, 129, 140
9:12   141 n. 48
9:12a   140, 140 n. 47
9:12b   136 n. 34, 141
9:12c   141
9:13   95 n. 18
9:13a   141
9:13b   141
9:14   142, 143, 166
9:15   136 n. 34, 142, 142 n. 50
9:16–18   142
9:19–22   170
9:20–21   7
9:20   258
9:21–22   169 n. 23
9:24   95 n. 18
10   133 n. 24, 150 n. 12, 154 n. 21, 170 n. 28
10:1–13   12, 148, 148 n. 8, 151 n. 13, 153 n. 18
10:1–11   8
10:1–5   150
10:1–4   152, 153 n. 18
10:1–2   148
10:3–4   152, 157
10:3   152
10:4   155
10:5–10   151 n. 13
10:5   149, 151, 154, 155 n. 24
10:6–11   149–53, 158, 159
10:6   149, 150, 150 n. 12, 151, 151 n. 13, 152, 152 n. 15, 153, 155, 157
10:6b   152
10:7–13   152 n. 15
10:7–10   152 n. 15, 157 n. 33
10:7–8   153 n. 20
10:7   19 n. 11, 148, 149, 150, 152, 152 n. 17, 153, 153 n. 21, 154, 154 n. 23, 156, 158, 159, 251 n. 13
10:7a   148, 152
10:7b   12, 14, 145–59
10:8–11   153–58
10:8–10   157 n. 32
10:8   149, 150, 153, 153 n. 21, 154, 154 n. 23, 155, 157, 157 n. 32
10:8c   154 n. 23
10:9   149, 150, 155, 155 n. 25, 156, 157
10:9a   155 n. 25, 155 n. 26, 156
10:9b   155, 155 n. 25, 155 n. 26

10:9c   155
10:10   149, 150, 156, 156 n. 30, 157, 157 n. 31, 157 n. 32
10:10b   157
10:11   149–50, 150 n. 12, 157
10:11b   157
10:12   187
10:15   185
10:16   8
10:19   164 n. 20
10:21   166
10:22   166
10:23–11:1   12, 163, 163 n. 8
10:23–25   163–66
10:23–24   164, 164 n. 10, 168, 169, 169 n. 23
10:23   163, 164, 164 n. 9, 168, 169, 169 n. 24, 169 n. 25, 198 n. 17
10:23a   164, 164 n. 10
10:23b   164 n. 10
10:24   163, 164, 168, 170
10:25–27   164, 167
10:25–26   166 n. 15
10:25   163, 164, 165, 165 n. 11, 166, 167, 170, 171
10:26   11 n. 26, 12, 14, 161–71
10:27–11:1   167–70
10:27   163, 164, 167, 167 n. 18, 170, 171
10:27a   167
10:27b   167
10:28–30   163 n. 8, 167, 170, 171
10:28–29a   163 n. 8, 168 n. 21, 169 n. 23
10:28   134 n. 29, 163, 167, 168 n. 20
10:28b   164
10:29   163
10:29a   164, 168
10:29b–30   163 n. 8, 168 n. 21, 169 n. 23
10:29b   163 n. 8, 164, 168
10:30   163, 168, 169 n. 24
10:31–11:1   164, 169
10:31   163, 164, 170 n. 28, 186
10:31b   169, 170, 171, 179, 180, 181, 185, 187, 188, 189, 190
10:32–33   170 n. 28
10:32   163, 169 n. 23, 170, 188
10:33   163, 164

(1 Corinthians)   10:33a   169
10:33b   170
11:1   163, 169
11:2–34   12–13, 15
11:2–16   12, 173, 175–88. 189
11:2   176, 177, 179, 187
11:3–15   187, 188, 190
11:3–7   176, 178, 179
11:3–4   176, 178, 179, 180 n. 9, 184, 189
11:3   176, 179, 181, 183 n. 16, 187, 188, 190
11:3a   179 n. 8, 180
11:3c   179 n. 8, 180
11:4–6   181 n. 11
11:4–5   178
11:4   176, 179, 180 n. 9, 186, 188, 190
11:5–10   184
11:5–6   176, 178, 180, 183 n. 16, 188, 189, 190
11:5   176, 180 n. 9
11:5a   180
11:5b   180, 180 n. 10
11:6   176
11:6a   180, 180 n. 10
11:6b   180, 180 n. 10
11:7–12   11 n. 26, 12–13, 15, 173–90
11:7–9   181 n. 11
11:7   176, 178, 181, 188, 189, 190
11:7a   173–74, 181, 187, 189
11:7b–9   183
11:7b   174, 181, 182, 183, 186, 187, 189
11:8–12   176, 178, 182
11:8–9   176, 178, 182, 185, 185 n. 25, 188, 189, 190
11:8   174, 176, 182, 185, 185 n. 24, 189
11:8b   185
11:9   175, 176, 182, 184 n. 23, 185, 189
11:10   176, 178, 183, 184 n. 21, 188, 189, 190
11:10a   183, 189
11:10b   183, 184, 184 n. 21, 189
11:11–12   176, 178, 184, 185, 185 n. 25, 188, 189, 190
11:11   175, 184, 185. 190
11:12   176, 178–79, 185, 188, 190
11:12ab   185
11:12a   185
11:12b   175, 185
11:12c   175, 185, 186
11:13–15   177, 178, 185, 187 n. 30
11:13   177, 178, 185, 186 n. 26, 187, 188, 189, 190
11:13a   185
11:13b   186
11:14–15   174, 180, 180 n. 9
11:14   177, 178, 186, 186 n. 27, 187, 188, 189, 190
11:15   177, 178, 187, 187 n. 29, 187 n. 30, 188, 189, 190
11:16   82 n. 13, 177, 178, 187, 188, 188 n. 31, 190
11:16b   188
11:18   23 n. 17
11:23–25   8
12:1–14:40   13, 15, 198 n. 15
12:1–31   63 n. 26
12:2   8, 135 n. 29, 151 n. 14
12:3   8
12:13   7, 8, 148
12:17   252 n. 19
12:19   252 n. 19
12:27   113 n. 20
13:8   112 n. 17
13:10   112 n. 17
13:11   112 n. 17, 199
14   198 n. 15, 198 n. 16
14:1–20   197–200
14:1   197
14:2   198, 198 n. 15, 200, 203
14:3   198, 198 n. 17
14:4   198
14:4a   198 n. 17
14:4b   198 n. 17
14:5   198, 198 n. 17, 199
14:7   198 n. 15
14:9   199, 200, 203
14:10   199
14:11   198 n. 15, 199, 200, 203
14:12   198, 198 n. 17
14:14–19   199 n. 18
14:14–15   71 n. 5, 198 n. 15
14:14   198 n. 15, 199
14:15   199
14:16–17   200, 203
14:16   198 n. 15, 199
14:17   198, 198 n. 17, 199
14:18   199

14:19   199
14:20–25   13, 191, 201
14:20   199, 200, 201, 203
14:21–25   201
14:21   13, 15, 19 n. 11, 191–94, 195 n. 8, 196–97, 198, 199, 200, 201, 201 n. 21, 202, 203, 251 n. 13, 258
14:22–25   200–202
14:22   200, 200 n. 19, 201
14:22a   200
14:22b   201
14:23–25a   202
14:23   23 n. 17, 198 n. 15, 200
14:24–25   194 n. 6, 201, 201 n. 20
14:24   194, 195 n. 7, 197
14:25   11 n. 26, 13, 15, 191, 194–96, 197, 201, 201 n. 21, 202, 203
14:25b   202
14:26   198, 198 n. 17
14:27–28   198 n. 15
14:28   198 n. 15
14:34   258
14:37   82 n. 13, 243
15:1–58   13–14, 15, 209 n. 12, 212 n. 21, 248 n. 3
15:1–2   225
15:1   227 n. 17
15:3–5   8
15:3   258
15:7–11   224
15:10–11   225
15:12–13   224 n. 7
15:12   223, 223 n. 6, 227 n. 14, 227 n. 17
15:12b   212, 227
15:13–28   227, 229
15:14   259
15:15   239
15:16–17   227
15:17   258
15:20–28   13, 212–18
15:20–23   212, 212 n. 22, 218, 219
15:20   212, 212 n. 22, 215, 216 n. 25
15:20a   210
15:21–26   253–54
15:21–22   212 n. 22, 236–37, 239, 258
15:21   212, 216
15:21a   210, 215, 237, 253
15:21b   211, 237

15:22–23   212
15:22   232
15:22a   237, 253
15:22b   211, 237, 244
15:23–24   213 n. 23
15:23   212 n. 22
15:23a   211, 211 n. 19
15:23b   211
15:24–28   212–19
15:24   112 n. 17, 208 n. 10, 210, 214 n. 24, 218 n. 27, 254, 254 n. 22
15:24ab   213, 215, 217
15:24a   212, 218
15:24b   208 n. 8, 212, 214, 218
15:24c   213, 214, 215, 217, 253
15:25–28   213 n. 23
15:25   11 n. 26, 13, 15, 162 n. 3, 205–11, 214, 218, 219, 247
15:25a   213, 214, 215
15:25b   213, 214, 215, 216
15:26   112 n. 17, 210, 213, 214, 215, 218, 219, 252, 253, 254, 255, 256, 257, 258, 259, 260
15:27–28   215, 216 n. 25
15:27   205–11, 216 n. 25, 218, 247
15:27a   13, 15, 206, 213, 214, 216, 217, 218, 219
15:27bc   214, 216, 217
15:27b   213, 214, 216, 217
15:27c   213, 214, 216, 217
15:28   208 n. 8, 213, 214, 216 n. 25, 217
15:28a   213, 217
15:28bc   218
15:28b   213, 217
15:28c   213, 214, 214 n. 24, 217, 218, 219
15:29–34   13, 222 n. 2
15:29–32a   223–26
15:29   223, 223 n. 6, 224, 224 n. 8
15:29b   224, 228
15:30–32a   226
15:30–31   228
15:30   224, 225 n. 9, 226, 228
15:31–32a   226, 228
15:31   225, 225 n. 9
15:31a   225 n. 9
15:32   11 n. 26, 223 n. 4
15:32a   225, 225 n. 12, 228
15:32b   13, 15, 221–29

(1 Corinthians) 15:33–34 226–28
15:33   226, 227, 229
15:34   229, 258
15:34a   227
15:34b   227
15:34c   227
15:34d   227
15:35–49   232, 237 n. 15
15:35–44   237–41
15:35–43   240 n. 21
15:35–36   224 n. 7
15:35   240, 241, 245
15:35a   239
15:35b   239
15:36–41   238, 138 n. 17, 239
15:36–38   237, 237 n. 16, 238, 239, 240, 245
15:36–37   128, 239
15:36   237, 239
15:38–44   234, 244
15:38   232, 232 n. 4, 237, 238, 239
15:39–41   238, 240, 241, 245, 254
15:39   232
15:40–41   240
15:40   233, 238, 242
15:41   233, 233 n. 41, 240
15:42–44   128, 239 n. 19, 240, 245
15:42–43   239 n. 19
15:42a   238, 240
15:42b–44a   238
15:42b–43   240
15:42b   238, 239, 240
15:43a   238, 239, 240
15:43b   238, 239, 240
15:44   239 n. 19, 241, 241 n. 23, 244
15:44a   238, 239, 240, 240 n. 21
15:44b–49   13
15:44b   240, 240 n. 21, 241
15:45   19 n. 11, 236, 236 n. 13, 236 n. 14, 237, 241 n. 23, 242 n. 25, 251 n. 13
15:45a   13, 15, 231–45
15:45b–49   234, 244
15:45b   231 n. 1, 233, 233 n. 7, 234, 235, 237, 241, 242, 243, 244, 245
15:46–49   241–44
15:46–47   240
15:46   241, 241 n. 23, 244, 245
15:47–49   234 n. 8

15:47   242 n. 25, 244, 245
15:47a   234, 241, 242
15:47b   242
15:48a   242
15:48b   242
15:49   234, 234 n. 9, 242–43
15:49a   243, 243 n. 27, 244, 245
15:49b   243, 244, 245
15:50–58   13–14
15:50–54a   254–57
15:50   254, 254 n. 22, 254 n. 23, 255, 256, 257, 260
15:51–52   256 n. 30
15:51   255, 255 n. 25, 256, 257, 260
15:52   255
15:52a   255
15:53–54a   255, 256, 256 n. 30, 257, 260
15:53   256, 256 n. 29, 257, 257 n. 31, 260
15:54   250 n. 10, 256 n. 29
15:54–55   251 n. 12, 258 n. 35
15:54ab   256 n. 29
15:54a   255, 256, 257, 260
15:54b–55   247–60
15:54b   14, 15, 247–50, 251, 252, 253, 255, 256, 257, 258, 260
15:55   14, 15, 249–51, 252, 254 n. 24, 257, 260
15:55a   252, 253, 255, 258, 259, 260
15:55b   253, 257, 259, 260
15:56–58   257–59
15:56   253 n. 21, 257, 257 n. 32, 258, 259, 260
15:56a   258 n. 35
15:56b   258 n. 35
15:57   249 n. 7, 258, 258 n. 36, 259, 260
15:58   258–59, 260
16:22   8

2 Corinthians
2:17   96 n. 23
5:4   252 n. 17, 257 n. 31
6:16   135 n. 29
9:6   128
9:10   128
10:10   104 n. 4
10:17   38 n. 5
12:19   198 n. 17

Galatians
2:17   115 n. 26
3:21   115 n. 26
4:30   206
5:9   95
5:21   254 n. 22
6:7–9 128
6:7–8 128
6:14   41 n. 15, 115 n. 26

Ephesians
1:20–21   206 n. 3
5:31   103 n. 1

Philippians
3:3   41 n. 15

1 Thessalonians
1:5   118 n. 34
1:9   135 n. 29
2:12   254 n. 22
4:5   228 n. 18
4:16   255 n. 27
5:11   198 n. 17

1 Timothy
4:4   166 n. 15
5:18   125 n. 1, 127, 206

Hebrews
1:13   206 n. 3
11:28 157 n. 31

1 Peter
2:5   198 n. 17
3:22   206 n. 3

Revelation
2:14   167 n. 20
2:20   167 n. 20
9:10   253 n. 21
9:20   135 n. 29

OTHER LITERATURE

2 Baruch
17:2–3   258 n. 34
50:1–51:10   255 n. 26

1 Enoch
51:2   45 n. 25
62:15–16   256 n. 30

4 Ezra
3:7   258 n. 34

Psalms of Solomon
4:25   57
6:6   56–57
14:1   57
16:4   253 n. 21

Testament of Reuben
5:5   118 n. 35

Rule of the Community
1QS 4:7–8   256 n. 30

Philo
Creation 134–69   258 n. 34
Questions on Genesis 1:51   258 n. 34

www.ingramcontent.com/pod-product-compliance
Lightning Source LLC
Chambersburg PA
CBHW032001220426
43664CB00005B/98